Nicholas Roerich

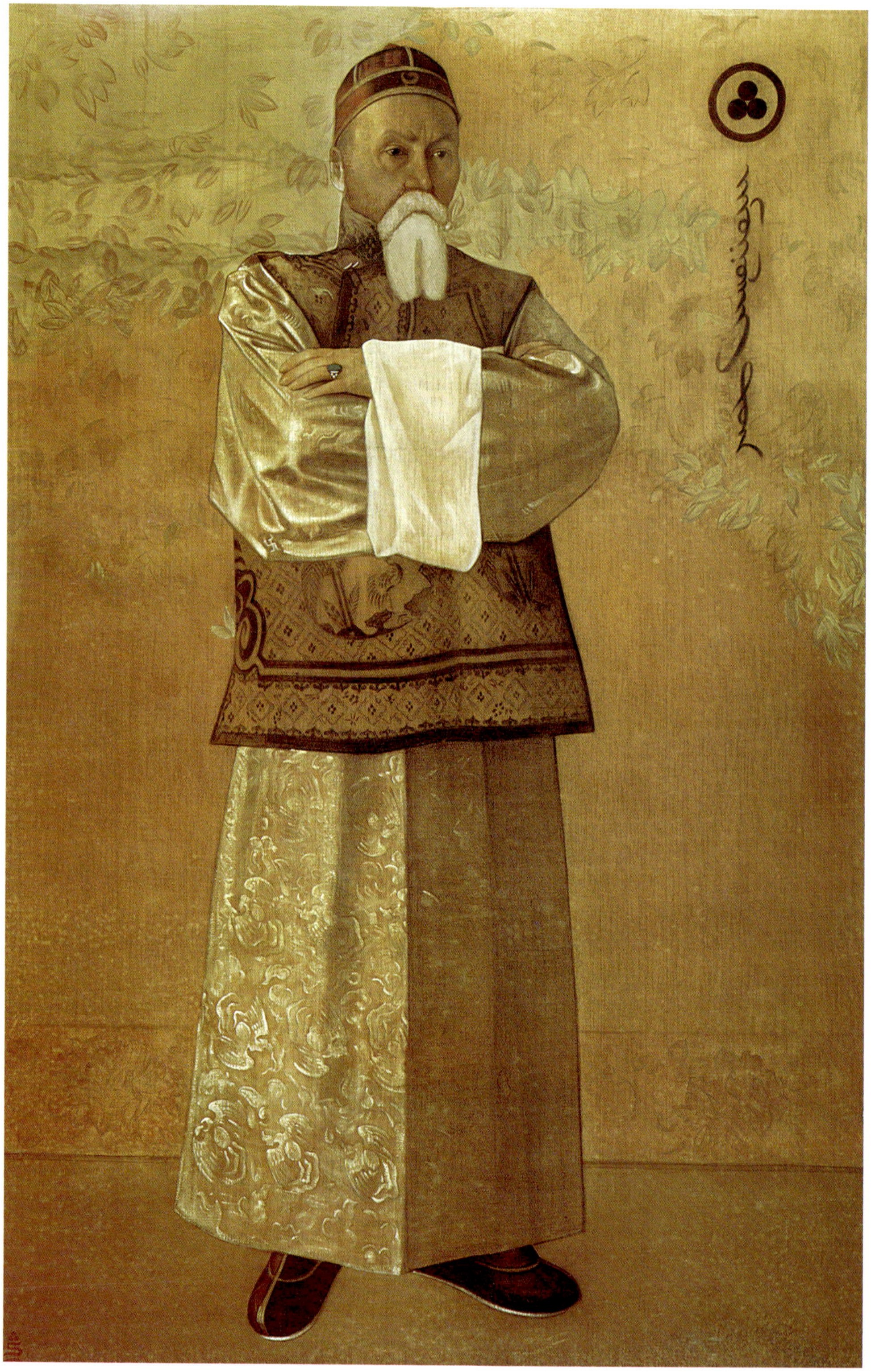

A portrait of Nicholas Roerich in Tibetan robes, by Svetoslav Roerich, 1933

Nicholas Roerich

A Quest & A Legacy

Edited by

Manju Kak

NIYOGI
BOOKS

Published by

NIYOGI BOOKS

D-78, Okhla Industrial Area, Phase-I
New Delhi-110 020, INDIA
Tel: 91-11-26816301, 49327000
Fax: 91-11-26810483, 26813830
Email: niyogibooks@gmail.com
Website: www.niyogibooksindia.com

Editor: Manju Kak
Design: Write Media

ISBN: 978-93-81523-52-0
Year of Publication: 2013

Printed at: Niyogi Offset Pvt. Ltd., New Delhi, India

Contents

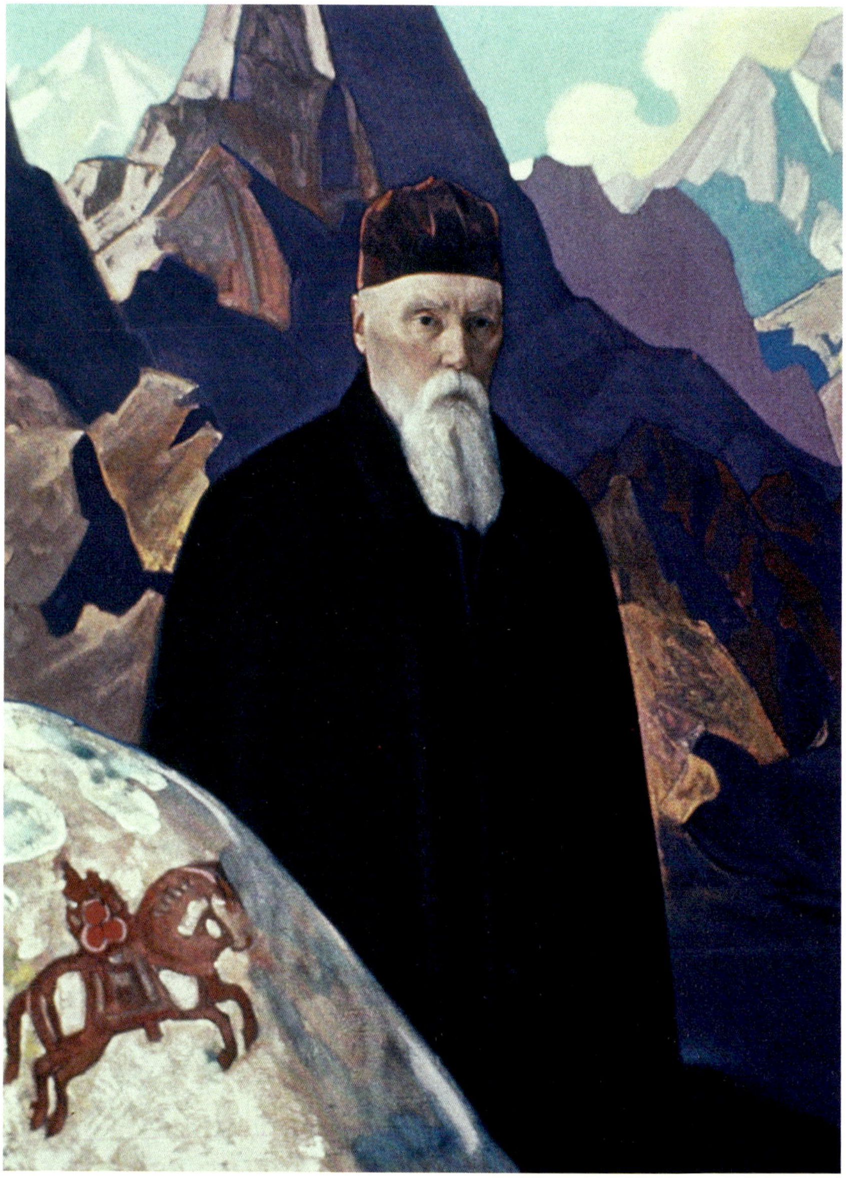

Portrait of Nicholas Roerich by Svetoslav Roerich, 1937
(Nicholas Roerich Museum, NY)

Foreword

Nicholas Roerich, for whom Mother India was as beloved as his Mother Russia, was one of the most talented artists of the 20th century. Born in Russia in 1874, he had, as a young man, a significant output of paintings representing rural life in that country. However, it was India that became his spiritual home, and the Himalayas his lifelong commitment, even obsession. After his arrival in Mumbai in 1923, he established friendship with many well known Indian intellectuals including Gurudev Rabindranath Tagore and Dr. Suniti Kumar Chatterjee. Over the years he undertook a series of remarkable and daring Himalayan expeditions in India, Tibet and Mongolia, and this resulted in a large number of extraordinary paintings of the Himalayas and the trans-Himalayan regions.

These paintings, many of which are in the Roerich Museum and in the Roerich Department at the State Oriental Museum, both in Moscow, represent a unique approach to the Himalayas, abode of Shiva, bringing out their inner spiritual significance that impelled the great Sanskrit Poet Kalidasa to describe them as '*Devatma*', a spiritual presence. They also teem with human figures—saints, prophets, seekers of the spiritual path and mystical figures drawn from many faiths including Hinduism, Buddhism, Confucianism and Christianity. His use of colour was extraordinary, especially his treatment of snow covered mountains and sunlit landscapes. In his profession of creativity he was able to capture even in a small painting, the subtle mystery that lies at the heart of the Himalayas and the great teachers who reside there. To quote him 'All teachers journeyed to the mountains. The highest knowledge, the most inspired songs, the most superb sounds and colours are created on the mountains ... Himalayas! Here is the Abode of Rishis. Himalayas—Jewel of India. Himalayas— Treasure of the World. Himalayas—The Sacred Symbol of the Ascent.'

The massive corpus of Roerich's work presents a unique dimension of spiritual striving and realization which will remain a source of inspiration for many years to come. His paintings of mountains have an inner luminosity and an aura of mysticism. Although I did not have the privilege of meeting Nicholas Roerich, I did meet his son Svetoslav in Bangalore along with his wife, the famous Indian actress Devika Rani. His paintings are also very dramatic, much larger than his father's and also dealing with the spiritual quest, especially a series on the great spiritual teachers of humanity.

Roerich was also an international peace activist, having presented the 'Roerich Pact' which was an International treaty to protect ancient buildings, works of art and cultural institutions in times of peace and war. He campaigned vigorously for this across the world and, in a way, prefigured UNESCO's Heritage programmes.

It is time now that we should rediscover the genius of Nicholas Roerich and revisit the saga of his amazing life. I welcome this book *Nicholas Roerich: A Quest and A Legacy* which brings together scholarly contributions from a number of different disciplines and effectively presents Roerich's life and his multifaceted personality. The illustrations greatly enhance the value of the book, and I am sure this handsome volume will be of great interest to admirers of Roerich's work in India and around the world, and also help to introduce his oeuvre to artists, art critics and art lovers from the younger generation. Dr Manju Kak is to be commended for putting together this well-researched and thought-provoking volume.

Dr. Karan Singh
New Delhi, 2012

Nicholas Roerich: A Quest & A Legacy—An Introduction

Manju Kak

India has been as much the spiritual home of Russian painter Nicholas Konstantovich Roerich (1874-1947) as Mother Russia. Roerich died without being able to return to his homeland, a citizen bereft of his nation. From the time of his childhood spent in the family estate outside St. Petersburg in 'Isvara'—reputedly once owned by an Indian Raja—India was firmly embedded in his consciousness. It was only befitting that when Roerich died in December 1947 at Kullu, Himachal, his simple grave, placed under willows, was marked by a monolithic rock that reads 'Maharishi', or Great Sage.

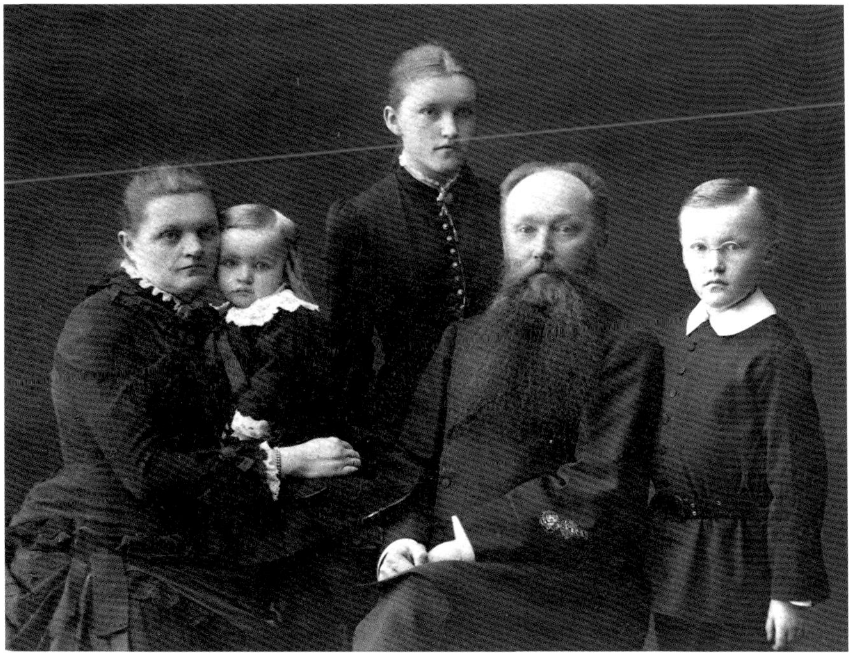

Left to right: Maria Rerikh, Vladimir Rerikh, Lidiya Rerikh, Konstantin Rerikh and Nicholas Roerich ca. 1883–84. Russia (Nicholas Roerich Museum Archive, NY)

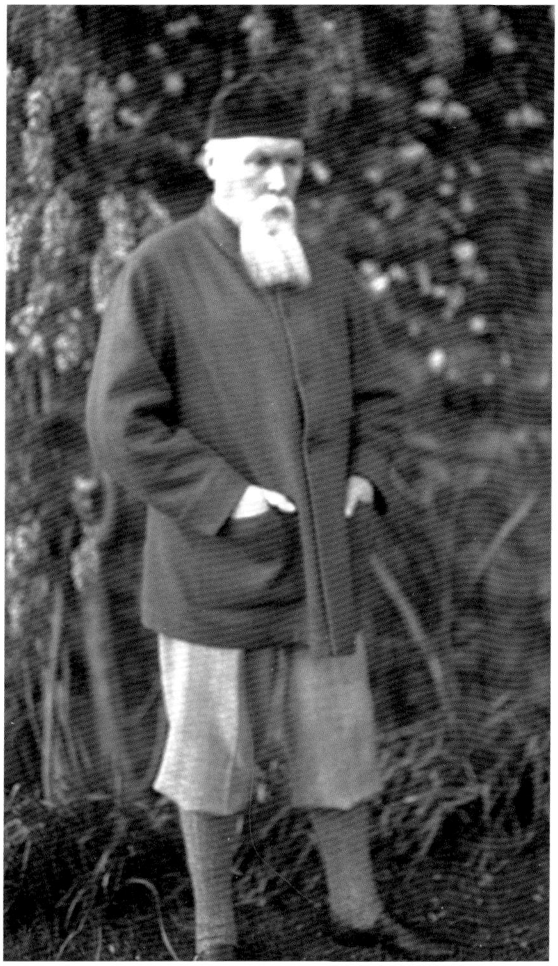

Nicholas Roerich, ca. 1936–42. Naggar, India (Nicholas Roerich Museum Archive, NY)

For this painter-philosopher who never returned to Russia—having lived in India for twenty-odd years—it is believed that more than five hundred Roerich societies have proliferated since the decline of Communism in 1991, in the Russian Federation alone. They are dedicated to the propagation of Roerich's ideas as a peace activist as well as the principles of his philosophical thought, Agni Yoga.[1] It is perceived, however, that they present a threat to the dominance of the Orthodox Church.

Early Life and Artistic Expression

Though Roerich remained essentially Russian, he was a cosmologist, his consciousness belonging to an international arena. When fascist governments and monarchies were destroying Europe, visionaries like N.K. Roerich, Richard von Coudenhove-Kalergi (Pan-Europa), Henry Dunant (Red Cross) were presenting ideas that crossed national boundaries.

Some writers, including Suchandana Chatterjee, a contributor to this anthology, slot Roerich's life in the larger collective of 19th and 20th century western adventurers, colonial military agents and surveyors, and iconoclasts who thirsted for the unattainable, far-fetched landscapes of the Orient, in particular Tibet. To name a few, British army officer and explorer, Francis Younghusband; Nain Singh and Kishan Singh Rawat, the Indian colonial surveyors who first mapped Tibet; Belgian-French spiritualist and explorer, Alexandra David-Neel; Alexander Csoma de Koros, the Hungarian Magyar wanderer and scholar; Albert Gruenwedel, the German Orientalist and explorer; Sven Hedin the Swedish scholar, around some of whom, cults have arisen.

Clearly in post-1991 Eurasia and beyond, Nicholas K. Roerich continues to arouse the interest of extensive scholarship, both adulatory and critical. Controversies aside, the question often asked is: what is the draw and pull of a man who was, in his final avatar, a painter of mountains?

This anthology of essays on the artist seeks to answer just this. The contributors—scholars, disciples, practitioners—have looked at Roerich's life from varying perspectives to explain his multi-faceted personality. Through these writings, one hopes to come to a holistic understanding of the man and his times.

Roerich's body of work has been divided into three periods by some critics—divisions that I look upon as progressing towards the same ideal or path.

His Russian period, that some call the 'stone' phase, sought to inquire into the common roots of the Russian peoples' Slavic heritage, their pre-Christian, that is, Celtic, Viking and Mongol traditions, and blood ties. (It is interesting to note here Roerich's mother had Mongol blood). He raised awareness that this ancestry of old Russia should not to be forgotten. He was deeply influenced by his teacher, the great Russian artist Archip Ivanovich Kuinji. Roerich was also close to some Slavophiles of the early 1900s especially Princess Maria Teneshiva, and her efforts at creating the experimental village, 'Talashkino'. Madavan Palat in his essay 'Nicholas Roerich: Artist and Messiah,' says that this experimental village belonged to a wider European movement, represented in England by William Morris and the Arts and Crafts Movement. He goes on to add that here, artists of the calibre of Aleksandr Benois, Mikhail Vrubel and Roerich, among others, gathered to produce everyday items of furniture, textiles, metals and much else.

His second so-called theatrical phase (especially in the 1920s) is seen in his oversized murals and decorative panels which express a continuum of inquiry into Russia's past, its animistic beliefs, its close unity with natural materials, implements and other objects. The quest for the heritage of his forefathers can be seen in his search for Russia's pagan beginnings, writes Lokesh Chandra in 'Mysticism and the Art of Roerich'. Joe Troncale in 'The Transcendent as Theatre in Roerich's Paintings' further discusses the enhanced role that painting was beginning to play in 'theatre'. Association with theatre's luminaries such as Sir Thomas Beecham (Covent Garden) in England, and Russian émigré impresario Sergei Diaghilev (Ballet Russes) as well as composer Igor Fyodorovich Stravinsky (Rite of Spring) brought Roerich European renown.

Troncale notes that during this period the work of Russian painters was intimately integrated and synthesised with the other elements of

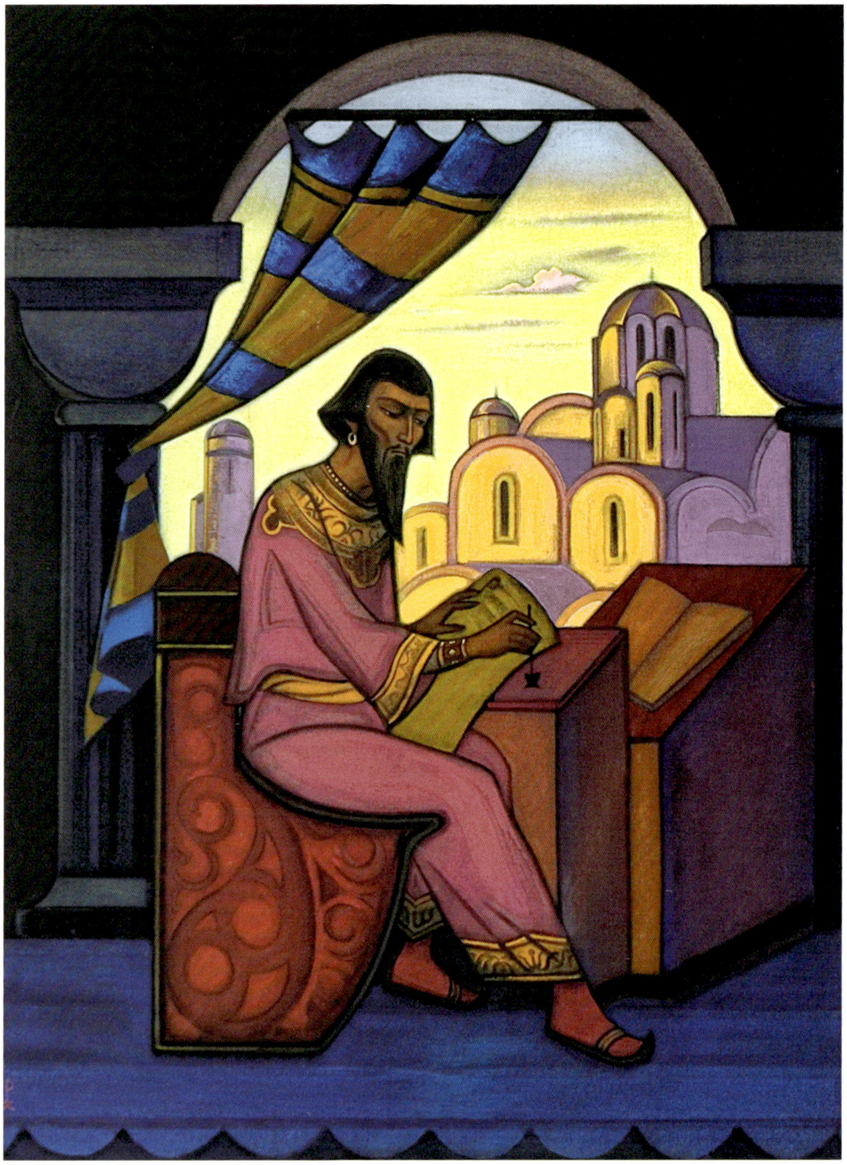

Yaroslav the Wise, 1941 (International Centre of the Roerichs, Moscow)

a theatrical production thereby highlighting the fundamental unity of the arts.

Roerich's arrival in Bombay, India, with his family on 30 November 1923, was followed by his daring mountainous expeditions. This makes up his third 'mountain' phase. His arrival was viewed with suspicion by the ruling British Raj. It was a period of frenetic anti-Soviet activity stirred by India's British colonial masters who were stakeholders in the 'Great Game' being played out for dominance in Central and Inner Asia, a point Suchandana Chatterjee elucidates in 'Glimpses of

Inner Asia'. To make matters worse, Roerich quickly established friendships with many well-known Indian intellectuals such as RabindranathTagore, Suniti Kumar Chatterjee, Kedarnath Dasgupta, among others, and despite the passage of time, continued to retain his Russian passport which made colonial rulers draw conclusions that he was a Comitern agent.

The culmination of this expedition was expressed in his transcendental paintings of the Himalayas and Trans-Himalayas, peopled with figures of enlightened saints, prophets, hierarchs, keepers of the spiritual path; the nineteen-canvas *Banners of the East* series drawn from many faiths—Christ, Confucius, Moses, Buddha, Mohammed on Mount Hira, Lao-tse, Russia's own St. Sergius, the Buddhist Shambhala king, Rigden Djapo. As the Indian saint, Shri Ramakrishna said, *Jata mat tata* path, so Roerich too believed that all religions are paths to one God.

Through his body of work Roerich advocated a return to the ancient roots of human wisdom, which asserted the importance of spiritual life and of peaceful co-existence based on a cosmic mentality. Towards this end he linked these prophetic messages of Judeo-Christian and Islamic faiths with those of the older religious traditions of Asia and of the indigenous peoples of the Americas.

Central Asian Expedition

It was this nascent quest and the search for the elusive Buddhist mythological land of Shambhala (Shangrila) that took Roerich first upon the Central Asian Expedition (1924–28) across the Chinese Gobi desert and later into the Siberian Altai (1930–31). Ruth Drayer writes in 'Across the Gobi Desert' that 'Roerich was aware that the regions of Mongolia and the central Gobi were an explorer's and archaeologist's paradise with whole cities hidden beneath the sands.' Ostensibly supported by the then American Secretary of Agriculture, Henry A. Wallace, (later Vice-President) as an Agrarian Expedition,[2] it had as its subtext this belief that 'Shambhala' did exist, a belief that was very similar to (the belief of) Belovodye, the land of Whitewater of Old Russian Believers who had fled to Siberia during the church reforms of Patriarch Nikon (1652–1666); the Christian Holy Grail; or the Hindu sacred geography of the mythical land of Meru. Both Suchandana Chatterjee and A.V. Ivanov throw further light on this.

The route the Roerichs took on this first expedition (1924–28) covered the vast and difficult geographical terrain of the Himalayas and of Central Asia from Kashmir, Leh, Khotan, Kashgar, Urumchi, Mongolia, Gobi and Taklamakan deserts, to Tibet and finally Sikkim, a distance of over 8,000 km, half the distance he was to later travel. Ian Heron writes on how the Roerichs acquired a mysterious piece of meteorite in France, 'The Chintamani Stone', which accompanied their travels and acted as a lodestar.

Roerich's philosophical ideas were honed and shaped by his Great Journeys. Roerich scholar, philosopher and Indologist L.V. Shaposhnikova in 'A Caravan through Time and Space' says he (Roerich) wished to learn about the origins of humanity. According to him, Russia needed a detailed study of her eastern roots—the ethno-genesis and migration of peoples who came and filled and recreated Europe as Chatterjee extrapolates. His training in the Imperial Academy of Arts (1893), St. Petersburg, and experience as an archaeologist came in handy. His jottings transferred to the books he wrote—*Altai–Himalaya, Heart of Asia*, etc., which form an important archive of happenings in this part of the world—Tibet, Mongolia, Buryatia, at that time—and how the region fitted into the future of pre-World War II Eurasia.

Many post-perestroika scholars have shown a cynical curiosity about this expedition. For example, Chatterjee writes that it 'hurled them into the cockpit of diplomatic gambling, occult mystery and alleged geopolitical scheming'. Conversely this critique has drawn much flak from Roerich Societies worldwide, who consider such interpretations as being a flawed understanding of the artist and his motives.

Nevertheless the expeditions formed the 'bridge' that connected his early explorations in Russia with his 'arrival' in his new home in Kullu (Himachal Pradesh) and in 'Urusvati', the inter-disciplinary Institute he set up. Writes Mikhail Chiryatyev in 'Urusvati: The Himalayan Research Institute,' that the novel concept here was the synthesis of natural sciences and humanitarian disciplines as well as that of traditional and modern knowledge was fundamental to the Institute. He hoped to diffuse the narrow pragmatic utilisation of science—which leads to the destruction of nature—with a crucible of conscious knowledge that would save humanity and pin it to the domain of ethical science. Following the expedition, Roerich remained in India yet continued to straddle the arc that seeped into

Russian consciousness in the severe Communist decades, as a reminder of her eastern heritage. Even earlier, from the time when Russian court culture was heavily Francophone, Roerich re-iterated through his work that one of Russia's emblematic eagles faced east.

Roerich's first Central Asian Expedition formed the bedrock of the oeuvre of his paintings. At Kullu he continued to express his 'findings' till his death, leaving behind a legacy of approximately 7,000 paintings in museums and private collections the world over. He painted majestic mountain peaks, distant landscapes and peoples, together with their history, legends and spiritual traditions. He visualised the Himalayas and by extension the Trans-Himalayan region as a shared spiritual possession of many countries, peoples and faiths. In them he explored the language of colour that was both extraordinary and unique. He captured that spiritual dimension that has made the mountains home of the seeker and the sage.

His paintings expressed a core philosophy that spoke of the deep connectedness of man to nature and also reinforced India's tradition for a culture of assimilation, explains L.V. Shaposhnikova. He reiterated an artist's belief that a perfect world does exist, if only we could find the path to it. While he did not find Shambhala, finally he knew it as a state of the mind, says Tashi Paljor in 'The Legend of Shambhala'.

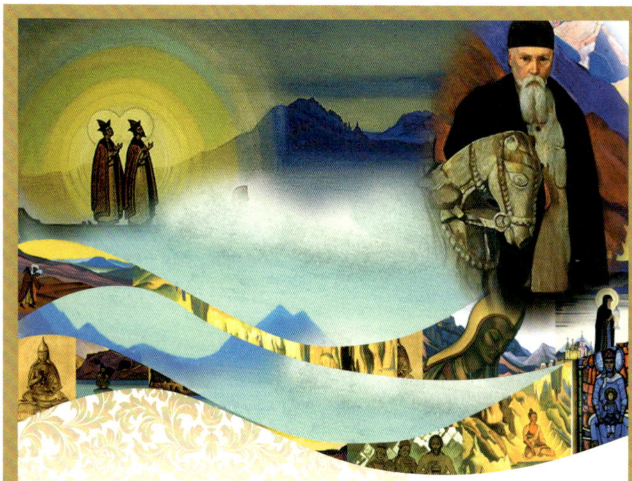

NICHOLAS ROERICH: A Quest & A Legacy

The Russian born artist, Nicholas Roerich (1874-1947), visualized the Himalayas and the Trans-Himalayan region as a shared spiritual possession of many countries. To him exploring the language of colour was a spiritual journey in itself. Through his paintings he expressed a core philosophy that speaks of a universal truth and the deep connectedness of man to nature. His legacy lies in his mountain landscapes, which are extraordinary. Through them he reiterates an artist's belief that perfect worlds must exist, if only we could reach them. In his own life he exemplified this search in a historic journey he undertook in search for Shambala. The journey took him over into a landscape in which he put to test both his response to colour and his beliefs.

The route he took on his first journey (1923-28) covered the vast and difficult geographical terrain of the Himalayas and of Central Asia, from Kashmir, Leh, Khotan, Kashgar, Urumchi, Mongolia, Gobi and Taklamakan deserts, to Tibet and finally Sikkim. A distance of over 8000 kilometers. This was the search for the legendary paradise of Shambala. The difficult terrain reinforced the sense of co-existence to him. The travellers delved into the spiritual underpinnings of Hinduism, Sufism, Theosophy, Buddhism and Christianity which influenced the artist's work.

The journey inspired the Peace through Culture movement. 'Pax Cultura' that became the legal instrument 'Roerich Pact' was later used as a basis for the international convention for the preservation of cultural heritage from armed conflicts, created in Hague in 1954.

At the end of his Central Asian expedition Nicholas Roerich, along with his wife Helena, and his two sons, George, and Svetoslav, settled in Naggar, Himachal Pradesh, in 1928 and produced hundreds of paintings that drew inspiration from that historic journey. He concluded that the artistic and spiritual heritage is the most potent binding force between cultures. The premise being belief and imagination can enhance political vision and open the door for co-existences in the Himalayan and trans-Himalayan tracts; that cultures can co-exist if one espouses the wise way; that artistic and spiritual heritage above all is the most potent binding force.

Spiritual Quest

In the years following 1918 to 1991, Soviet Russia remained spiritually barren. The erstwhile Communist leadership had closed doors firmly upon all organised religions. The more esoteric faiths and societies suffered a similar blackout—be it Buddhism, Theosophy, Agni Yoga, etc. Particularly in the Stalinist years, Buddhist monasteries, schools and temples were brutally destroyed and monks repressed.

After a long hiatus a resurgence of religiosity occurred in 1987 when the then Russian Premier Mikhail Gorbachev invited N.K. Roerich's son Svetoslav to Moscow with the aim of establishing a Roerich Centre there.[3]

Soon after, a spiritual thaw set in. The law 'On Freedom of Conscience and Religious Organisations' was enacted in 1990. The doors had been flung open. Since then many esoteric organisations have been revived or established in Russia including the Russian Society of Theosophy and the one devoted to the teaching of Roerichs' Agni Yoga or Living Ethics. Groups of devotees and admirers of the Roerich family legacy continue to spread across the Central Asian Republics, America, Eastern Europe, Brazil, Argentina, Italy, France and above all, India.

Most of Roerich's paintings were brought to cyberspace post-1991 because of his immense following. Yet in current and older western scholarship, it is generally believed Roerich has not been awarded his rightful place by the West in the world of art. The previous century was a time when western artists, connoisseurs and scholars had publicly rejected spirituality and God. Roerich's work did not quite fit into contemporary western trends. 'He was not a cubist, fauvist, Dadaist, surrealist, or any other 'ist'.'[4]

There was nothing here of the quest for the unknown found in Tibetan Buddhism or the Upanishads. Another reason for this could be that there is often a marked difficulty expressed by western viewers in understanding Roerich's paintings. Possibly the average western viewer sees his work purely in the light of 'mere' painting without its philosophic, esoteric connotation and contextualisation. I use mere not to deny the elevated space of art, but to express a view that Roerich's oeuvre is 'beyond art', that is, not a *value* but a *dimension* or space easier understood by Indians whose everyday lives are indoctrinated by spiritual lacings. In contrast, his work has seen unqualified admiration in India, the sort accorded to the poetry of

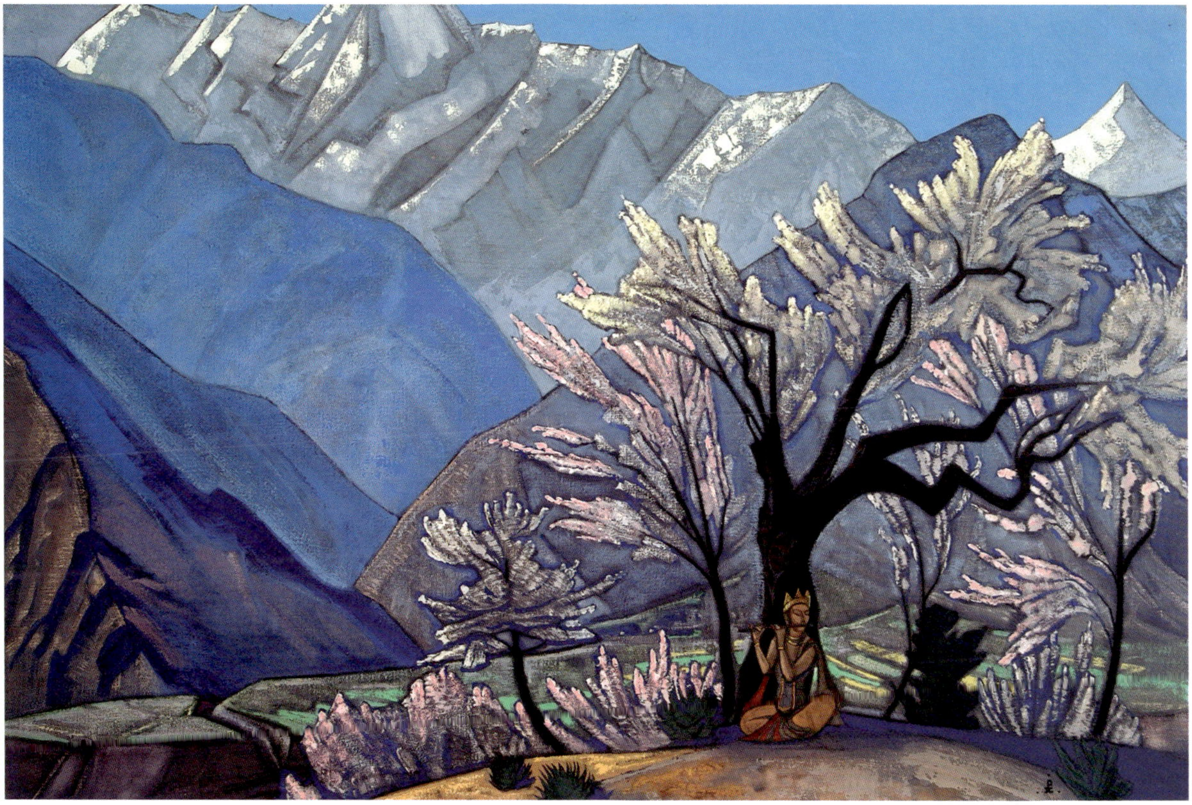

Krishna, from 'Kullu' series, 1929 (Nicholas Roerich Museum, NY)

celebrated Bengali poet-laureate Rabindranath Tagore. His paintings are understood by even those Indians who are not connoisseurs of art; for they symbolise that which Indians hold close to their spiritual consciousness—the mighty Himalayas.

Essentially Roerich's paintings demonstrate the power of human consciousness to penetrate the fundamental unity of things, explains L.V. Shaposhnikova. In a sense they seek to ask—what is our connectedness to the impulse that created us. The fulcrum of Roerich's entire body of work lies in just such subtle messages that are imbued with the history of civilisation, the connection with the divine, to our many karmic lives.

They are rooted in the ancient *aranya* texts that uphold the keel of nature which economists now acknowledge as indispensable to the future basis of world civilisation. They also display what Buddhist scholar Andrea Loseries calls a unique luminosity. Roerich said 'Culture is the worship of light.' He captured landscapes where man was alone and dominated by cosmic forces. According to him, wild, untouched spaces like the Siberian taiga—mountains, glaciers, rivers, lakes—were sanctuaries; the life source of civilisation—vital organs of the earth that need protection and care, to remain so—write A.V. Ivanov and I.V. Fotieva in 'The Roerich Family and Altai'. 'Alas, man has reached everywhere—there are fewer and fewer wild spaces left; today inaccessible regions are in jeopardy. The cognition of beauty is what will save mankind,' said Dostoevsky. Concurs L.V. Shaposhnikova, when we are exploring our consciousness of cosmic space the Oneness of Nature manifests as taught in Indian spiritual texts of the Vedanta and Upanishads. As much as political boundaries separate, it is the awareness of the contiguous bonds of air, space and water that bind.[5]

It is said the biggest challenge to this century is the quest for universality peace, sustainable ecology and the eradication of poverty. Nature cannot thrive without peace—echoed in Roerich's statement, 'Where there is culture, there is peace.' The sages of the Hindu Upanishads too uttered *Pritvi Shantih, Antariksha Shantih, Om! Shantih Shantih Shantih.*

Roerich's Peace Pact—Pax Cultura

The architectural quality of Roerich's work is seen in his paintings, *Island of Rest, Great Spirit of the Himalaya*, etc. Through his work as a painter and archaeologist, he shows his concern for material culture: buildings, ancient churches, city walls, etc.

It has always been believed that artists have a special calling for they are particularly sensitive to the cause of culture. From the Russo-Japanese War (1905) onwards, the early 20th century was devastated by war on a scale not seen before, leaving the world fraught with paranoia. Europe and by extension Russia lived in a cauldron of hate and destruction that resulted in the outbreak of the two World Wars. It was during his student years, that Roerich began working for world peace. Even before the Bolshevik Revolution broke out Roerich had already laid his ground work for activity through his mobilising of artists. Here he held a number of positions that were to prepare him for the leadership he showed later, says Kenneth Archer in 'The Roerich Pact—Original Collaborators.'

Roerich had secured a reputation in Imperialist Russia as a painter, archaeologist and philosopher, but once the Bolshevik Revolution of 1917 gained ground, he left Russia. Earlier, in 1916, Roerich's family moved to Finland following his diagnosis with a serious disease of the lungs, and lived on the seashore of Lake Ladoga. In 1918, Finland declared independence and Russian borders were closed. The Roerichs were cut off and they moved to England in 1919 and from there to America.

It was 1929, when he had settled down in India that he proposed the Peace Pact Committee and the Roerich Banner of Peace. The Roerich Peace Pact Committee was based in New York. The Banner of Peace was a white flag with three magenta spheres enclosed in a circle that are said to represent science, religion and art. They also symbolise the past, the present and the future in the overarching circle of eternity, says Marga Koutsarova in 'The Roerich Pact and the Banner of Peace.'

On 14 April 1935, the Pact was signed in Washington at the White House by American President F.D. Roosevelt and twenty Latin American countries of the Pan American Union. Later in India, in 1948, the newly formed Indian government agreed to adopt it as well. The contribution of the Roerich Pact to the articles of the 1954 Hague Convention for the Protection of Cultural Property in the Event of Armed Conflict and recently to the Second Protocol of 1999, both of which form the basis of our cultural treaties, is well documented. But, though the 1954 Hague Convention prohibits the deportation of cultural property from the region, many states do not have the requisite legal framework to protect this. International law can only establish framework for legislation, but measures have to be taken nationally to make it a ground reality.

After the Iraq National Museum was looted (2003), the Kabul Museum defaced and Bamiyan Buddhas obliterated in Afghanistan (2001), Serbia's 16th century Stari Most across Neretva River destroyed in a Croatian attack (1993), and in India the demolition of Babri Masjid at Ayodhya two decades ago, Roerich's global ideas on cultural preservation have acquired greater current significance. In Russia, too, paradoxically, while the Russian Soviets preserved Moscow's legacy of Czarist buildings, today as new wealth dominates this luxury-crazed city, worries over the preservation of historic architecture loom large. Clearly, cultural property is non-renewable. Between the decades 1940 to 1990 we have destroyed fifty percent of our cultural heritage, says Archduke Karl von Hapsburg-Lothringen, President of the International Committee of the Blue Shield.[6]

In the past, international or national conflicts targeted infrastructure. But today when strife is increasingly based on ethnicity, cultural property becomes the object of rage. In post-1991 Eurasia, International Roerich Societies emphasise the protection of just such material architecture and cultural heritage in times of war, natural disaster and armed conflict.

Shambhala—the Quest for the Land of Dharma

Roerich's influences were largely from eastern philosophies. In 1901, Nicholas Roerich married Helena Shaposhnikova, born to an accomplished St. Petersburg family. She shared his interest in art, music and Chinese, Tibetan and Indian philosophy and possessed an immense knowledge of Buddhist philosophy. Helena Roerich had translated two volumes of H.P. Blavatsky's theosophical treatise *Secret Doctrine*. Many of Roerich's paintings were a result of their common creativity, he said. It is said that the continuity of the theosophical outlook from Tsarist time to post-Communist Russia was established through the Roerichs.

In 'Living Ethics', Marina Bernardi explains the kernel of the philosophy of Agni Yoga. V. Khvorostov further discusses the underlying principles in his essay 'Diamond of Consciousness.' He elucidates how the practice enhances 'awareness of subtle energies in strengthening people's hearts.' They held many common beliefs with the Theosophical Society which also emphasised universal brotherhood and the comparative study of religion.

The young couple co-operated with the Buriat Lama Dorzhiev in building a Tibetan Buddhist Temple in St. Petersburg. Dorzhiev saw the possibility of an alliance of the Buriats, Kaimyk and other Buddhist tribes living in the eastern part of Russia with the thirteenth Dalai Lama, who was the most politically aware of the Dalai Lamas then. Lama Doboom Tulku, in 'Nicholas Roerich: Influences and Experiences,' writes that from Dorzhiev, the Roerichs learned of the Tibetan text and ritual, the *Kalachakra* (The Wheel of Time) and of the coming of a new historical-astrological cycle, 'The New Age' to be marked by a new Buddha, Maitreya. Contemporary scholars state Roerich's own spiritual and philosophical aspirations are said to have been to establish a neo-Buddhist state in which Russia would have a place that would secure it as an eastern power. Tsar Nicholas II as the Buddhist Tsar would have been a counterweight to English and Chinese influence in Tibet before plans fell through and the Bolsheviks drove the family of Romanovs out of Soviet Russia. It is to be remembered between the two World Wars—the conflicting ramifications of universal socialist ideas were propelling the growth of peoples' movements in China, India and Russia in the same time frame. The question often asked was, what shape and role should the Americans carve for themselves? Roerich sought perhaps to show them a direction, explains Palat.

Nicholas II, however, was not to become the 'Bodhisatva Tsar'. Much of this has come under speculation of being part of a grand territorial ambition, his larger than life obsession. But Roerich's admirers have always said he was a visionary. They claim that his pursuit was for a land of dharma—the physical manifestation of a veritable Shambhala, where man could return to the earth its pristine and divine beauty, protect its isolated prairies, allow for nature to breathe, hence his repeated assertion that 'Beauty is Culture'. For him the anti-imperialist movement could provide an excellent opportunity to carve a pan-Mongol space or a pan-Buddhist space—where there could be such a cultural and philosophical environment, is evident in his diaries and writings. It would serve as the bridge between a Tsarist and new Russia.

Motives of artists are not easily understood; how their seemingly conflicting thoughts and ideas fuse upon a central goal. Says the Nobel

Path to Tibet, 1925 (Nicholas Roerich Museum, NY)

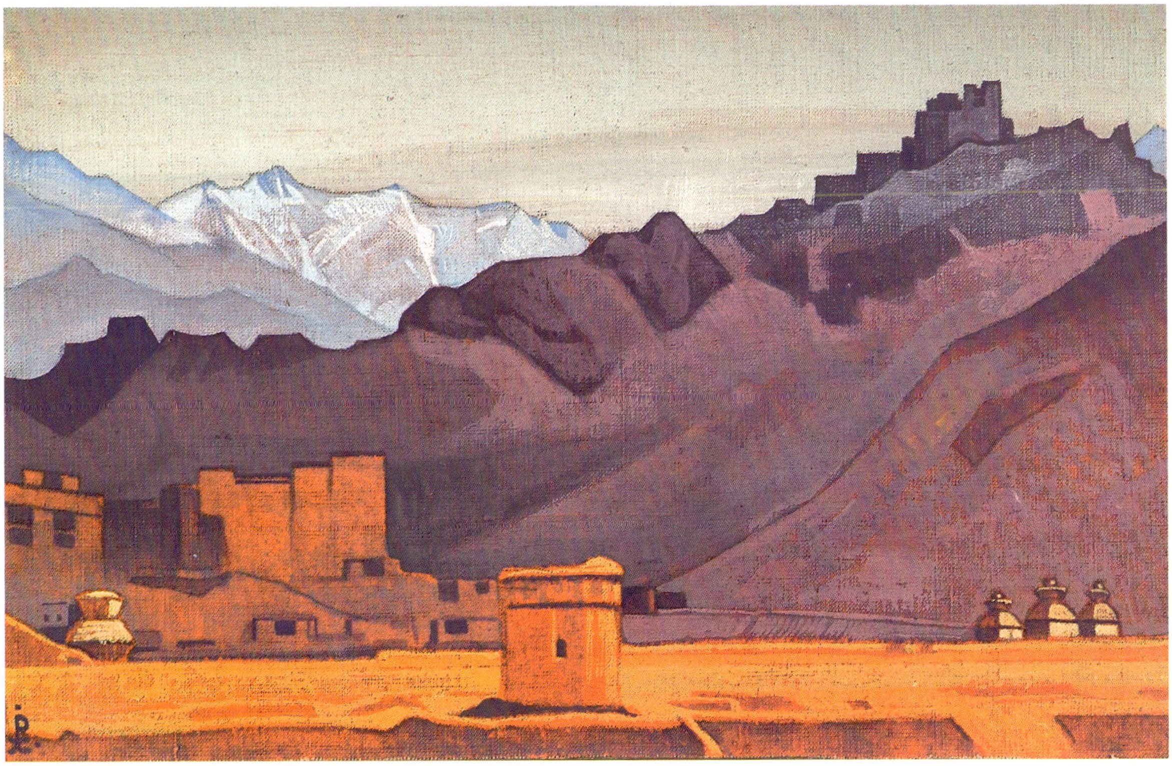

laureate and writer Orhan Pamuk, 'Men have the capacity to entertain contradictory thoughts with much more capacity than 19th century writings have told us is possible.'[7] That we do not have to follow them sequentially, or for them to be in logical progression, for the mind to sift them and perceive their connectivity, he explains.

Roerich continued to watch the international scenario develop between the 30s and 40s from his perch in the mountains of Kullu in India, still with his Russian passport, not ceasing to consider himself a *bonafide* Russian. At this point again Roerich's paintings, such as *Gesar Khan* and *News from the Himalayas* were considered in some way to be prophetic. In 1941, amidst the Soviet army's defeat, 'Alexander Nevsky' rides in the middle of a battlefield of soldiers. It was soon after the end of the War, in 1947, that Roerich passed away quietly in his Indian mountain home.

Roerich in India

It is often said that Russia and India are old souls. In their quest for modernity they shared the same time line. When Tsarist Russia went to war with Japan, there were reverberations in India in the Partition of Bengal (1905). As the Bolshevik Revolution gained ground, the Khilafat movement boosted the nascent Indian Congress Party after 1917.

However, in his essay 'Conditional Love', John McCannon writes of Roerich's 'western dismay' when he first arrived on seeing Indian poverty and the abysmal conditions of people under British rule, but those outcries are bedded amidst other observations where the *apna pan* of self-critique is clear. Roerich certainly saw the inequities, the degradation, and he makes mention of an India chafing under the British yoke. But he believed Russian culture had very strong Indian roots and that the world too was indebted to Indian philosophical and cultural traditions.

Today Roerich's legacy strengthens the case for India's traditions for composite culture and internationalism. Innumerable inspirational paintings of Roerich are found at museums and institutes in Benaras, Chandigarh, Delhi (Pusa), Allahabad, Chennai and Naggar aside from those in private collections. The International Roerich Memorial Trust is headquartered in Bangalore and at Naggar, Kullu. At a time when, post 9/11 religious and ethnic strife are tearing apart Eurasia, and Central and South Asia, and the world is increasingly being viewed as bi-polar, and sometimes even uni-polar. Roerich's work, rooted in the sense of common

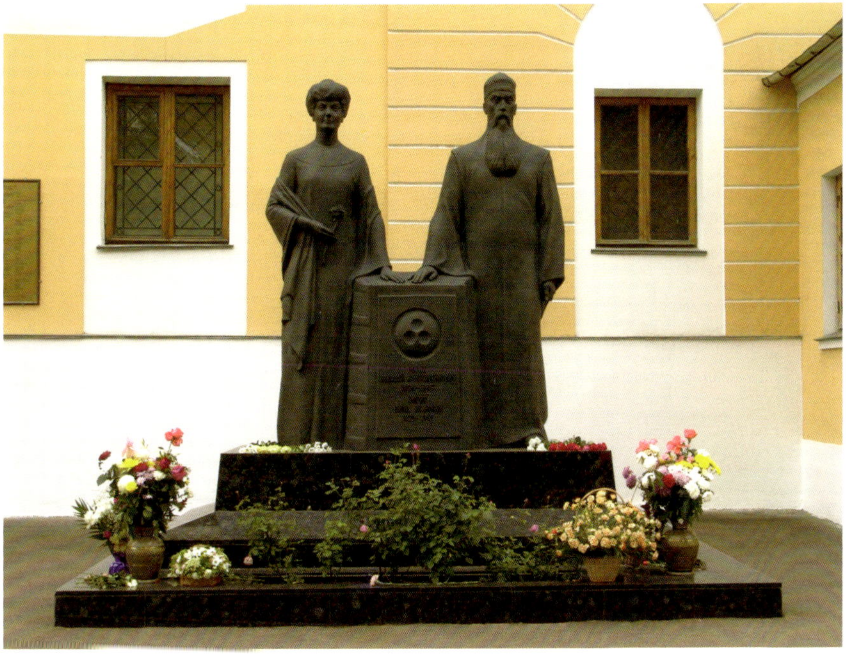

Monument sacred to the memory of Helena Roerich and Nicholas Roerich (International Centre of the Roerichs, Moscow)

religious beliefs and shared cultures, is relevant in our increasingly fragmented society. Through his paintings, the Roerich Peace Pact, his delving into the philosophy of Living Ethics and his journeys, one thing comes true and clear is that he was looking for the essential unity of life, its intermingling with a common universal soul.

End Notes

1. The Soviet government flatly forbade theosophy and the association of Russian Theosophist. A few members were forced to emigrate abroad after 1938. (www.hctheosophist.com/archives/pdf/hc200301.pdf, p3.2/9/2011)
2. Reproduced from the holdings of the Franklin D. Roosevelt Library, 504.418 B I/89
3. Raisa Gorbachev was involved in starting a fund in the name. (www.hctheosophist.com/archives/pdf/hc200301.pdf, p4, 2/9/2011)
4. Partha Chatterjee, http://www.thehindu.com/thehindu/fline/f2625/stories/20091218262509200.htm 5/22/2010
5. The 2010 Europa Nostra, Europe's foremost prize for culture was awarded to Mme. Shaposhnikova for making the dilapidated Lopukhins Estate into one of the finest museums dedicated to N. Roerich's work both as a painter and cultural/peace activist. Established in 1963, EUROPA NOSTRA represents 400 organisations across Europe and is headed by the Spanish tenor Placido Domingo)
6. Established in 1996, the 'Blue Shield' Committees aim to be for cultural heritage what the Red Cross is to human life.
7. Orhan Pamuk, *The Naïve and Sentimental Novelist*, Penguin India, New Delhi, 2010.

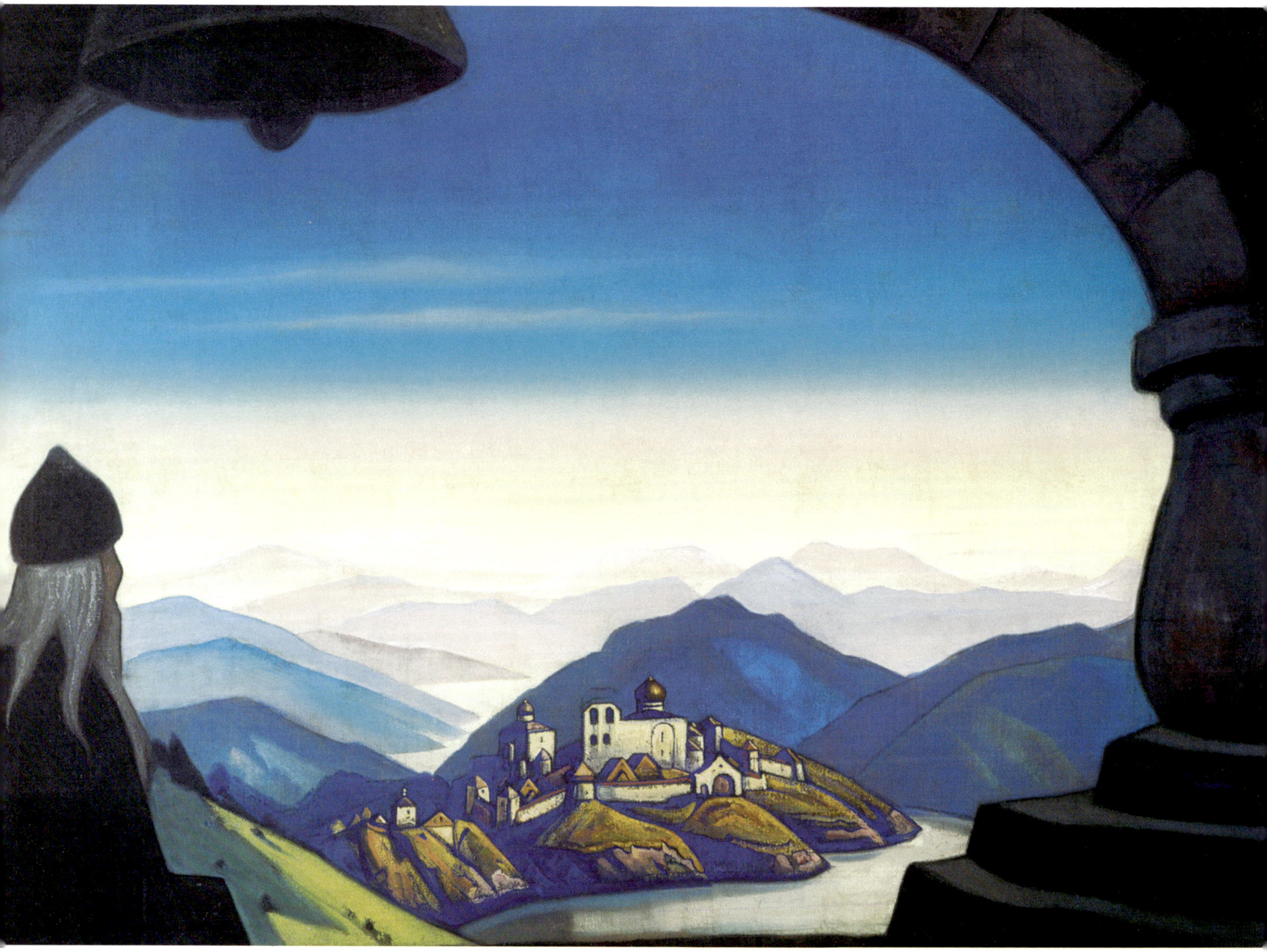

Terra Slavonica, 1943 (International Centre of the Roerichs, Moscow)

Nicholas Roerich: Artist and Messiah[1]

Madhavan K. Palat

Nicholas Roerich matured in a generation that rejected the past and much of tradition with an exuberance that was as essential to its proponents as it seemed irrational to its critics. The forms of radicalism that surfaced were bewildering in their variety, but for the present purpose they may be condensed into two. The first of these turned to the external environment for solutions to the problems afflicting human society and depended on the certitudes of science and rationality. They pursued their remedies through the state, the economy and the social structure, the law, the bureaucracy and social institutions. Armed with these concepts, the state and its establishment dragged Russian society through a forced industrialisation from the 1890s until the 1930s. The oft-recounted story of the revolutionary drama of this period which tore Russia apart and reconstructed her as the former Soviet Union

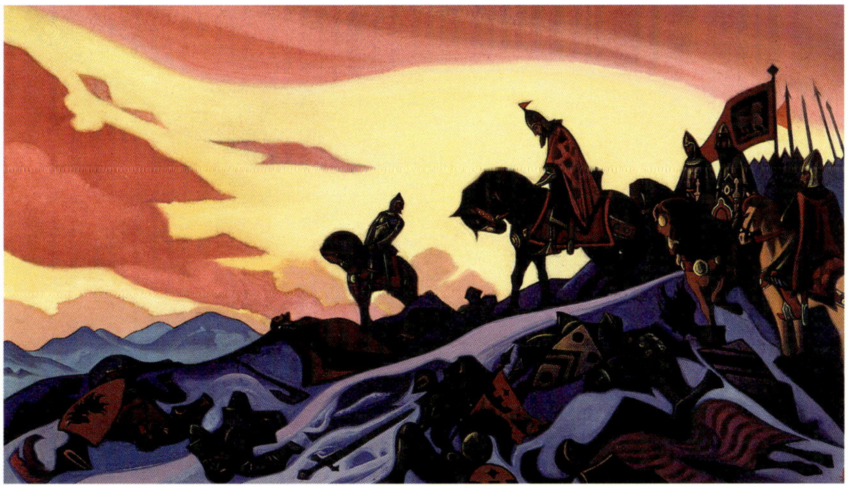

Alexander Nevsky, 1942 (International Centre of the Roerichs, Moscow)

is one of a series of revolutions and wars between 1904 and 1945, including the two World Wars, the disastrous famines which starved millions and the terrors of the *gulag*.

The other series of radicalisms looked for salvation in the inner self rather than in the external environment of social and political institutions in order to investigate all that modernity imagined had been irrevocably superseded. They investigated the irrational, plumbed the depths of the unconscious, crossed over into transgression, sought out 'higher forms of consciousness' and attempted to divine cosmic mysteries. They were represented ideologically through various forms of conservatism like Slavophilism, Eurasianism, Byzantinism, Panmongolism, civilisation theory, much else, including Nietzschean trends within Marxism like Gorky's and Lunacharsky's Godbuilding. In the world of art and culture they were located in Symbolism, Russian Art Nouveau, the World of Art, Decadence, much of what came to be called the avant-garde, and included at the extreme spiritualism, mysticism, Satanism and occultism, theosophy, anthroposophy and messianism. They distanced themselves from academicism in art, as also from the critical realism of the Wanderers of an earlier generation and most often from the socialist realism of the subsequent, post-revolutionary generation.

The first set of trends resulted in what is historically known as the revolutionary epoch in politics; the second ushered in the Silver Age of Russian culture, the two of them coinciding, and often overlapping in time with many of the same *dramatis personae*. Roerich squarely placed himself, and has been placed by historians and critics, in the latter category as he expressed himself chiefly through primevalism, Symbolism, occultism and messianism.

The first painting that brought Roerich renown and entry into the hall of fame, the Tretiakov Gallery in Moscow, was *The Messenger* (1897), depicting two men in a boat approaching a Slavic settlement upstream with the news of the coming of the Varangians or Vikings. The theme was severely historical, the style remarkably realist, exuding a sense of foreboding. This was the closest he came to celebrated painters like Ilya Repin, but marked his distance from them by not engaging in patriotism. This was intended to be one of a series of twelve paintings called the *Slavic Symphony*, the story of the coming of the Varangians as told in *The Primary Chronicle*; but he did not proceed with it. Two years later, he produced another comparable

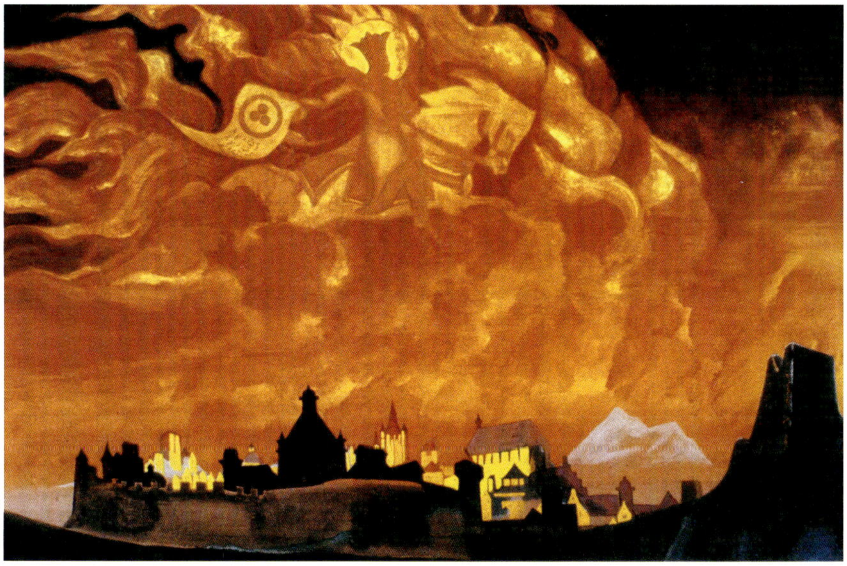

Sophia the Almighty Wisdom, 1932 (Nicholas Roerich Museum, NY)

and thematically similar historical painting, *The Campaign* (1899). The pessimistic air upset the critical realists led by V. Stasov, but it pleased Sergei Diaghilev, the enthusiastic propagator of all that was new, of Impressionism, post-Impressionism, Symbolism and Art Nouveau. Historical Russia was a starting point, but Roerich preferred legend to researched history—it led him to origins, to the mysteries of life and allowed an exploration of spiritual life and of a harmonious integrated existence. His depiction of the coming of the Varangians, their exchanges with the local population and their settlement along the Dnieper were cheerful, brilliant with colour and bustling with activity. It derived from a vision that was utterly Narodnik, of co-operative and non-alienated labour in everyday life. It also belonged to a wider European movement represented by William Morris and especially by the Arts and Crafts Movement in England. This was domesticated in Russia by Princess Maria Tenisheva at Talashkino, where artists of the calibre of Aleksandr Benois, Mikhail Vrubel and Roerich among others gathered to produce everyday items of furniture, textiles, metals and much else, many of them of exquisite museum quality.

Roerich's search for harmony in the troubled modern world was a journey from Russian history to Slavic myth and legend, to a pagan sensibility, further to Scandinavian, Eurasian, Hindu and Buddhist legend and eventually to the unlikely setting of the Old Stone Age. He claimed that our ancestors then lived as one community in a single

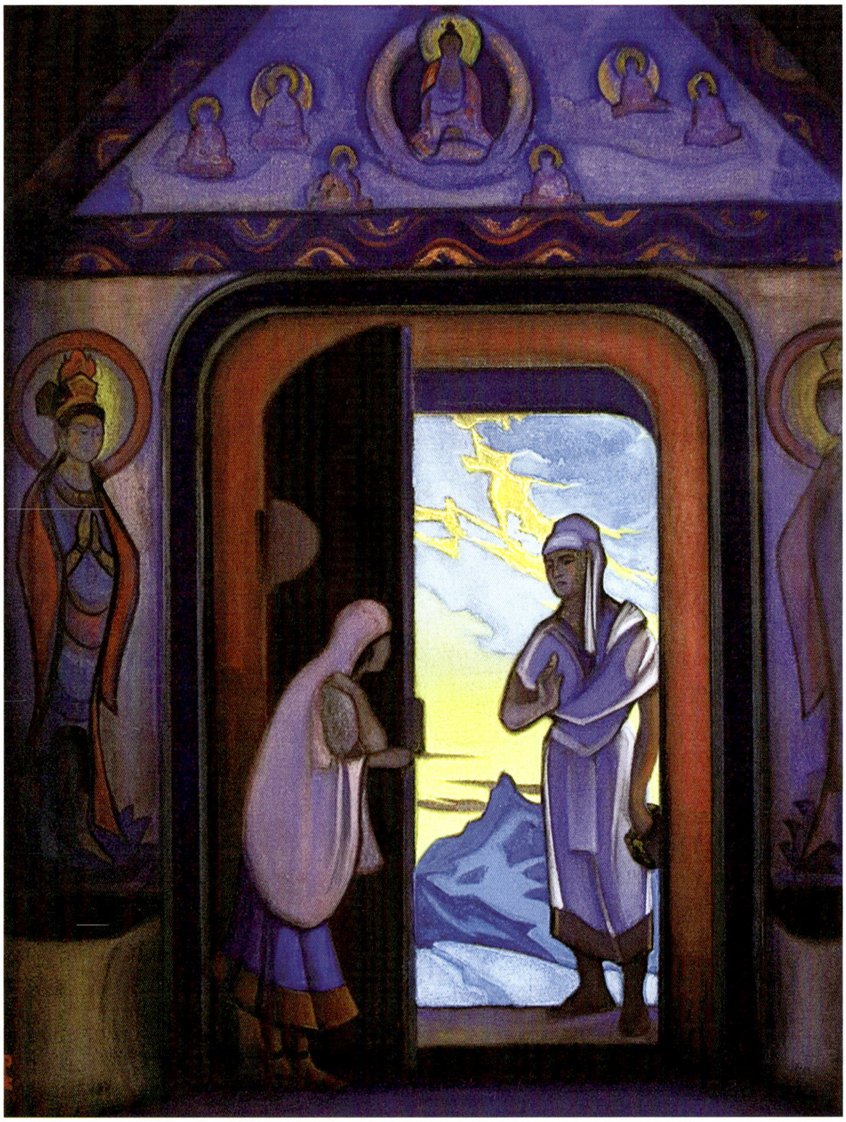

The Messenger, 1946 (International Centre of the Roerichs, Moscow)

geographical space, at peace with themselves and the universe around them with a feeling for the mystery of the divine and the sacred. In a famous essay of 1909, he argued that the modern world had lost the joy of art, of the capacity to live in it and experience its immediacy He deplored mass production, the origins of which he traced to metal casting of moulds. The Old Stone Age was the most creative for this reason, for objects of everyday use were individually made and decorated and decorative art was necessarily creative.

The idea of the 'primitive' community or of a primitive communism was common to most of the speculative histories of the 19th century in

Europe and Russia. He saw himself as both agent and witness to that impending millennial transformation. In this respect, he differed little from dreamers like Bakunin and Kropotkin, or Lenin and Martov, who were firm in their conviction of ushering in the millennium. While the socialists sought a revolution in all external power structures that would create the conditions for such enlightenment in communism, Roerich looked to the inward transformation of the individual through spiritual exercises. All his art was a means to such a revolution through the spirit.

The pagan sensibility, the cosmic mystery, the feeling for the sacred, and of man as wholly a part of nature were all explored in a large number of canvases. In the first of such canvases, *The Gathering of the Elders* (1899), a group of tribal elders is deep in consultation around a cult site in a forest clearing. The most famous canvas, *The Idols* (1901), depicts an ancient cult site with white doves overhead as a symbol of harmony with nature. It was followed by *Conjuration by Water* (1905), in which an elder causes the waters to rise by ritual movements of his arms and perhaps incantations. And again, in 1911, in *Human Forefathers*, a Slav youth playing a reed pipe is lulling to sleep a circle of bears, in Slav legend the ancestors of humanity, in a gentle landscape of harmony and peace. Between 1907 and 1910, he painted the Bogatyr frieze of seven panels based again on Slavic mythology, an evocation of prehistoric life at its most vigorous and fulfilling.

From 1907, he painted numerous highly acclaimed stage sets besides designing costumes for operas, ballets and plays; he continued to explore Slavic pagan themes, but but its specifically Slavic content atrophied. As a contemporary observed, 'Roerich's 'man' is not Russian, Slav, or Viking. He is ancient man, the primeval barbarian of the earth.'[2] In 1907, he was commissioned by the Opéra Comique of Paris to design the stage sets for Rimskii-Korsakov's *The Snow Maiden* (*Snegurochka*). It was a very Russian tale and sets had been designed in the 1880s by Vasnetsov; but Roerich now produced them with more Eurasian elements in costumery, the feeling was pantheistic and very pagan and it was utterly fantastical. He continued in a similar vein for the sets of Polovtsian Dances, which were a sequence in Alexander Borodin's *Prince Igor*. It opened in the Théâtre du Châtelet in Paris in 1909 to delirious audiences, an important element in the success being Roerich's sets. Their towers, forts and churches were Slavic; but the limitless steppe, the brilliant skies and once again an indeterminate and primordial landscape, all moved the viewer beyond, toward a universal spiritual quest.

However, the sensational and revolutionary event of the decade in the world of art, and perhaps the culmination of Roerich's set designing career, was Stravinsky's masterpiece, the *Rite of Spring* (1913). It is the tale of the sacrifice of the maiden who must dance to her death for the sun god Yarilo. With the encircling bears as the ancestors of the human species, it was certainly very Slavic. Stravinsky's score and Nijinsky's choreography were variously discordant and disorienting, and the audience was ecstatic and outraged in equal measure; but a new age had dawned with this event. Roerich's designs evoked everything that was Slavic, pagan and mysterious, and it all seemed to belong to the dawn of time. He deployed his well-known themes, the sacred circle of palisades and the dead horse heads from *Idols*, the elders in bearskins from *Human Forefathers*.

Disturbingly, it seemed to prefigure the coming age of inhumanity and barbarism. The dancers formed in circles that closed into themselves, with their feet turned inward, the opposite of the ballet dancer's graceful outward flow of the arms and spring of the body. An outraged critic wrote that the Chosen One looked like a 'knock-kneed idiot contorted by paralysis, before she abandons herself to a massive attack of epilepsy.'[3] There is no record of human sacrifice in Slavic folklore and with his encyclopedic knowledge of the subject, Roerich could not have erred. Did the sets then portray the viciousness of the epoch and an end to Europe's expansiveness, or the harmony of communal existence in god and nature periodically reestablished through ritual? The uncertainties and ambiguities they induced, were revolutionary at the time, even if they may not appear so radical today.

Roerich duly moved from the Slavic to other myths, especially Nordic mythology. Canvases like *The Ominous Ones* (*Zloveshchie*) (1900-1901) showing a flock of ravens, birds of ill-omen, or *The Herald* (*Vestnik*) (1914), a black ship, a bearer of bad news, approaching a high cliff with a puny settlement atop it, derived from that source. *The Herald,* similar to his first work, *The Messenger*, was less realistic and distinctly ominous, as if foretelling the catastrophe about to descend on Europe and Russia. His enthusiasm for *The Valkyrie* led him to produce sets in 1907, although he had not even been commissioned for them and they were never in fact used. Most unusually, the critical acclaim was extraordinary, and in 1921 the journal *Kunst und Dekorazion* published in Darmstadt declared it was the best that had ever been produced for a Wagner opera. Similarly, his sets for the Moscow Art Theatre's production of Ibsen's *Peer Gynt* in 1912 were highly acclaimed and rated as the most faithful to the Nordic environment, although, unlike the rest of the cast, he had refused to travel to Norway to inspect the landscape or study customs. He preferred to seize 'reality' through the imagination rather than observation.

As he penetrated the infinite distance of time, precise geographical location and landscape became of declining significance and suggestions of the primeval world the primary focus. Travelling through the deserts of New Mexico and Arizona in the early 1920s, he was drawn to the tribal customs of native peoples and produced a series of paintings called *Messiah*; similarly he was attracted to the wild seascapes of the coast of Maine in 1922 on which he painted an entire series called *Ocean*.

Despite the pronounced pagan sensibility, Roerich smoothly integrated Christian themes into his quest for the primordial. After a trip through twenty-seven historical towns during the summers of 1903 and 1904, he painted a large number of canvases of Russian medieval churches, forts and towns that were far more than mere depictions of Russian historical sites. Representing the unity of nature in which all of human life and its products seamlessly belonged, they were more in the spirit of a universal belief system than of specifically Christian worship and reverence. These paintings celebrated the lapidary power of the churches, and their embedment in Russian soil. Thus the *Cross*

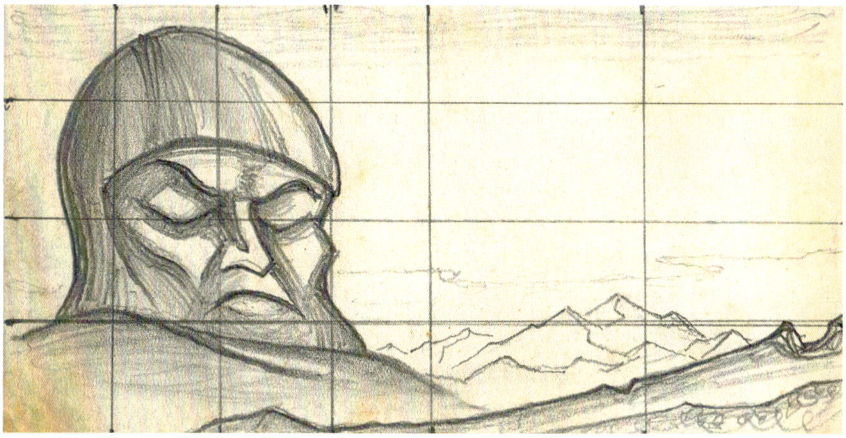

The Dream of the Orient, 1920-1921, sketch for a painting of the same name (International Centre of the Roerichs, Moscow)

at Izhorsk (1903) stood all alone like an ancient ruin or a solitary idol in an empty landscape, the broad brush strokes suggesting powerful currents of energy building up from the left and heading toward the cross which bends slightly to the right, apparently under this pressure. Another cross seems to lie half-buried on the left in that same mound. As a contemporary observed of his depiction of these Christian sites, 'He scrutinised the stone face of ancient times and grasped its expression.'[4]

His most Christian moments were reflected in his paintings of Madonnas and female deities. However here, too, he searched for a universal, and not specifically Christian, embodiment of female virtues and sensibility; he was not obsessed with sensuality and military prowess, with a Salome, Ishtar, Kali or Durga. He found his ideal in the Virgin Mary. This was probably due more to personal and psychological inclination than religious devotion. He was by no means misogynistic, but his ideal women were more spiritual than sensual. His search during the first decade of the 20th century culminated in the fresco of the *The Queen of Heaven* (1912) in the Church of the Holy Spirit at Talashkino. This deity, which had been rejected in 1906 for violating the canon, is highly syncretic even if superficially Christian. The crown presented a traditional Catholic image of the Virgin, but she looked more like a Byzantine empress, whether Christian or otherwise, or a pagan river goddess watching over the river flowing at her feet. Her hands are set in a *namaste*; and the Buddhist and even Hindu icon of the lotus appears in place of the infant Jesus. His other Madonnas are similarly syncretic. *The Mother of the World* (1924 and 1937) is seated on rocks which may be a stylised lotus in a water body; and his *Sophia the Almighty Wisdom* (1932) is a matronly warrior blazing through the skies.

A number of paintings used Christian imagery to record the horror that was taking place or to clairvoyantly portend what was about to occur in Europe. In 1912, he saw the imminent holocaust in a dream and heard a voice proclaim 'the end of times.' Like Coleridge, he put down what he saw, and like Blake, he painted the vision: *The Last Angel* (1912) descended onto a city aflame, marking the end of time as in the Book of Revelation (in 1942, he returned to that subject to record the horror that was taking place in his homeland). Between 1912 and 1914 he painted overpowering canvases of doom: *The Sword of Valour, The Pure City Tormented by Enemies, The Battle in the Heavens, The Herald* and

The Doomed City. Gorky was so attracted by the sensational *Doomed City* that he bought it with the very un-Marxist comment that Roerich was an 'intuitivist' and 'above reason.' The symbolism and meaning of this renowned canvas were ambiguous. As the Christian metaphor of evil, the serpent could have trapped the city in its coils; as representing the *kundalini*, hence divine wisdom, the serpent alone was possibly aware of what the feckless citizens were not. A year earlier he had painted another canvas, *The Cry of the Serpent*, where an enormous snake at the base of a cliff lets out a cry, possibly as a warning of an impending disaster. Again, this serpent was more *kundalini* than Satan. However, his visions of imminent catastrophe were not cast exclusively in Christian symbolism. He produced many 'prophetic' paintings, just as Alexander Blok was to compose his prophetic poetry; his angels could be demonic and his work was increasingly marked by pantheistic visions, supernatural elements and metaphysical landscapes.

World War I confirmed the worst fears of many. Swedenborgism, spiritualism, occultism, astrology and the like became major obsessions in those tense years. Christianity, or its symbols and myths, was merely one of the many vehicles to express foreboding and seek reassurance. Saints appear in their roles as protectors, like *St. Nicholas* (1916), *St. Mercurius* (1917), *Procopius the Righteous Averting the Stone Cloud from the City of Ustiug* (1914) and *Procopius the Righteous Praying for the Unknown Travellers* (1914). Perhaps the most soothing is *Panteleimon the Healer* (1916), who is appropriately enough collecting restorative herbs in a peaceful and cheerful garden. Many others suggest the calm and peace of the sanctuary, as in *House of the Spirit* (1915); *The Hiding Place* (1915); *Repentence* (1917) and *The Holy Island* (1917), presenting a chapel on a cliff, hermits' cells, a monastery and a rock island. A number of works, however, express the atrocity of war: *The Glow* (1914), a city in flames; *Conflagrations* (1914), a castle goes up in flames; *Shadows* (1916), a distorted city; and *Human Deeds* (1914), a city destroyed.

As Roerich moved away from history, archaeology and folklore into the distant realms of mythology and origins, he gravitated toward Symbolism to express the mysterious. In the literary world of the late 1890s, Symbolism had attracted some of the most erudite, daring and innovative of Russian writers, condensing much of what is known as the Silver Age. It was more a movement than a doctrine and asserted the superiority of intuitions over empirical observation to grasp the essence of things, similar to the Romantic movement at the beginning

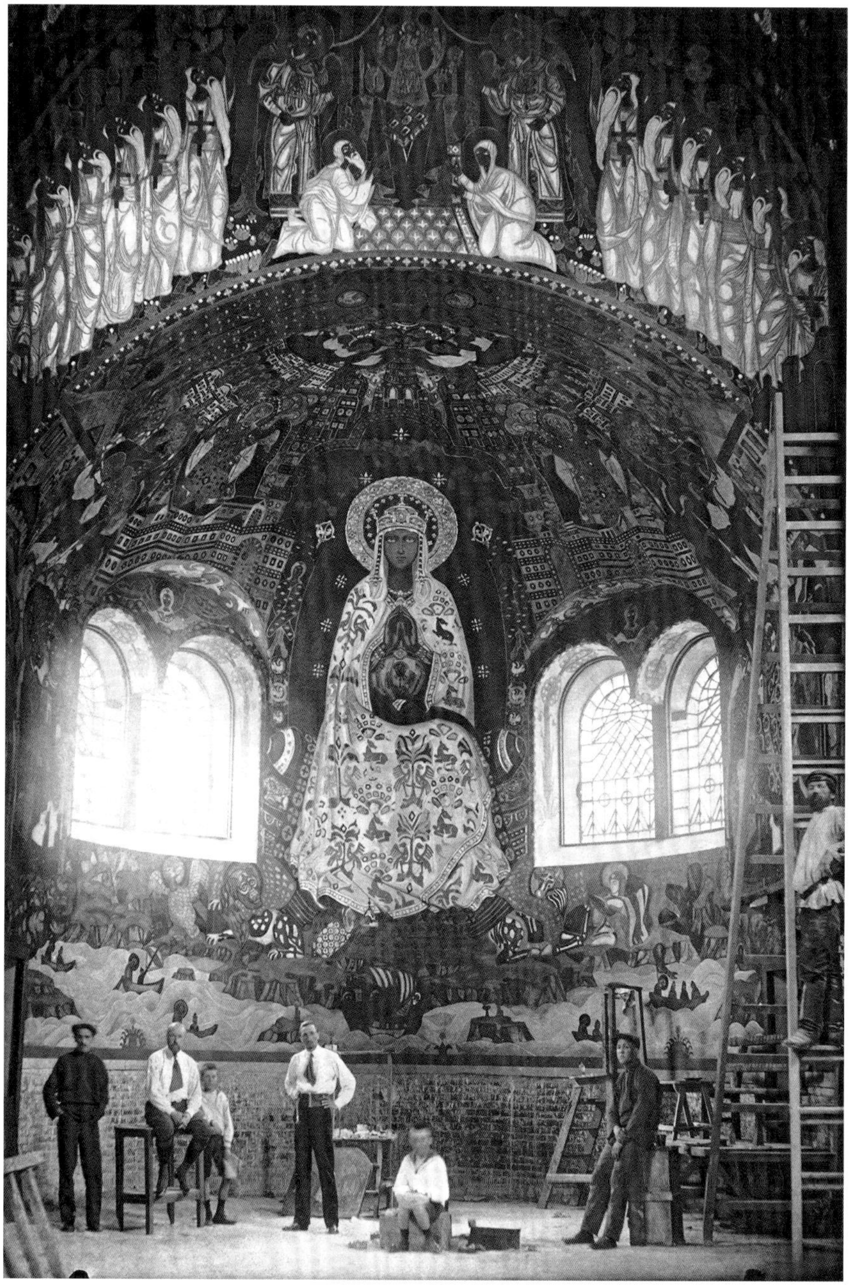

The Queen of Heaven fresco in the Church of the Holy Spirit in Talashkino. Sitting on a bench: Nicholas Roerich, Svetoslav Roerich (beside him), George Roerich (seated in front) 1914. Talashkino, Smolensk province (Nicholas Roerich Museum Archive, NY)

of the 19th century. The phenomenal world was considered a reflection of a higher reality; Symbolists were therefore highly attuned to the irrational, the subconscious and the unconscious, the spirit, the occult and with mental instability, decay, and morbidity. Their literary inspiration came from Baudelaire, Verlaine, Mallarme, and especially Maurice Maeterlinck, who interested Roerich immensely.

Accordingly, from about 1900, his people and landscapes begin to lose their specifically Russian and Slavic features. The figures become more stylised, the colours more arbitrary and ambiguous symbols impart meaning to the canvas. Thus the symbols of the raven, the white doves, the serpent and the angel in a series of canvases before and during the War, appear mysterious in the manner so beloved of the Symbolists. His Christian subject matter, too, is handled in a manner more Symbolist than Christian. His theatre sets, especially for the *Snow Maiden*, the *Polovtsian Dances* and the *Rite of Spring*, exhibit these features remarkably. In the paintings *Human Forefathers* (1911) and *Procopius the Righteous Praying for the Unknown Travellers* (1914), for example, the flat and widely spaced surfaces and the greens, violets and pinks, convey an infinite calm and spiritual repose. One of his most overpowering works, *The Heavenly Battle* (1909, 1912), suggests the immensity of nature and the titanic struggle in the sky as the storm clouds approach a puny human settlement at the corner of the painting.

His most Symbolist canvases are closely associated with Maurice Maeterlinck, especially as he explored the symbol of the cavern and the mountain to depict processes of awakening from an unconscious or unaware state to full consciousness. (It is astonishing how the radical intelligentsia, from Belinskii to Lenin, constructed the education and emancipation of the Russian people in almost identical terms.) A series of canvases marked the progress through the cavern up to the mountain, the mind's advance to illumination. This motif was also explored in the sets he designed for Maeterlinck's play, *Sister Beatrice*. Maeterlinck, like his contemporaries, drew on Dante's descent into Inferno and the subsequent rise to Purgatario and above. Roerich painted the negative attributes of the cavern in his sets for *Peer Gynt*, where the trolls lived in them like the modern bourgeois of two-dimensional self-sufficiency and philistine smugness, but *Peer Gynt* emancipated himself from this world. Descent into the subterranean world focussed the mind, compelled it to meditate on its condition and prepared it for its emancipation from its own blindness. Many sources of such symbolism were available to Roerich: ancient Greek and Roman myths, the catacombs of early Christians, the Russian Orthodox anchorite tradition of cells in monasteries of Kiev and Pskov, Siberian shamans imagining their journey into subterrestrial darkness to gain wisdom before gaining the mountain heights. Hindu and Islamic mythology also contains such stories, and in modern times, even Cold War history and mythology have treated Solzhenitsyn's *gulag* as one of a passage to enlightenment.

In the opposition of the cave to the mountain, the cavern, like the womb, also represented the assumed feminine principles of the spiritual, intuitive and the irrational against the masculine one of rationality. Another deeply significant meaning of this symbol was of the *axis mundi*, which conceived the world as positioned anywhere along the line from the deepest cavern to the most exalted mountain peak. Roerich maintained that the preoccupation with vertical structures in all human civilisations, be they towers, pyramids, ziggurats, trees or mountains like Kailas, Olympus and so many others is explained by this symbol. Mysteries are hidden deep underground, in the criss-crossing network of caverns as in the Chud legends of Siberia from there they rose into the light above, the mountain tops and eventually to his new world, Shambhala.

At this point Roerich moved into the world of the occult. Occultism is said to be distinguished from mysticism and religion by four properties: 1) correspondences, between the visible and the invisible world, and signs that reveal; 2) the concept of living nature, as held together by a system of sympathies and antipathies; 3) imagination and mediation to see and to guide; 4) transmutation of elements from one level to another. All this was esoteric knowledge, available only to the adept and seer.

Through such occult devices in Central Eurasia, he identified the original home of the human species in the space between south Siberia and the Himalayas or the Tibetan plateau and believed that the key to the future and salvation of mankind was to be found here. Like many of his contemporaries, Roerich was obsessed with the problem of the East and the West, and identification of the territory that would end conflict on earth melded perfectly with the current geopolitical theory. It identified Anglo-Russian rivalry in Central Asia as a major source of worldwide conflict and advocated the urgent necessity of resolving that tension through the conquest and firm political control of this territory by either the Russian or the British Empire. Roerich preferred the Russian Empire and, after 1917, he foresaw himself as inaugurating the new conflict free utopian state, the Sacred Union of the East.

He cast himself as a prophet and along with his wife, Helena Ivanovna, founded a new sect called the Agni Yoga. They awaited the

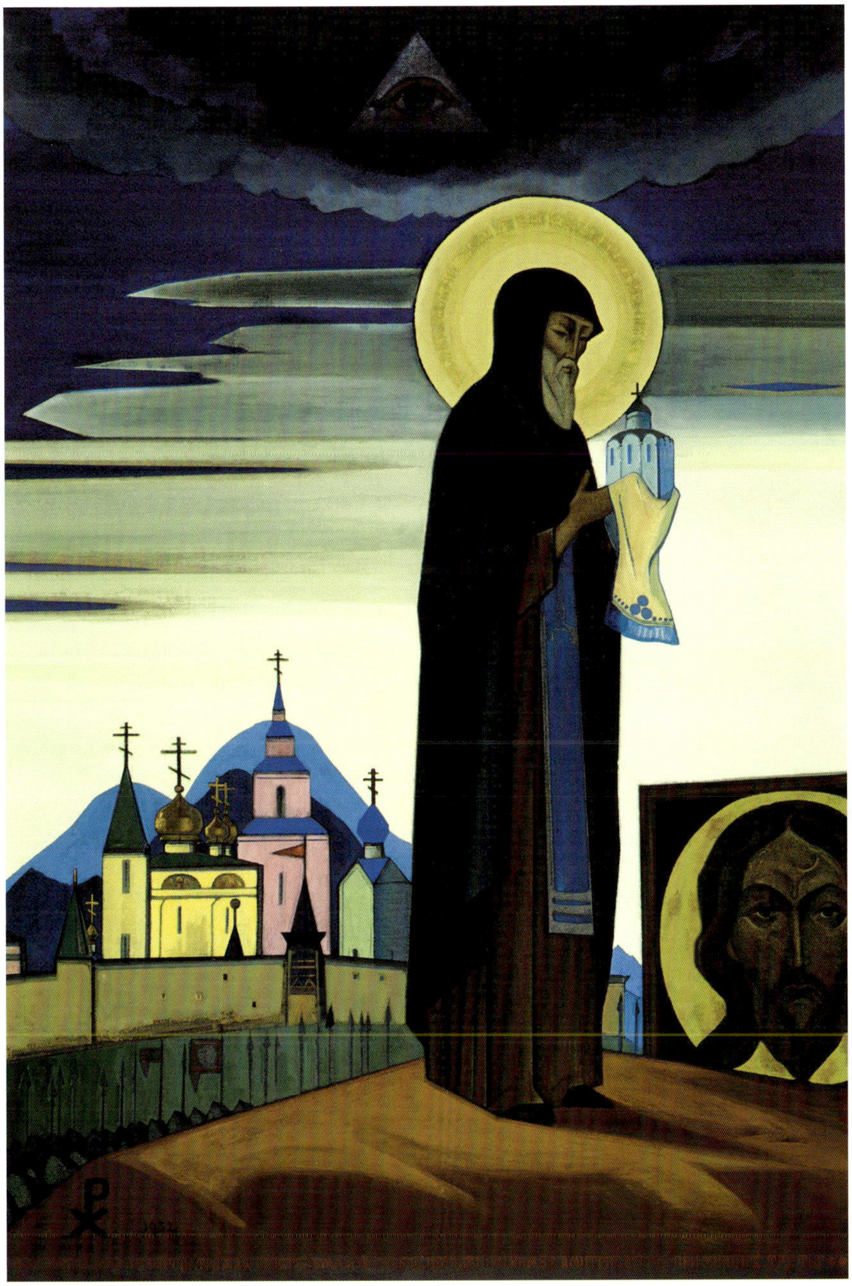

St Sergius Radonezhsky, 1932 (International Centre for the Roerichs, Moscow)

coming of a messiah called Maitreya, the Buddha of the future, and the founding of a new land of love, beauty and truth called Shambhala somewhere in the Himalayas. They received messages from the 'astral plane' from spiritual masters, especially Master Allal Ming, who convinced them of their mission to usher in this New Age of Peace and Beauty. Other masters were Koot Hoomi and Morya who seem to have

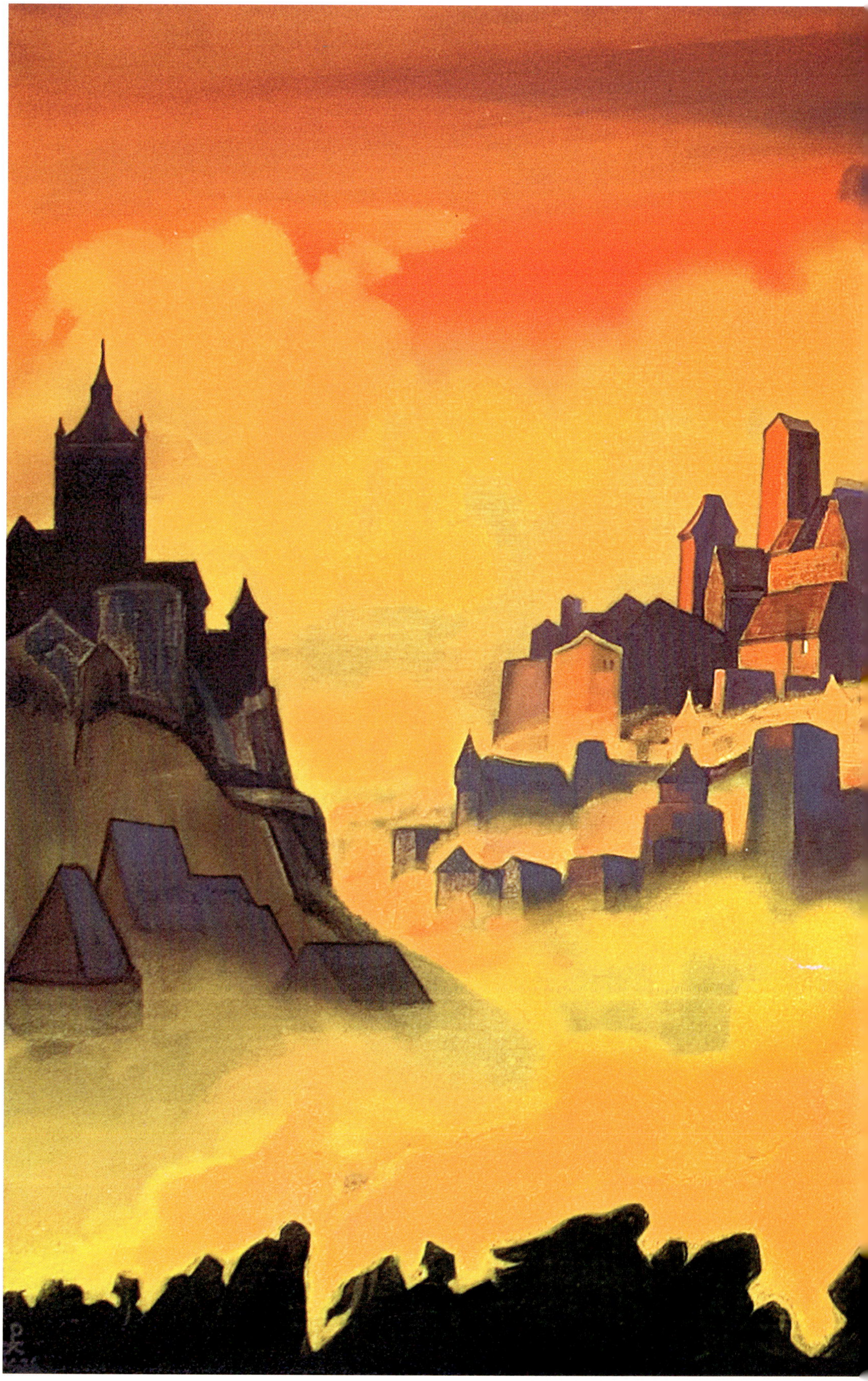

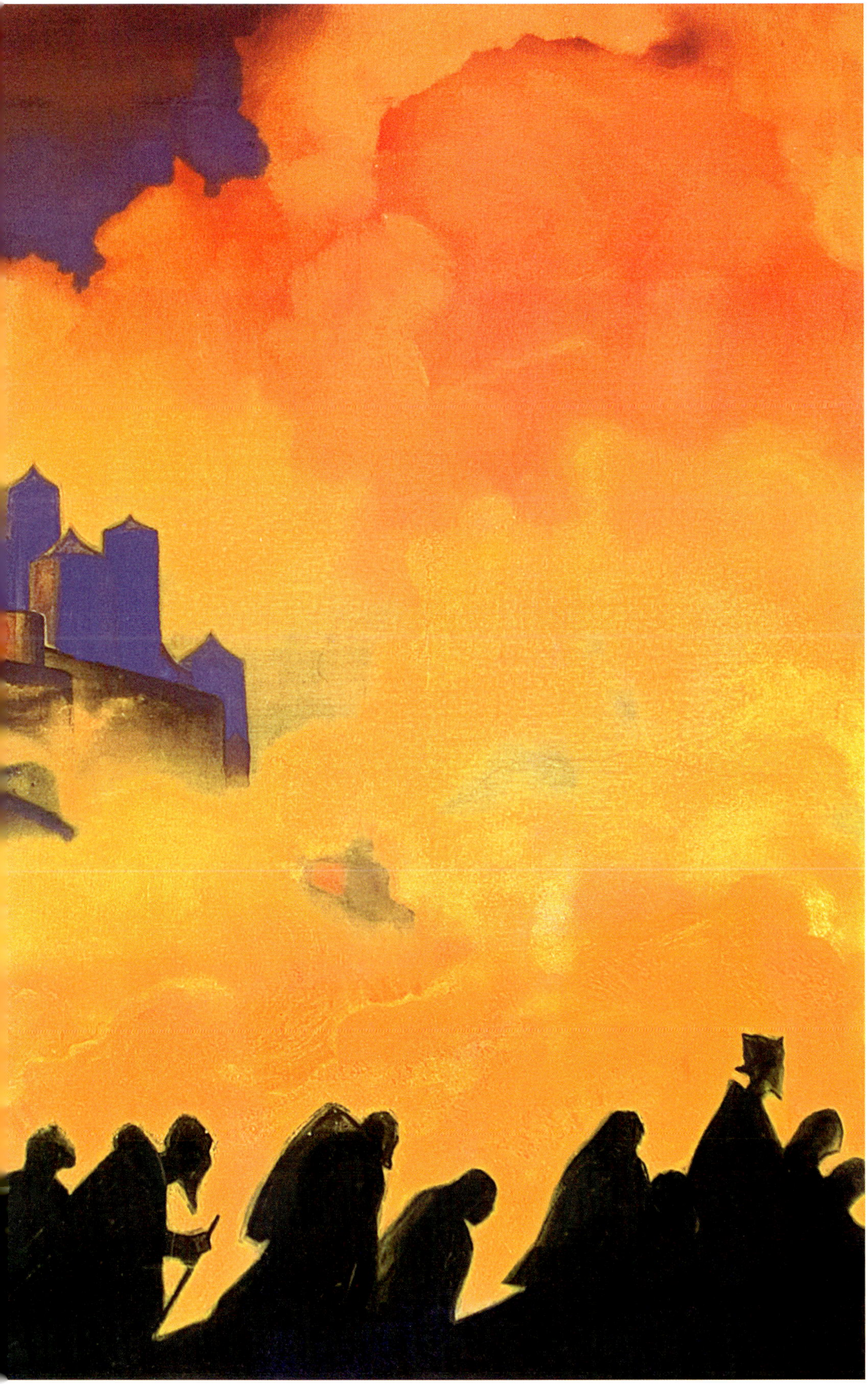

Armageddon, 1936 (International Centre of the Roerichs, Moscow)

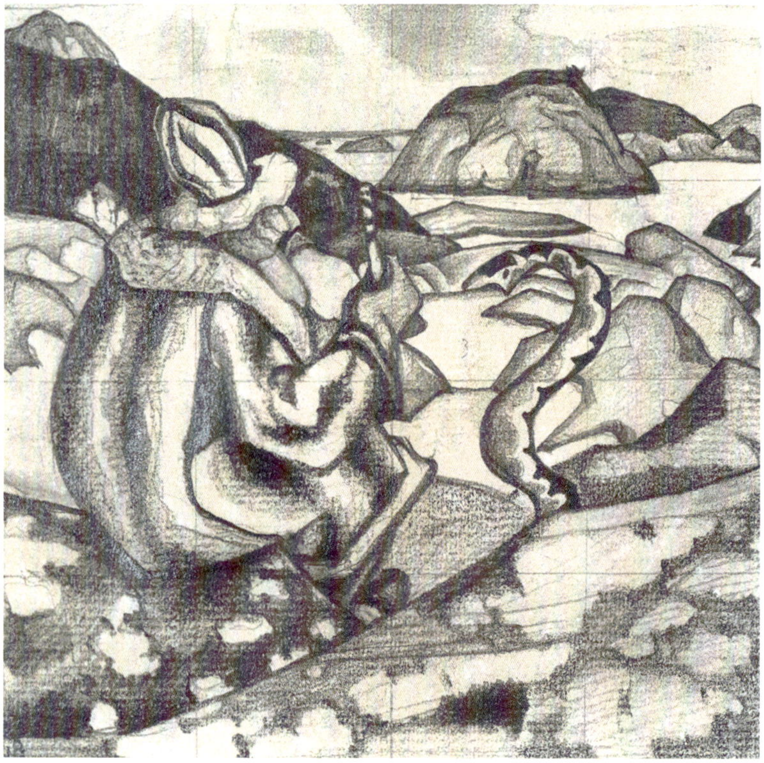

The Snake Charmer, 1920-21 (International Centre of the Roerichs, Moscow)

guided them through the years and even specified the year 1936 for the appearance of Shambhala and the coming of the Maitreya Buddha. (Astonishingly, that was the year that Stalin declared that socialism had been established and class antagonism overcome, an event that he celebrated with a new constitution.) These masters were providing regular instruction on the creation of the great Buddhist state in Eurasia; and it seemed to come with the benediction of either the Soviet Union or of the United States or quixotically enough both, with much tactical guidance on how to approach the rulers of either state. For his first expedition to this Eurasian world of the Altai, Mongolia, China and Tibet in 1925–1928, he received all clearances from Chicherin, the Soviet Commissar of the Nationalities. He had to visit Moscow in 1926 for the purpose and he was a canny enough politician to present paintings of the Maitreya Buddha who bore the features of none less than Lenin! For his second expedition in 1935, he mobilised finances from the American followers of his occultism, led by Henry Wallace, Roosevelt's Secretary for Agriculture and later the Vice-President of the USA.

As he engaged in allegedly obscure political manoeuvring, he painted his way into the ideal world. During the First World War, the landscapes shift from a visibly Russian and northern location to something more eastern as in *The Boundaries of the Kingdom* (1916); *The Summoned* (1916); *The Hunter at Rest* (1916); *The Wisdom of Manu* (1917). A growing number of paintings depict revelation, as in *The Sorceress* (1916); *The Command* (1916); *The Commands of Heaven* (1915); thereafter gods physically appear, arrows fall from the sky, hunters sight a quarry, all suggesting an advent. Fascinated by the tale of Gesar Khan in Ladakh, he made Gesar an avatar of Maitreya, and painted a series on the Gesar epic, *Host of Gesar Khan* (1931); *Sword of Gesar* (1932); *Signs of Gesar* (1932). During an enforced halt in Khotan, he painted a series of seven canvases that were explicitly messianic, on the coming of Maitreya.

As he moves fully into Tibet, the sublime mountainscapes, the immense height of the mountain range in hundreds of his paintings suggest the arduousness of the spiritual quest. At the lower levels, human beings, the preceptor and acolyte, the messenger, the seer illumined by unearthly flames, or somebody akin to them receive or impart occult knowledge through devices like the Chintamani stone. In the forbidding ranges also appear oases with lush subtropical vegetation, hot springs, watercourses and palm fronds, so unlikely in those mountain deserts as to be visions of paradise for spiritual seekers. The seers, holy men, mahatmas or teachers were depicted as famous religious leaders, be it Jesus, Mohammed, Zoroaster with the sacred flame, Lao-Tse, Moses, Buddha, Confucius, Milarepa, St. Sergius, St. Francis, St. George, Oirot of the tribe of that name in the Altai. As also chaste Madonnas in *Mother of the World* and *Madonna Oriflamma* (1932), repeating his earlier vision, *The Queen of Heaven*.

Roerich was a product wholly of his times. He pursued his quixotic ambition of establishing that earthly paradise as a territorial state in the unpromising emptiness between Siberia and the Himalayas just as so many of his contemporaries hoped to found their socialist paradise in the equally unpromising territory of underdeveloped Russia. Roerich attracted a devoted band of followers and the sect continues to flourish in our times, we may or may not be drawn to it, but it gives meaning to that sparkling artistic output and permits us to enjoy it all the more.

End Notes

1. I am heavily indebted to John McCannon's interpretation of Roerich's art, as will be evident from the text. His list of publications may be found at http://www.usask.ca/history/faculty_jmccannon.shtml. I am most grateful to him for having sent me copies of his articles as also to Mehrdad Samadzadeh of the University of Toronto for considerable bibliographic help.
2. Sergei Makovskii, 'N. K. Rerikh,' Zolotoe runo, 4 (1907), pp. 3-7, here p. 5.]
3. By Gaston Carraud in *La Liberté*, see Millicent Hodson, 'Sacre: Searching or Nijinsky's Chosen One,' *Ballet Review*, Fall 1987, pp. 53-66.
4. Jacqueline Decter, *Nicholas Roerich. The Life and Art of a Russian Master* (Rochester, Vermont: Park Street Press, a division of Inner Traditions International, distributed by Harper and Row, 1989), p. 59.

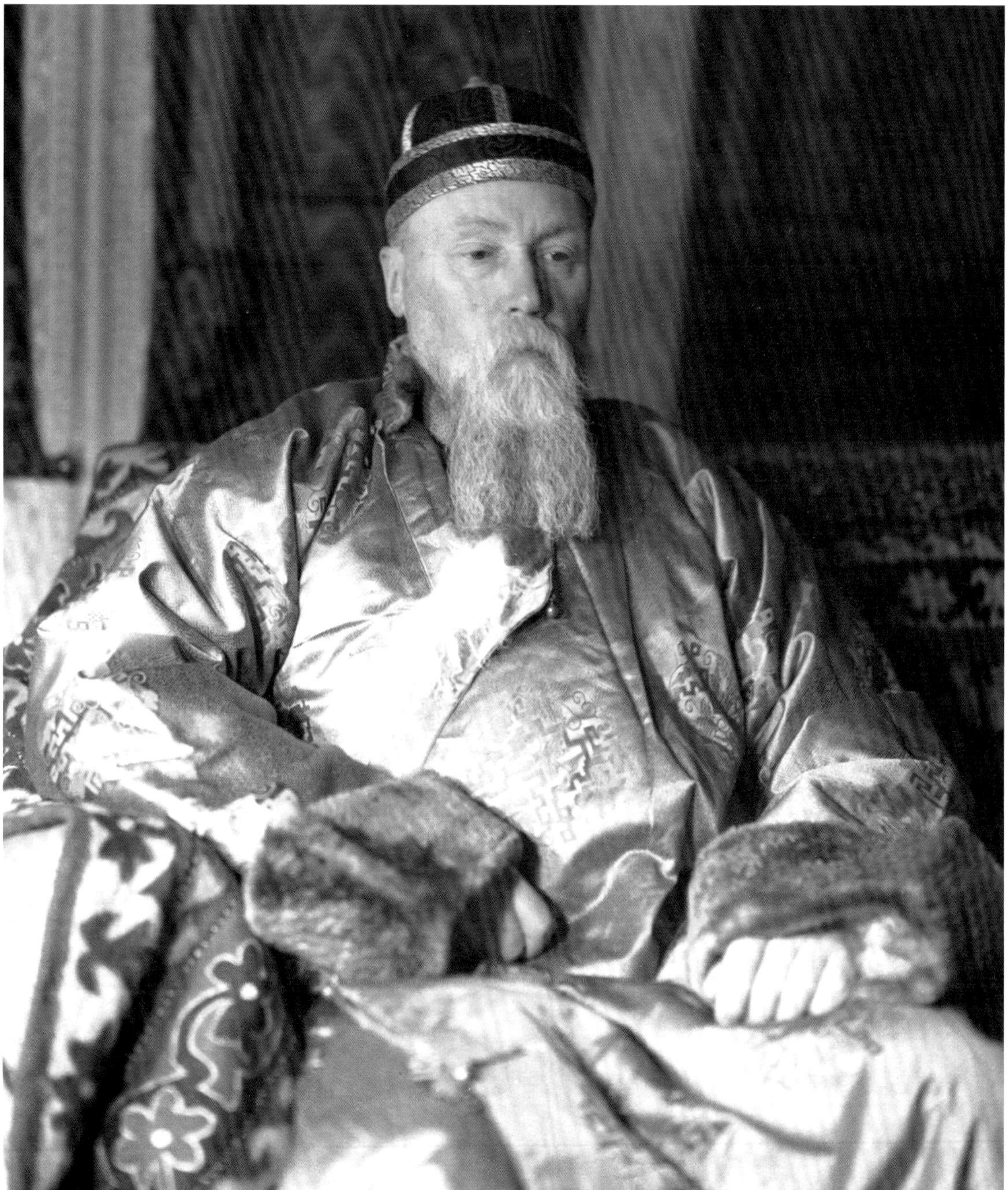

Nicholas Roerich, ca. 1933–37. Naggar, India (Nicholas Roerich Museum Archive, NY)

Glimpses of Inner Asia

Suchandana Chatterjee

In recent times, there seems to be a widespread dissemination of knowledge about Inner Asia, not merely as the colonial backyard of the Chinese, Russian or British empires but as an interactive and cultural space with global exposure and immense scope for the fusion of ideas of tradition and modernity. Though Tibetan Buddhism seems to be the bonding element between South Asia and Central Asia, several parallel links have also surfaced that explain the region's survival as a post-colonial Asiatic borderland.[1] There are fresh images of the region north of the Himalayas, representing it not as the vestiges of the colonial past but as an idyllic terrain for pilgrimage and scholarly enlightenment. The people who visited the region were not ordinary travellers but

The Greatest and Holiest of Tangla, 1932 (Nicholas Roerich Museum, NY)

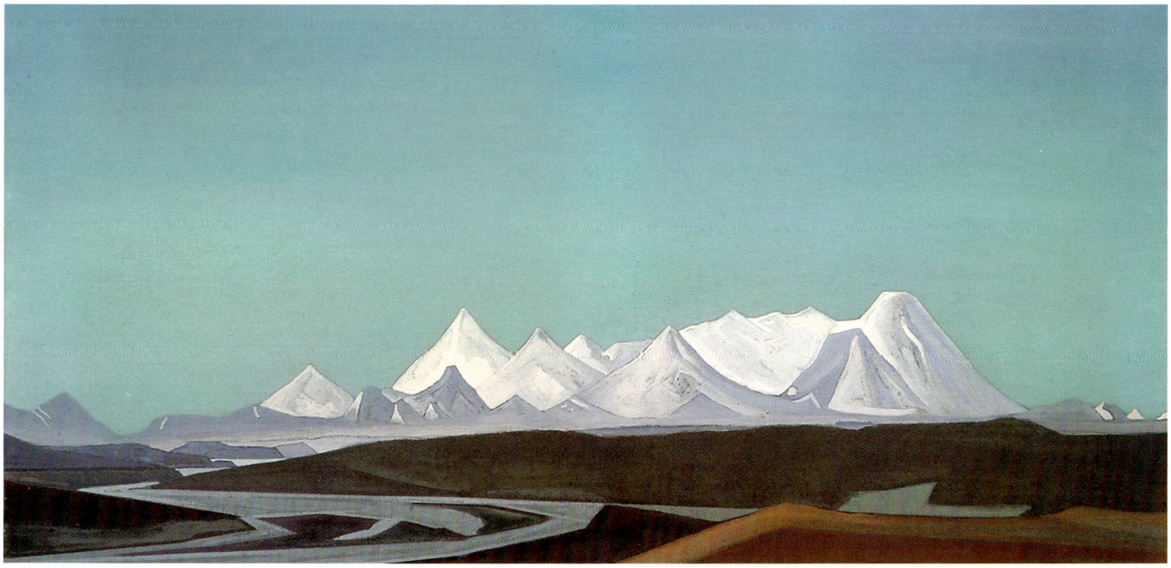

colonial surveyors, Buddhist pilgrims, traders and scholar-travellers from the South Asian region en route to their sacred destinations in Tibet or to other regional hotspots in Central Asia. Some of these rare visitors were from the Indian subcontinent who traversed northerly routes to examine various facets of this difficult terrain. Nicholas Roerich (1874–1947), the Russian painter and spiritual master, belonged to this category of visitors whose impressions about local politics and spiritual regeneration are valuable evidence on the post-1917 regional dispensation. What also cannot be ignored are his impressions about an idyllic space in a contested terrain. His journey, which he called the Central Asiatic Expedition, was conducted in two phases, from 1924–28 and 1930–31. The trips were the outcome of diverse but inter-related interests—artistic ambitions and spiritual quests in the Trans-Himalayan mountain territory. Roerich's synergy as a traveller with ethnographic pursuits and his involvement in the 'spiritual geopolitics of Inner Asia' are critically reviewed by the post-perestroika generation of scholars.[2]

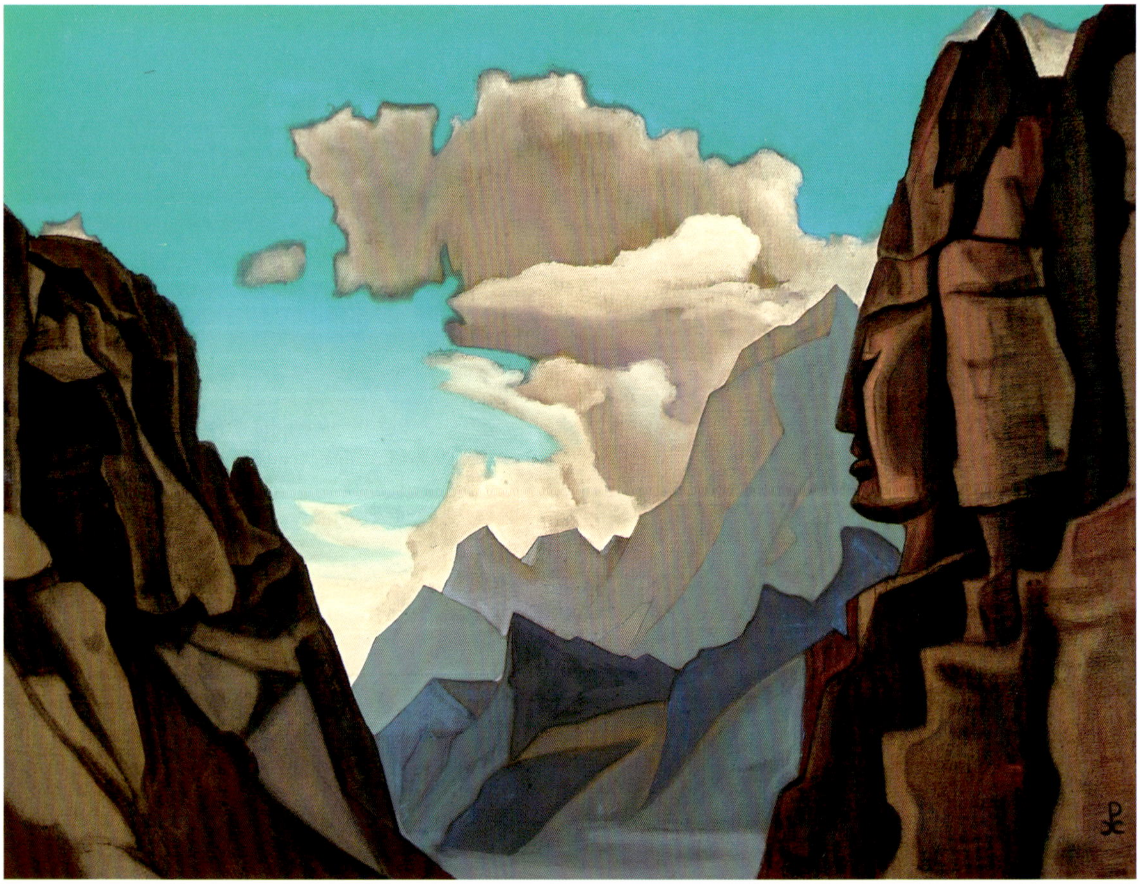

Great Spirit of the Himalayas, 1934 (Nicholas Roerich Museum, NY)

It is true that Nicholas Roerich's spiritual convictions and 'world view' of the 1920s were clearly different from his original painterly style. However, his interest about the ethnogenesis of the Eurasian people, and his archaeological training in the Imperial Academy of Arts motivated him on his Central Asiatic Expeditions. He searched for 'lost cities' and 'secret lands' of Eurasia that had deep connections with the lamaistic tradition, blending legends and myths about the renewal and spread of Buddhism in the land north of Tibet and the region between the Altai and the Tien Shan. Roerich's engagement with metaphysical discourse was the outcome of his interest in the origins of humanity. This was perfectly consistent with the anthropological and ethnographic enquiries made by his contemporaries in the Imperial Academy of Art.

His associations with ethnographers gave him a worldview about diffused Eurasian cultures that spread westward.[3] He had a searching mind that looked for answers to questions about migratory movements of Turkic and Mongol tribes across Eurasia (represented by the lineage of the mighty Chingiz Khan). These tribes had spread their influence up to River Irtysh in the south and in the Transbaikal region in the east by eliminating rival clans and tribes (like the Tatars). Militarily, they had incorporated territories adjacent to the Altai mountains, East Turkestan, Tibet and northern China, ravaging the caravan trade between China and the Altai. At the same time, they had also utilised opportunities to improve commerce with settled neighbouring tribes and finally, brought into vogue a very able system of administration with the assistance of Chinese astrologers, scribes, secretaries and intelligence officers. In *The Heart of Asia*,[4] Roerich describes the ways in which the Altai emerged as the origin of such migratory routes. Religions and creeds, myths and legends across the steppes of Central Asia, Mongolia and the Himalayas testify to this singular fact—that the Altai, a borderland of Asia and Russia, was the cradle and original homeland of tribal groups that were dispersed in the region.

In Roerich's perception, the Altai was 'an untouched treasure'—it was a cauldron of various ethnicities and combined several artistic influences (both linguistic and folkloric) from the neighbourhood that needed to be explored. Altai represented cultural diffusion. This idea was strongly entrenched in Roerich's mind by the 1920s. But intertwined with this understanding of cultural diffusion were his convictions about pristine beauty, humanity and harmony that were

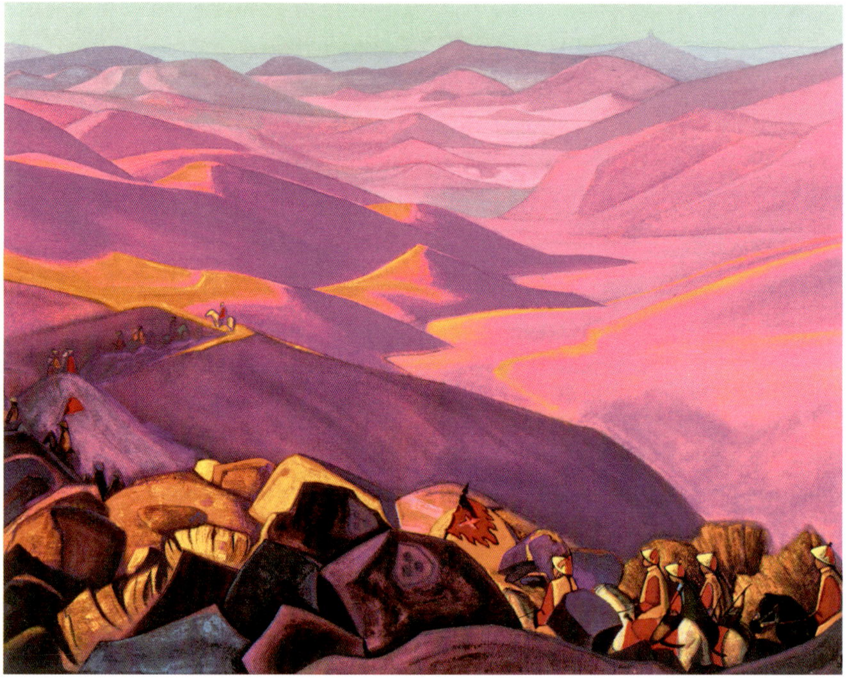

Mongolia. (Chingis Khan March), 1937–1938 (International Centre of the Roerichs, Moscow)

represented by the highlands of Asia. Roerich was not only sketching the diffuse ethnographic character of the Altai, but was also orienting towards 'a metaphorical generality'. His new frame of mind focussed more on the singularity of a mountain landscape, stretching across High Asia up to the Himalayas and Tibet, than on differences among the diffuse cultures of the Altai region. This singular approach was reflected in whatever Roerich wrote or preached around this time. His metaphorical interpretations about the Altaian landscape, his identification of the Altai as the real-life location of the land of the Shambhala, fabled in Buddhist mythology, were the beginnings of his exploration of the mystical Orient as he began his sojourn towards the highlands of Asia. So, mysticism and artistic pursuits made Roerich's Central Asian Expedition of 1924–28 a much-publicised affair. Roerich's spiritual rhetoric was expressed in imageries, legends and tales that reiterated Eurasia's mystical and messianic traditions.

Roerich's two expeditions in 1924–28 and 1930–31 reflect his mental transition from imagination to reason. The first Expedition, directed along the Srinagar-Leh-Ladakh route to the Altai via Chinese Turkestan (Khotan-Karashahr-Aksu-Urumchi-Kashgar), immortalised in his travel diary *Altai–Himalaya* (1929), gives us various images of spirituality, authority and defiance in Inner Asia. During his journeys he came in direct contact with varied sects and faiths of Inner Asia—the Red Cap sect of Padma Sambhava in Sikkim, the yellow faith of Tsong kha pa, the extremely radical Bon po sect in Ladakh as well as the rock-culture tradition in the trans-Himalayan region. He scanned the main arteries of migration via Urga and the Yum Beise monastery across the deserted land between Mongolia and Central Gobi until he reached the main artery of migration in the Altai region.

It is worth discussing the context in which this Expedition began. As leader of the Expedition, Roerich was committed to the 'goodwill undertaking' that began with the artistic aim to create a pictorial record of lands and peoples of Inner Asia. It began as a cultural enterprise but it has been implied that the primary motive of the journey may have been to establish a web of links in a chaotic regional environment. Roerich had a good sense of the intricacies of regional developments in the aftermath of 1917, especially as Central Asia and its southern and eastern borderlands were rocking with such rapid-pace developments as Chinese warlordism, the spread of the Bolshevik banner, Civil War intervention, the growing influence of émigré ideas, Buddhist reformism and occult beliefs. Roerich's realistic assessment of a turbulent period is also evident in his diaries and travel notes that recount various stages of the mammoth undertaking which spanned three continents, more than 16,000 miles and gained the Roerich family worldwide fame, hurled them into the cockpit of diplomatic gambling, occult mystery and alleged geopolitical scheming in which Roerich's 'masters' were involved. There has been a lot of curiosity about the intentions behind his spiritual quests in Inner Asia (mostly related to his imagination about the dreamland of Shambhala, that is, the land of the Maitreya or the incarnation of the Buddha, and his perceptions of the Altai region as a replica of Shambhala).[5] However, his Moscow-based disciples and Naggar-based devotees in the Indian state of Himachal Pradesh have vowed to defend the legacy of the Roerichs, emphasising Nicholas's intense obsession with pristine and divine beauty which he discovered in the mountains of High Asia.[6]

But what goes undetected is his pragmatism. Roerich had a correct sense of the uncertainties and ambiguities in the aftermath of the Revolution of 1905 and the First World War and seemed to be inclined towards alternative paradigms of anti-imperialism, Bolshevism, theosophy, pan-Mongolism and pan-Buddhism. Roerich seems to have been in close touch with various options—the Soviet option (as

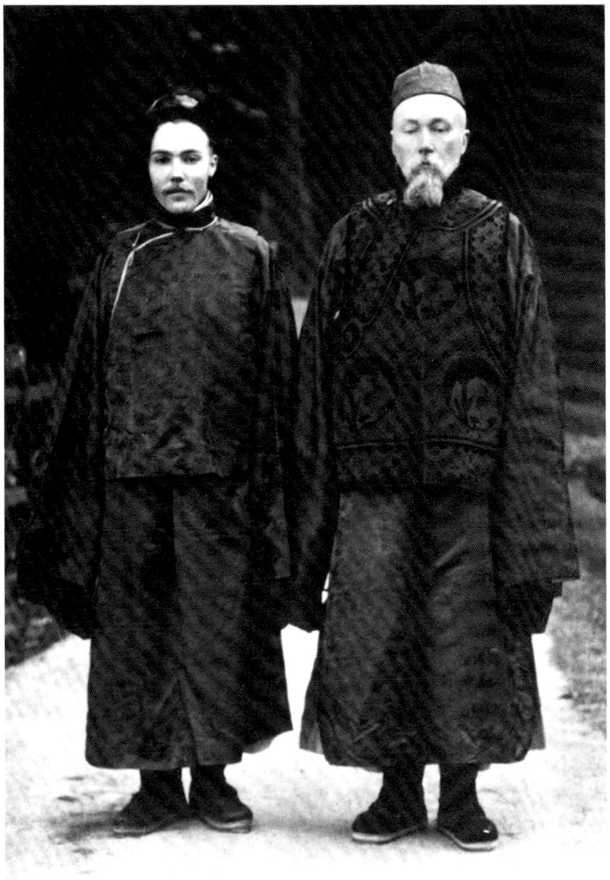

Left to right: George Roerich and Nicholas Roerich, 1924. Darjeeling, India (Nicholas Roerich Museum Archive, NY)

he involved himself in a series of Soviet geological missions in the Altai region that would have the resultant effect of extending Soviet sphere of influence in Asia beyond Mongolia), the nationalist option (as he nurtured special feelings for the Turko-Mongol people of Siberia, East Turkestan and Mongolia), the American option (as he is believed to have established a vast network of allies and followers in the West and even had a 'corporate' vision, thinking seriously of a Belukha Corporation with American collaborators), the Altai option (as he fantasised about a spiritual abode in the Altai mountains with fascinating ideas about a radiant lake of Belovodye, the spiritual replicas of the Buddha in the Altai and Tibet and so on). Added to this was another option, that is, the Buddhist option as he tried to work on the idea of a pan-Buddhist state and tried to reach out to the Siberian lama-intellectuals like Agvan Dorjiev, Pyotr Badmaev and others who also supported a similar idea. Connected to this was the Tibetan question due to British imperial designs and lama activities in Tibet, inner strains within the lama community reflecting two figureheads: Dalai Lama as the Tibetan spiritual head and Panchen Lama who, according to Kate Teltscher, often parleyed in the diplomatic settlements between the Manchu Emperor, the British Governor Generals, the Russians and several intermediaries.[7] From Roerich's scattered comments, we get an idea of the range of diplomatic activity centring Mongolia, Buryatia and Tibet.

What is significant about Roerich is his uncanny ability to extrapolate these options. Because of his daring pursuits in unknown lands of the North, both bigger and smaller truths were revealed. These were contestations of power among imperial and regional authorities, provincial rivalries in Chinese Turkestan and the end of prosperity of the Turkic *begs* (chieftains) of Yarkand, Khotan and Kashgar, tenuousness of Mongolian borders, the new prospects of

Mongolia as Soviet protégé, the new age thinking about a messianic upheaval and an urge for Buddhist spiritual brotherhood in the Himalayas that would challenge the imperial ambitions of the British Indian empire. It is intriguing how and why, as an émigré from Soviet Russia, he tried to represent himself as a supporter of Soviet development-oriented programmes in Tibet and Central Asia. So, his art-based expedition also had other tags and there are implications that Roerich was a political player in the highlands of Asia who moved in and out of Soviet-dominated Mongolia (Outer Mongolia), Chinese-dominated Mongolia (Inner Mongolia) and British-influenced-Tibet.

It is useful to reconstruct the narrative and route of his first trip and examine his experiences of travel as well as the impact of his cultural journey. What is revealed is his training and deep-rooted interest as an ethnographer. During the course of his journey from Chinese Turkestan beyond Urumchi, he gets intensely involved in several aspects of Siberian antiquity and the main arteries of migration in Eurasia as well as the faiths and beliefs that remained in oblivion due to political uncertainties of the post-1917 phase.

The broad span of Roerich's interest ranged from the diversity of Eurasian cultures, the great migrations of nations to the inner rhythm of the 'heart of Asia', the vibrant culture of mountain people and the mountain eco-system and the spiritual, mystic and serene world

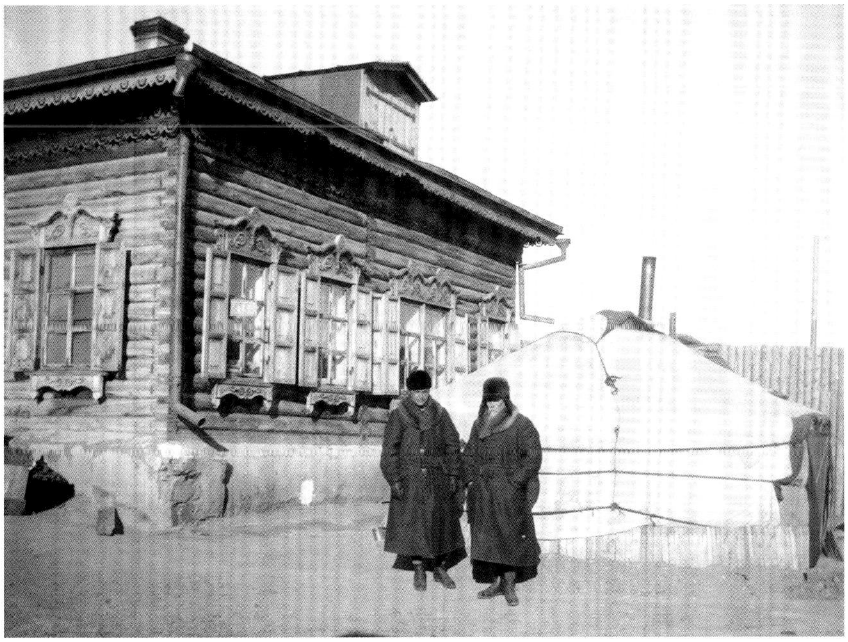

Left to right: Maurice Lichtmann and Nicholas Roerich March–April, 1927. Ulan Bator, Mongolia (Nicholas Roerich Museum Archive, NY)

of the Himalayas. These aspects are revealed in his travel notes, *Altai–Himalaya* and in his philosophical anecdotes about the Himalayan sojourn, titled *The Heart of Asia*. The former reveals the hidden truths of a very different world—the Altai, and is written as fragmented thoughts. The latter, a philosophical review of the Himalayan uplands that he visited, articulates the natural flow of his ideas. Adherents of Nicholas Roerich argue that he was not merely on a physical journey to the mountains—he was on a mental search for enlightenment and *The Heart of Asia* reveals his inner quest. He was deeply engrossed in philosophical questions about the cultural spaces of Asia and what they represented—the land of powerful governors as in Khotan or the land of 'extraordinarily rich artistic and historic material'.[8] The Himalayas, according to Nicholas Roerich, was a cultural enigma and he was constantly visualising a cultural world that was juxtaposed to the austerity of the local *ambans* (high officials) of Chinese Turkestan. Roerich associates his readers with an extraordinary landscape that was brimming with Tibetans, Kalmyks, Dungans who inhabited the entire stretch of caravan territory of Chinese Turkestan. To Roerich, the eastern margins of the Ili district, towns like Chuguchak, Karashahr and Kuldja with Buddhist affiliations are far more attractive in comparison to the decadent world of Kashgar and Sinkiang. Roerich is wary of the man-made difficulties while travelling in a Chinese land, but that does not lessen his enthusiasm about the tribes inhabiting these lands, especially the Kyrgyz.

The accounts are a major departure from earlier perceptions about Chinese hegemony and prosperity. These reflect the chaos and disturbances in the eastern regions that were under imperial control. What is alarming especially is the decadence and injustice in Sinkiang, the mischief of the *ambans* and so on. Khotan and Aksu, in Roerich's account, represented decadence. They ceased to be flourishing trade depots under Chinese *taotais* (heads of military or civil circuit) and *ambans*. Another grievance of the visitors was the suspicious attitude of the Chinese governors in Khotan, Urumchi and Kashgar.

These realistic assessments reflect Roerich's awareness of ground realities. Roerich experienced the widespread effects of decadence in Chinese Turkestan, the erosion of the once-prosperous Tibetan-Mongolian trade and communication routes, the ambiguities of military rule by the Chinese warlords in Mongolia and the fading of monastery towns in ancient Mongolia from public memory. The demoralising effects of the Russian Civil War also impacted on Roerich's mindset. Roerich's 'esoteric' side came in the limelight in the post-1917 years, giving him recognition as an unusual character who was completely immersed in the 'sublime scenery, new human types, strange manners and customs, and under the assaults of hardship, danger and the stresses and strains of exploration in almost untrodden lands.'[9] It is this phase of his life—the phase that marked the 'rebirth' and 'transformation' of Roerich as a spiritual guru and reflected his synergy as a traveller in Asia's geopolitical landscape—that had a larger impact on the post-perestroika generation of scholars and writers to whom diaries, personal recollections and afterthoughts of the Roerichs gave an idea not only of Roerich's pre-1917 frame of mind but also his inner realisations about Inner Asian dispensations in the post-1917 period.[10]

Roerich's sojourn to Tibet, Mongolia as well as Buryatia in the Altai was linked to his contacts with spiritual masters who wanted to create a spiritual community of the Buddhist faith. Roerich believed that the days of despair would end one day and that a new 'order' would emerge. He believed in the messianic traditions of Asia and was optimistic about spiritual regeneration among the Mongols, Kalmyks and the Oirats. Similar revivalist agendas were echoed by the Buddhists and the Old Believers. Roerich was trying to adapt himself to these and the Altaian ideals of a new spirit that would rise from the caverns and enlighten the world. There were echoes of revival in different parts of Asia and Roerich tried to establish a universality of such ideas.

Roerich's Central Asian Expedition was not a relentless search for hidden tracts and treasures. There was an urge to compare different worlds: (a) the Soviet fortress in Siberia and Mongolia (b) the character of Chinese warlordism in Eastern Turkestan and (c) the spread of spiritualism in Tibet and the Altai region.

Very distinct from Roerich's impressions about Central Asia are the descriptions of his elder son George (Yuri) Roerich who was his travelling companion. The two Roerichs had very different perspectives; the father engrossed in the artistic and spiritual traditions in Eurasia stretching from Tibet to Siberia and the son deeply involved in acquisition of trade items and other expedition-related material along old and new trade routes of Central Asia via Sikkim, Kashmir-Ladakh, Khotan, Urumchi, Urga, Yum Beise and the Gobi Desert. The father's motive was to study the vestiges of a past culture in the Eurasian borderlands as well as to establish a spiritual brotherhood comprising of Tibetans, Mongolians and Siberians (Altaians, Buryats). This was the place where Roerich focussed his spiritual dreams and envisioned the destiny of the Maitreya. So, for Nicholas Roerich, it was an artistic enterprise. The son was more concerned with specifics of trade and had a keen eye about every item of trade in the New Dominion that was being controlled by the ruthless Chinese warlords, be it antiques or silk carpets or precious stones like jade. The affluence of Khotan was the major point of reference for George Roerich. For Nicholas Roerich, the focus was Altai, resonating with legends about underground tunnels and chambers that represented the pivot of diffused Eurasian cultures. In contrast to his father's artistic and spiritual pursuits, George Roerich had an eye for realities of trade. From Yuri Roerich's account, we get an impression of Inner Asia's political transition and dramatic interludes in the aftermath of the 1911 revolt in China and the Bolshevik takeover that had reset regional ambitions of the neighbours and accounted for global friction during the interwar period.

The Siberian plateau and adjoining steppe territory was *The Heart of Asia*, from where the Roerichs were to begin their explorations of nomadic migratory routes. The artistic aim of the explorations in the Altai was a survey of the funeral mounds and other vestiges of nomad culture in the Tien Shan, the Jair Mountains and the Altai. The travel would take place along the Trans Siberian Railroad and Lake Baikal. Beyond the Baikal, they were to visit centres of Buddhist learning in Buryatia, the residence of Buryat intellectual or the *khan-po* and

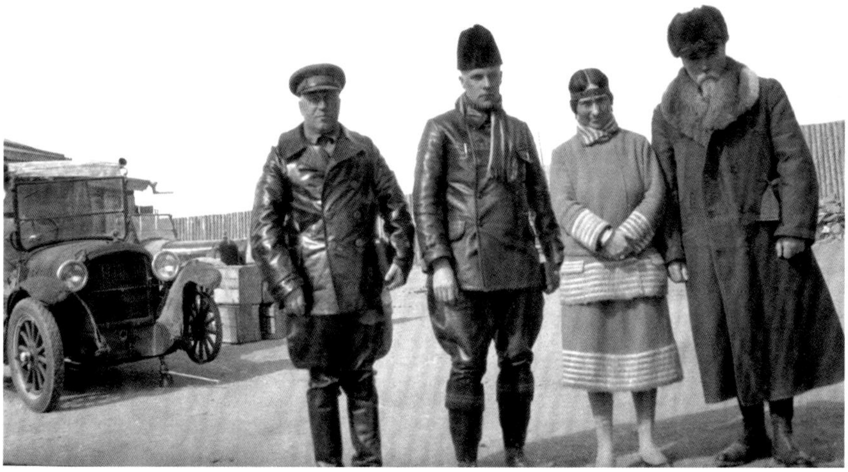

Left to right: Maurice Lichtmann, Nicholas Roerich March–April, 1927. Ulan Bator, Mongolia (Nicholas Roerich Museum Archive, NY)

the printing establishments that disseminated Buddhist teachings in Siberia and Mongolia. The other purpose of the visit was to explore the Altai as the replica of Shambhala, decipher commonalities between the two sacred lands. In Altai, there was Belukha, the sacred peak of the Altai, which was 'so clear and reverberant',[11] similar to the Kailash in the Himalayas and therefore the two were 'geographical and metaphysical twins'. Similarly, there was the legend of Belevodye (Land of the White Waters) in the Altai which had special or secret passages from where the protectors emerged on horseback.[12]

Mongolia was to be the real surprise for the Roerichs. Because of their ethnographic research, they were able to enlist the assistance of the Mongolian authorities. The caravan journey along the unexplored terrain of Central Gobi up to the Mongolian outpost of Yum Beise monastery that was rich and alive with legends of the warrior priest Ja Lama, his fortress city, Tempei Jaltsen, and stone-relics and carvings that immortalised legends about the nomads' heroism and prophesised the resurrection of a saviour and protector was an eye-opener. In their search for options, the Roerichs were inspired by the life of the warrior priest, his Russian upbringing, his travels to India, China, Tibet, his knowledge of Buddhist metaphysics and secret Tantric teachings and his innovative mind. The onward journey from Yum Beise to the direction of Tsaidam was more revealing because it gifted the explorers with many 'colourful combinations'—the multi-coloured stone surfaces, legends about fiery dragons that separated souls and spirited birds that combined them.[13] In the Tibetan upland they once again confronted the 'dark odds'[14]—the military generals' treachery. Juxtaposed to the omnipresence of the 13th Dalai Lama was the new popularity of the Tashi Lama who was destined to be the new spiritual leader and would 'reconstruct Tibet' along the lines forecast by the 'enlighteners'.

Prophecies about the future messiah were no less evident in Lamaist Urga. Therefore, Mongolia had two significant nodal points—'modern' Urga/Ulan Bator, the capital of outer Mongolia where reconstruction work was in progress after the civil war of 1919-21 and Lamaist Urga where Buddhist legends about reincarnation were predominant. Lamaist traditions were firmly entrenched all over Outer Mongolia and the Republican Government of Mongolia in no way interfered with monastic life. The civil war of 1919-21 brought to an end the Chinese dominance of the frontier towns and the Roerichs were struck by the character of deconstruction and reconstruction: how Chinese trading joints were replaced by Mongolian frontier towns and how the Mongol workforce dominated their Chinese and Russian counterparts, how the Mongol Frontier Commissariat wielded significant authority and how Mongol prophecies about a new messiah, the incarnation of Bogdo Gegen, tended to influence young minds in the lamaist establishments. It appeared that all places from Tibet to Mongolia were connected by common strands—Buddhist lineage, Mongol history, Mongol architecture, nomadic living, intermingling of Mongol, Chinese, Tibetan, Manchu and Buddhist texts, legends of Emperor Genghiz Khan, the cult of the sacred mountain, etc. Side by side the pristine Lamaist world is the real world of reconstruction, set to tune by the communist regime's reorganisation programme in the realm of education, administration, health services, communication and trade.

From the Roerichs' accounts, we get an idea about an Inner Asian spiritual mindset that was very close to the Lamaist tradition. We also get indirect evidence about differences among Lamaist sects and spiritual leaders and a Bolshevik attempt to establish a common cause between Communism and Buddhism through mediators and loyalists like Agvan Dorijev, Mongolian writer Zhamtsarano (Jamtsarano) and the Roerichs. In the Soviet Union, Inner Asia was studied as an extension of Siberia. The entire corpus of Soviet literature was a tribute to Soviet socialism and Central Asia and Inner Asia were showcased as a Soviet success story of development and transformation. Special categories like 'Buryat Autonomous Republic' and 'Mongol Autonomous Republic' highlighted the Sovietised apparatus in regions with a Mongol lineage. In retrospective analysis, this had a special effect of letting the world know that the first-ranking intellectuals of Buryatia were Buddhist educators who were trained in the Russian milieu of reform and collaborated with their mentors in St. Petersburg. The Roerichs also belonged to this circuit of intellectuals and through their travels in Inner Asia, got an impression of the mystic world of the Buddhist lamas who were not bound by traditional Buddhist principles but tried to break free of the shackles of orthodox monastic life by associating with a broader community of believers and soul seekers. In their artistic explorations, they also set their eyes on 'trade highways', spanning the southern peripheries of Central Asia.

Roerich's *The Heart of Asia* combined spiritual enquiry with artistic visions and social awareness. In one single volume, he portrayed the spiritual world of Buryat lamas, their adherence to the 13th Tibetan Dalai Lama Thubten Gyatso, the opulence of Tibetan merchant families, the prosperity of Mongol traders and works of art by conventional artistic groups of Urga, particularly the semi-Tibetan and semi-Chinese image-makers. According to the post-perestroika generation of scholars, however, the implications of a 'Buddhist alliance' were manifold. Tibet was not the only spiritual guideline for Nicholas Roerich. The Roerich formula of finding peace lay elsewhere—in the Altai and Mongolia.

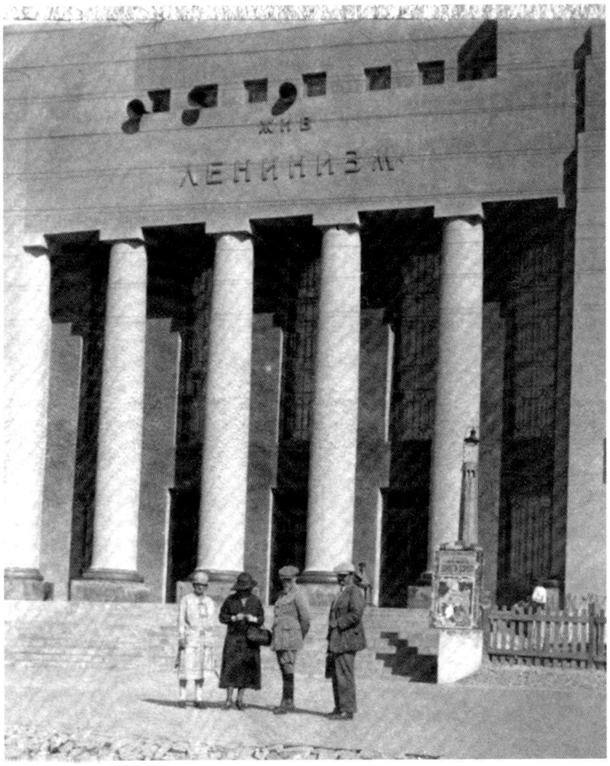

Left to right: Sina Lichtmann, Helena Roerich, Nicholas Roerich, Maurice Lichtmann, August–September, 1926. Novosibirsk (Nicholas Roerich Museum Archive, NY)

Altai Himalaya, Roerich's travel diary, reflects his deep insight about Asia's spiritual world that harmonises various beliefs. Roerich's diary is a 'symphony of Asia'. Altai, to Roerich, reflected harmony and was the replica of Shambhala, the imagined new kingdom of peace in the Northern Himalayas. In the Altai, there were legends of the White Burkhan, caves with secret passages where people, belonging to the migratory tribes, found protection. This was the land of the Belovodye, the original homeland of the Kalmyk and the Mongol tribes. So, Belovodye in the Altai is an imaginary world, a world of believers belonging to the Buddhist faith. It is an inner world that is serene and calm, while the world around it is filled with intrigue, deception and chaos. Chinese intrigues in Tibet, the Mongolian revolt, the Dalai Lama's spiritual authority, the alternative lamaist sects, British misconceptions about trespassers on the roof of the world, the New Dominion's cold-blooded motives are juxtaposed to the inner visions of the spiritual master, Nicholas Roerich.

According to the post-perestroika generation of scholars, the implications of a 'Buddhist alliance' were manifold. Over time, however, questions have been raised about a Buddhist framework and ideas about 'a Eurasian future'[15] have percolated in Inner Asia. Inner

Asia's cosmopolitan image has reappeared indicating its span across territories belonging to at least three time zones of Russia, China, Mongolia, Tibet and India. This re-conceptualisation of Inner Asia has brought back to life Nicholas Roerich's ideas about diffused Eurasian cultures. So, we are faced with multiple hypotheses about the space that Inner Asia represents—a pan-Mongolian space, a colonial space representing competing interests, a dynamic cultural space depicted in the travel narratives of Nicholas Roerich and a Buddhist space of the lamaist tradition and a Buryat space. The unusual Buddhist locales visited by Roerich indicate the prominence of those sacred sites in a large Buddhist space. Roerich's account reflects the transnationality of Buddhism and pan-Mongolism on the one hand and hybrid local sentiments of Inner Asia on the other.

End Notes

1. There is awareness about opportunities for literary reform among Tibetan minority linguistic groups (like the Sikkimese). Kalzang Dorjee Bhutia's upcoming lecture *Fusing language and modernity-Sikkimese language (Lho skad) and literary reform*, 6 November 2010, Trace Foundation lecture series programme in Latse Library, New York.
2. John McCannon, 'By the shores of white waters: the Altai and its place in the spiritual geopolitics of Nicholas Roerich', *Sibirica*, Vol. 2, Issue 2, October 2002.
3. Described by John McCannon in 'In search of primeval Russia: stylistic evolution in the landscapes of Nicholas Roerich, 1897-1914', *Ecumene*, 7 (3), 2000.
4. Nicholas Roerich, *The Heart of Asia*, New York: Roerich Museum Press, 1929; Reprint in Varanasi: Pilgrims Publishing, 2007.
5. Markus Osterrieder, *From Synarchy to Shambhala – the role of political occultism and social Messianism in the activities of Nicholas Roerich*. www.celtoslavica.de/bibliothek/osterrieder_shambhala.pdf.
6. The International Roerich Memorial Trust in Naggar (Kullu, Himachal Pradesh), India, organises special shows and exhibitions on the ethnographic and artistic collections of Nicholas Roerich and his family. The Himalayan Research Institute 'Urusvati', has established worldwide contacts in order to revive the intellectual tradition of Roerich and synthesise his scientific views on ethics, spirituality, folk art and eastern philosophy. This tradition, interrupted during the Second World War, has been revived and widely researched upon by scientists all over the world. Such revivalist projects have been described by Mikhail Chiritayev and Georgy Fursey in the seminar *Nicholas Roerich – his legacy and quest*, Jamia Millia Islamia, New Delhi, 12-13 November 2009. The Roerich Museum in Moscow also collaborates with its Indian counterparts to promote Roerich's spiritual and artistic visions and preserves a wealth of ethnographic material the Master collected during his Central Asian Expeditions.
7. Kate Teltscher, The High Road to China-George Bogle, The Panchen Lama and the First British Expedition to Tibet, London: Bloomsbury, 2006.
8. *The Heart of Asia*, p. 8.
9. Introduction by Claude Bragdon in Nicholas Roerich, *Altai-Himalaya: A Travel Diary*, New Delhi: Book Faith India, 1996, p. xxii.
10. Letters of Nicholas Roerich in *Peterburgskii Rerikhovskii Sbornik,Vypusk 1-5*, 1998-2002 gody. Website: http://www.spbu.ru/Science/Centers/RoerichCenter/SCREENS.
11. Nicholas Roerich, *Altai – Himalaya: A Travel Diary*, New Delhi: Book Faith India, 1996, p. 349.
12. *Altai-Himalaya: A Travel Diary*, p. 337.
13. *Altai-Himalaya: A Travel Diary*, pp. 60-62.
14. *Altai-Himalaya: A Travel Diary*, pp. 73-76.
15. Anya Bernstein, 'Pilgrims, fieldworkers and secret agents—Buryat Buddhologists and the Eurasian Imaginary', www.princeton.edu/~restudy/soyuz_papers/Bernstein.pdf. Republished as 'Pilgrims, fieldworkers and secret agents—Buryat Buddhologists and the history of a Eurasian Imaginary' in *Inner Asia*, Vol. 1, No. 1, 2009.

A Caravan in Time and Space

L.V. Shaposhnikova

In the 20th century, a caravan went across planet Earth, both in time and space. Known as the Central Asian Expedition, it was led by one of the major figures of the century, artist, scientist and thinker Nicholas Roerich. The caravan included his wife, the philosopher, Helena Roerich, and their son Yuri (George) Roerich, a young scientist-Orientalist. The caravan started in 1924 in Sikkim and ended in the same place in 1928. This circular route comprised: India, Chinese Sin-Tsian, Soviet Middle Asia, Siberia, Altai, Mongolia and Tibet. On the face of it there seems little difference between this expedition and the previous

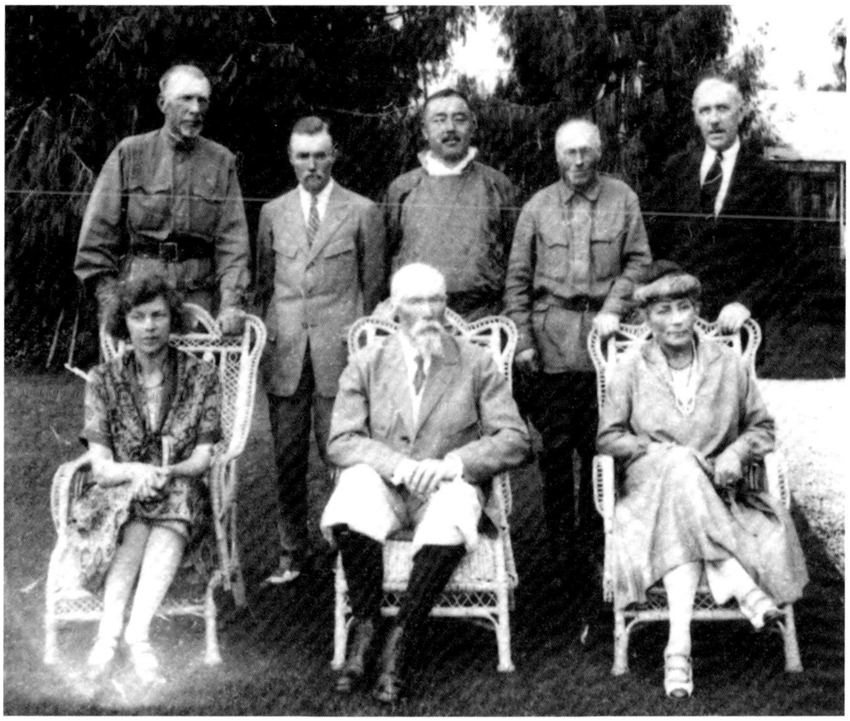

Left to right, sitting: Mrs. F.M. Bailey, Nicholas Roerich, Helena Roerich; standing: Nikolay Kordashevskiy, George Roerich, unknown, Konstantin Ryabinin, Frederick M. Bailey, May 24–26, 1928. Gangtok, Sikkim. At the British Residence, headed by Colonel F.M. Bailey, Political Officer in Sikkim (Nicholas Roerich Museum Archive, NY)

ones which traversed across Central Asia. As in the earlier expeditions, unknown Himalayan passes and peaks were mapped, monuments of culture and history studied, specimens of flora and fauna collected, and expressions of folklore noted. However, something about this Expedition made it different from the others.

The material accumulated and the experiences en route were interpreted from a broad historical and philosophical point of view based on cosmic cognition. Also, no other Expedition in the whole history of mankind has given birth to so many paintings. A part of those canvases is testimony to some secret goals pursued by the Expedition's caravan. But before proceeding towards any analysis of

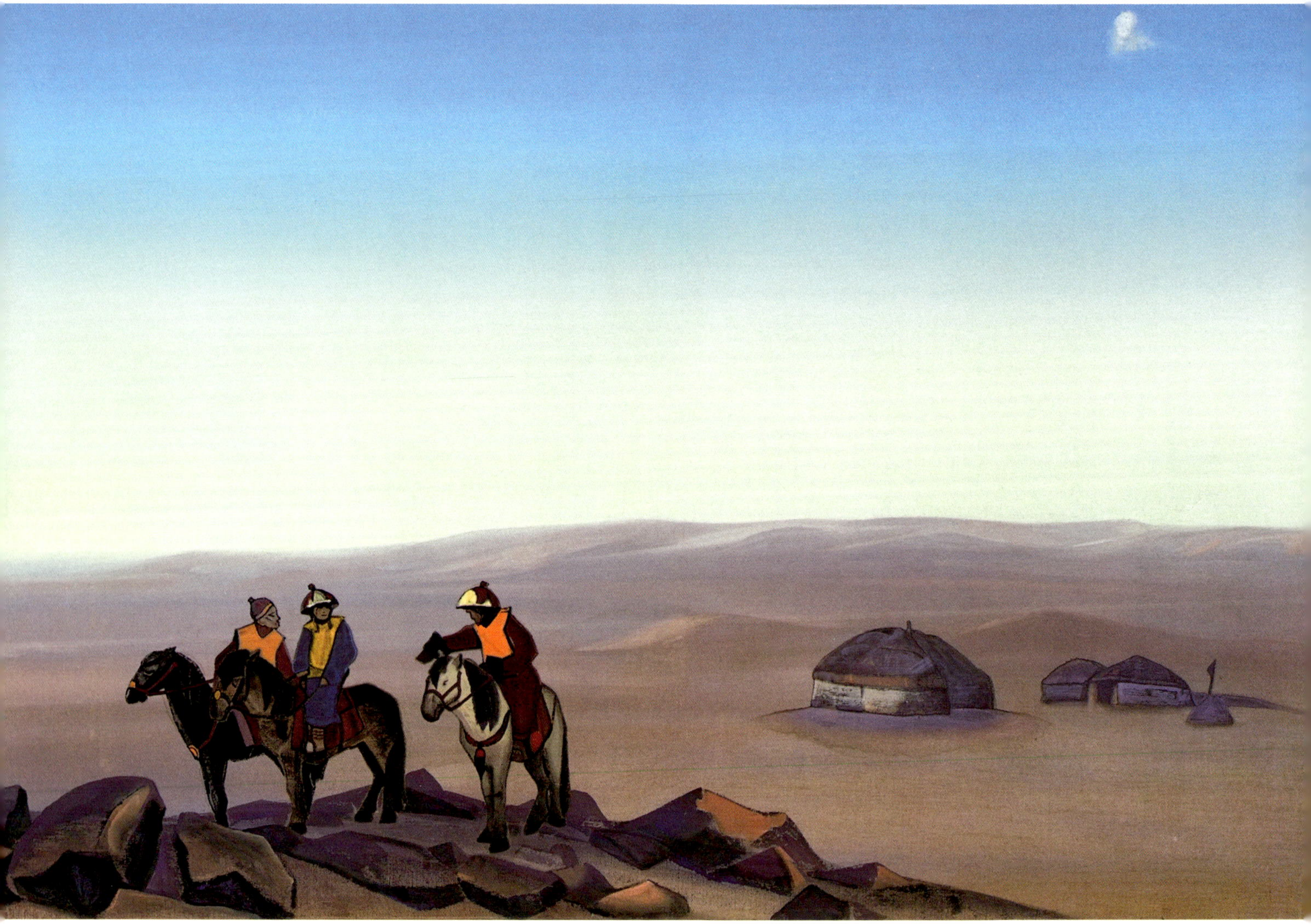

Mongolia I, 1938 (International Centre of the Roerichs, Moscow)

those goals which constituted, to my mind, the main purpose of the Expedition, it is necessary to make a small excursion and examine the methods of achieving them.

By the 20th century two trends of cognition—scientific and extra-scientific, or meta-scientific had clearly been established. Meta-science's terms of research were different both in obtaining knowledge and in tracing its sources. Since antiquity the method of cognition and knowledge through spiritual space of man has been acknowledged. This knowledge is revealed through intuition, insights, dreams, visions and, finally, through a mysterious process that can be termed 'evidence of a witness'. Such evidencing involves a direct relation and interaction with personalities of a higher level of cosmic evolution.

The 20th century witnessed such a process in the lives of both Helena and Nicholas Roerich. They accomplished this by establishing contact with their Teacher, a Cosmic Hierarch, and maintaining the closest spiritual collaboration which resulted in the creation of the treatises of Living Ethics, a philosophy of Cosmic reality. This philosophy of the Roerichs synthesised science and meta-science, and proposed a system of cognition necessary for forming a new cosmic mentality. In all Roerich's creative work and activities, the attempt always was to explore and seek what I term, the meta-historical reason. Just as any field of science has the aspects of empiric science and a meta-scientific one, similarly there is history and a historical process, and also meta-history and a meta-historical process. And it may be said that the reason for the historical process lies in the meta-historical process, in a knowledge higher than earthly. As Roerich visualised it, this process works in complete agreement with cosmic evolution and creates its images through the spiritual fields of great artists. Time and Space in these images are different; past, present and future are expressed as a unified entity. And in turn this renders a prophetic character to the process. This is clearly reflected in Roerich's creative work.

It may be mentioned here that any higher impulse sent by cosmic matter to the Earth is transferred through specific people. It is through such messengers of cosmic evolution, that the latter affects its creation on Earth. Evidently, the level of spiritual development and degree of consciousness of such a person would be far higher than that of an ordinary person. Helena and Nicholas Roerich, in my understanding, fall into this category.

Roerich's talent was unique, rich and versatile. In his perception of history and historical thinking, spirit and matter interacted in great harmony. With a mental level in tune with his spiritual space, a deep sense of intuition (or a high degree of intuitiveness), dreams about the past, afflation, visions and later 'witnessing', all these aided him in experiencing 'direct communication with long passed epochs'. The Russian archaeologist A.P. Okladnikof, a man of deep scientific intuition, sensed this character in Roerich's studies and called them 'historical reveries'.

Roerich's passion for history started with an interest in archaeology at an early age and then developed into a professional occupation. He studied the Stone Age and started excavations in Novgorod and Pskov. Archaeology provided him not only with historical information, but led to a unique way of experiencing history. Roerich described it as a "pinchingly pleasant feeling to be the first to take out of the earth some antique curiosity, to experience direct communication with a long passed epoch. So much mystery! So much wonder! In death itself—there is eternal life!" In a series of canvases painted before the Revolution, Roerich captured visions of the past in precise and rare imaginative detail.

Nicholas Roerich, February, 1926. Yarkand, Chinese Turkestan (Nicholas Roerich Museum Archive, NY)

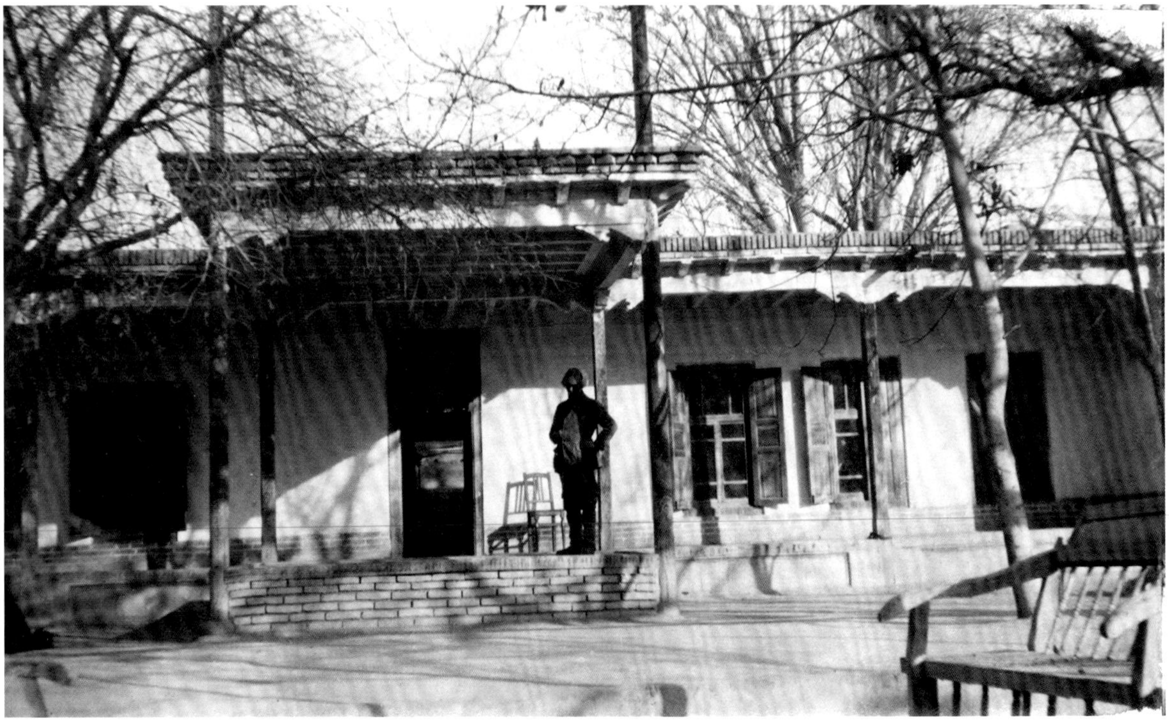

The bedrock of all Roerich's creative work may be described as 'beyond world' or 'other being'. Without recognising this fundamental point of view, the uniqueness and spiritual depth of his body of work cannot be fully appreciated. And perhaps his responsiveness to, and interest in India's culture, history and art was due to the multi-layered meanings resonating there. One could argue that there was nothing unusual about this. At the beginning of the 20th century, many westerners were attracted by India. Possibly, Roerich's interest in India was initially to explore the common historical source of Slavic and Indian people. What intuitively attracted him to India, however, was that unlike many other countries, here history and culture were lit with a 'beyond world' experience that continued to be part of daily living.

It is this process that determined what seemed mysterious, often inexplicable in India, and appeared sometimes just miraculous to Europeans. Time in India had its own specific understanding. Ancient Egyptians, Sumerians, Toltecs have disappeared from the face of this planet without any trace. Only relics excavated from dry and scorched earth are reminders of them. While in India, the resonance of all those who once walked along its ancient roads pulsates in the living. The ancient cultures of Mohenjo-Daro and Harappa, buried and covered in sparsely vegetated hills of the Indus Valley, continue to seep into the souls and customs of people inhabiting modern Indian cities and towns. The early dawn of Australoid tribes of the Stone Age are still expressed in the folklore and dances of South India, for example.

This kind of integration and cultural continuity has unfailingly worked for millennia and has formed the 'great rhythm' of the Indian cultural phenomenon. There is an important issue in this phenomenon without which it is not possible to understand either the country itself or its spiritual tradition. Like other countries, India was subject to attacks, invasions and even conquests. But, unlike other countries, it quickly assimilated the culture of the invaders turning it into an organic part of its cultural complex. This mysterious ability can neither be explained nor can it be studied. Jawaharlal Nehru's words that, at the dawn of history, India was already "mature in many respects" throws some light on this ability, though it does not explain the phenomenon itself.

"...In the past," Nehru wrote, "the dominating feature of the Indian culture and even ethnic development was some internal inclination for synthesis rooted mainly in the Indian philosophical outlook. Each new invasion of foreign elements was a challenge to this or that culture, but it was successfully countered with new synthesis and process of absorption. This was also a process of rejuvenation on the soil of which new flowers of culture grew, though the basis in general was left without changes."

Nehru ascribed the "inclination for synthesis" to the Indian philosophical outlook. Undoubtedly, it constituted the essence of the ancient spiritual tradition of India that absorbed into itself seemingly different components, such as philosophy, beliefs, religious systems and folklore.

Various Indian philosophic systems sprouted afresh on the centuries-old tree of spiritual tradition, nourished by the same roots. The old was not negated, or cut off, but was canonised in the new, as part of further advancement and transformation. For example, in Vedantic studies, we find a mature analysis of other philosophic systems, such as Charvaka, Buddhism, Jainism, Sankhya, Yoga, Mimansa, Nyaya and Vaisheshika.

This concept of the dialectical unity of past, present and future formed the Indian spiritual tradition. No contradictions existed between the elite and folk culture. The same ideas and truths were perceived and applied on all layers of Indian society in correspondence to their mental evolution and education. India's rich oral tradition played a most important role in this process.

These philosophic truths permeated and seeped into people's lives through the epic poems, *Mahabharata* and *Ramayana*, the myths of the Puranas and incantations of the Vedas, through oral stories, from the Buddha's life. However, the philosophical spine of the nation mentioned by Nehru was nurtured by the ancient spiritual tutorship of the gurus. The Sanskrit word guru (spiritual teacher), in the course of time, became as widespread as the Russian word sputnik.

The gurus did not let the spiritual tradition die but carefully passed it on from one generation to another, creating and sustaining an endless chain of cultural continuity. Despite differences in approach, they retained and preserved the intransient features of Indian philosophic thought.

While ancient Greeks worshipped gods and heroes, in India, gods and *rishis* are worshipped and only then heroes. *Rishis*—developers and creators of the spiritual tradition of India—are its special phenomenon. According to the mythological tradition, *rishis* of the first generation were not just cultural heroes who educated people, but they had links with the Cosmos. The Great Bear stellar constellation is called the *Saptarishi* in India or Seven *Rishi*s. And these Seven *Rishi*s belong not only to Indian mythology, but to its history as well. Their genealogy spans centuries and has survived until the 20th century. In any other country today, the existence of *rishi*s would be subject to explicit doubt or just negation, but not in India, where the 'whisper of centuries' is distinctly audible. Among the historical *rishi*s of India, there have been philosophers, religious reformers, and political leaders. Buddha and Mahavira, Nagarjuna and Nagasena, Shankara and Ramanuja, Ramakrishna and Vivekananda, Aurobindo Ghosh and Mahatma Gandhi, so different in terms of their ideas and activities, were united by their humanism. Their constant attempt was to comprehend the cultural and historical evolution of mankind, and more importantly, to help man evolve and achieve perfection.

Some of those *rishi*s are known to us, others remain anonymous, concealed by an opaque curtain of myth. Some of them, when they appeared in the world, often held important social positions; for

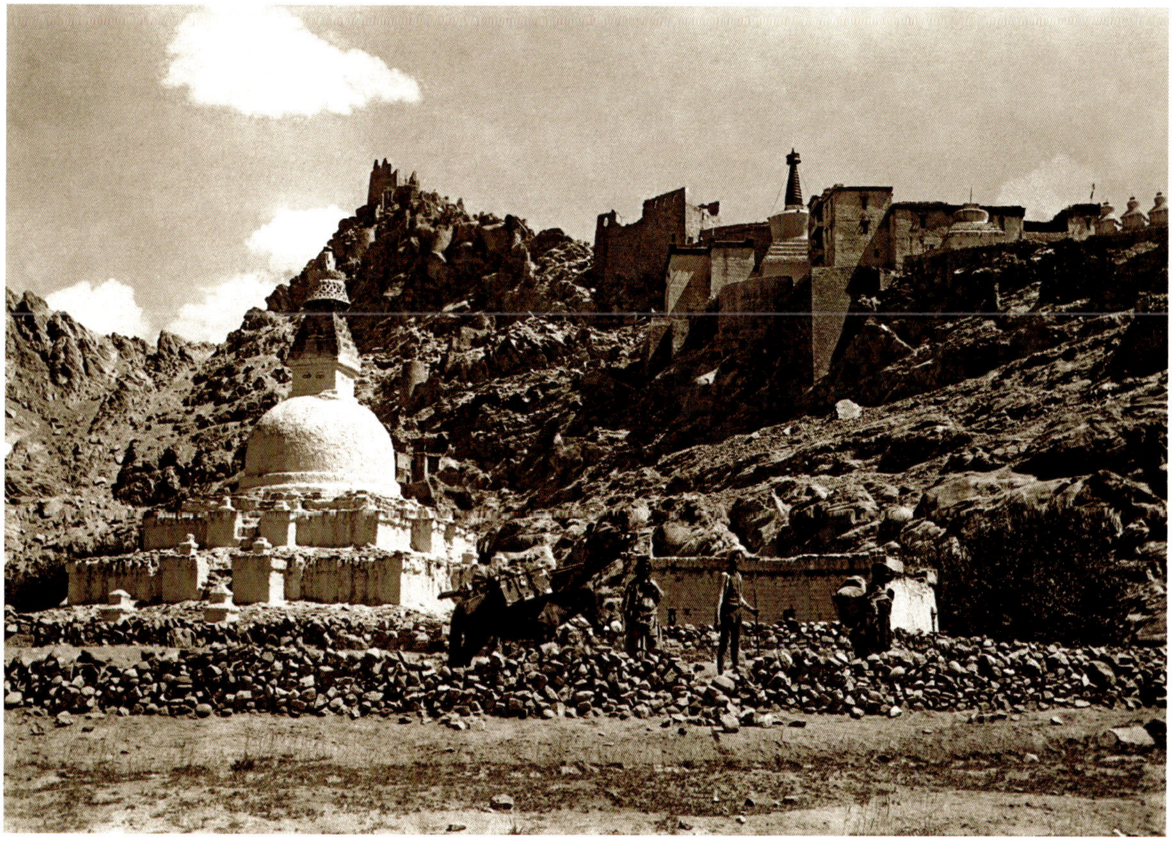

Stupa in Shey, 1925 (International Centre of the Roerichs, Moscow)

example, Ashoka from the Maurya dynasty, or Emperor Akbar from the dynasty of Great Mughals, exemplifying that power combined with wisdom brought fruitful historical results.

Roerich aspired to experience such an India. Initially it was an intuitive process. But later, after his encounter with the Teacher, a Cosmic Hierarch, it was a conscious process and the method of 'witnessing' became the final one in his meta-historical process. It would be relevant to say that Roerich explored and applied this process to its fullest in India.

The Central Asian Expedition, the focal point in the lives of the Roerichs, was scheduled to begin from the neighbouring Indian kingdom of Sikkim. However, while in Darjeeling, an event took place which determined Nicholas Roerich's whole life and creative work. This event is described by Roerich:

> "After midday, the four of us were going by car along a mountain road. Suddenly, our driver slowed down; we saw a port-chaise carried in a narrow place by four people in grey clothes. A lama with long black hair, and unusual for lamas, black beard was sitting in the palanquin. He had a crown on his head, and his red and yellow garments were extraordinarily clean. The port-chaise caught up to us and the lama, smiling, nodded to us a few times. We passed and remembered the beautiful lama for a long time. Then we tried to meet him. But what was our amazement when local lamas told us that no such lama existed in the whole region." [7, c. 158–159].

The lama was their spiritual Teacher who hurried to the meeting with them, which took place at a small roadside temple in front of the monastery of Gum. The Teacher, who had a direct relation to cosmic evolution and meta-historical process, set before the Roerichs the task that was to take the shape of the Central Asian Expedition.

Along the route of the Central Asian Expedition, the focal point in the lives of the Roerichs (both Nicholas and Helena) created the energetic field of the New World in those countries where they felt the necessary conditions existed for such creative work. This work was enacted in closest collaboration with the Cosmic Hierarch.

Three canvases painted by Nicholas Roerich in pre-revolutionary Russia acquired reality during the Central Asian Expedition. The *Treasure of the Angels* turned into a fragment of a meteorite said to contain subtle cosmic energy. It is said to have been delivered to the Roerichs by the Teacher himself. The *Book of Doves* turned out to be an allegory on cosmic reality, and, finally, the *Lords of Beyond* appeared as the very same Cosmic Hierarchs who had for centuries contributed to mankind's evolution.

The caravan unfolded a grandiose and rich picture of two flows of life in Asian cultures. Not only was there no clear division between the two flows, but they constantly interacted with each other. This interaction revealed to Roerich—historian and artist—a rich and unique prospect for research. He researched the historical migrations of peoples across mountains and deserts. The traditional historical explanation of this movement was to him, unconvincing. He felt it was a cosmic rhythm and cosmic energies that moved those masses of people. Essentially, Roerich aimed at comprehending cosmic evolution and its laws as revealed to him and Helena Roerich by their spiritual Teacher.

Proceeding on this line, so precisely and clearly explained by the Teacher, Nicholas Roerich penetrated into the great historical essence of the nomad world covering the vast Eurasian steppes—a world of dynamic activity, and of intensive energetic exchange. The contact with nomadic and agricultural peoples, not always peaceful, infused fresh energy into them. A huge world, ancient and modern, across which the caravan moved, resounded with a sense of past unity and integrity. In Tibet, the Roerichs discovered megalithic monuments, similar to those of ancient Europe. In the Tibetan northern uplands, 'animistic style' ornaments of Eurasian nomads were found. What Roerich looked for were not differences, but commonalities in cultures; he believed that an awareness of this, in the course of time, would help overcome separation and hostility. He sensed that unity belonged to meta-history, and separation came from the earthly historical process that slowed down the course of cosmic evolution.

The time continuum of past, present and future is perhaps inapplicable in the worlds of a higher state of matter. But Time is of invaluable aid in studying the historical process and determining what is good for humanity—what is necessary in it for its future evolution, and what can be cast into oblivion. Based on this view Roerich divided everything that was existent and happening into: that which is permanent, and that which is transient. Meta-history mostly consisted of intransient elements, and these constituted Roerich's search during the Expedition. He found them in ancient

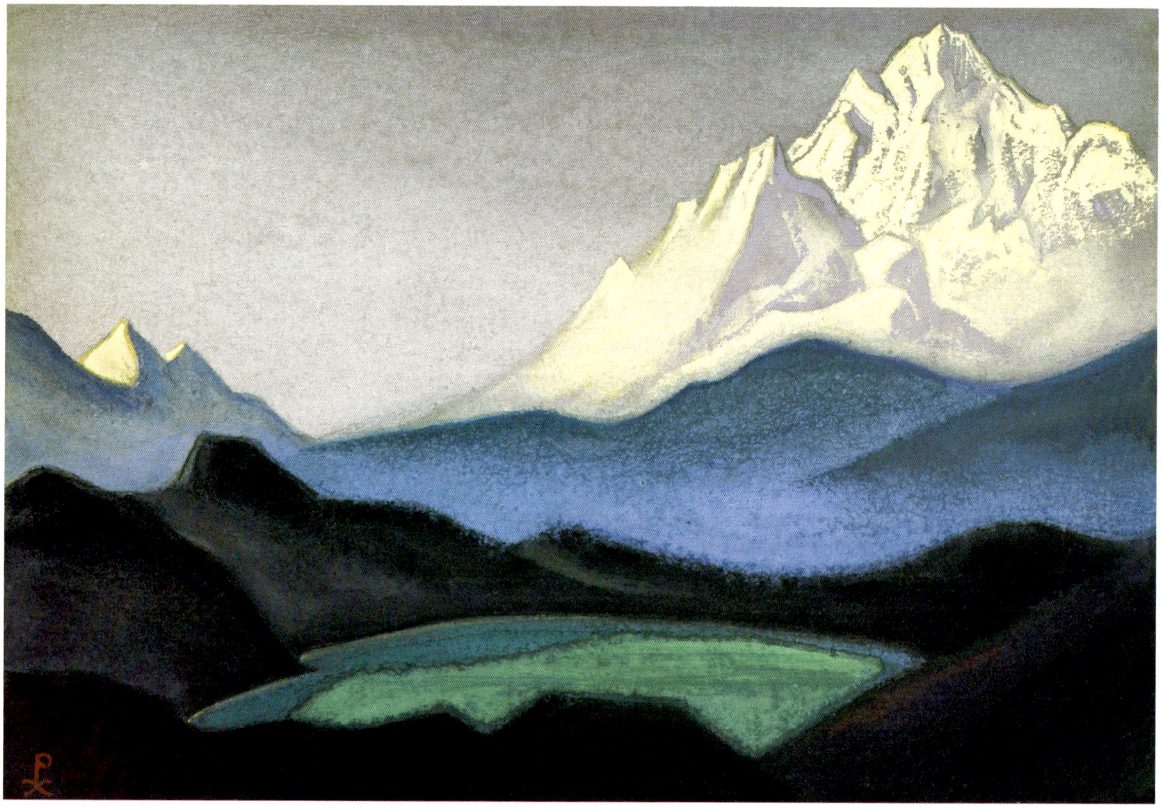

The Power of Snows, 1945 (International Centre of the Roerichs, Moscow)

sacred books, spiritual teachings, myths of cosmogony, legends about *rishis* and cultural heroes, artistc creations, and numerous other phenomena which have survived through centuries, and which serve as a scaffolding for the future.

The idea that "there is no future without the past" formed the base concept inRoerich's work from the very outset. He looked in the past for what could serve as a support for the future. He visited temples and monasteries—Hindu, Buddhist and pre-Buddhist. They housed unique libraries, and ancient manuscripts lay beside the altars. In his Expedition diaries, Nicholas Roerich mentions many intransient elements that would prove indispensable for the future. He called these elements 'wonderful stones'.

An important act, directly related to cosmic evolution's creative work, was undertaken during the Expedition—the laying of 'magnets'. This act, according to Living Ethics, provides the necessary impetus to lower energies from higher energies, thus giving a momentum to cosmic evolution. In the philosophy of cosmic reality such a magnet or 'stone' implies an energy structure of space.

Such a structure is a result of the energetic creation of those who carry forward the so-called 'dictates of cosmos' or a mission of inner cosmic evolution within. Nicholas Roerich's paintings during the Expedition and Helena Roerich's 'fiery centres' (developed under the tutorship of the Cosmic Hierarchs) are believed to be related to the formation of such energies.

So what was there in the Central Asian Expedition corresponding to this? First of all, there was the 'stone' or a fragment of a meteorite referred to in Roerich's Expedition diaries, and evident in his paintings. But the unique energies of this meteorite needed to be combined with other energies so that a 'space magnet structure' could be formed. The 'fiery experience' of Helena Roerich which developed under the guidance of Cosmic Hierarchs, started during the course of the Expedition itinerary in 1924. And Nicholas Roerich created on the same itinerary not only sketches, but a great number of large scale canvases. The conditions along which the caravan moved, were hardly favourable to such creative work.Undoubtedly, their activities were related to the formation of the energies of the 'magnets' that were being laid.

During the Expedition under extremely difficult conditions, Nicholas Roerich painted three significant series: *His Country, Banners of the East* and *Maitreya*. To these we can add the following: *Command of Rigden Djapo, Legend of Shambhala, The Entrance Keeper* and *Unspilt Vessel*. These paintings were created between 1924–1927.

Thus, when laying the 'magnets', the Roerichs used three sources of energy, all related to cosmic evolution: the energy sources of the meteorite evident to Roerich in mythology, legends and beliefs; the 'fiery centres' of Helena Roerich, and the paintings of Nicholas Roerich.

The question arises: at which places were the 'magnets' laid along the route of the itinerary? There is no specific answer to this question so far, though some suppositions may be confirmed through the hints given in Roerich's diary. I believe that the laying of 'magnets', which was directly related to the meta-historical process, took place along the whole Central Asian Expedition. An attentive reading of Nicholas Roerich's diaries, reveals the author's attitude to a particular space, or country. It is obvious that the first laying of magnets took place in India—the country towards which the Roerichs had a special inclination.

The second place where the magnets were laid may have been Moscow. What indicates this is that the *Maitreya* series of paintings, which were directly related to this process, were left in Moscow as also earth brought here in a special casket from a sacred place and finally, the book, *Community*, in which the Teacher had expressed his prophetic ideas about Russia.

The year 1926, when the Roerichs visited Moscow, was a turning point for Russia when a choice that would determine its future lay before the government. All objects brought by the Roerichs were rejected by the State. His paintings were put away in State storages. Later they were rescued by A.M. Gorky and ended in Nizhniy, Novgorod; the casket with the earth disappeared; the book *Community* was not published. Years later in 1957, the process of reinstating Nicholas Roerich was begun when his son, Yuri Roerich set in motion the establishing of a Nicholas Roerich Museum in Moscow. His early death interrupted these activities. They were resumed when, in 1989, the Soviet Foundation of the Roerichs was created in Moscow with the main purpose of organising the Nicholas Roerich Museum. Finally, due respect and honour was accorded to Nicholas Roerich.

After Moscow, the 'magnet' was probably laid at Altai, and in the Uymon valley. Mongolia was the second country where Roerich left his painting. It was called *The Great Horseman* and had an obvious relation to the secret country where *ashrams* of the Teachers—Cosmic Hierarchs—were located. After Mongolia, they went to Tibet where the Expedition suffered many calamities and hardships. The cultural condition of the region was not highly rated by Roerich. However, despite being critical of the situation in Tibet, Roerich wrote extensively about its future renaissance.

As the Expedition advanced, the word 'Shambhala' appeared frequently in Roerich's diaries, implying a secret country of *rishis* and righteous living. In Roerich's diary, *The Heart of Asia*, he mentions that the geographical indications of the place "are deliberately confused or mispronounced. But even in this wrong pronunciation, you can discern the true geographic direction, and this direction, don't be surprised, again leads you to the Himalayas". The secret country, according to Nicholas Roerich, had a definite geographic location. "Some indications, obscured with symbols, testified to the location of Shambhala in Pamir, in Turkistan and in Gobi". All those areas were mentioned because, near Shambhala, people live in yurts and breed

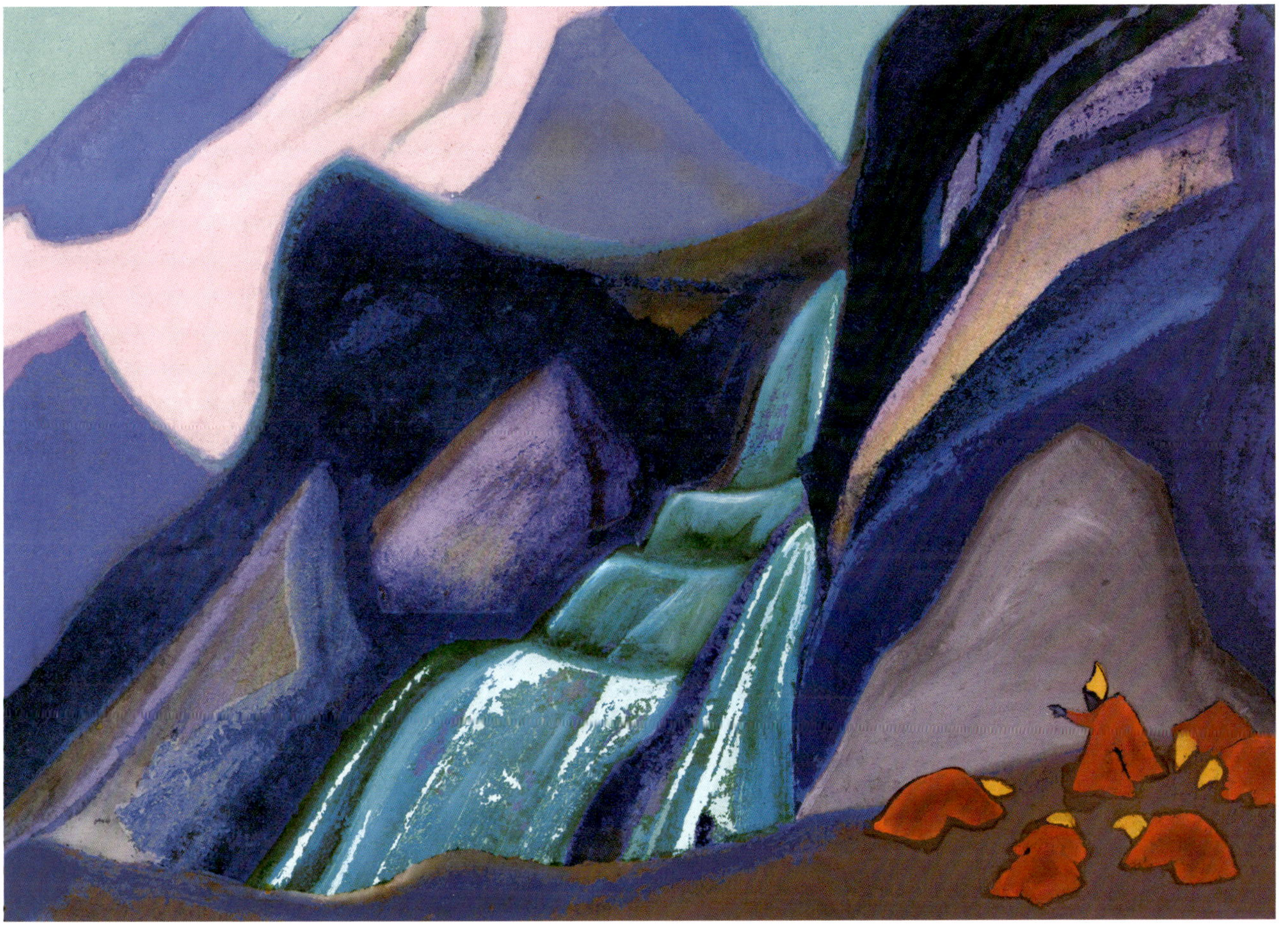

Monks returning from Lahaul (International Roerich Memorial Trust, Naggar, Kullu)

cattle. "...But do not let us forget," Roerich continued, "that mountain Kirgyzs in Kunlun neighbourhood also live in yurts and breed cattle."

Kunlun was mentioned more than once by Roerich in connection with the Secret Country. The same ridge appeared in Altai as in the legendary stories of wanderings in search for Belovodye. It is this route, geographically deciphered by Roerich that formed part of the Central Asian Expedition.

Perhaps Roerich's belief in Shambhala and the Mahatamas is best explained in his own words:

> "You, maybe, will ask me why, talking of Shambhala, I mention the great Mahatmas? Your question may be justified because before, in literature, these great notions became absolutely separated due to the lack of information. But, knowing literature about the Great Mahatmas and studying information

about Shambhala in the locality, it is highly instructive to see these notions unifying signs and, finally, understand how close they are in reality.

"It is a strange and outlandish feeling to go through the same places where the Mahatmas passed. There was a school founded by Them. Two day's trip from Sagdzong, there was one of the *Ashrams*, not far from the Brahmaputra. If necessary, they passed unnoticed, like ordinary travellers....All that they offer is not illusory, not ephemeral, but real and relating to most comprehensive study of possibilities offered to us by life."

Behind all this, the Roerichs felt there was a greater reality related to both the mundane and supra-mundane worlds. To them it seemed evident that a secret path ran parallel to their own itinerary. Along this, walked strange figures, lamas, story tellers, fellow travellers who warned them of impending disasters, brought them mysterious communiqués. And sometimes, serendipitously eased and facilitated

Tibet (International Roerich Memorial Trust, Naggar, Kullu)

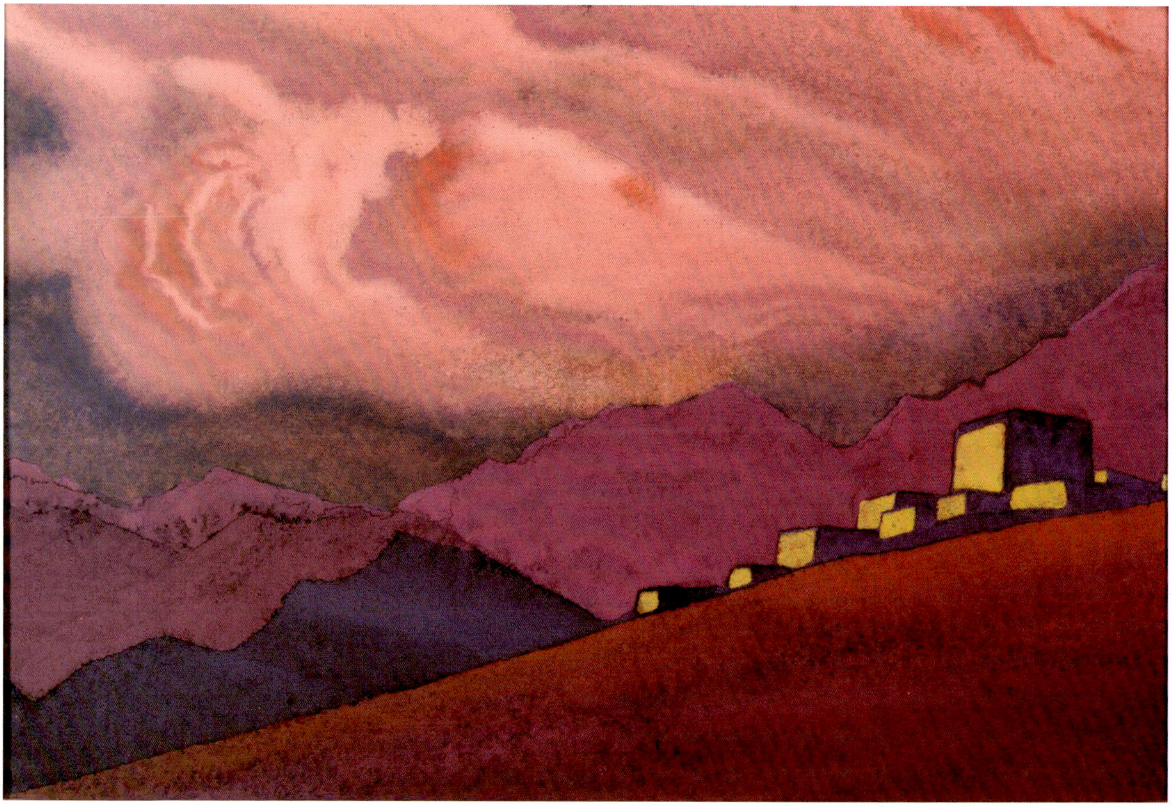

their journey. At each stage of the itinerary, in each country or area, something happened that required further interpretation and comprehension. His diary records many events of this kind. Roerich reflected upon Time and Space legends and a higher consciousness mysteriously coalesced between mountain valleys, distances and snow-capped peaks. The 20th century with its significant turning points is over. The Soviet Union has fallen apart, its ideology has lost its value. Many things have changed. But the struggle of the old with the new continues and traditional science and the church seem to be permanent allies in this struggle. In new Russia, Roerich's philosophy of cosmic reality is still not understood. In fact, Roerich has come under severe criticism from certain Russian academia by detractors such as V.A. Rosov, N.E. Samokhina, S.R. Ableyev, etc.

Rosov grossly distorted the image and tasks of the Central Asian Expedition in his doctoral thesis. Ignoring Roerich's cultural, artistic and scientific achievements, he projects him as a pitiful political adventurer: preparing an armed attack against Tibet; trying to create an independent state in Central Asia which would include Soviet Siberia; speaking against the USSR; colluding with Japan on the eve of the Second World War, etc.

Helena Roerich, the Teachers' creative collaborator in spreading the teaching of Living Ethics, was not spared either. N.E. Samokhina who proclaimed herself to be the first expert of the Roerichs' philosophical heritage, termed the philosophy of cosmic reality as mediocre esoteric writing. It seems obstacles are being deliberately planted in the path of a new cosmic mentality.

Two other unique acts of the Roerichs may be considered as aspects of meta-historical creation: Roerich's Pact on the protection of cultural and historical values at the time of armed conflicts; and the Institute of Himalayan Studies established in India, in the Himalayan valley of Kullu. It is of deep regret that neither Roerich's Pact nor the Institute of Himalayan Studies have had an appropriate and worthy continuation. Perhaps it would be correct to assume that through the Expedition he created a new "Empire". The creative work that was the outcome of this Expedition reinforced Nicholas and Helena Roerich's lifelong effort towards a new cosmic consciousness that was so far not accepted or understood in Western civilisation.

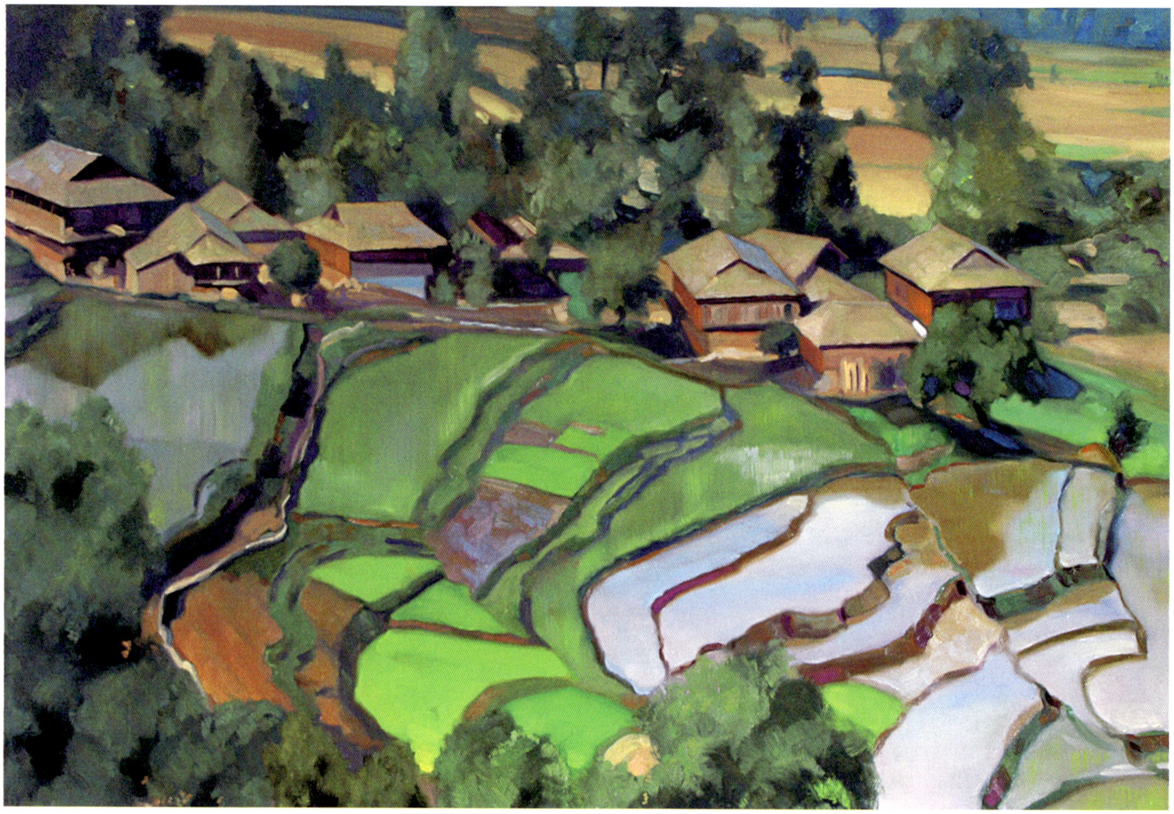

Naggar Kullu, 1938 (International Centre of the Roerichs, Moscow)

Select Bibliography

N.K. Roerich. *Collected Edition*. V. 1. Petrograd: Publishing house of I. D. Sytin, 1914.
Zolotoye Runo. 1907. No. 4.
D. Burlyuk. *Roerich*. New York, undated.
Perezvony. *Riga*, 1926. No. 13 (5).
Roerich's *Empire*. M.: ICR, 2004.
J. Nehru. *Discovery of India*. M., 1955.
N.K. Roerich. *Selection*. M., 1979.
N.K. Roerich. *Kindle the Hearts*. M.: Molodaya Gvardiya, 1975.
N.K. Roerich. Letter to V. A. Shibayev dated 27.07.25 // ICR MD. F. 1. Inv. 1. (Temp.) No. 2531.
N. Roerich. *Diary Pages*. In 3 v. V. 1. M.: ICR, 1995.
N.K. Roerich. *Altai–Himalayas*. M., 1974.
N. Roerich. *Diary Pages*. V. 3. M.: ICR, 2002.
Рерих Н. *The Heart of Asia*. Southbury (Conn.): Alatas, 1929.
Рерих Н.К. *Altai–Himalayas*. Travel diary. Riga: Vieda, 1992.

Luminosity and the Natural Mind

Andrea Loseries

In discussing 'Luminosity and the Natural Mind', one can lay emphasis or point at the paintings of Nicholas Roerich. Particularly, his body of paintings of Tibet and Mongolia, carry this quality of pure mind par excellence. To explain this further one could look into some crucial practices and aspects of Tibetan Buddhism.

The notion of the natural luminosity of mind occupies an important position in Tibetan Buddhism, and in the ancient religion Bon, especially in the teaching of the Great Perfection (*rDzogs pa chen po*), which belongs to both spiritual mainstreams.[1]

In early Buddhist Sutras such as the *Prajñāpāramitā*, the ultimate nature of mind is attested to be clear light (*sems kyi rang bzhin no 'od gsal ba'o*).[2] On this basis the Secret Mantra Path (*gSangs sngags kyi theg pa*) or Vajrayana (*rDo rje theg pa*) was developed using the method of

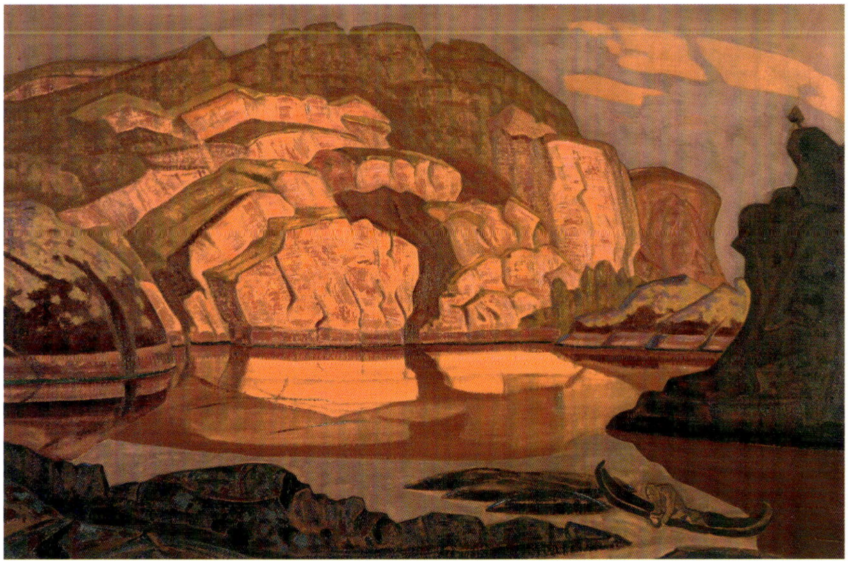

Hidden Treasure from 'Heroica' suite, 1917 (Nicholas Roerich Museum, NY)

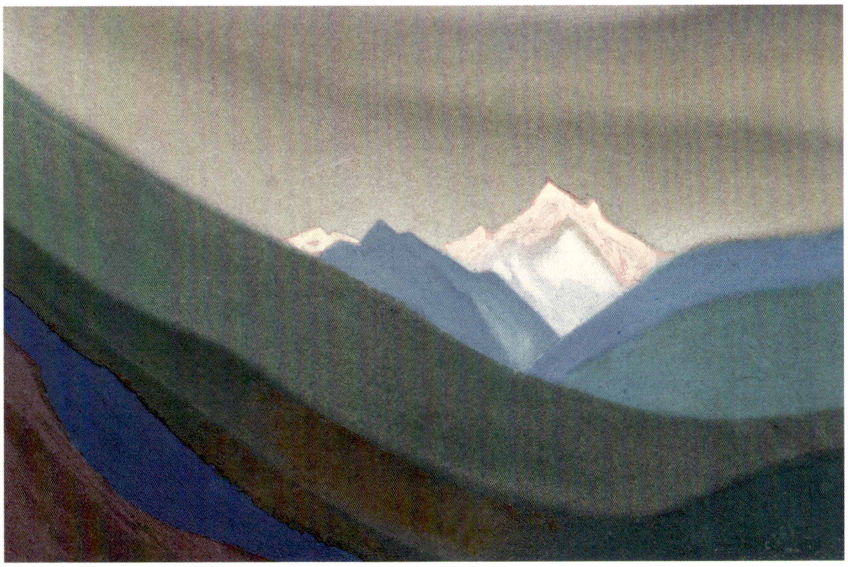

Study of Mountains (series) (International Roerich Memorial Trust, Naggar, Kullu)

visualisation expounded in Tantric Sadhana practice. The practitioner creates, in stages, a luminous appearance of a Buddha or deity out of the primordial void. The practitioner then identifies with the created vision by an exchange of light rays streaming out of the vital centres of the body of the created visions and out of oneself (*skyes rim*). This clears him/her of all veils of ignorance. Authenticated with the power of seed syllables and Mantras the translucent visual appearance, which is seen like a reflection in a mirror, is then reabsorbed into the natural state of void experienced as clarity and bliss (*rdzogs rim*).[3]

The inherent luminosity of mind applies also to the gross elements of the inner and outer world, that is, living beings and their environment consisting of the five elements. In various practices such as the alchemis fasting practice called 'Sucking the Essence' (*bcud len*)[4] or the Direct Leap (*Thod rgal*)[5] as expounded in the Heart Drop (*sNying thig*) teachings compiled by Longchenpa (*kLon chen Dri med 'od zer*), one takes into experience (*nyams su blang ba*), the essential nature of light of all phenomena as self-awareness (*rang rig*). When awareness (*rig pa*) integrates into the pure vision (*dag snang*) before one in space and becomes that vision, one eventually realises the rainbow body (*mja' lus*) or body of light (*'od lus*).[6]

Moreover, this awareness is sustained and persevered in not only during meditative practice, but also in all activities during the day,[7] during the dream stages, while asleep,[8] in the process of dying, and also during the intermediate stage (*bar do*). The cultivation of clear light, (*'od gsal*) that is the essential nature of our mind, if practiced and experienced during this lifetime, will eventually culminate in enlightenment and the realisation of Dharmakaya (*chos sku*) at the moment of death when the 'luminosity of the path' (*lam gi 'od gsal*) merges with the 'luminosity of the ground' (*gzhi gi 'od gsal*). If one is unable to bear the clear light due to the stranglehold of ignorance (*ma rig pa*), the consciousness will then co-emergently give rise to the five wisdoms (*ye shes lnga*) in the form of the Five Transcendental Buddha Families (*rgyal ba rigs lnga*) and the five mind poisons (*sems dug lnga*). If the deceased has the capacity to merge into the dazzling wisdom light of the respective Buddhas and shake off his inflicting emotions that divert him into the dullness of Samsaric realms, he will attain full enlightenment at this stage and realise Sambhogakaya (*longs sku*). If not, he may still use skilful means for attaining liberation and realise Nirmanakaya (*sprul sku*) by wisely recognising and keeping up the luminosity of intrinsic awareness during a human rebirth.[9]

In Tibet many examples exist of a successful completion of the process of transformation into light. And even in recent years Buddhist as well as Bon practitioners in Tibet manifest signs of the rainbow body at the end of their lives.[10] This transformation is neither artistic nor mystic, but a process of purification that eliminates the causes of all obscurations (*sgrib pa*), which have shadowed the luminosity of the mind since time immemorial.

The high altitude of the Tibetan Plateau and the seemingly endless horizon of the Mongol steppes, where only space and sky prevail

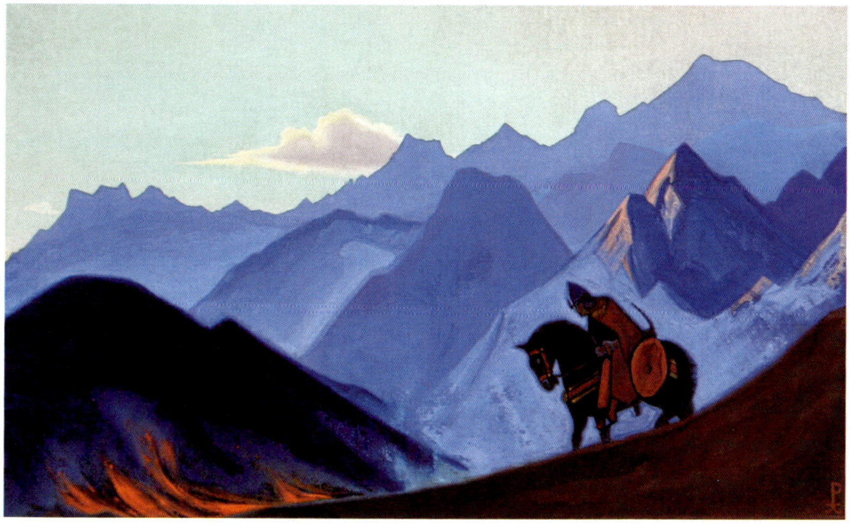

The Signs, 1937 (International Centre of the Roerichs, Moscow)

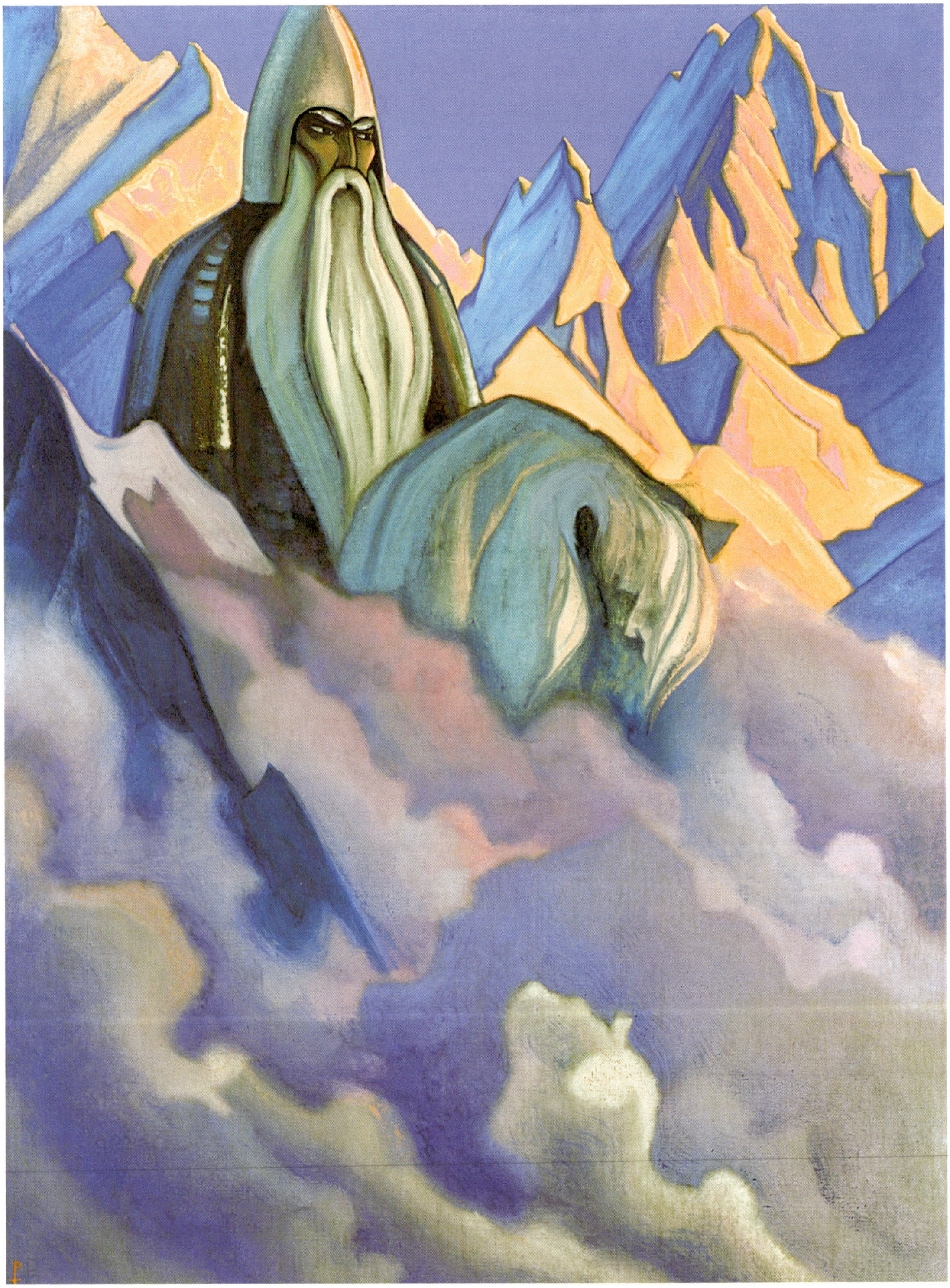

Sviatogor, 1938 (International Centre of the Roerichs, Moscow)

without much of a change in lifestyle or material diversity, may have enhanced the mastership of its inhabitants in contemplation of this kind. Rainbows often fill the sky and visions, based on either fabrication (*dmigs pa*) or poetic reveries, arise easily. Moreover, in the natural calmness of mind even an apparently gray and lonesome landscape starts to glow, with all appearances bathed in a brilliance (*dvangs*) that is but the reflection of the inner luminosity of one's Buddha nature.

The most dominant feature of Nicholas Roerich's art is this intrinsic luminosity. His quest for and exploration of his innate awareness (*rang byung rig pa*) and maintaining (*drvang pa*) its aspect of clarity (*gsal ba*) are mirrored in his landscape paintings of Tibet and Mongolia. He often chose as a theme rocky hills and snow-capped mountain peaks bathed in veils of mist against a skyline, where the evening light casts the scenery into a dazzling glow. In a similar manner, the naked state of awareness sets fire to inflicting emotions (*nyon rmongs*), which pervade the mind, and merges in a single sphere (*klong du gcig*) with the wisdom play (*rtsal*) of outer appearances (*snang ba*) manifesting such as they are, a decorum, an ornament (*rgyan*). The play with shadow and darkness against light and brilliance in Roerich's landscape paintings reflects his internal struggle with karmic impediments (*las kyi sgrib pa*) and his longing to merge into bliss (*bde ba zung 'jug dmyer med*). The depiction of a monastery or mountain hermitage far off on high cliffs expresses a cry for liberation from worldly bondage and suffering. A tree in the crisp freshness of spring in a still frozen landscape raises hope and determination. Azure blue lakes in the depths of valleys against the might of eternal snow on seemingly endless rock ranges are reminiscent of the uncontaminated state of one's own mind (*yang gad pa rang sems kyi gnas lugs*) within the solidness of habitual traces (*bag chags*). Roerich seldom paints figures. It indicates his lone pursuit for perfection. However, the outlines of a temple or the summits of *mChod rten* in his all pervading mountain sceneries refer to his refuge into the Triple Gem, or the Tri-ratna (*dkon mchog gsum*) that sustained him on the Path.

The luminosity and brilliance apparent even in shadow and darkness in these paintings touch the heart of the on-looker, and uncover a deeply veiled longing for wisdom and for peace with each and everything in this phenomenal light and sound show of illusion.

Such phenomena are self-evident in the paintings of Nicholas Roerich. His works show rare incandescence that captivates the beholder.

End Notes

1. See f.i. Tenzin Wangyal 1993, Shardza Tashi Gyaltsen 1993, Namkhai Norbu 1986.
2. *The Tibetan Tripitaka*, Tokyo, Vol 21, No. 734, p. 59, 3-7.
3. Guenther 1971, Davidson 2008, Guenther & Trungpa 1975.
4. kLong chen rab 'Byams pa: *Tshig Don mDzod* ii.3.1.b.2.i.a.2.1; Walter 1980:28; Wills 1995:71, White 1998.
5. rDzogs pa chen po'I lhun grub thod rgal gyi'i glu dbyangs by Tshogs drug rang grol; Rig 'dzin gTer bdag gLing pa: rdzogs chen Kun bzang dgongs 'dus las: nying po rab gsal.
6. Dalai Lama 1995: 143.
7. Rang grol Lode, 5th Thugse Rinpoche: dus bshi sangs rgyas nyams byor; in: Dzogs chen kun bzang dgongs 'dus.
8. Namkhai Norbu & Reynolds 1987.
9. Reynolds 1989, Bar do thos sgrol chen mo, Tse le Nagtsok Rangdrol 1989.
10. Reynolds 1989; Dargye 1977:222, Wills 1995:71, Ricard 1994.

Select Biography

Bar do thos sgrol chen mo.
Tibetan Tripitaka, Tokyo, Vol 21, No. 734.
kLong chen Rab 'Byams pa (1308-63): *Tshig don mDzod.*
Rang grol Lode, 5th Thugse Rinpoche: dus bshi sangs rgyas nyams byor; in: rDzogs chen kun bzang dgongs 'dus
Rig 'dzin gTer bdag gLing pa: rDzogs chen Kun bzang dgongs 'dus las: nying po rab gsal.
gTer ston Padma Gling pa: Rig 'dzin padma gling pa'i zab gter chos mdzod rin po che, 20 vols. Delhi 1976.
Tshogs drug rang grol:rDzogs pa chen po'i lhun grub thod rgal gyi'i glu dbyangs.

English Sources

Dalai Lama, XIV: The World of Buddhism. An Overview of its Philosophy and Practice. Somerville 1995.
Dargye, Eva: The Rise of Esoteric Buddhism in Tibet. Delhi 1977.
Davidson, Ronald M.: Tibetan Renaissance. Tantric Buddhism in the Rebirth of Tibetan Culture. Delhi 2008 (Columbia 2005).
Guenther, Herbert v.: Buddhist Philosophy in Theory and Practice. Baltimore 1971.
Guenther, Herbert v. & Chogyam Trungpa: The Dawn of Tantra. Berkeley & London 1975.
Namkhai Norbu: The Crystal and the Way of Light. London 1986.
Namkhai Norbu & John Reynolds: The Cycle of Day and Night. New York 1987.
Reynolds, John M.: Self-Liberation Through Seeing with Naked Awareness. New York 1989.
Shardza Tashi Gyaltsen: Heart Drops of the Dharmakaya. New York 1993.
Tenzin Wangyal: Wonders of the Natural Mind. New York 1993.
Tsele Natsok Rangdrol: The Mirror of Mindfulness. The Cycle of the Four Bardos. Boston 1989.
Tulku Thondup: Hidden Teachings of Tibet. London 1986.
Walter, Michael: The Role of Alchemy and Medicine in Tibetan Buddhism. London 1980.
White, David Gordon: The Alchemic Body. Siddha Traditions in Medivial India. Chicago 1998.
Wills, Janice Dean: Enlightened Beings. Life Stories from the Ganden Tradition. Somerville 1995.

When the Expedition started out in 1924, Nicholas Roerich was fifty years old. His achievements were already of considerable significance. He was an Academician of the Russian Academy of Arts; his paintings had been exhibited in many major museums of the world and enjoyed much acclaim. A museum named after him had been opened in New York; its exposition included a large number of his paintings. In archaeology, he had laid foundations of a complex historical and cultural study on Russian antiquity, on the basis of the excavation of materials from ancient Russian cities of Novgorod, Pskov, etc. Roerich embodied his discoveries on canvas. In him the great talent of an artist was combined with amazing clear-sightedness of a scientist, and remarkable foresight of a wise sage. 'One who doesn't know the past, can't think of the future,' he wrote in 1910. 'A [sic] Nation must know its history expressed in the ancient monuments. A [sic] Nation must own all best achievements of the previous epochs. We must seek with great care for antiquities untouched by barbarian hand and return them long deserved significance.'[1]

This idea was based on the concept of the essential unity of the past and future. The application of this idea to the activities of the Expedition, added newer dimensions to their discoveries.

Nicholas Roerich was actively involved in diverse cultural and educational activities. He collaborated with the magazine *Art and Artistic Industry*. He was an active member and later the leader of the association 'The World of Art'. In 1906, Roerich was the head of the Drawing School of the Emperor's Society for Promotion of Arts guiding it to become one of the most famous artistic educational institutions of Russia. In 1915, the Russian public widely celebrated the 25th anniversary of Nicholas Roerich's creative activities.

He called upon the state to participate in the protection of historical and cultural monuments. The idea of cataloguing architectural monuments was his brainchild. Roerich thought it was equally necessary to educate and involve the public in this enterprise. After completing the Expedition, he returned to the idea he had earlier conceived of an international agreement on protection of cultural values. 'The Roerich Pact', named after him, proposed the organisation of an international public movement for the protection of mankind's cultural property.

Helena Roerich, Nicholas Roerich's spouse, was forty-five years of age when the Expedition began. She came in contact with what they termed the Cosmic Hierarchs, the guards of, and contributors to the evolution of earthly mankind. The Roerichs called them their Teachers and they were guided by them in all their endeavours. All their main achievements, including the Central Asian Expedition, were in relation to messages received from them. Helena Roerich kept records of conversations with her Teacher, which later formed the treatises of Living Ethics, a philosophy of cosmic reality that outlined mankind's evolutionary path for the next millennium. Yuri , the Roerichs' elder son, was twenty-two years old when the Expedition started. He was an indispensable co-worker. Yuri was an Orientalist, educated at the Hindu and Iranian Department of the School of Oriental and African Studies, London University. Proficient in more than thirty languages and dialects, he was of invaluable help with the varied populace encountered during the Expedition. Yuri's education in military science at the Paris University's Military Department proved extremely essential as well in defending the Expedition's caravan more than once from attacks of armed gangs and marauders. India played the role of a powerful cultural and historical phenomenon in the life of the Roerichs, and in bringing all they already know and understood to a higher level of cognition. Nicholas Roerich wrote:

> 'All around India, from the scorched South to the soaring Himalayas, there live signs which you remember in any country. You will justly pay reverence to the subtlety and elevation of thought in all of them. Any Hindu, from the most learned one to the commonest *coolie*, will be glad to talk about high subjects. Even in a short time, you will understand that, above mundane life, above public and state issues, highly spiritual subjects are most significant for a Hindu.'[2]

Nicholas Roerich had always wished to visit India. Initially it attracted him as a field for historical studies. In 1914, Roerich met Russian Orientalist, V.V. Golubev in Paris. Both being interested in India, they planned an Expedition which did not take place for a number of reasons. India was then a British colony with serious disagreements with Russia. Quite some years passed before Nicholas Roerich would be able to visit India.

When the Revolution took place in Russia, the Roerich family was in Finland where Nicholas was undergoing treatment. Finland proclaimed its independence and broke away from Russia. Thus, the

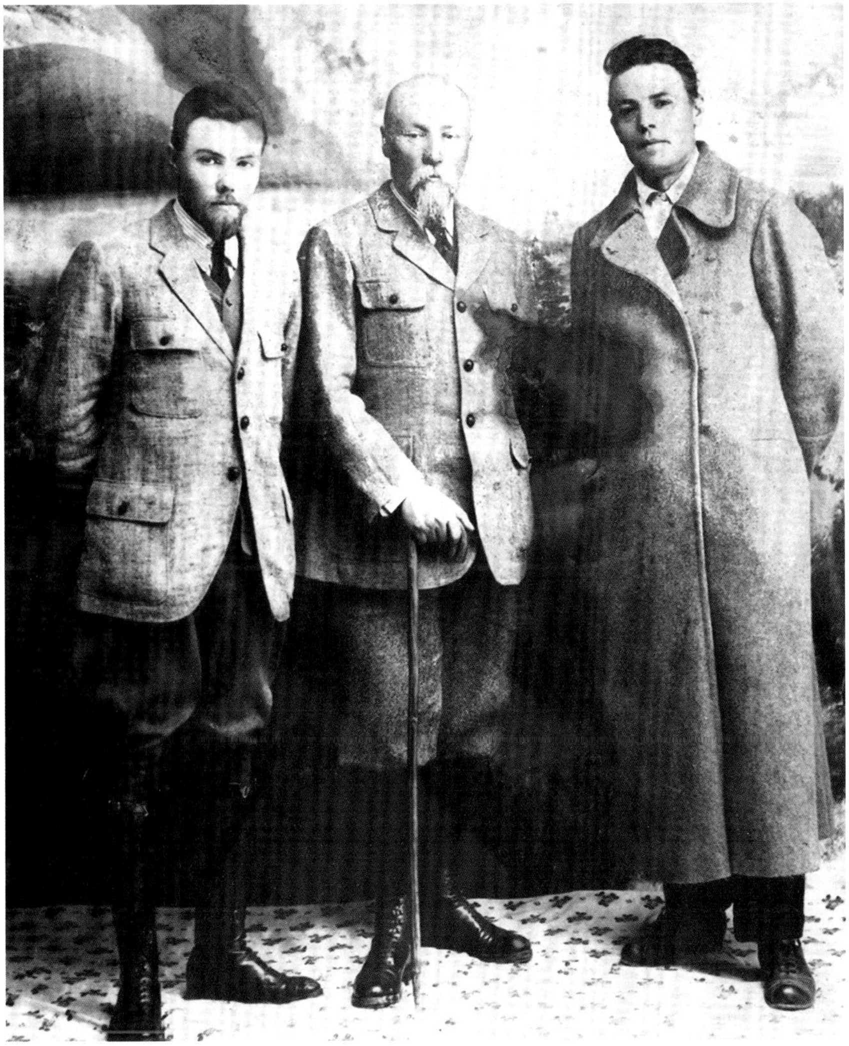

Left to right: George Roerich, Nicholas Roerich, Aleksandr Bystrov, April–May, 1926. Urumchi, Chinese Turkestan (Nicholas Roerich Museum Archive, NY)

Roerichs found themselves stranded beyond Russian shores. Soon, Nicholas Roerich received an offer to hold his exhibitions in Sweden, Denmark and England, and accepted.

While in England, Nicholas Roerich was invited to exhibit his paintings in the United States. He agreed and the Roerichs arrived in America. Roerich was soon established as a renowned artist whose work made a strong impact on the cultural scene. A museum named after Nicholas Roerich was established in New York, to which Roerich donated a large number of his paintings. Besides the museum, Nicholas Roerich organised several cultural and educational institutions to promote culture. All this while, Roerich continued to dream about India. And soon the opportunity presented itself.

In 1923, the Roerich family arrived in France, and left by sea for India from Marseilles. A life-long dream was coming true. After spending a year travelling around the well-known historical sites of India, the Roerichs settled in Darjeeling in the North-east. Here Nicholas and Helena Roerich had their second significant meeting with the Teachers (the first meeting had taken place in London). All Roerich's future activities were now conducted under the guidance of the Teachers and their influence can be traced through the whole stream of Roerich's heritage. The meeting with the Teachers in Darjeeling determined the future plans of the Expedition.

It was Roerich's inherent belief that, 'No museum, no book gives the right to portray Asia or other countries if you have not seen them with your own eyes, if you did not take at least memorial notes on the spot. Persuasiveness, this magic quality of creative work, inexplicable with words, is created only by stratifying true impressions of the reality.'[3] He further elaborated the aims of the Expedition: 'Besides artistic

Study of Mountains (series) (International Roerich Memorial Trust, Naggar, Kullu)

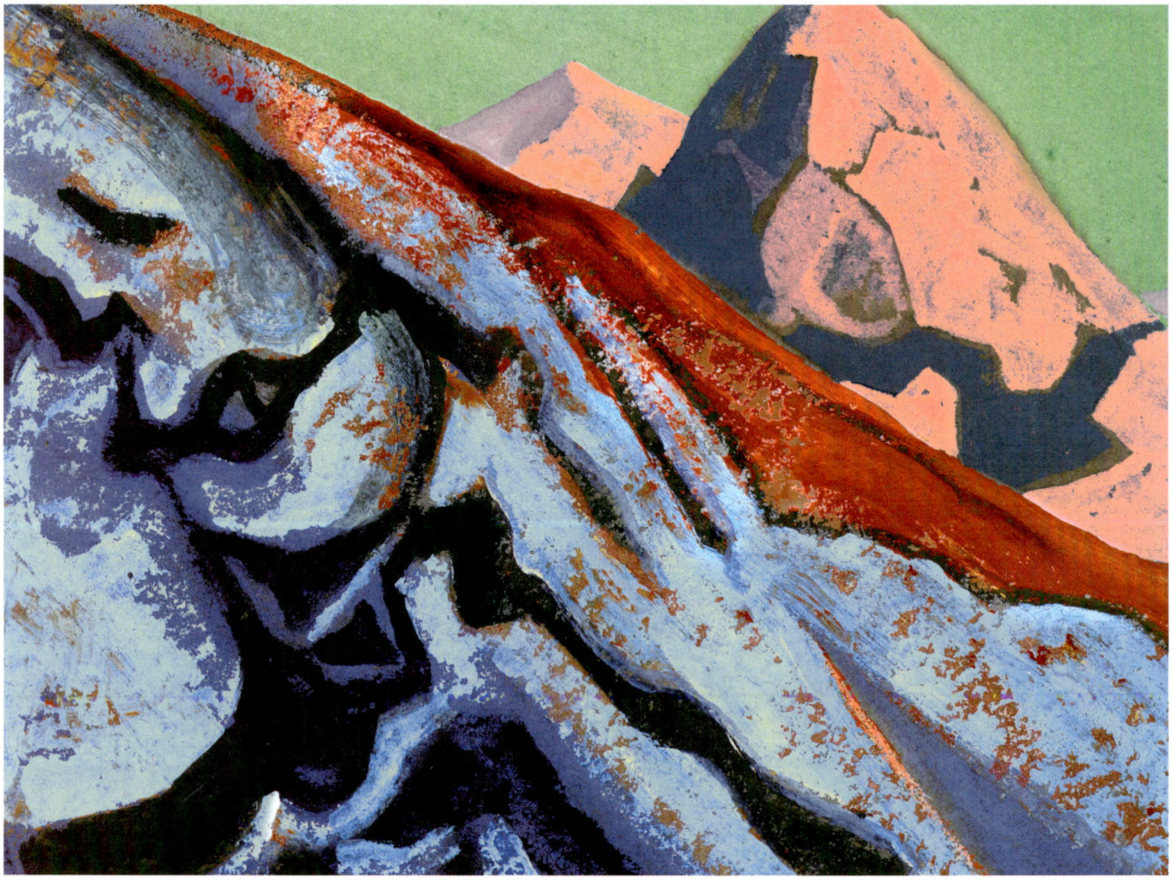

tasks, we plan to learn about the situation with antique monuments of Central Asia, to observe the modern state of religion, customs, and to mark traces of the great migration of peoples. The last task had been akin to me for a long time.'[4]

The itinerary covered by the Central Asian Expedition spanned several vast unexplored regions. It started in 1924 from Sikkim, then a small kingdom near British India in the North-east of India. It proceeded to the erstwhile Indian Princely state of Kashmir and then to Ladakh and Karakorum. It crossed the North-western part of the Taklamakan desert and continued along the Chinese territory of Sin-Tsian. Moving along the Eastern slopes of Tian Shan, near the Chinese city of Urumchi, the Expedition crossed the border with Soviet Middle Asia and arrived in Moscow. From Moscow, it headed for Siberia, Altai, and through Buryatia, near the city of Kyahta, it entered Mongolia. From there, moving through the Gobi desert, the Expedition entered Tibet. It returned to Darjeeling after traversing scarcely known Trans-Himalayan regions. In four years the Expedition had covered more than 25,000 km, crossing thirty-five hazardous high mountain passes, between 4,000 to 6,500 m high.

In Sikkim, Roerich visited the ancient monasteries Pemayangtse, Tashiding, Sanga Cheling, Dubling and held discussions with their head lamas, hermits and sages. Ancient legends, sagas about the sacred mountain Kanchenjunga—the mountain of Five Treasures—and of the sacred, legendary country Shambhala were collected. To the Roerichs all these legends and sagas were somehow reminiscent of the legends of Belovodye commonly heard in Russia.

Roerich noted in his diary, 'In 1924 a new era started according to Tibetan chronology.'[5] The beginning of the new era many felt was directly related to the rise of a new cosmic mentality in the cultural space of Russia. It was evidenced in the studies of Russian scientists Vernadsky, Tsiolkovsky, Chizhevsky and many other outstanding representatives of a galaxy of philosophers, poets and artists of the Russian Silver Age, a galaxy to which Nicholas Roerich belonged as well. What Roerich looked for and what was discovered during the Expedition, was directly linked to the issues these Russian scientists worked on, the recognition of the laws of unity between Man and the Universe.

Passing through terrain that echoed with the footsteps of the Great Teachers of humanity, such as the Lord Buddha and Christ, Roerich recovered fragments of long forgotten knowledge. Roerich's notation in his diary crystallises his creative and spiritual accomplishments: 'By your own you will cross the entire path following landmarks,' he wrote. 'Yourselves, with human feet. You will collect your own pearls befitting your size. You will pick the pearls with your fingers. Develop dynamics by your own hands. 'Give away,' eradiate your will....This way, mere curiosity will be separated from the true aspiration....There are paths to be crossed with pure hands and by one's own will'.'[6] 'And if you are able, through the shell of mundane things, to see the heights of Cosmos,' continued Nicholas Roerich in his diary, 'what a new, wonderful, inexhaustible aspect the world will take for a liberated eye.'[7]

In India, time and again, Roerich witnessed these resonating philosophical and spiritual leanings. In the spring of 1925, the Expedition arrived in Kashmir. 'As in Sikkim,' Roerich wrote, 'spiritual comprehension strikes you in Kashmir. Hardly do you think, and the person you talk to already makes a corresponding gesture. How many good thoughts can be sown by these strings of keen feelings.'[8] A true measure of spiritual comprehension can be found in people whose consciousness is not subject to ignorance or prejudice, concludes Roerich:

> 'Thus, eight Muslims sitting on a red carpet, unexpectedly, without being asked, glorify Christ and the Universe until midnight. Following them, all boatmen move their white turbans and sway, singing along. Then, the gramophone repeats Shalyapin's 'Lel's Song' by Rimsky-Korsakov, and Kashmir men's turbans nod keenly. Single mentality! We finish with a song about Akbar. And the whole midnight passes without any negations. Everything mutually found is accepted with a good smile.'[9]

All these experiences strengthened his integral belief in the unity between Man and the Universe and the existence of a pervasive cosmic mentality.

In Kashmir, Roerich formulated the title for a long-planned series of paintings dedicated to the Great Teachers of humanity — *The Banners of the East*, which included nineteen wonderful canvases.

With the experienced eye of an artist, the intuition of a scientist, Roerich noticed similarities in the art of Russian and Indian people, preserved even today:

> 'Paunchy white columns of the temples; details of ornamental patterns; steep stone stairs; gilded roof; creaking painted window shutters; rusty locks; low little doors 'with a bow', carved balustrades, stone floor lopsided plates, old varnish smell, small window glasses. So where we are? In Rostov Kremlin? In Suzdal monasteries? In Yaroslavl cathedrals?…This is the main palace of Kashmir Maharaja.[10] 'In the character of the temples and mosques, in the carved corner dragons, in the hip-roofed tower, we find an unexpected combination of wooden churches of Norway and Chinese pagodas. A Roman chimera, animal design of Altai, beasts of Chinese-Turkistan and China, are scooped from the same well. Siberian ways of the peoples have carried far the same meaning of decorations.'[11]

These observations would lead Roerich to the conclusion that all cultures stream from a single source disseminated during the great migrations of people in distant historical times.

In 1925, the Expedition entered Ladakh. In Roerich's Expedition diary, we find many records dedicated to the teachings of the Buddha,

Study of Mountains (series) (International Roerich Memorial Trust, Naggar, Kullu

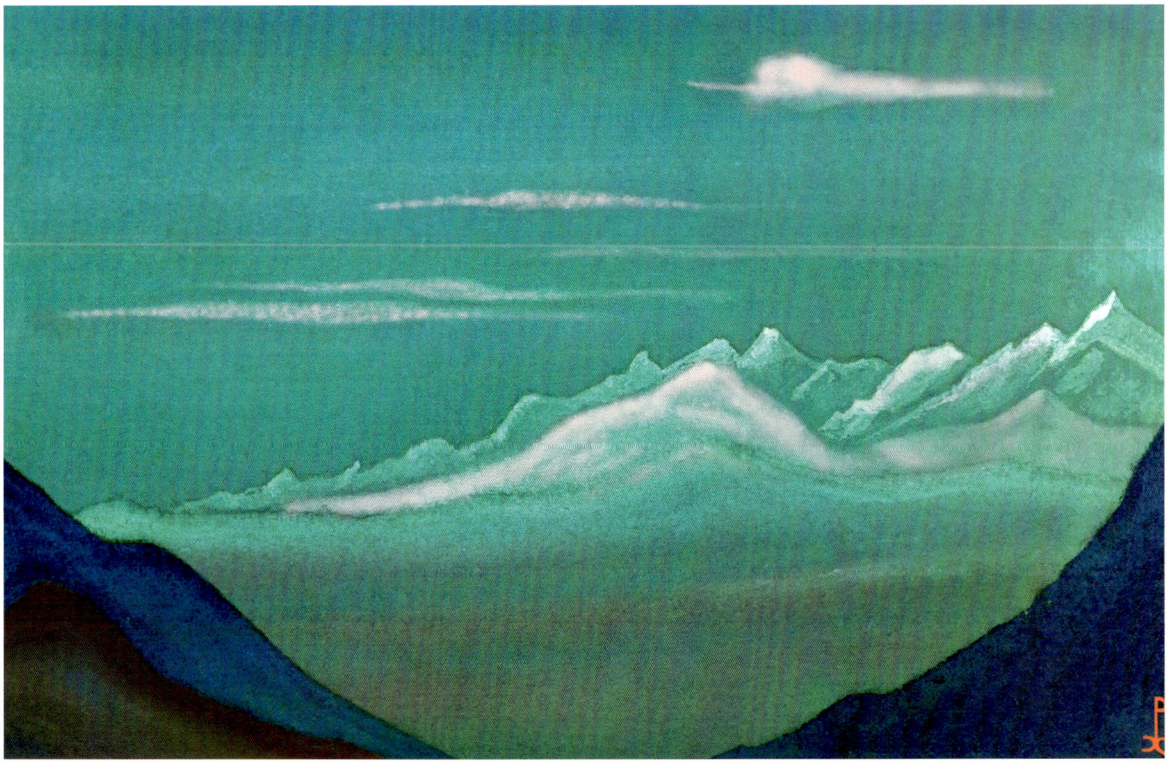

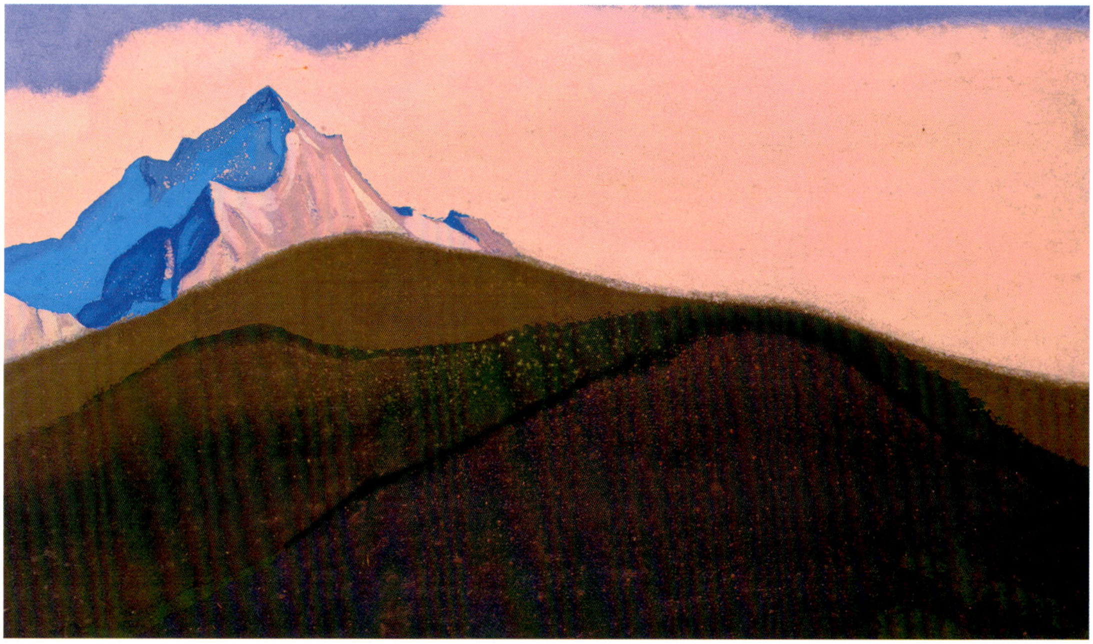

Study of Mountains (series) (International Roerich Memorial Trust, Naggar, Kullu)

Confucius and Jesus. In the monasteries, Nicholas Roerich studied ancient manuscripts over fifteen hundred years old. He also recorded what appeared to be the evidence of Jesus' stay in India, Nepal, the Himalayas and Tibet:

> 'So high and dear to all peoples image of Jesus is preserved by Buddhists in their mountain monasteries. It's no wonder that the teachings of Christ and Buddha bring all the peoples into one family, but that noble idea of community is expressed so clearly. Who can be against this idea? Who will belittle the simplest and most beautiful solution of life? So easily and scientifically flows the earthly community into the great Community of all worlds. Jesus' and Buddha's behests rest on the same shelf.'[12]

In the autumn of 1925, the Expedition's caravan left Ladakh's capital Leh and in twelve days, after crossing five high mountain passes of Karakorum, it descended to the plains. After facing sheer cliffs of ice and raging snow-storms of the Himalayan passes, they entered the huge plains of Asia where the great Taklamakan desert begins. Here the Chinese local authorities met the Expedition with hostility. On 14 September, the Expedition entered Hotan where the travellers found themselves prisoners of the ignorant and cruel Amban.

Nicholas Roerich realised the urgency of departing from hostile territory. However, they could not leave. Criticising life in Hotan, a rare thing for Roerich to do, he describe it as one of impenetrable darkness, deceit and betrayal, and without any dignity of labour.

> 'What do we understand more by sitting in Hotan? It becomes clear once again that such life as in Hotan must not exist. Imagine, the life of one hundred thousand people is turned into impenetrable darkness. From darkness, diseases, vice, lies are born. People are left just with petty trade, secured by deceit and betrayal. Understanding of the product quality is dead. Understanding of the urgency of work is gone. Understanding of the victory of labour is emptied. Immersion into the slime of the bazaar pools and mutual strangling is under way. It can't continue like this.'[13]

Despite these adverse circumstances, Nicholas Roerich continued his work, creating the *Maitreya* series of paintings that were later left in Moscow. Thanks to the Expedition leader's resolute actions, and supported by the Soviet Consul in Kashgar to whom Nicholas Roerich sent a telegram asking for help, the Expedition managed to break away from imprisonment.

In April 1926, the Expedition entered Urumchi. Through Soviet Consul, A.E. Bystrov, Roerich applied for permission to enter Soviet Russia. After receiving permission on 13 June, the Roerichs arrived in Moscow, and stayed there for a month. From Moscow they went to Altai and continued their scientific work: collecting minerals, medicinal herbs, examining ancient burial sites, collating local legends and traditions. Here Nicholas Roerich made sketches for his future paintings. The mysterious and enigmatic legends of the snow-white mountain of Belukha, stories about the sacred country of Belovodye heard from Old Believers were reminiscent of legends about the Buddhist pure land of Shambhala that the Roerichs had heard of in the Himalayas. Based on the discoveries and experiences during the Expedition, Roerich came to the conclusion that the source of Altai, Himalayan and Buddhist legends, is a common and universal dream of the eternal land of Justice.

On 19 August, the Roerichs set off for Mongolia through Buryatia. In Urga, the capital of Mongolia, preparations were made for the next

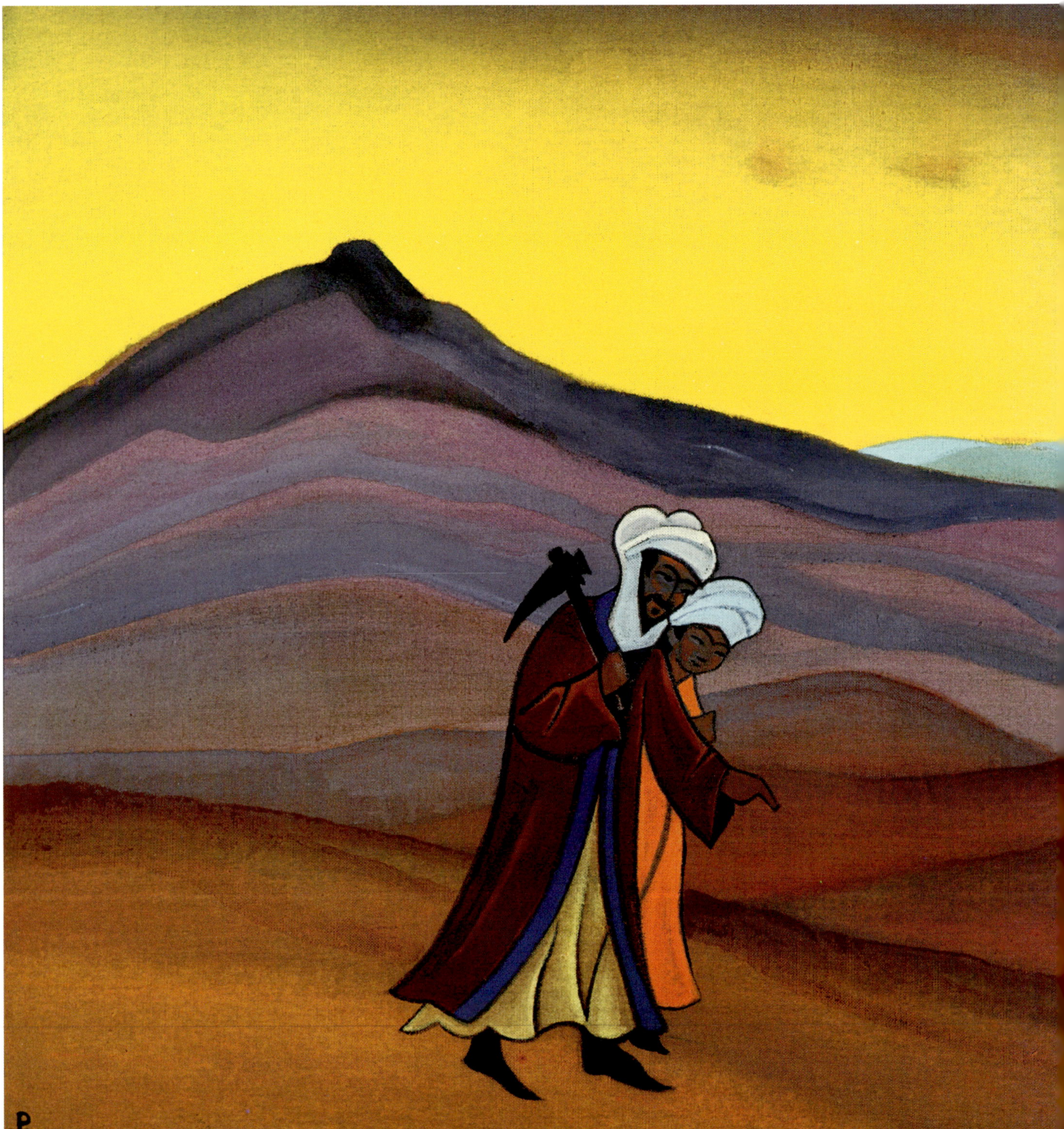

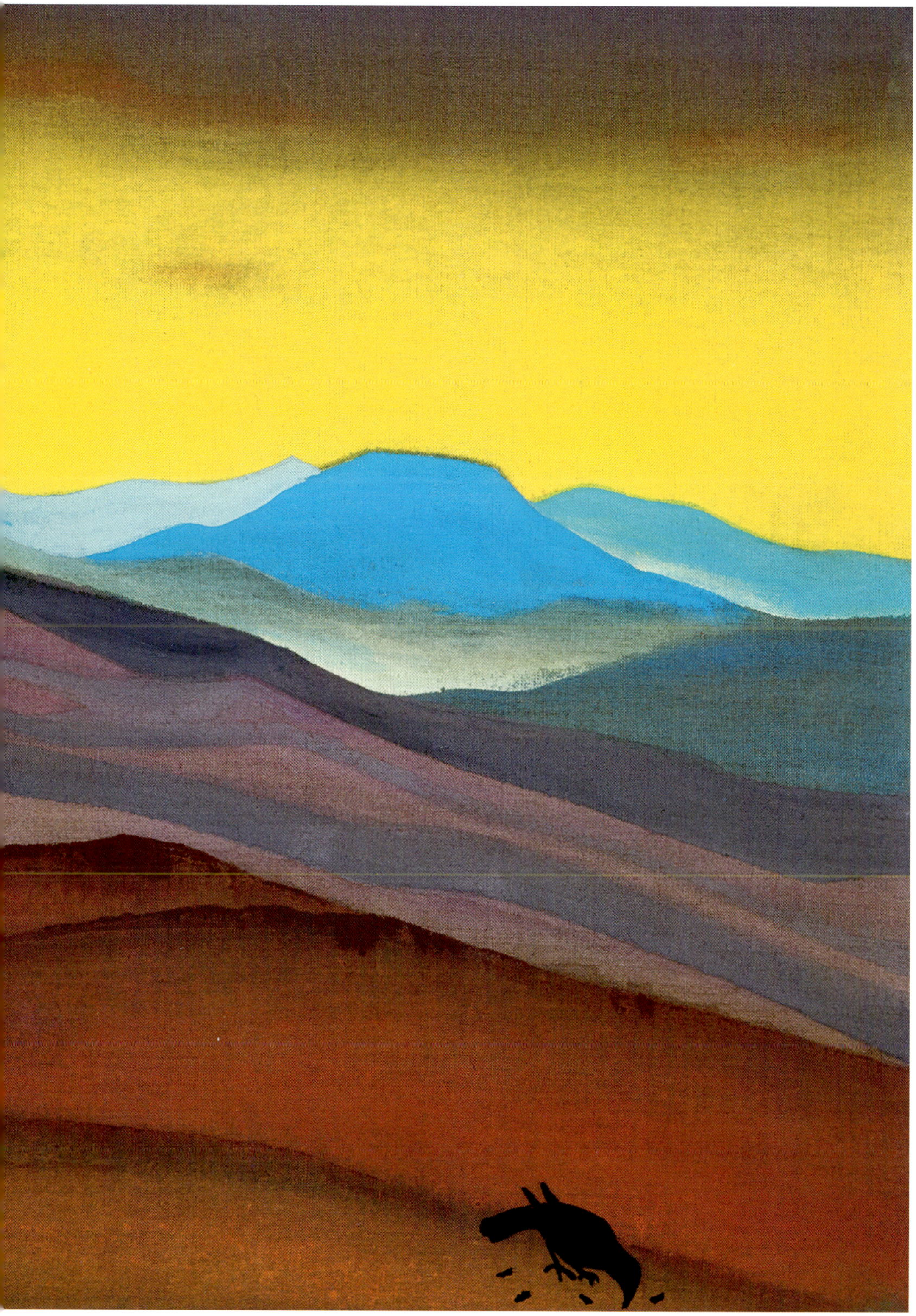

Khusru and Shirin, 1938 (International Centre of the Roerichs, Moscow)

leg of the Expedition's journey to Tibet. On receiving permission from the Tibetan Government to visit Lhasa, in April 1927, the caravan headed for Tibet. The route went across Gobi desert and Tsaidam. Near Shragol, their camp was washed off by a mud stream, resulting in the loss of some of the collections and Expedition property.

In September, approaching Tibet, the Expedition ascended to Tang-La pass and entered Shendi valley where the caravan was stopped by a detachment of Tibetan soldiers. This meant an unplanned stopover. The Expedition was forbidden to enter either Lhasa or Nagchu. They had to spend the severe winter in summer tents blasted by howling winds and hurricanes on the high Chantang mountain plateau located at the height of 4,000-4,500 m above sea level. In the entire Central Asian Expedition, this winter was the most terrible and dangerous encountered. Caravan animals perished in large numbers and they also lost some of their caravan members. Describing this perilous period Roerich writes:

> 'Two gentle days turn into severe five months staying in summer tents with frost temperatures lower than 0°C, with hurricane whirls at the height of 15,000 feet. Constantly drunken Major and wild ragged soldiers are left with us. It is forbidden to talk to passing by caravans; it is forbidden to buy food from the locals. Caravan slowly perishes. Every day there are new dead bodies by the tents, and packs of wild dogs loudly share their meal. Out of 104 caravan animals, ninety perished. Five people have died: three Mongolian lamas and two Tibetans. Malonov swells from heart attacks and finally dies too. Wife of the assigned to us Major got pneumonia and died. Vultures and eagles argue over the prey with the packs of dogs.'[14]

It was almost as if an invisible enemy had planned to sabotage the Expedition.

Forty years later, when the veil of secrecy was lifted from the British archives, it became known that the British Intelligence Service had forced the hand of the Tibetan authorities, leading to these incredible, unnecessary hardships.

It was the Roerichs' strength of purpose and courage that helped them endure and win over the elements of nature and human hostility, and break away from the mortal embrace of frosty imprisonment. In the beginning of March 1928, moving along the itinerary prescribed by Tibetan authorities, the Expedition headed for Sikkim. Ahead was Eastern Tibet and the unexplored areas of the Trans-Himalayas through which the caravan approached the area of the Great Lakes, then onto river Brahmaputra, after crossing unmapped passes about 6,300 m. high.

Nicholas Roerich, April, 1935. Tsagan-kure, Inner Mongolia (Nicholas Roerich Museum Archive, NY)

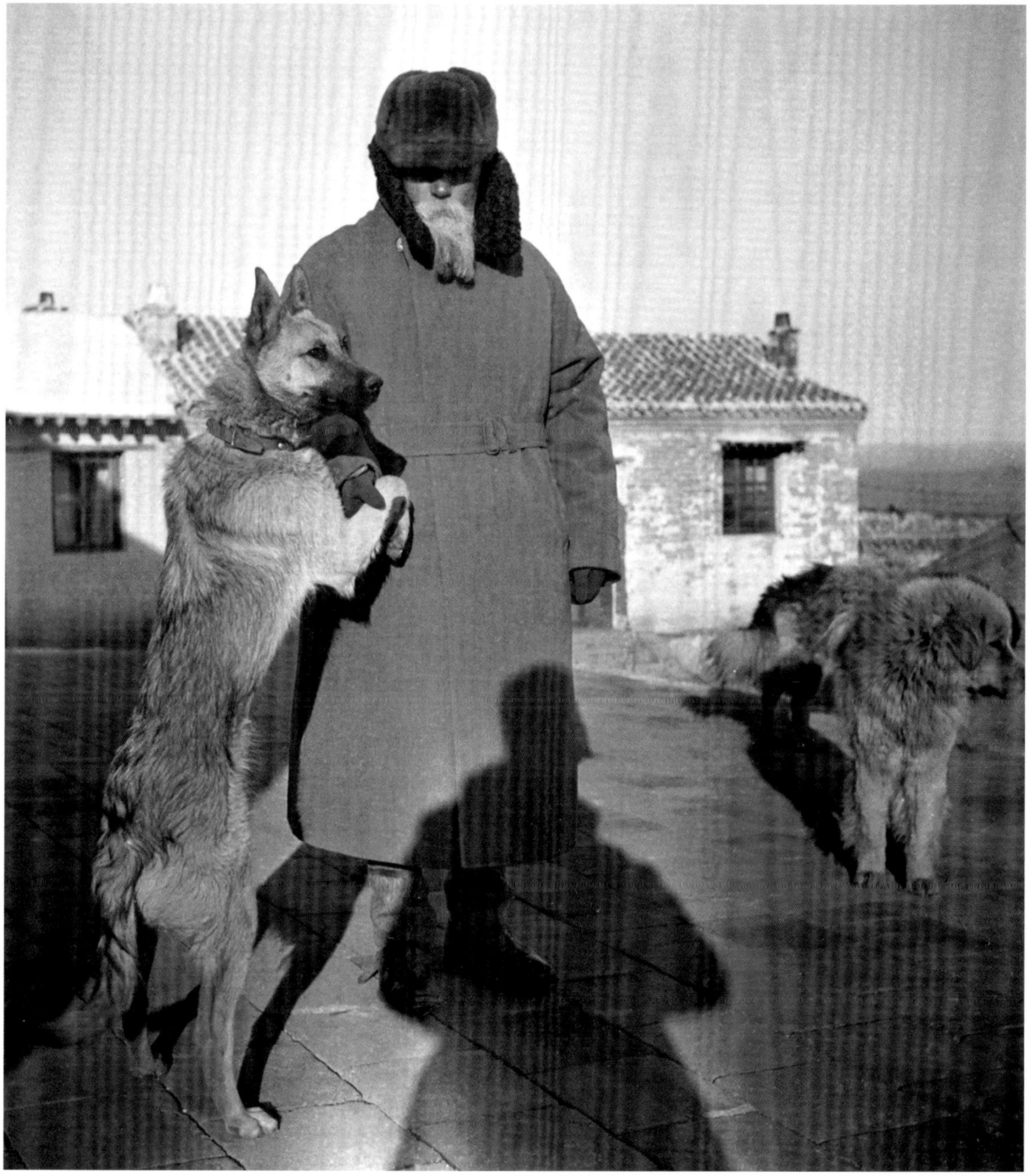

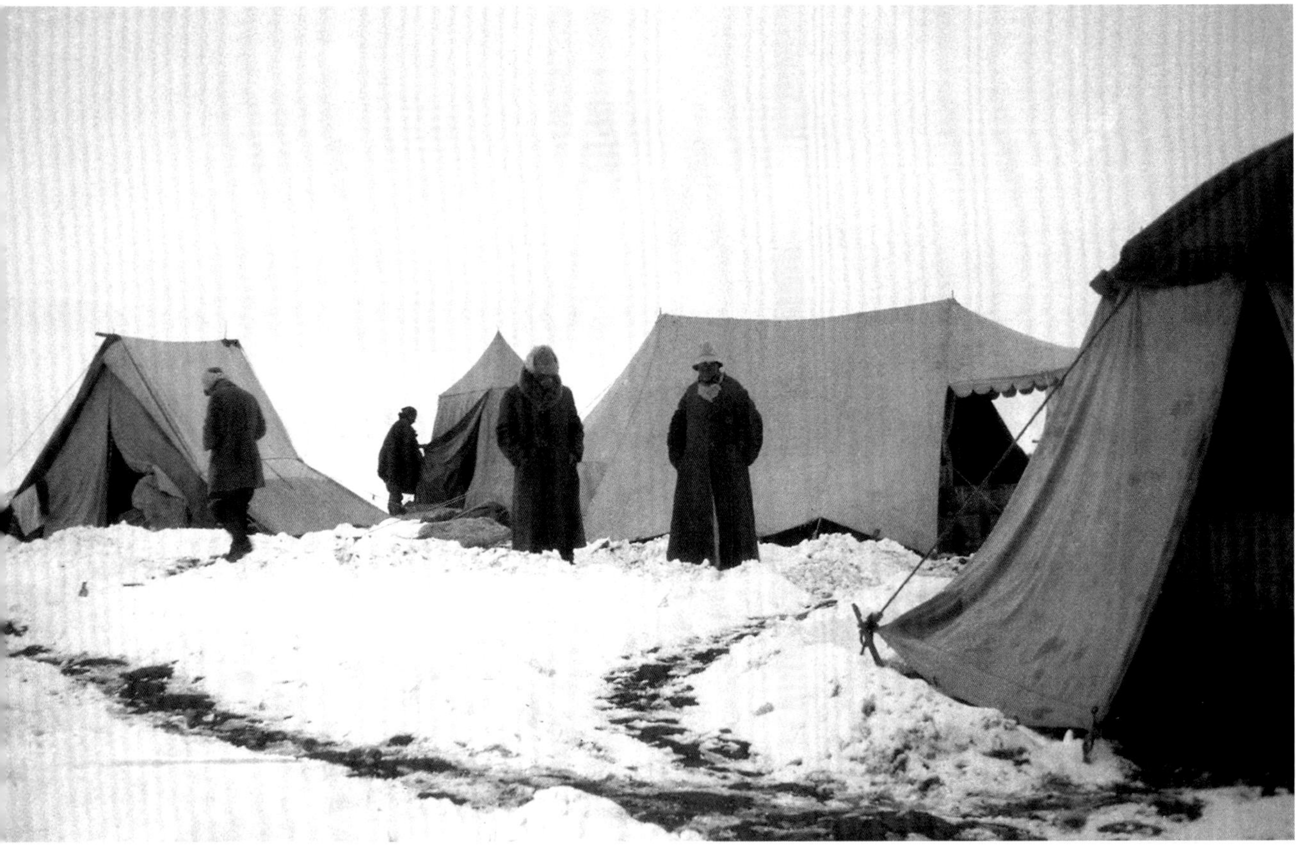

Right to left: Konstantin Ryabinin, Nicholas Roerich, October–December, 1927. Chu-na-khe, Tibet Expedition camp during the detention at Chu-na-khe (Nicholas Roerich Museum Archive, NY)

On 24 May, the caravan entered Gangtok, the capital of Sikkim. The same day the Roerichs sent a telegram to the New York museum: 'N. Roerich's expedition, after great difficulties, reached Himalayas. Thus, a major expedition to Central Asia is accomplished. A lot of scientific material was collected and many paintings painted.'[15]

On 26 May, the Expedition arrived in Darjeeling. In the same year, the Roerichs settled down in the sacred Himalayan valley of Kullu. A small estate was purchased on its southern slopes where the Roerichs lived till mid-December of 1947.

More than five hundred paintings, studies, drawings were created by Nicholas Roerich en route and presented to the Nicholas Roerich Museum in New York. No other expedition has been represented by artistic material to such an extent as the Central Asian Expedition. They not only supplemented accumulated scientific material, but formed an independent body of high artistic and scientific value. Journeying often through trackless terrain, the Expedition broadened geographical research on Central Asia, having proceeded along a

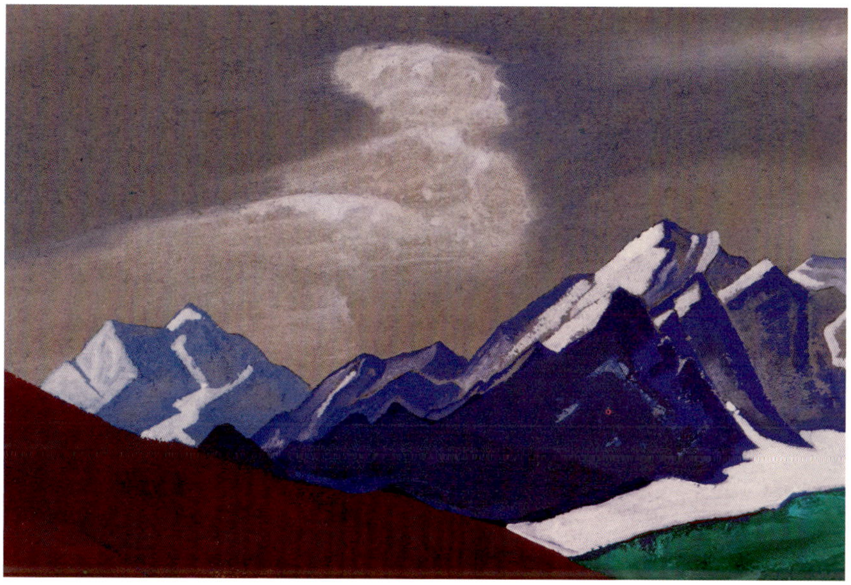

Study of Mountains (series) (International Roerich Memorial Trust, Naggar, Kullu)

route, which no other expedition had ever undertaken. It resulted in the mapping of new mountain paths and passes. Many archaeological monuments, enormous ethnographic folklore, and linguistic materials were discovered, collected and studied. After a comprehensive study of collected material, Nicholas Roerich came to the conclusion that ancient cultures originated from a single common source—which should be searched for in Asia. As such, the Eurocentric idea of civilisation, as held today, was erroneous.

End Notes

1. N. Roerich. *Safeguard the Antiquity*. M., 1993. p. 32.
2. N. Roerich. *The Gate to the Future.*// Quot. after: *L.V. Shaposhnikova*. Wisdom of Centuries. M., 1996, p. 43.
3. Nicholas Roerich. *The Heart of Asia*. Saint-Petersburg. 1992. p. 4.
4. *ibid*. p. 4.
5. Nicholas Roerich. *Altai–Himalayas*. Riga. 1992. p. 45.
6. *ibid*. p. 48.
7. *ibid*. p. 48.
8. *ibid*. p. 73.
9. *ibid*. p. 73.
10. *ibid*. p. 68.
11. *ibid*. p. 68-69.
12. *ibid*. p. 85.
13. *ibid*. p. 154-155.
14. Nicholas Roerich. *Altai–Himalayas*. Riga, 1992. p. 305.
15. The N. Roerich Museum. Guidebook. M. p. 260.

The Mountain of the Five Treasures

Ringee Eden Wangdi

In December 1923 Nicholas Roerich, with his wife Helena and son George, arrived in Darjeeling, in front of Kanjenchunga, the Mountain of the Five Treasures. At that time Darjeeling was part of Sikkim, the small kingdom located on the border between Bengal, Nepal and Tibet. In Ghoom, close to the old monastery built by a Mongolian Lama, who placed there a huge statue of Maitreya, the Roerich family met their Himalayan Master.

Drops of Life from 'Sikkim' series, 1924 (Nicholas Roerich Museum, NY)

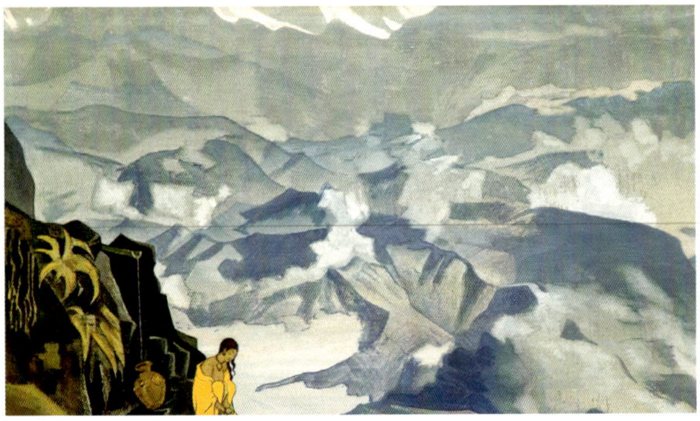

They lived in Darjeeling for about fifteen months in a house with a breathtaking view called *Talai Pho Brong*, which belonged to the renowned XIII Dalai Lama.

They travelled around west Sikkim, visiting old monasteries and meeting the most erudite and holy Lamas. Among them was Lama Minjur Dorje, who decided afterwards to follow the Roerich family to the Himalayan Research Institute Ursuvati, in Kullu.

The first view of Kanjenchunga and the Himalayan peaks impressed Nicholas so deeply that he repeatedly painted the mountains. In 1924 he painted four series of canvases inspired by the beauty of the place, its history, legends and its spritual ethos: *His Country*, twelve canvases on the sacred land of the Master; *Sikkim* and *Himalayas* (small watercolours); *Banner of the East,* nineteen canvas portraying the spiritual Masters of the Oriental part of the world.

During their time in Sikkim, they also planned a Central Asian Expedition and their visit to the bottom of Kanjenchunga became the first part of a long trek. On 5 March 1925 the Roerichs left Darjeeling in

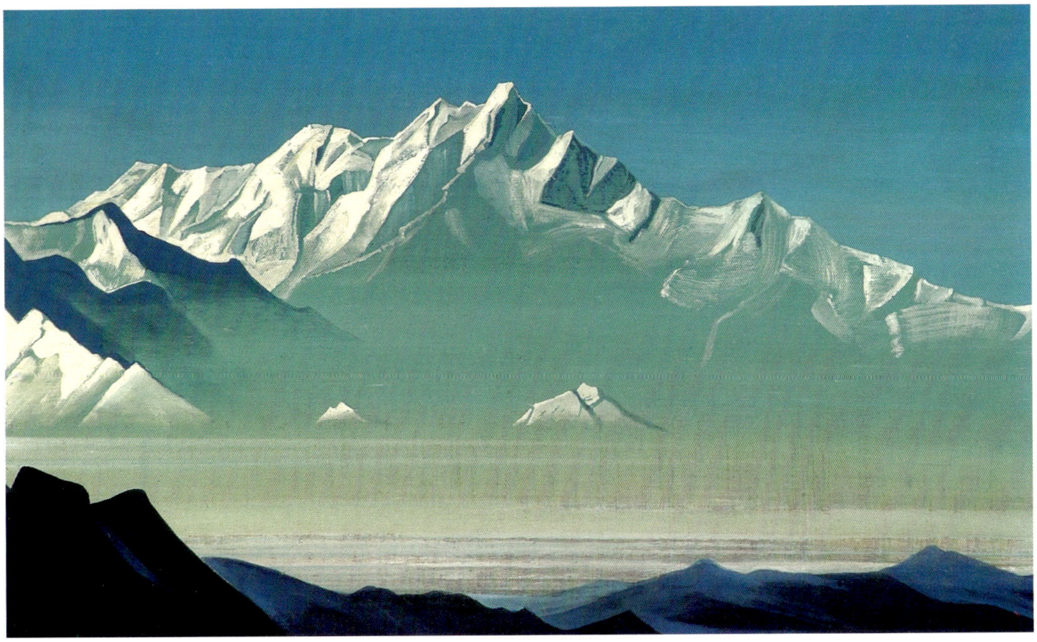

Mount of Five Treasures (Two Worlds) from 'Holy Mountains' series, 1933 (Nicholas Roerich Museum, NY)

order to begin their expedition. More than three years later, in May 1928, the caravan returned to Gangtok, finally reaching Darjeeling, where they lived for another six months, joined by their American co-workers and Svetoslav, their youngest son. Here, on December 1928, the establishment of the Himalayan Research Institute, Ursuvati, was formally decided upon and it was thereafter built in Kullu valley because of its better climate. In January 1929 the Roerich family left Darjeeling for Kullu.

Helena and George returned to Darjeeling in 1949, after Nicholas' death, with the intention of finding a house in Sikkim to live in. But instead they discovered Crookety House in Kalimpong, where due to Helena's poor health, they decided to live until Helena's passing away in 1955. More than eight decades after their first arrival in Darjeeling, witnesses and memories of their presence and work, vouch for the deep and lasting impression of the Roerich family in both Darjeeling and Kalimpong.

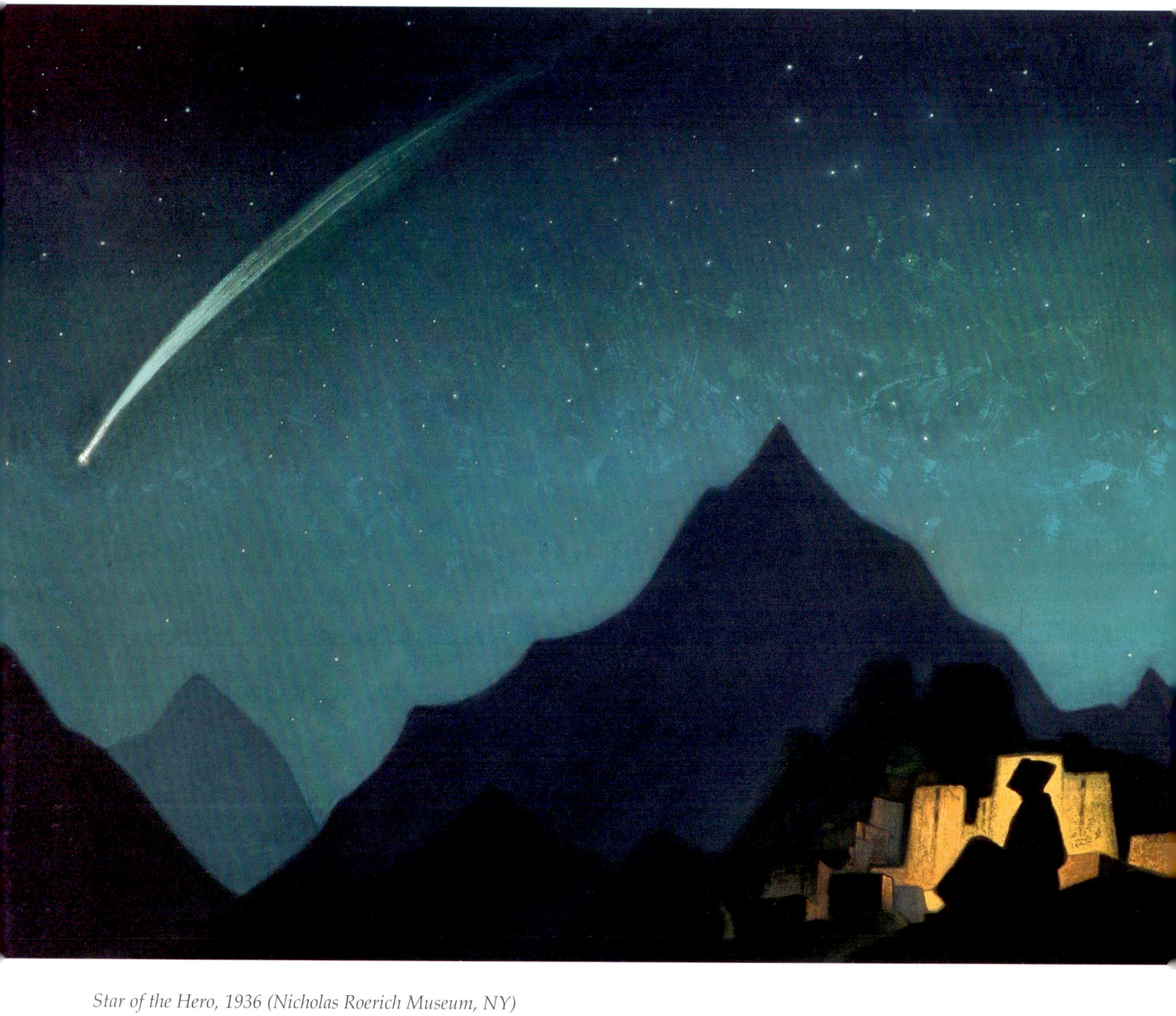

Star of the Hero, 1936 (Nicholas Roerich Museum, NY)

The Chintamani Stone

Ian Heron

Saturday, 6 October 1923, was a momentous day for the Roerich family. Residing at the Lord Byron Hotel in Paris, Nicholas Roerich, his wife Helena and their elder son George awaited the arrival of a precious talisman which held great meaning for the ambitious enterprise they were about to embark upon. In the writings of the Roerichs they often called it simply 'the Stone', but sometimes the 'gift of Orion' and 'Treasure of the World'. A Russian researcher, Alla Shustova, used the name *Treasure of the World* as the title of an entire book she devoted to it, which was published in Moscow in 2005. She understands, as do many of those who are interested in the subject, that the talisman was a piece of a much larger stone called Chintamani, and for this

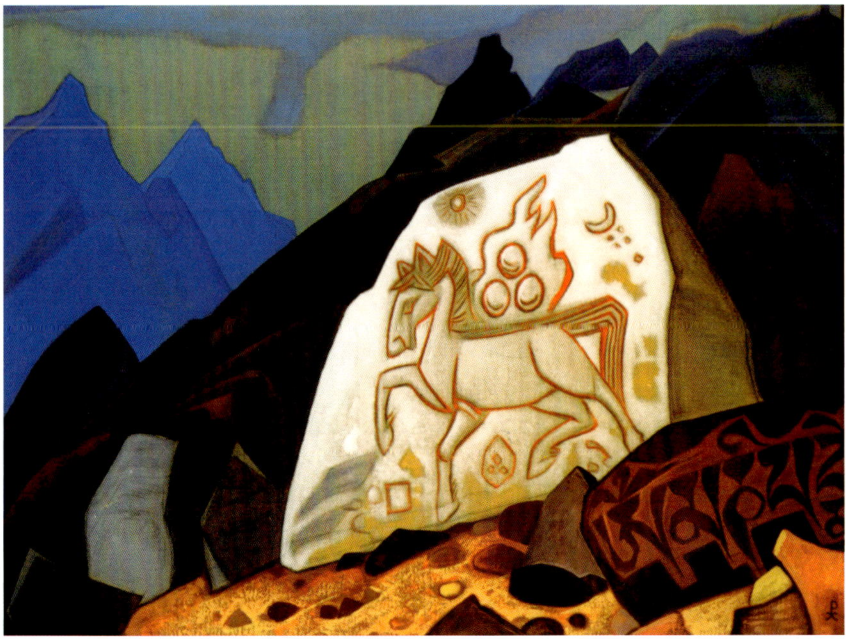

White Stone, 1933 (Nicholas Roerich Museum, NY)

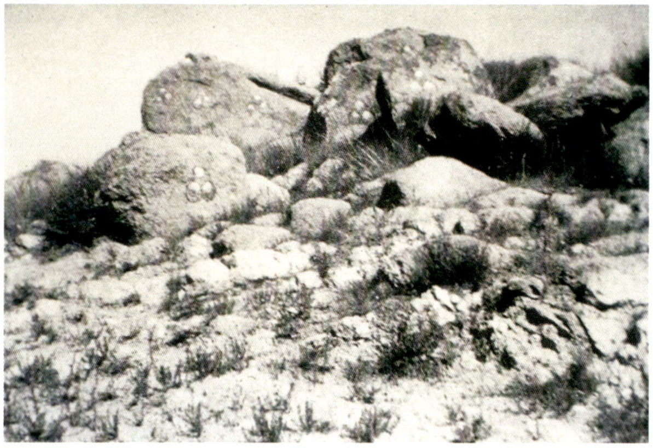

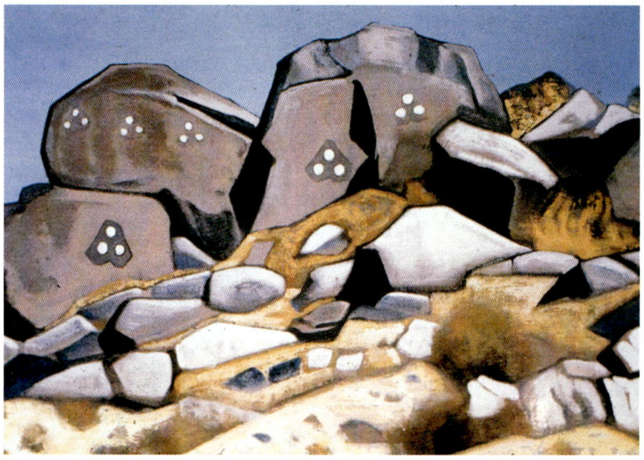

The photograph of the place that became a plot for the painting of Holy Stones, 1933 (Nicholas Roerich Museum, NY)

reason the Roerichs' Stone is known by this name also. Shustova concludes that the Stone was 'a piece of a meteorite', which again concurs with the view held by many of the Roerichs' followers, and which is derived from primary sources, namely the writings of the Roerichs themselves.

According to Shustova, the Roerichs understood that what they were about to receive was one of a number of such talismans. More than a mere symbol, it would provide for them both powers of protection for their journey, and powers of divination, enabling them to focus on their aspirations, and so helping to bring about their success. Shustova says that the Stone was 'a pure gift of Morya'—the name of Helena Roerich's spiritual teacher—and they were instructed by him to bring it to 'the fatherland', which lay 'in the East'. Importantly, they also knew from him in advance of this journey, that their mission there with the Stone would signify for the East 'a new development'. We are also told that the main stone was located in the East (by which is meant Central Asia) and for this reason the Stone, being derived from it, was returning there with the Roerichs. Significantly Helena Roerich writes in the book *Supermundane* about the main stone that 'The place where it was revealed became the foundation of Shambhala'.

The Roerichs had been expecting to be sent the Stone in Paris and on account of its importance, the arrangements needed for them to receive it seemingly involved one or more intermediaries. Shustova says the Stone was sent to Paris by post, but there is also speculation that while in France it was held by an esoteric fraternity prior to the Roerichs receiving it. The story resumes a more certain line, however, when Shustova states that on 6 October, a messenger from the Bankers' Trust office in Paris delivered to the Roerichs' hotel the parcel containing the Stone.

What appeared before them was firstly a robust pine box, on the lid of which was written the recipients' names—'Monsieur et Madame N Roerich' and the line *de la part de MM*, 'on behalf of MM'. On opening the box it was found to contain an antique casket, seemingly of German provenance, whose exterior edges were formed by metal strapwork of gilded appearance. Between the strapwork, which divided the front and back faces of both the lid and the box itself into four panels, were inlaid pieces of antique leather. On several of the panels were discernible embossed images of sages or religious figures. Adjacent to the images on two of the panels the 'triad' device could be seen, about which we know that, in addition to being adopted later on by the Roerichs for the Banner of Peace symbol and other motifs, it was depicted in the top right-hand corner of Svetoslav's well-known portrait of his father holding the casket, painted in 1928. The four panels on the rear of the casket depicted the letter 'M' in old German script, repeated in alternate colours. Significantly, it was this face of the casket, not the front, which is shown in another picture of Svetoslav's entitled *Sacred Box*, also painted in 1928. Opening the casket disclosed a bundle carefully wrapped in an embroidered cloth. The cloth was spread out to reveal its intricate design of intertwining rose-like blooms, at the centre of which was sewn in bold gold letters a motif of Christian iconography, the IHS monogram, surrounded by a blazing sun. And now too was manifest the treasure the cloth was protecting—the Stone itself.

There is seemingly incontrovertible evidence of the existence of the Stone in a photograph, which Shustova informs us was taken soon after the talisman was received, in the Roerichs' apartment at the hotel. At least two copies of the picture are said to have been made, since we are told that one was sent to Vladimir Shibayev in Riga and another to Sina Fosdick in New York. So what does the photograph tell us about the nature of the talisman? Certainly it may plausibly be a piece of a meteorite. The image depicts a palm-sized mineral object whose appearance is broadly consistent with descriptions found in Mme. Roerich's writing entitled *Legend of the Stone*, where she writes of a talisman 'shaped like a human heart' and having 'the shape of a flat fruit or heart, oblong in form'; further on she describes how a fragment seen by the writer was 'the length of [a] little finger' and had the appearance 'of greyish lustre [sic] like a dried fruit'. The descriptions differ slightly, but it may be reasonable to conclude she was not describing unrelated objects.

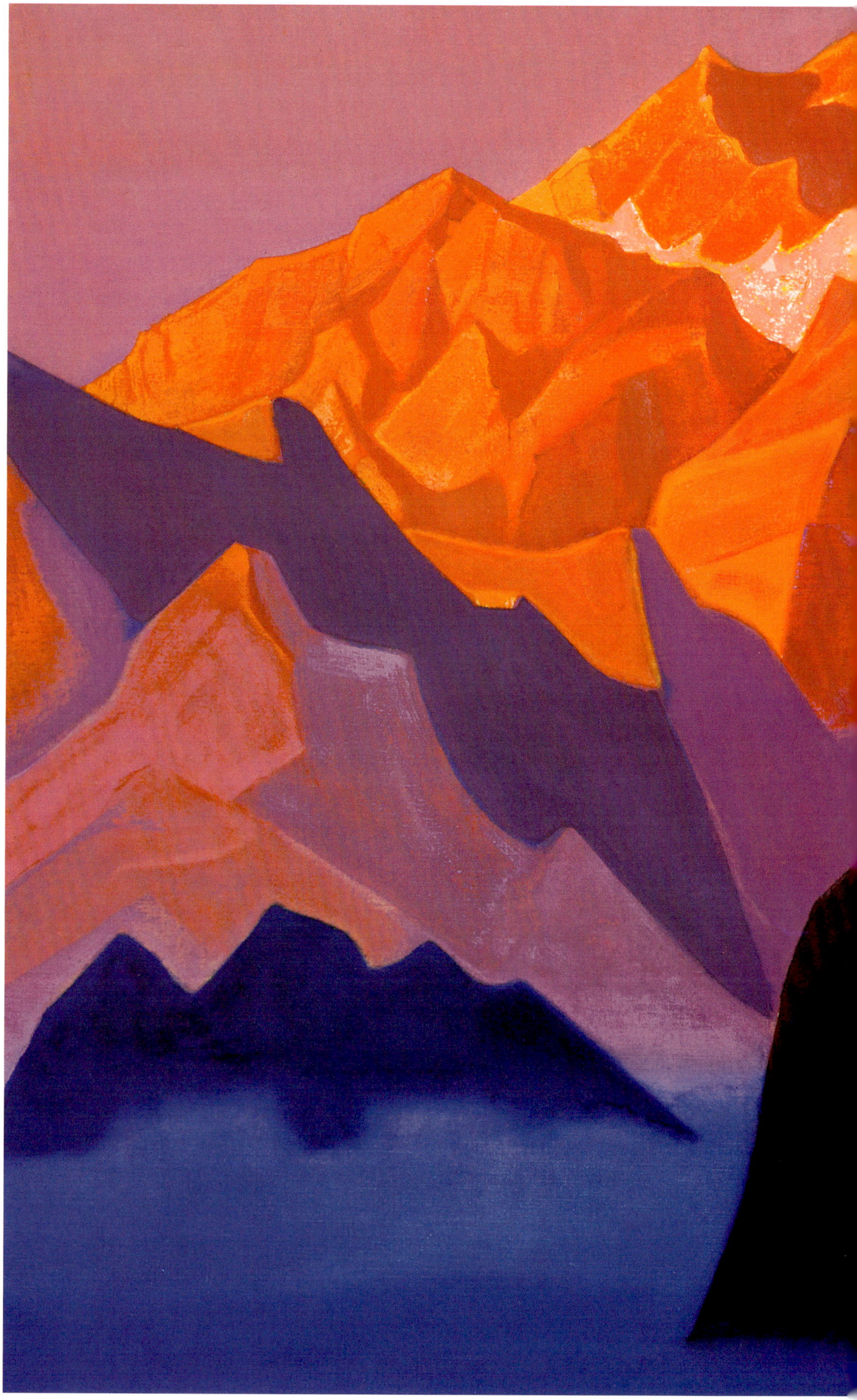

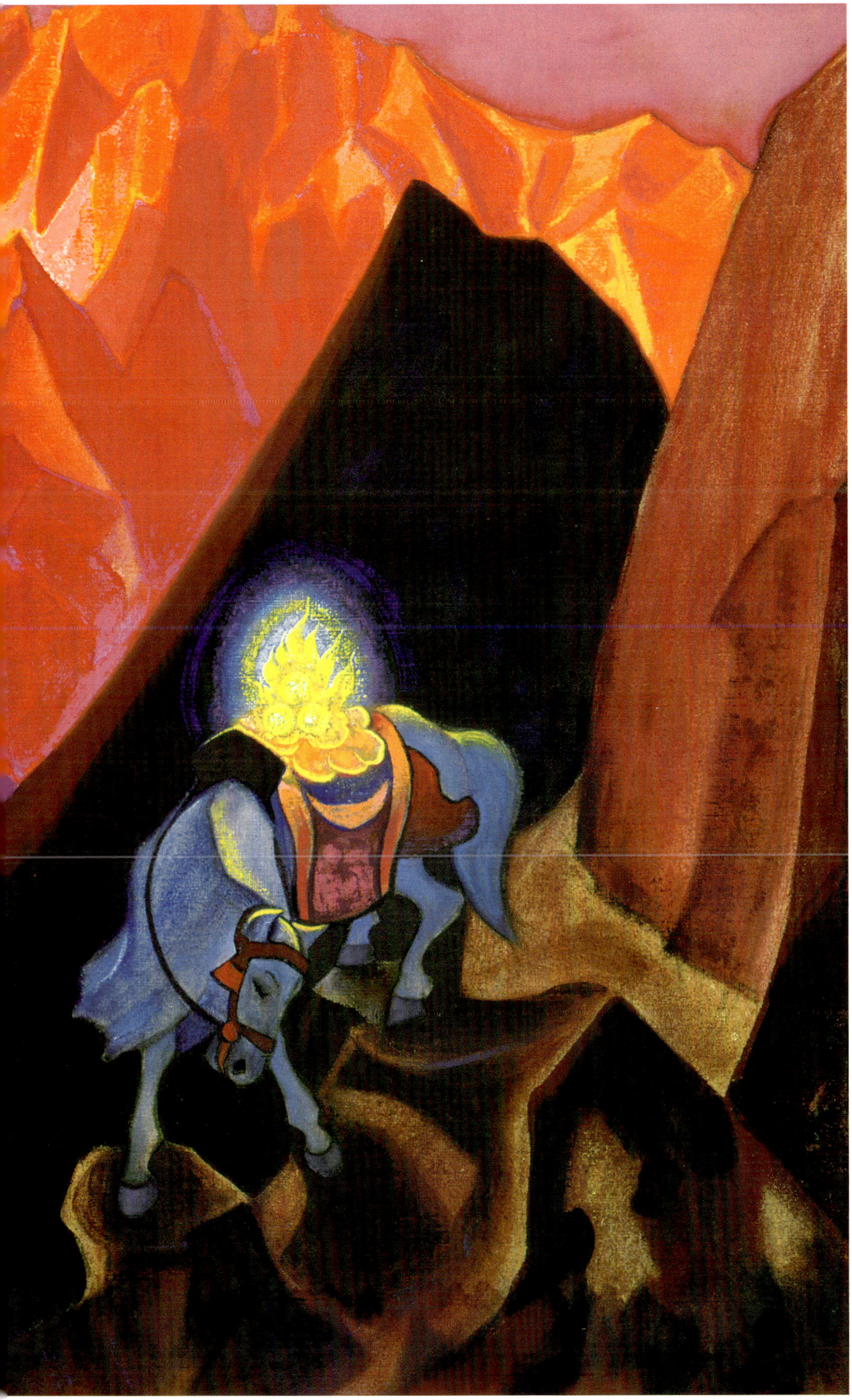

Chintamani, 1935-1936 (International Centre of the Roerichs, Moscow)

Unusually for a meteoritic fragment, we see that the talisman has a general axial symmetry and an overall form which is specific enough to suggest that it may have been worked on and shaped at some stage. The quality of the photograph makes it difficult to discern its surface characteristics, but a generalised mottling and some surface features can be seen. Were it to have been an iron meteorite, for Roerich mentions in *Himalayas Abode of Light* that the Stone was linked to the main stone by a 'magnetic' connection, and magnetism is a property of iron meteorites and were we able to discern whether it is smoothly polished, its surface would exhibit the unique *Widmanstatten* structure which is a characteristic of this type.

Many of Roerich's followers today accept that the Stone had a legendary origin, because Helena Roerich had called it the 'gift of Orion' and had encouraged the idea of the origin of the parent stone in the constellation of Orion. Shustova reiterates the idea of the source of the Chintamani stone in Orion, as other authors have done before her, such that the belief has gained a popular currency. Andrew Tomas, for example, in his book *We Are Not the First* states that 'the Chintamani stone is alleged to have been brought to Earth…from one of the solar systems in the constellation of Orion, probably Sirius…by a space voyager…' The Chintamani stone having now somehow come to the Earth, Shustova states that it was received by the Brotherhood of Light during the age of Atlantis. She then sets out the various complex and sometimes problematic lines of the legendary history of the talisman—the wandering fragment of the Chintamani stone—up to the point when the Roerichs are said to have become its custodians, so bringing its story into the present era. She states that the main Chintamani stone now lies concealed in a special underground repository, where it is unavailable to 'ordinary people', including scientists, because, as she says, it belongs to esoteric tradition, and such people are unable to believe in it.

In this essay, the Stone is discussed in two distinct contexts: one its verifiable reality, insofar as the photographic evidence is to be believed; two the legendary history of both the main stone, Chintamani, and that of the talisman, which was supposedly once part of it, prior to being received by the Roerichs. Nevertheless, given that beyond reasonable doubt the Roerichs' Stone existed as a material object, so must the Chintamani stone itself have existed in material reality, at least, at the time the Stone was derived from it. Furthermore, we are entitled to assume that the Stone still exists, and to ponder this same

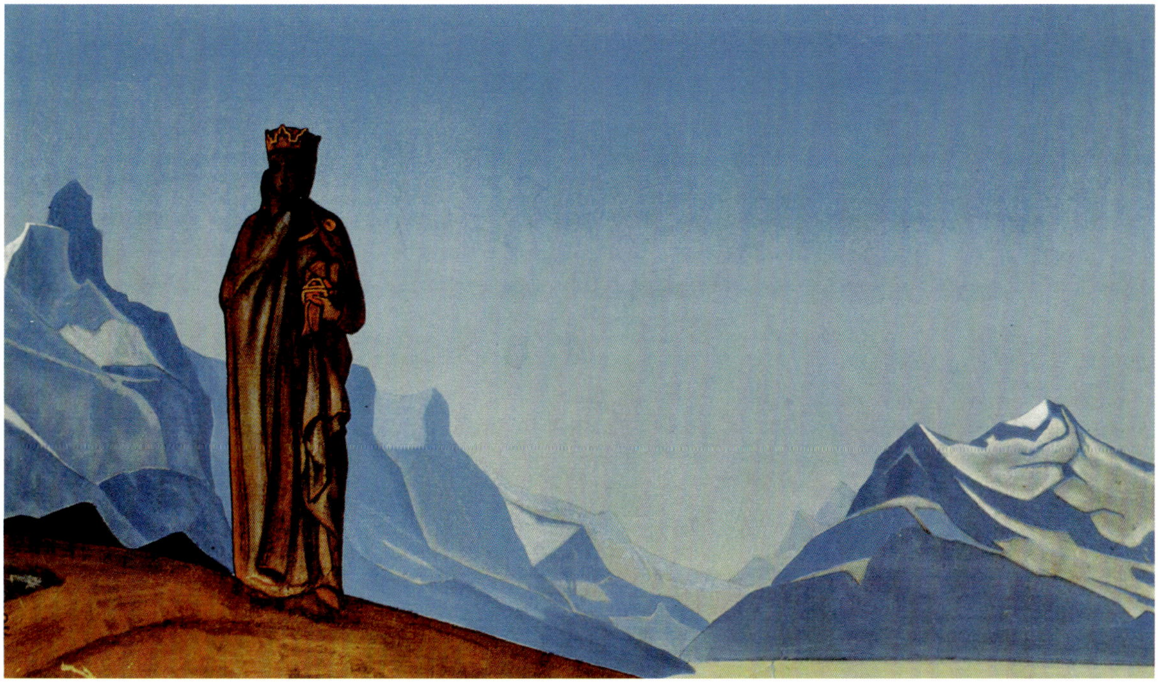

She Who Carries the Stone, 1933 (Nicholas Roerich Museum, NY)

question concerning the parent stone also. Our enquiry leads to the following obvious question—if the Stone was a piece of a meteorite, from which larger meteoritic stone did it derive? The key point here is that all meteorites of any consequence which are known about in our era have been recorded scientifically. Therefore, if we were to discover sufficient evidence relating to the main stone, we would be in a position to search the scientific record to try to identify it.

In fact we are in a position to ask a number of basic questions relating to the Stone during the period of the Roerichs' activities and their custodianship of it, namely, what is the identity of the main Stone; what can be said about the location of the main Stone; who was principally involved in sending the Stone to the Roerichs; and what were the aims in sending it to them and the purposes of the Roerichs in having it? We are also entitled to ask information about a further significant matter, namely, where is the Stone located at the present time, and who has custody of it? Other than informing us about the connection of the Stone with Morya, and the guidance received by the Roerichs from their own spiritual teacher and other teachers in the esoteric tradition, regarding their mission with the Stone, Shustova does not give us verifiable evidence-based answers to any of these questions.

Furthermore, it is worth pointing out that the reader of the Roerichs' books encounters in the Stone an historical issue of great significance. In his book *Himalayas – Abode of Light*, Nicholas Roerich mentions the Stone in the context of the stone of the *graal* — the Christian symbol as it is given to us in Wolfram von Eschenbach's epic poem *Parzival* — from which it might be implied that he sees a relation between them. This idea is also touched upon in the chapter entitled *The Stone* in Roerich's book *Himavat*, and in Mme. Roerich's book *Supermundane*. Therefore, given that the Stone is generally believed to be meteoritic, the questions of its identity, and so also of the location of the main stone, may cast light on the nature of the graal itself.

In 1991, the author's research arrived at a firm answer regarding the identity of the main Stone, based on the assumption that this meteorite is one which is catalogued in the scientific record. According to the evidence available, the author suggests it derived from the stone known in the catalogue as *Armanty*. It is worth bearing in mind the very significant point, given that the artist writes in *Himalayas – Abode of Light* that 'the chief body of this stone is lying in Shambhala', that the site of the main stone would represent the focus of the earthly

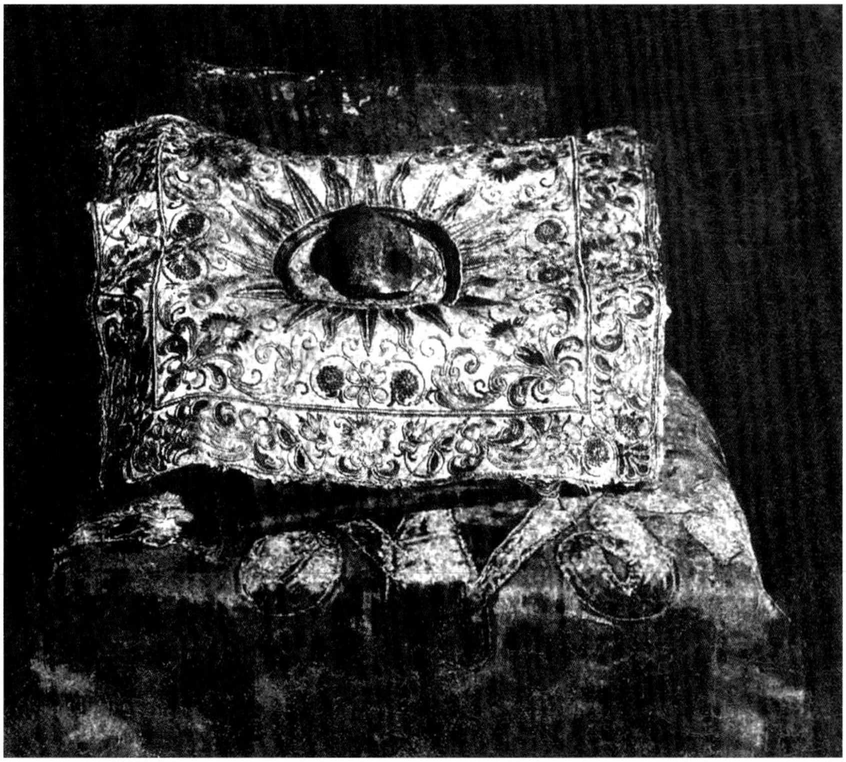

Chintamani Stone (International Centre of the Roerichs, Moscow)

Shambhala as the Roerichs understood it. Rather than being concealed in a special underground repository, as stated by Shustova, my findings suggest that it lay visible on the web of its native land, in Mongolia. If also the question is asked, whether Roerich ever painted an image of the main Stone, the author would suggest there are good reasons for looking at his scenic designs for Act One of *The Rite of Spring*. Regarding a possible relationship between the Stone and the stone of the *graal*, it would seem, considering scholarly research into literary sources for the idea of the *graal* in *Parzival* that the Roerichs' notion should be taken as metaphorical.

The question of the sender of the Stone seems to the author a more intractable problem, but focusses on the cloth in which it was wrapped as a crucial piece of evidence. Among several eligible candidates, the author would suggest that one figure in particular meets most of the necessary criteria, namely Dr Alexander Barchenko, a colleague of Roerich's from the pre-Revolutionary period. The question of the purpose of the Stone for the Roerichs in the East can, as the author understands it, only be fully answered using knowledge of Roerich's ambitious vision for Central Asia, about which previously unpublished aspects are gradually being researched, notably by Russian scholars.

Select Bibliography

Eschenbach, Wolfram von: *Parzival*: trans. A.T. Hatto, London 1980.
Grady, Monica, ed.: *The Catalogue of Meteorites*: Cambridge 2000.
Roerich, Helena: *On Eastern Crossroads*: New York 1931; *Supermundane*: New York 1994.
Roerich, Nicholas: *Himavat Diary Leaves*: Allahabad 1946; *Himalayas – Abode of Light*: Bombay 1947.
Shustova, Alla: *Treasure of the World*: Moscow 2005.
Tomas, Andrew: *We Are Not the First*: London 1971.

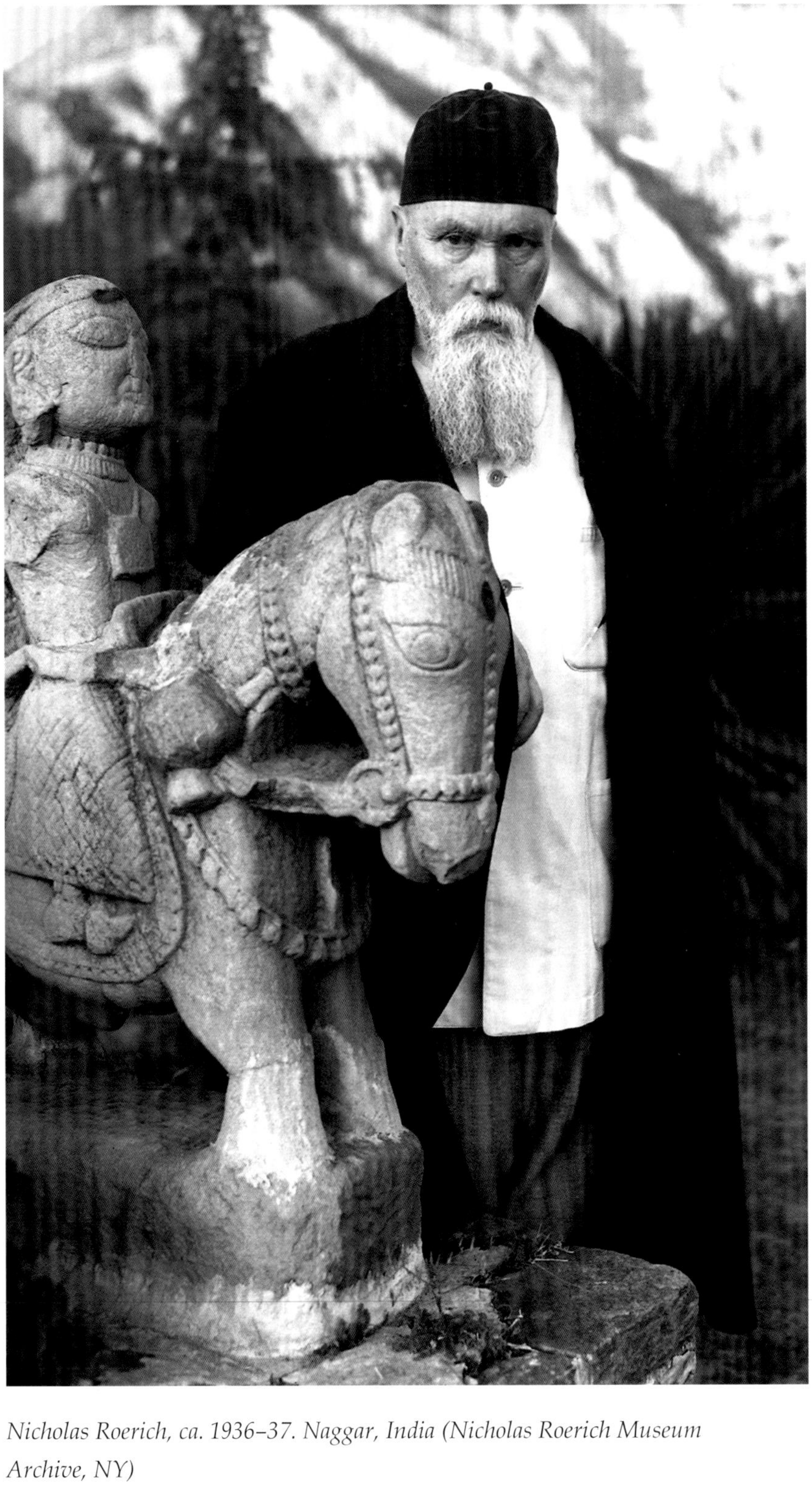

Nicholas Roerich, ca. 1936–37. Naggar, India (Nicholas Roerich Museum Archive, NY)

Conditional Love

John McCannon

When biographies of Nicholas Roerich discuss the artist's painterly, political and spiritual engagement with India, they frequently quote excerpts—expressions of delight—from his essays and journals, such as this passage, written in late 1923, when he and his family first stood in the shadow of the Himalayas, the fulfilment of a long-held ambition:

Study of Mountains (series) (International Roerich Memorial Trust, Naggar, Kullu)

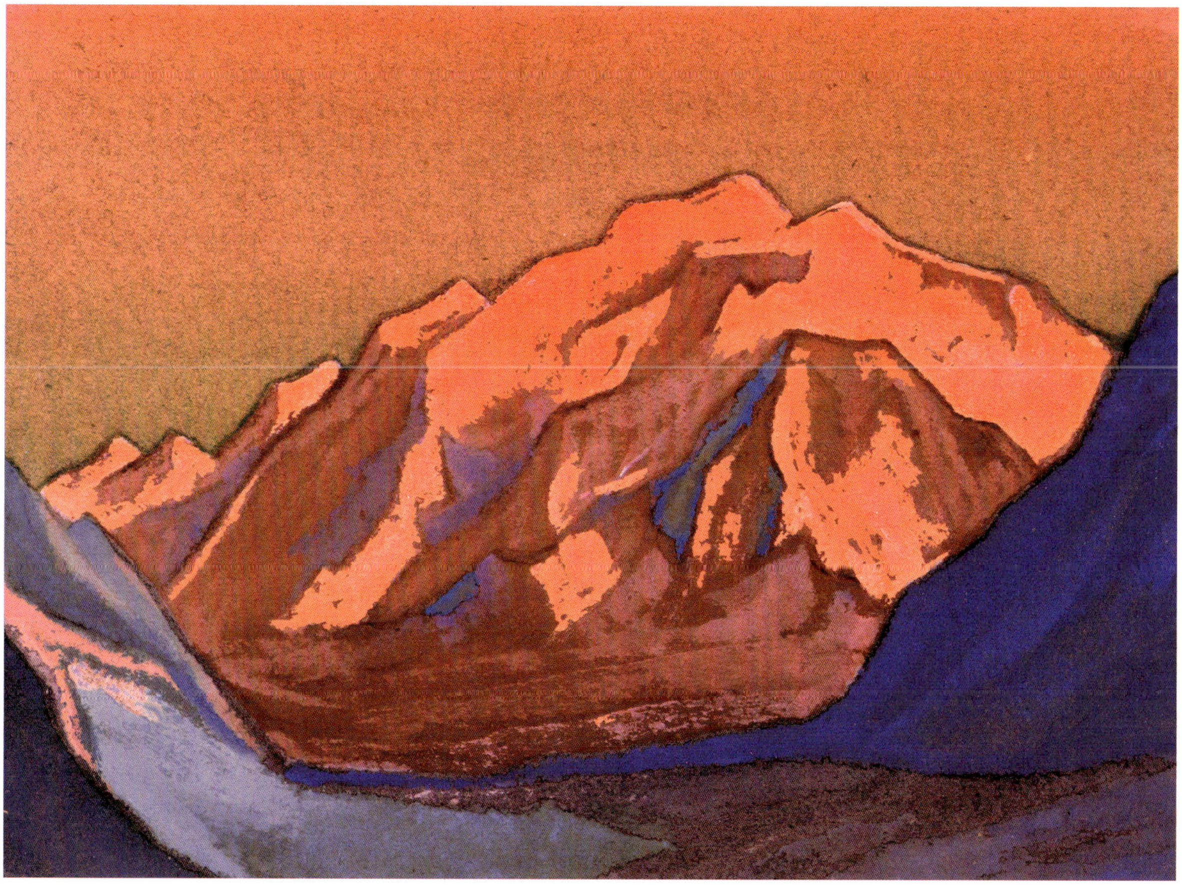

'Here is the abode of *rishis*,' Roerich marvelled. 'Here resounded the sacred flute of Krishna. Here thundered the Blessed Gautama Buddha. Here originated all Vedas...here lived the Pandavas and Gesar Khan. The Himalayas [are the] Jewel of India [and] the Treasure of the World.'[1]

This is but one of hundreds of expressions of what appears to be boundless and undiluted praise on Roerich's part—an unconditional love for India as the source of all that was wise and virtuous in Eurasian culture. This is the sentiment that receives most attention from those who study Roerich's religious and intellectual relationship with the faiths and folklores of Asia, and it is popularly believed to be the *only* way he felt about places like India. In reality, Roerich's attitude toward Asia was far more complex. There is no doubting the sincerity of his admiration and affection for India. Indian and Tibetan Buddhism formed one of the core elements of his universalist philosophy and the Agni Yoga doctrine that he and his wife Helena articulated from the early 1920s onward. And, of course, Roerich made India his home for nearly half his life. But admiration and affection were only part of what the artist felt for India, and to focus exclusively on them is to leave oneself with an incomplete understanding of his worldview and intentions. As much as Roerich condemned British imperial rule in India, he had his own geopolitical agenda to work out there. India itself was to play a crucial role in the Roerichs' chimerical and constantly shifting 'Great Plan' to found a pan-Buddhist commonwealth in the far reaches of Asia. As much as he valued eastern faiths, he believed that in many respects he possessed a truer understanding of them than their native practitioners, and he presumed to teach Indians and other Asians how to be better Buddhists. He cherished Asia's ancient ways, but felt that Asia itself needed nothing so much as a jolt of modernising reform. But often he experienced massive disappointment whenever the *actual* Asia—mundane and filled with all the flaws of human existence—failed to live up to the idealised expectations that he and his family had built up in their minds for so long.

When Roerich and his family first set foot on the shores of India, having arrived in Bombay (Mumbai) on 30 November 1923, what manner of place were they expecting to encounter?[2] Roerich and Helena had had more than twenty years to construct in their minds a simulacrum of India—a mix of fact and imagination that did not prepare them altogether perfectly for the actual place once they got there.

Roerich's absorption with India dates back to his student days, when he turned to the critic Vladimir Stasov for advice on how best to lend authenticity to the scenes from Russian prehistory he was then painting. Famously, Stasov suggested that the young artist look to Asia if he wished to uncover the true roots of ancient Slavic culture. From that moment forward, Roerich immersed himself in the scholarly works of Indologists, Mongolists and Tibetologists. With his fiancée and young bride Helena, he deepened his acquaintance with Indian religious thought via Vedantism, as preached by Vivekananda and Ramakrishna, and less directly through the Theosophical writings of Helena Blavatsky. It is generally agreed that the first major artwork to reflect this growing interest was Roerich's 1905 canvas *Treasure of the Angels*, which, although ostensibly Christian in its iconography, contains subtexts that are thought to be informed by Asiatic faiths. That same year, in the pages of the literary almanac *Vesy (The Scales)*, Roerich published the short story 'Devassari Abuntu', which narrates the process by which an Indian woman attains enlightenment and inner peace.[3] Two canvases based on the story followed in 1906—*Devassari and the Birds* and *Devassari Abuntu Transfigured into Stone*—both modelled on the Buddhist paintings in the Ajanta caves near Aurangabad.

India figured with increased prominence in Roerich's art and worldview during the half-decade leading up to World War I. Alongside Russia's most renowned orientalists, Roerich served on the commission that, between 1909 and 1915, oversaw the construction of St. Petersburg's first Buddhist temple—and while the project's denominational orientation was Mongol-Tibetan, under the leadership of the Buryat monk/diplomat Agvan Dorjiev, it caused Roerich to think seriously for the first time about the possible political ramifications of millenarian Buddhism.[4] As Roerich strove to fit all Eurasian religions into a universalist framework, in which the faiths of the east shaped the faiths of the west, thanks to a long process of cultural diffusion, Asiatic themes appeared more frequently in his art. To take one India-specific example, he repeatedly equated the demigod Krishna with the shepherd boy Lel from the classic Russian folktale 'The Snow Maiden'. In addition, a particular influence on him at this time was the Indologist Viktor Golubev, who encouraged Roerich to mix Asiatic motifs with Christian ones as he completed his *Queen of Heaven* fresco for Princess Maria Tenisheva's Church of the Holy Spirit at Talashkino, one of Roerich's most profound depictions of the principle of feminine divinity. It was after touring a spring 1914 exhibition of South Asian art organised by Golubev at Paris's Cernuschi Museum that Roerich was first seized by the desire to travel to India himself, and he communicated this new wish in his 1914 essay 'Path to India'.[5]

Desire flared into yearning during the war itself, and especially during the revolutions that tore Roerich's homeland apart.[6] As Russia careened toward military defeat, political collapse and civil war, Roerich took solace in the *Gitanjali* poems that had earned Rabindranath Tagore the Nobel Prize for Literature, as well as in the *Bhagavad-Gita* and *The Sayings of Sri Ramakrishna*. As he advised his fellow artist, Alexandre Benois, near the end of 1917, 'If you have some quiet time, you should turn to these indispensable books....They are serious teachings, and they have much to say about the present state of humanity.'[7] In his own diary from October 1917, Roerich, reacting to the Bolsheviks' seizure of power, recorded the following entry, which shows how he retreated mentally to the east in the face of what he regarded as calamitous realities: 'I prostrate myself before the Teachers of India. Into the chaos of our lives they have brought works of truth, a joyfulness of the spirit, and a fruitful silence. At a time of extreme need, they have sent us a summons: one that is serene, full of conviction, and wise.'[8] Roerich and his family were more eager than ever to answer that call, and their longing to voyage to India is achingly clear in paintings like *Karelia – Eternal Expectation* (1918), in which three male figures and a woman—stand-ins for Roerich, Helena, and their sons, the budding orientalist Yuri (George) and the future artist Sviatoslav—sit on a deserted shore, staring out at the horizon. The Roerichs left Soviet Russia in early 1918 and spent their first years of emigration in Karelia, Finland and Scandinavia, striving to reach England, where they hoped to receive permission to enter India and to raise enough money to pay for passage there. However, these plans were derailed by financial difficulties and the Roerichs took a fateful three-year detour to the United States, and did not reach Asia until the end of 1923. While in England, though, the family made the acquaintance of many Indians, thanks partly to their membership in the English chapter of the Theosophical Society, and partly to George's being enrolled in London University's School of Oriental Languages. Among the luminaries Roerich came to know at this time were Kedarnath Das Gupta, the linguist Suniti Kumar Chatterjee, and

Kalidas Nag, the historian. Most life-changing of all was his meeting with Rabindranath Tagore in July 1920, when the poet came to call on the artist's family at their Queen's Gate Terrace flat. Tagore praised the Indian-themed paintings Roerich was working on at the time—*Song of the Morning* and *Song of the Waterfall*—although neither of the two men could have guessed that they would remain in contact until Tagore's death in 1941, or that their families would intermarry, with Sviatoslav (Svetoslav) Roerich taking Tagore's great-grandniece, the actress Devika Rani, as his wife in 1945.[9]

All these experiences and impulses shaped for Roerich a particular India of the imagination, whose contours overlapped only partly with those of geographic reality. Roerich's India was unspoiled by industrial-era 'progress' and the grasping acquisitiveness of contemporary commercialism. Roerich had long been in the habit of condemning what he saw as the amoral, socially-atomising materialism of his own day by contrasting it with past eras—ancient Russia, for example, or the Stone Age—that, in his estimation, had been blessed by greater social cohesion, greater human dignity, and greater innate virtuousness. As a corollary, then, Roerich's imagined India was by definition a holy place. Here, in the birth site of Hinduism and Buddhism, he expected to find nothing less than a living shrine, where the air reverberated always with the sound of temple bells and ritual chants, and where the land and its inhabitants were suffused with profundity and spiritual vitality. Thirdly, Roerich's India was a land of historical destiny: as an archaeologist and ethnographer—but also as a practicing Theosophist who adhered to Madame Blavatsky's doctrine of 'root races'—Roerich valued India and the Central Asian lands to its north as the supposed *fons et origo* of the Indo-European Aryans.

Fascination with the Aryans took many forms in the late 19th century, and Russian intellectuals were no less influenced than their counterparts elsewhere in Europe.[10] With his decades-long interest in what he saw as a vast religio-cultural continuum spanning Eurasia, with east and west bridged by civilisations like Zoroastrian Persia and old Russia, Roerich hoped to find in India a source of the *ur*-culture from which it had sprung. So long as the India of real life conformed to the India of his expectations, Roerich was pleased with it. And there is no doubting the long-term and heartfelt esteem he held for the country.

After arriving in Bombay, the Roerichs cruised to the nearby island of Elephanta, to see the temple there honoring the god Shiva. Originally, they had planned to visit the Theosophical Society headquarters in Adyar, but because Tibet was by now so clearly their favoured destination, they trekked instead to Jaipur, then to Agra, where they drank in the loveliness of the Taj Mahal. Proceeding along the Ganges valley, the family stopped at Benares, as well as the holy cities of Gaya and Sarnath, where the Buddha attained enlightenment and preached his first sermons. Before turning north to the Himalayas, they visited Bengal's metropolis of Calcutta.

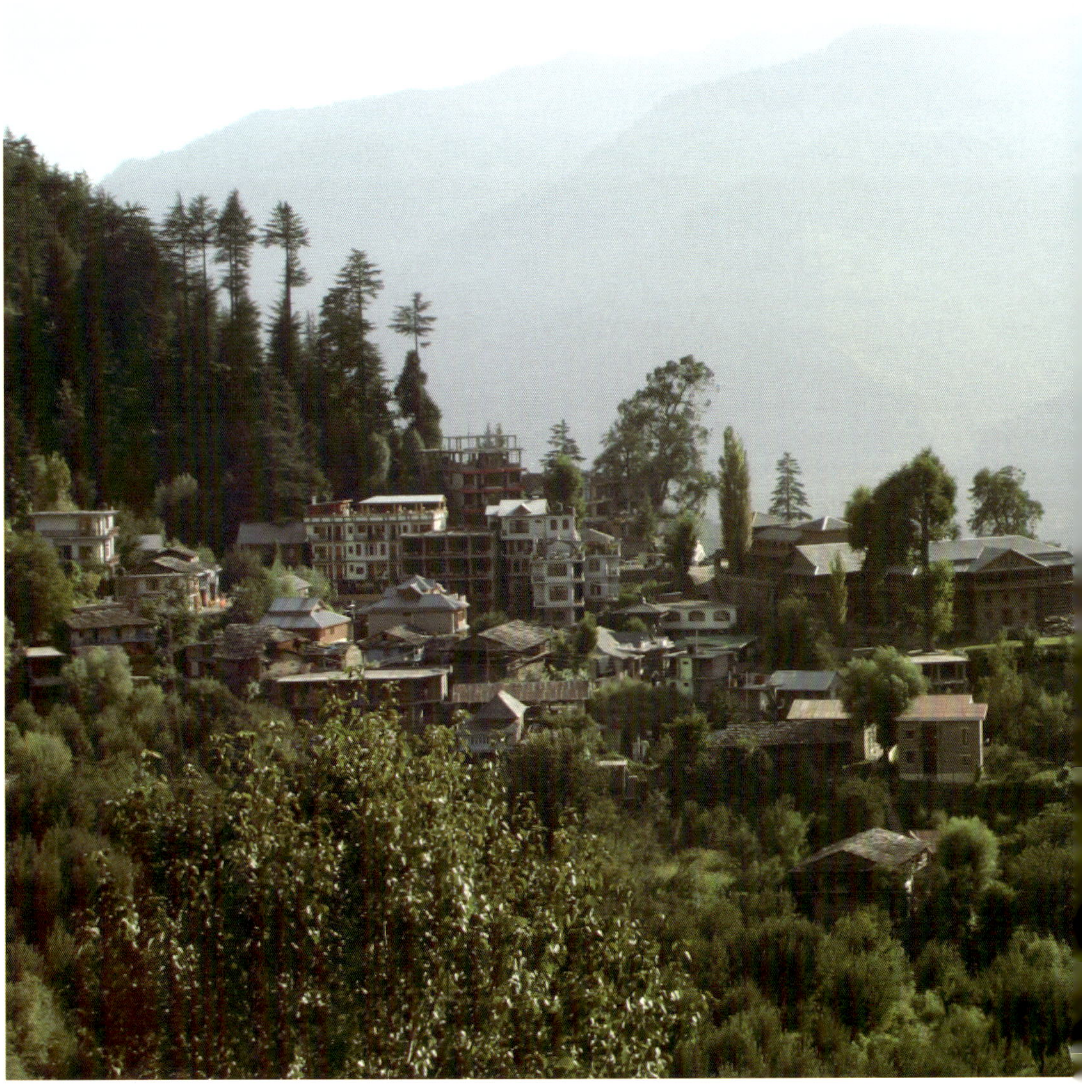

Kullu Valley (International Roerich Memorial Trust, Naggar, Kullu)

Many sights pleased the family during these first weeks—a tiger in the forest, moonlight on the Ganges—and Roerich produced a sublime nocturnal scene of Benares. But his acquaintance with the India of his dreams did not prepare him adeqately for the hardships of its daily existence. Since he had fantasised for so long about a uniformly transcendent and beauteous Orient, Roerich felt let down by this first encounter with the actual Asia. 'Where are the palaces and pagodas? Is it really India?' he asked in *Altai–Himalaya*, his famed travelogue.[11] 'A thin shore. Meagre little trees. Crevices of dessicated soil. So does India hide its face from the south.' The 'desecrations' of

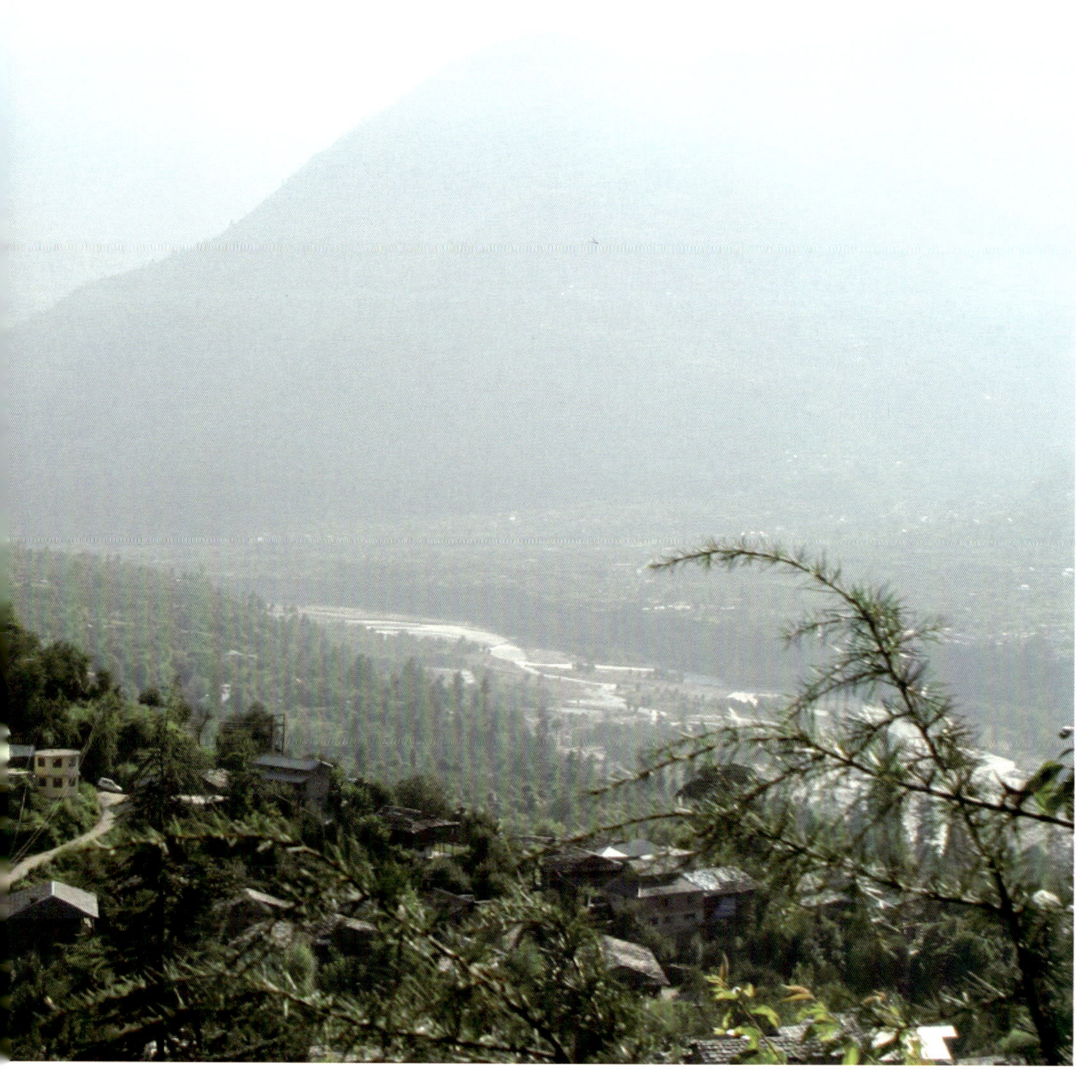

poverty and prostitution shocked him, and, noting with melancholy how 'Sarnath and Gaya, sites of the Buddha's glorious deeds, lie in ruins,' he concluded that spiritual vitality in these parts of India had dried up like sap in a drought-withered tree.[12]

In other words, for all his immersion in things Asiatic, Roerich came to India as a European. With respect to Asia, an entire scholarly subfield is dedicated to analysing the many disappointments experienced by Western visitors who come to the east seeking, but failing to find, spiritual truth.

An instructive comparison can be drawn here between Roerich and the celebrated Jesuit priest and paleontologist Pierre Teilhard de Chardin, who was active in Asia as a researcher and traveller at the same time Roerich was. Like the painter, de Chardin, one of the originators of the noösphere concept, strove to find some way to reconcile faith and science in an age when secularism appeared to be inexorably on the march. Both in China and in India, de Chardin believed at first that he might encounter the sort of ancient grace and profundity needed to restore religious vitality to the modern world. As he noted in October 1923, 'What better opportunity…than to go and lose myself for weeks on end in the fermenting mass of the peoples of Asia? There I could count on meeting the new currents of thought and mysticism in process of formation, which were preparing to rejuvenate and fertilise our European world.'[14]

Just as de Chardin's hopes were frustrated, so were many of Roerich's. Roerich treasured the time he spent among the intellectual elite of Calcutta—including Tagore's family and the world-famous botanist Sir Jagadis Bose—in late 1923. And he mixed well with the populace in Darjeeling, where he and his family lived between December 1923 and the final preparations for their departure to Ladakh in early 1925. Excursions to Ghoom Monastery near Darjeeling gave the family great pleasure, as did visiting other religious centres in Sikkim and neighbouring regions.[15] Roerich's sense of satisfaction, religious and aesthetic, is amply expressed in his paintings from late 1923 and early 1924, one of the most creatively productive periods of his career. During these months, he completed the *Himalaya* and *Tibetan Path* series, consisting of forty-one and eight landscapes, respectively, as well as the *Sikkim* and *His Country* series, which feature mountainside stupas and temples, seekers of wisdom scaling the heights, and depictions of Chintamani, the 'radiant thought-gem' from Tibetan myth that Roerich called 'the treasure of the world'. Also in early 1924, Roerich began the nineteen-canvas *Banners of the East* series, whose subjects form a pantheon of gods and *gurus* from many faiths, including Christ, Confucius, Moses, the Buddha, Mohammed, Lao-tse and Russia's own St. Sergius. Roerich also painted Tsong-kha-pa, founder of Tibet's Gelugpa sect; the Tibetan poet-hermit Milarepa; Padma Sambhava, who brought Buddhism from India to Tibet in the 8th century; and the *Mother of the World*, a pantheistic madonna meant to symbolise the eternal feminine principle for all Eurasia.

But Roerich's contentedness extended only so far as India reflected back to him the image he wanted to see there. When it turned any face to him that he found unattractive, his judgment was swift and harsh—and more so than de Chardin's, for the simple reason that the Jesuit was an outsider disappointed by the failings of faiths that were not his own. Roerich, by contrast, felt himself to be a true Buddhist, just as many Western occultists and orientalists did.[16] Since shortcomings in India were, in Roerich's mind, the shortcomings of his own co-religionists, he naturally took them more to heart.

Just as pertinent, Roerich's thirst for change was motivated by his interchange with prominent Asians who themselves wished to reform Buddhism or Hinduism. Roerich had spoken with Tagore about his involvement with the Brahmo Samaj movement. He was aware of, and may have actually met, the anti-colonial agitator Mahendra Pratap, who preached a 'religion of love' and dreamed of incorporating Mongolia, Tibet, China, Japan, Korea and India into a 'golden district'—an aspiration not unlike (and perhaps with some influence on) Roerich's Great Plan.[17] Further afield, Okakura Kazuko, author of the much-admired *Book of Tea* and a personal friend of Tagore's, pondered—in a manner that seems to have had an impact on Roerich—ways in which Asia might mix tradition and modernity in the 20th century.[18] However, the most direct influences on Roerich by far were exerted by the Mongol folklorist Tsyben Jamtsarano and the famed Buryat monk Agvan Dorjiev, a longtime confidante of the Thirteenth Dalai Lama and an equally longtime advocate of Russo-Tibetan friendship. Soon after the Russian revolutions of 1917, both men, already predisposed toward the modernisation of their faith, became proponents of reforming Buddhism in such a way that would make it more philosophically compatible with socialist principles and even Marxist-Leninist ideology. Both on the philosophical and political level, such a plan was more feasible than it might seem on the surface, but it was still a long shot and eventually failed, with dire consequences for both Dorjiev and Jamtsarano.

Although there are those who interpret Roerich's Plan as a tightly-coordinated conspiracy planned before the 1917 revolutions by a close-knit cabal of occultists and neo-Buddhists, and carried out as part of a single unbroken effort after 1917, it seems more correct to see it as Roerich's own initiative, even if it was shaped by dialogue with friends and colleagues, and even if Roerich sought the assistance of different followers and partners (some of whom he was more forthcoming with than others). Also, rather than there having been a master plan of long duration, it seems obvious with hindsight and with close examination that many elements—including some fundamental ones—of the Great Plan were adjusted or improvised on the spot, based on unforeseen or changing circumstances. Much of this had to do with the realities Roerich encountered both in India and in 1923–1925, as he travelled back and forth between India and the West.

The Great Plan appears to have taken shape in Roerich's mind in the spring of 1920, when he and his family were living in London. At this time, which coincided with the foundation of their own doctrine, Agni Yoga, the Roerichs are said to have received the following 'First Message to the New Russia' from Master Morya (the same spiritual adept purported by Theosophists to have instructed Helena Blavatsky in the 1800s): 'You who have been given a church, you who have been given two lives, raise up the church.'[19] If we read such 'sendings' as semi-conscious expressions of the fears and hopes that haunted the Roerichs' minds, we see obsession over Russia's fate intertwined with an intense version of the pantheistic mysticism that had guided them for years. Messianic ideas were already stirring within Roerich. For example, the hero of his 1918 short story 'The Flame', a thinly disguised autobiography, discovers that his destiny is to erect a temple that will serve humankind as 'a hidden source of learning.'[20] This same message is painted into *Nicholas of Mozhaisk* (1920), in which the saint holds a sword in one hand and a church in the other. Both objects are part of Estern Orthodox iconography, but this is a self-portrait of Roerich as the leader of a new church—larger and more inclusive than Orthodoxy, and the only creed capable of placing Russia's steps, if not the world's, on the path of righteousness.

In its first iteration, the Great Plan was part of a larger anti-Soviet strategy, in which pan-Buddhist confederation would allow opponents of the communist regime to gain a foothold in Asia and at least keep Siberia free of the Leninist menace. By 1920, it looked as though European Russia was lost to the White cause, at least for the time being, but the Bolsheviks had a long way yet to go before the Far East was pacified. At this early stage, both in London and after relocating to New York City, Roerich coordinated his efforts with White Russian émigrés in Europe and especially in the Manchurian city of Harbin—including his younger brother Vladimir, who had fought in Siberia and Mongolia during the Civil War under the leadership of the infamous and enigmatic White warlord, Baron von Ungern-Sternberg. Roerich and this cadre dreamed of uniting China, Mongolia, Tibet and India with as much of Siberia as possible, and Roerich preached the coming of a new capital, Zvenigorod, a 'city of bells' that was to appear in the Altai Mountains as a mirror image of Shambhala in the Himalayas.

Although some are convinced that Roerich's shift to a pro-Soviet stance took place early on—in 1921 or 1922, while he was still in

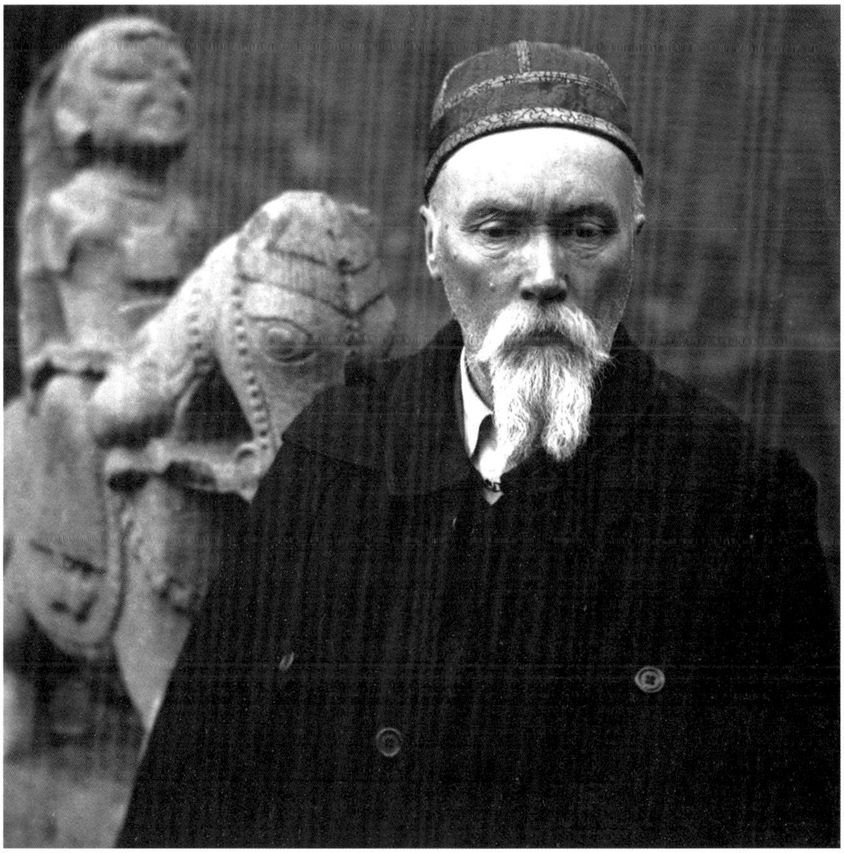

Nicholas Roerich ca. 1931–33. Naggar, India (Nicholas Roerich Museum Archive, NY)

New York—this is based principally on émigré-community rumours and after-the-fact speculation, as opposed to the diary entries and letters which indicate that this change of heart more likely began in 1923 or 1924. Roerich had a busy itinerary during this crucial period of 1923–1925. Having left New York in May 1923, he, Helena, and George—whose knowledge of oriental languages was to prove indispensable—spent the summer and fall in Paris, where they met with friends and helpers and, in October, took possession of what they asserted, and seemingly believed, was a sacred stone, the 'treasure of the world,' with paranormal properties. As we have seen, they voyaged to India by the end of the year, passing through Bombay and Calcutta on their way to Darjeeling and the Himalayas. After visits to Sikkim and nearby regions in early 1924, and after the family settled into their residence outside Darjeeling, Roerich and George returned to America that fall to confer with the family's 'inner circle' in New York: Frances Grant, Zinaida (Sina) Lichtmann and her husband Maurice, and Louis and Nettie Horch, who provided most of the financial backing for the Roerichs' ventures until their acrimonious falling-out in the mid-1930s. Roerich and George were in the US from October to December. It is at this point, after what seems to have been a month-long period of vacillation, that they committed fully to a pro-Soviet course of action. They returned to India via Berlin and Paris and, during these stopovers, conferred with highly-placed Soviet diplomats. Once back in India, Roerich and George visited Pondicherry, where they introduced themselves to the critic and activist Aurobindo Ghose; Adyar, where they visited Theosophical Society vice-president Jinarajadasa and the twenty-year-old Krishnamurti; and Calcutta, where they apparently met with Tagore's great-nephew Soumendranath, a known communist with ties to M.N. Roy. In March 1925, the Roerichs left Darjeeling for Srinagar, in preparation for their expedition to Central Asia. Their first destination was Ladakh, toward which they set off in August.

It was clear by 1923 and 1924 that the Soviet state was in place to stay, and that military opposition to it was futile. Combined with homesickness and the stress and impoverishment associated with life in exile, this was enough to cause many formerly anti-Soviet Russians to return home or at least wish they could. But more importantly after 1921, the USSR had embarked upon the relatively moderate New Economic Policy, which backed away from the breakneck revolutionary radicalism of 1917 and made the regime more palatable to some of its former opponents. Lenin's sudden death in early 1924 played a role in this as well. The history of the Russian emigration is crowded with examples of artists and intellectuals who had second thoughts in the 1920s about their estrangement from their homeland.

Circumstances in Asia, and the things Roerich learned about it during his early months in India, factored into his decision as well. This is a significant point about his relationship with India: the Great Plan, far from being fixed in advance, evolved quickly and radically thanks to the sense of potentialities and limitations Roerich gained once he was on the ground there. The rupture between the Thirteenth Dalai Lama and the Ninth Panchen Lama, made known to all the world when the latter fled Tibet at the end of 1923, as well as the death of the Jebtsundamba Hutuktu, Mongolia's chief cleric, a few months later, opened up huge power vacuums in the Buddhist world, causing much apocalyptic anxiety. Whether Roerich sincerely saw these events as signs of the coming new age or cynically perceived the stress caused by them as a useful tool to exploit for his own ends, his plans were certainly changed by them. Nor were his visits to Indian and Sikkimese monasteries and temples in late 1923 and early 1924 strictly cultural or religious. At a minimum, these were fact-finding missions to test out the salability of the Great Plan; they may also have involved active efforts to recruit Buddhist clergy to his cause. How much this was the case, and how successful Roerich may have been, are open questions. In attempting to answer them, some have focussed on a particular moment from the spring of 1924, when a trusted associate of the Panchen Lama, Geshe Rinpoche of Chumbi Monastery, is said to have ordained Roerich as a Buddhist lama, with the spiritual name Reta Rigden.[21] However, it is not easy to judge this episode's significance. Was it a full-throated endorsement of the Great Plan by Buddhist leaders, including the Panchen—perhaps even an acknowledgement of the claim Roerich had begun to make that he was a reincarnation of the Fifth Dalai Lama? Or was it a more symbolic gesture, similar to the honours conferred upon the French adventuress Alexandra David-Neel by the Panchen Lama in the 1910s, or even upon present-day, pro-Tibet celebrities like the martial-arts movie star Steven Segal? It is not implausible that Roerich persuaded key lamas that he was a religiously and even politically sympathetic figure. But for Buddhist clergy to accept Roerich's spiritual credentials did not require them to go along with his practical plans, and it seems unlikely that they did to any meaningful extent.

If they did, it would have been due to one more Asia-based factor that appears to have altered Roerich's plans considerably. Although the evidence here is fragmentary, it appears certain that sometime during the early 1920s, Roerich reestablished contact with one or more members of the commission that had built St. Petersburg's Buddhist temple prior to the 1917 revolutions, and particularly with Dorjiev. By this juncture, Dorjiev, along with the circle of Russian, neo-Buddhist orientalists still working in the USSR, was trying to ensure Buddhism's survival there by appealing to Kremlin moderates on two levels. They argued first that it was feasible to modernise Buddhism in such a way as to reconcile it ideologically with Soviet socialism, in much the same way that the renovationist 'Living Church' was attempting to make Russian Orthodoxy palatable to the Soviet authorities. In addition, Dorjiev and company attempted to persuade the Soviet leadership that a show of religious tolerance toward Buddhism would be a politically expedient way to win the allegiance of Buryats, Kalmyks and other Mongol Buddhists living under Soviet rule or in communist Mongolia (where Tsyben Jamtsarano was pursuing a strategy similar to Dorjiev's)—and also to realise Lenin's dream of 'setting the east ablaze' by exporting the revolution to Asia at large. This was, in essence, the reasoning Roerich used in his attempts to secure Moscow's support from the fall of 1924 onward, and it is all but certain that he was influenced by, if not collaborating actively with, Dorjiev in this matter.

Obstacles to travel (bureaucratic confusion, bribe-taking, or bad roads, for example) and the seamy side of life in Asia (poverty and corruption) were attributed by other Western explorers of Asia to social and economic undevelopment and taken in stride as part of the normal business of journeying in that part of the world. For Roerich, they were signs of spiritual degeneracy, as well as proof that a firm leader needed to take moral and political affairs in hand and change 'bad' Asia decisively. In Chinese Turkestan, where he had a particularly wearying time, he compared his experience to being stranded among savages in the Solomon Islands, and not a day went by that he did not rage about 'the Sinkiang dance of death' or curse the Chinese government for its 'buffalo'-like obstinacy.[22] Travelling between Kashgar and Ürümqi in early 1926, he dreamed of importing Western technology to eliminate the toil of travelling through 'this dusty cemetery':

> This is especially absurd when you realise that a whole day of exhausting travel is equal to two hours' ride by automobile or to an hour by aeroplane. I remember reading that Sir Aurel Stein was afraid the building of railroads and other signs of

Nicholas Roerich with a leopard, ca. 1937. Naggar, India (Nicholas Roerich Museum Archive, NY)

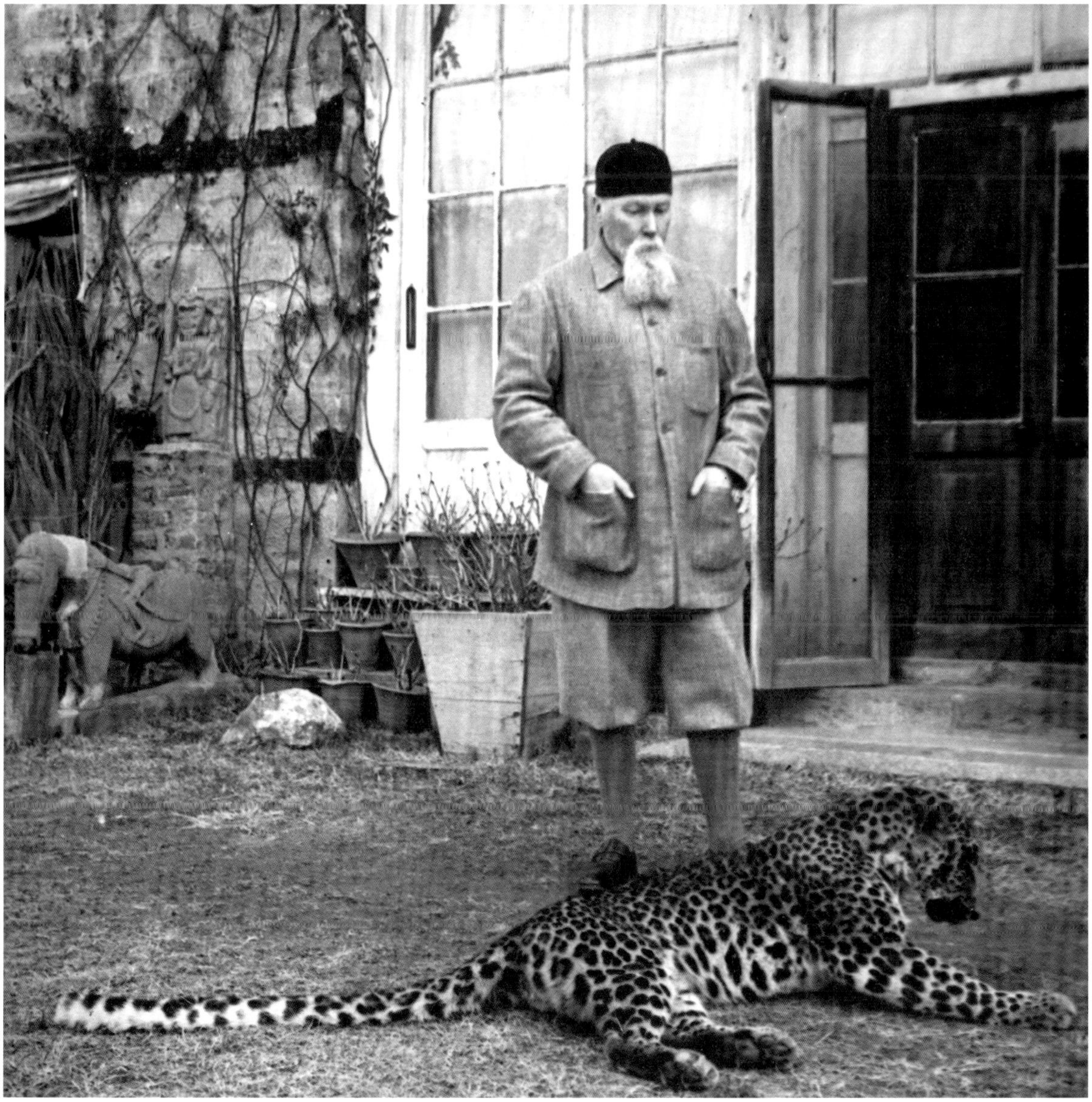

> civilisation would disturb the primitiveness of this country. And I have always been against the ugly evidences of civilisation. But this country is so paralysed that it needs a supermeasure of enlightenment.[23]

Not that this was simply a question of comfort. He was also holding present-day reality up against his vision of what Asia *should* be like, and *would* be like. On that happy day, there would be one community, governed by a single authority and speaking a single language—George recommended Hindustani—with no poverty, no graft and no injustice. Before him now, Roerich saw a broken kaleidoscope of nationalities 'dispersed in an unfathomable manner,' divided by 300 dialects in need of 'reconciliation,' and ruled abominably by corrupt tyrants or rapacious Western imperialists.[24]

From 1935 onward, Roerich and his family remained in India, becoming a fixture in the life of the Kullu Valley in the far northwest and also in the artistic life of the country as a whole. And so it would seem that, in later life, Roerich's feelings for India settled into the groove that they are generally thought to have: unconditional love and adoration. To an extent, this was indeed the case. As noted above, the Roerichs' esteem for India was genuine, their friendships with the Tagore family and with luminaries like Nehru were heartfelt, and the contributions made by Roerich and, increasingly, his son Sviatoslav to the Indian artistic canon were important. The pain the family felt upon witnessing the violence and trauma that accompanied Partition in 1947—an event Roerich repeatedly referred to as the 'vivisection' of India—was absolutely genuine. India was indeed their home; indeed, Helena never set foot outside the country between 1928 and her own death in 1955.

However, two things should be noted. First, the artist certainly never lost a chance to criticise the Raj from the time of his expeditions to his old age and eventual death in 1947. Second, and on the other hand, while India was the Roerichs' home by default, and largely out of affinity, it never displaced Russia in Nicholas's or Helena's heart. Throughout the late 1930s, and even more so during the 1940s, their feelings of homesickness grew ever more acute, and they made repeated attempts to petition the Soviet government to allow them to repatriate themselves. However much the Roerichs loved their adopted homeland, they never ceased to dream of returning to their original one.

End Notes

1. Nicholas Roerich, Himalayas: *Abode of Light* (Bombay: Nalanda, 1947), 13. Translation altered to better fit the Russian original.
2. The date of the Roerichs' arrival is variously given as 2 December and any one of several dates in November. British Government of India reports refer to a 30 November entry.
3. N.K. Rerikh, 'Devassari Abuntu,' Vesy 8 (August 1905).
4. On Dorjiev, the temple's construction, and the circle of orientalists associated with it, see John Snelling, *Buddhism in Russia: The Story of Agvan Dorzhiev, Lhasa's Emissary to the Tsar* (Rockport, Mass.: Element Books, 1993); David Schimmelpenninck van der Oye, *Russian Orientalism* (New Haven: Yale University Press, 2010); and A.A. Andreev, *Khram Buddy v Severnoi stolitse* (St. Petersburg: Nartang, 2004).
5. N.K. Rerikh, *Sobranie sochinenii: pervaia kniga* (Moscow: Sytin, 1914), 258-61.
6. On Roerich's psychological reactions to WWI and revolution, see John McCannon, 'Apocalypse and Tranquility: The World War I Paintings of Nicholas Roerich,' *Russian History* 30 (Fall 2003): 301-21.
7. N.K. Rerikh to A.N. Benua, 5 December 1917 (old style). Cited in E.G. Soini, *Severnyi lik Nikolaia Rerikha* (Samara: Agni, 2001), 59.
8. Cited in P.F. Belikov and V.P. Kniazeva, *N.K. Rerikh* (Samara: Agni, 1996), 139.
9. N.K. Rerikh, *Listy dnevnika* (1936-1941) (Moscow: MTsR, 2000), 85-92; idem, *Iz literaturnogo naslediia* (Moscow: Izobrazitel'noe iskusstvo, 1974), 111; Krishna Dutta and Andrew Robinson, *Rabindranath Tagore* (London: Bloomsbury, 1995), 225; and Bikash Chakravarty, ed., *Poets to a Poet*, 1912-1940 (Calcutta, 1948), 227. 10. The July date comes from Dutta and Robinson, while Chakravarty, relying on testimony from S. K. Chatterjee, says the meeting took place in June.
10. See Marlène Laruelle, Mythe aryen et rêve impérial dans la Russie du XIXe siècle (Paris: CNRS, 2005).
11. Nicholas Roerich, *Altai–Himalaya* (Brookfield, Conn.: Arun Press, 1983) [orig. 1929], 2-3.
12. *ibid.*, 6; Belikov and Kniazeva, *N.K. Rerikh*, 160.
13. Pierre Teilhard de Chardin, *Letters from a Traveller* (New York: Fontana, 1973), 59-61. Quotes that follow come from *ibid.*, 42, 59-61, 84-85, 168.
14. *ibid.*, 42, 59-61, 84-85, 168.
15. Roerich, *Altai–Himalaya*, 26-27.
16. See A.A. Andreev, *Soviet Russia and Tibet* (Leiden: Brill, 2003).
17. Roerich is not mentioned in M. Pratap, *My Life Story of Fifty-Five Years* (Dehradun, 1947), but speaks of Pratap approvingly in the Russian version of *Altai–Himalaya*. However, he does not say enough about Pratap to indicate whether he met him personally or only knew of his ideas. O.P. Shishkin, *Bitva za Gimalai* (Moscow: OLMA, 1999), the author most determined to see Roerich as a Soviet spy in the conventional sense of the word, asserts that Roerich and Pratap actively plotted together, but offers no proof. Scholars taking a more sober approach, such as A.A. Andreev and V.A. Rosov, tend to be more cautious about such assertions.
18. Mentioned in both versions of *Altai–Himalaya*, but at greater length in the Russian original.
19. N.K. Rerikh, *Pis'mena* (Moscow: Profizdat, 2006), 89-90.
20. N.K. Rerikh, 'Plamia,' reproduced in *Izbrannoe* (Moscow: Sovetskaia Rossiia, 1979), 55.
21. This event is alluded to by Belikov and Kniazeva, *N.K. Rerikh*, 130-31; Karl E. Meyer and Shareen Blair Brysac, Tournament of Shadows (Washington, D.C.: Counterpoint, 1999), 457; and Shishkin, Bitva za Gimalai, 110-12, although details vary. British authorities knew about the ceremony, and of Roerich's assertion that the moles on his neck (which they understood to be his cheek) marked him as the herald of Maitreya, the Buddha of the future. It is not clear exactly when or how the ritual actually occurred. Nor is there evidence that Rinpoche or the Panchen affirmed or even reacted to Roerich's claim to be a new incarnation of the Fifth Dalai Lama.
22. Roerich, *Altai–Himalaya*, 221, for example.
23. *ibid.*, 226, 235.
24. Quotes from the Russian original of *Altai–Himalaya*.

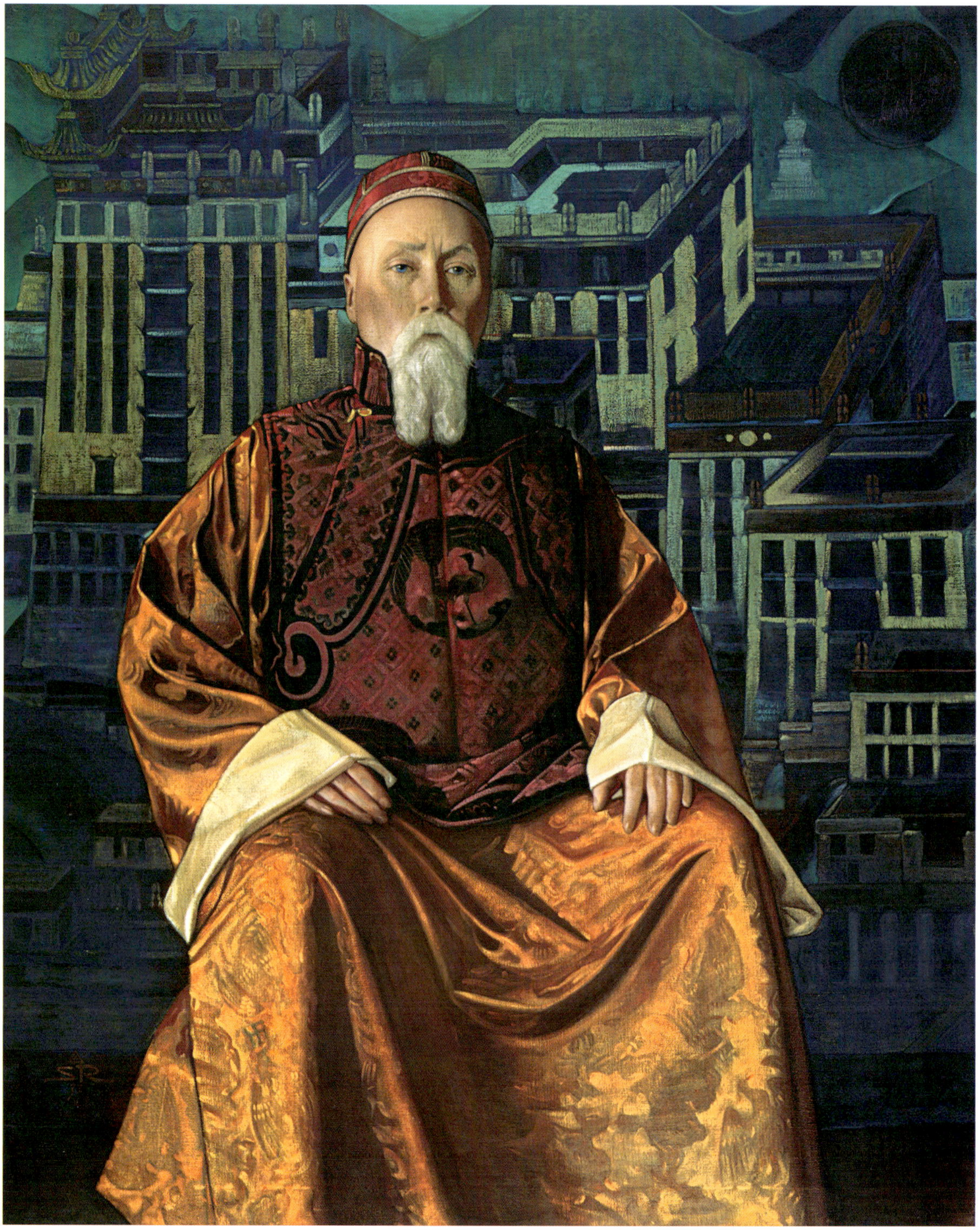

Portrait of Nicholas Roerich in a Tibetan Robe by Svetoslav Roerich 1933
(Nicholas Roerich Museum, New York, USA)

Meeting my Master

Sina Fosdick

I believe that in every life there is an outstanding, striking event, which often completely changes one's life, leading it into new channels, hitherto undreamed of. That is what happened to me on the day of my meeting Prof. Nicholas Roerich.

Madonna Laboris. 1936. (Latvian State Museum of Art, Riga, Latvia)

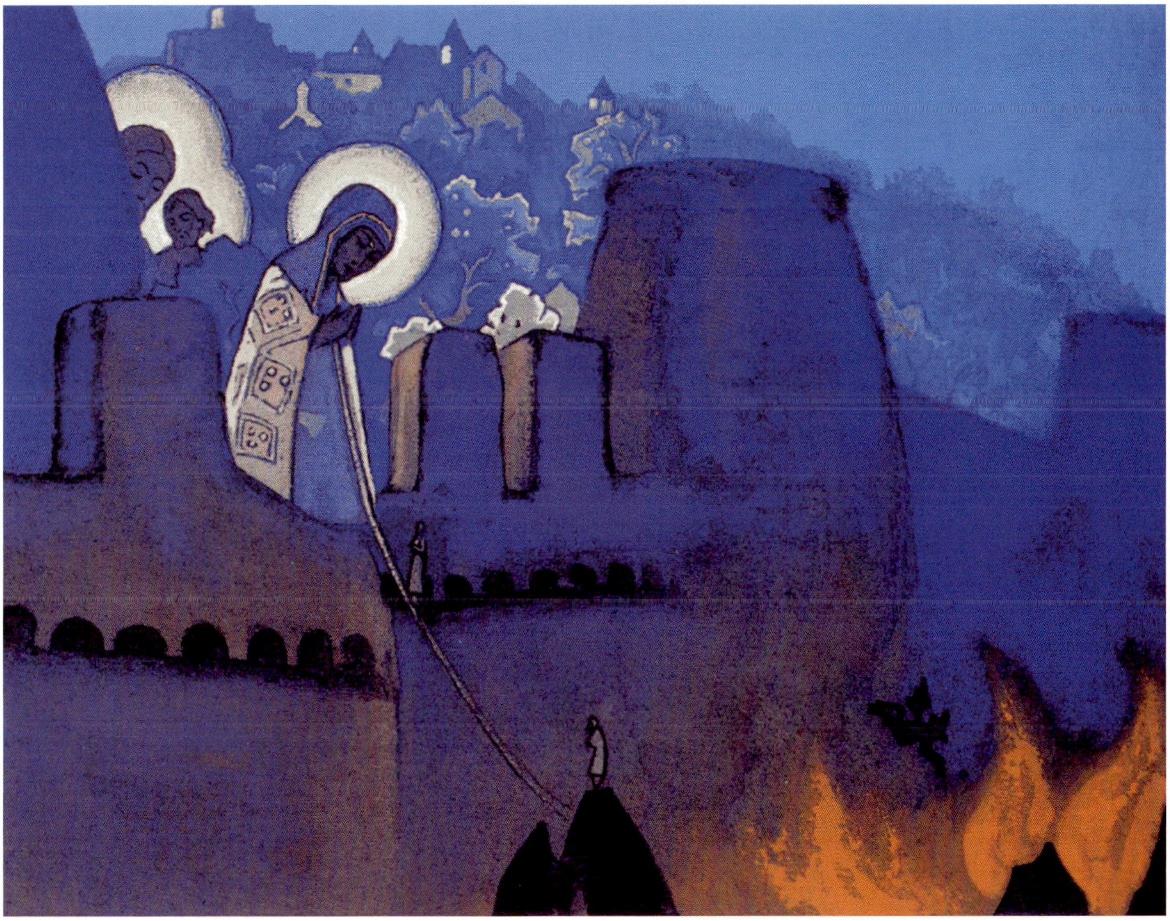

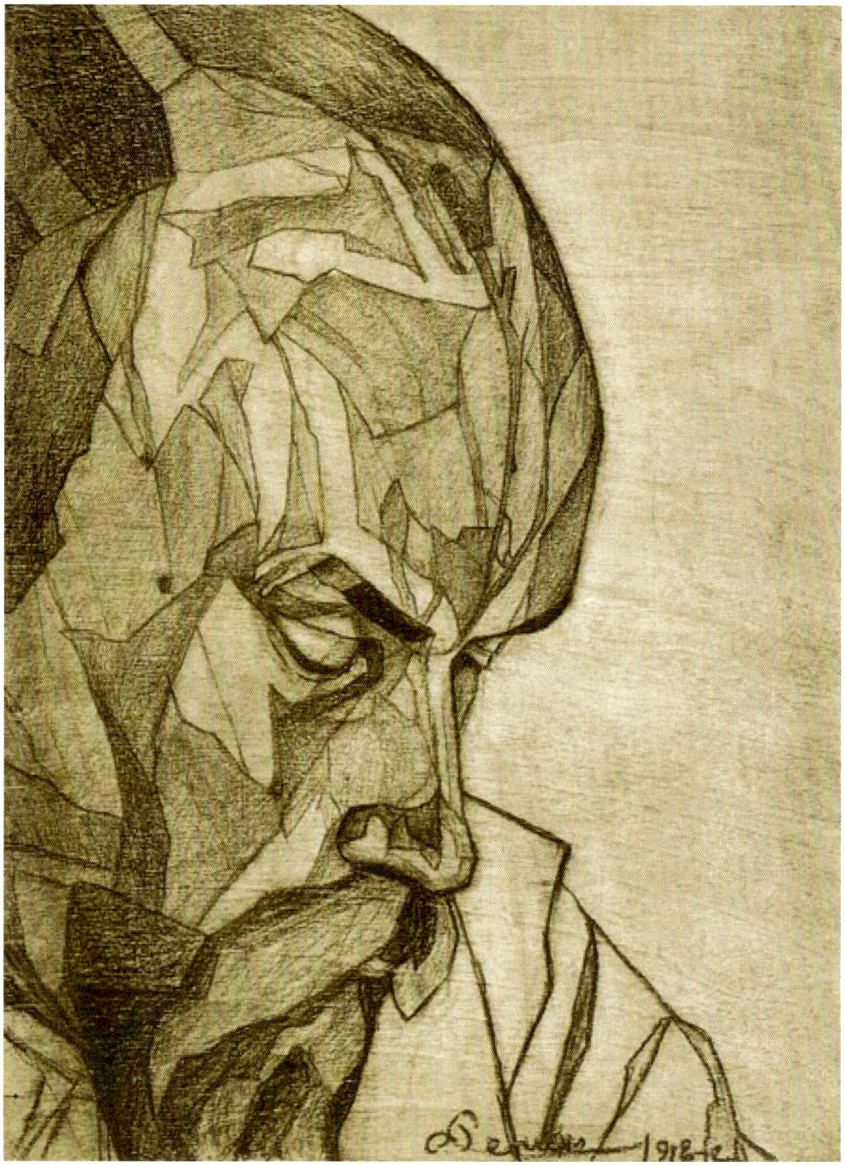

Portrait of Nicholas Roerich, 1916 (International Centre of the Roerichs, Moscow)

It was announced that the first exhibition of this internationally known artist would open in New York, in the winter of 1921. I knew there would be a great crowd on the day of the opening, and hesitated, thinking perhaps I should go on the next day, but, as if drawn by some powerful force, I decided to go. Later I read in the papers that the crowd had been estimated at about 10,000 people, but all I experienced when entering the halls of the gallery was a vast, majestic world, with great mountains, azure skies, with clouds suggesting images not of this plane, and a singularly peaceful, harmonious, indescribably beautiful realm, all new to me. I stood before the *Treasure of the Angels, Pagan Russia* and *Ecstasy*—three huge canvases of super human beauty and serenity, such as only a master-mind, akin to Leonardo da Vinci, could conceive and project in colour.

I was face to face with Infinity; with the first man, building his dwellings, worshipping divine forms and communing with God. Great spaces of cosmic significance, mountains, waterways, massive rocks, earthly and heavenly messengers, humble saints and heroes, peopled the world of Roerich, which he in turn gave to man with that generosity which is the distinction of the truly great in art. I felt choked, with tears filling my eyes, thoughts and emotions welling up in my heart. My hitherto secluded world was giving way to one of unearthly Beauty and Wisdom.

I was torn from my absorption in all this glory by someone who insisted upon introducing me to the artist. There he stood, of medium height, with luminous blue eyes, beard shaped to a point, noble head, radiating some invisible benevolent force, and with a most penetrating look in his eyes as if he could see deep into one's soul and find the very essence of it. Next to him stood his wife, Helena Roerich, so strikingly beautiful that one caught one's breath. I was invited to visit them that same evening in the Hotel des Artistes. They began to talk to me about their future plans, their mission in the United States, and what was to follow afterwards, at the same time professing deep interest in my music and teaching work. And, most astounding, our paths were to converge; the work of bringing art and knowledge to the Youth of America was to tie me closer to them!

The same evening thoughts were laid for common work—the foundation of the first of our institutions founded by Prof. Roerich—Master School of United Arts. Many more of these cultural centres were to follow; Cor Ardens, Corona Mundi, and later Roerich Museum, Roerich Museum Press, numerous Roerich Societies in all parts of the world, and others. That evening marked the beginning of my apprenticeship, which grew from then on into discipleship under Nicholas Roerich and in closest co-operation with him and Mme. Roerich.

But the deepest joy of that first evening of our meeting was the realisation that I had found my Master. By the very first words he spoke, filled with profound wisdom, and telling me ever so simply and gently about Beauty and Labour. His was the wisdom of both the earthly and heavenly planes, ever-compassionate, alleviating heartaches of those who came to him. He magnified all goodness, finding in ever-so-small a consciousness, a seed of good.

From my Master I learnt how to deal with others, in conflict and in sorrow; how to forgive but not to compromise; how to feel joy, but also perceive reality without closing one's eyes to it; how to love beauty, accepting it as one of the highest expressions of the human spirit; how to cognise and revere the Great Teachers of humanity.

He combined the all-pervading knowledge of an ancient sage with the synthesis of a genius—a combined artist, instilled in them indomitable courage and daring to battle life's obstacles. His was the pronouncement, 'Blessed be the obstacles, through them we grow.' He praised generously where even small progress was in evidence, thus prompting to still greater service. Joyously he welcomed a good soul, and grew silent when evil made itself known in his presence. And by this silence one grew to sense evil, when it approached him. A great builder, he brought people together for common work 'for general good.' Superhumanly patient, indefatigable in his creativeness which embraced such a vast sphere of human endeavours, he taught those near him to serve culture and love the joy of service, and through culture to battle for peace, for all men, for all times. He never belittled, and was a philosopher, writer, scientist, discoverer and possessor of a

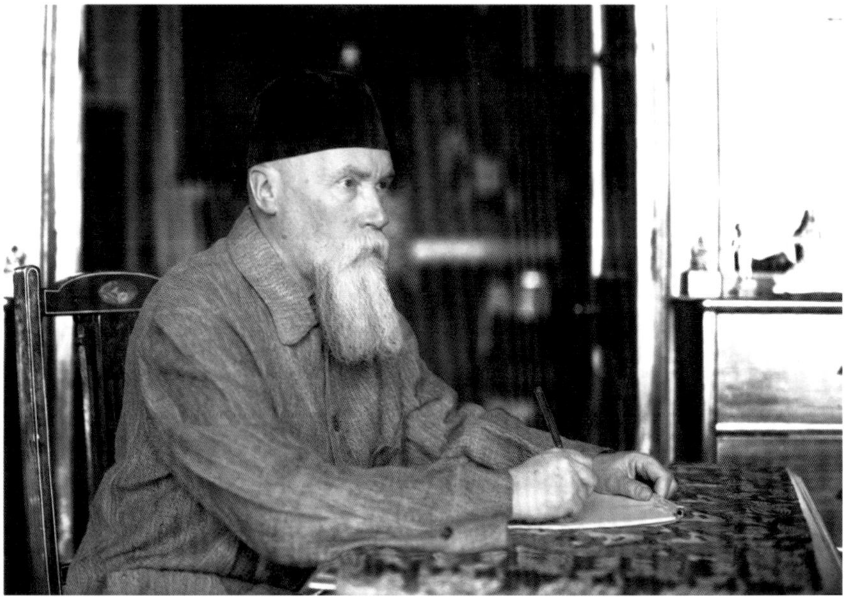

Nicholas Roerich ca. 1937. Naggar, India (Nicholas Roerich Museum Archive, NY)

vast realm of ideas whose profundity reach into the distant future. He brought joy, health, harmony and peace to many who sought him, as he radiated all these forces. He gave untold spiritual wealth to many, thus making their lives immeasurably rich. He gave of himself and his great treasures of spirit untiringly, bringing greatest sacrifices with complete selflessness. He was a sower, not for himself, but, for humanity. Communing with the Higher Worlds, he never forsook the earth, serving the General Good.

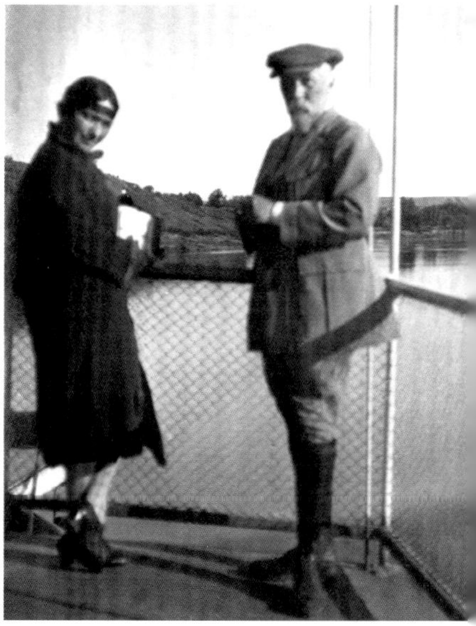

Left to right: Sina Lichtmann, Nicholas Roerich, July–August, 1926. The Ob, Siberia (Nicholas Roerich Museum Archive, NY)

He spoke of peace, creating the universally known Roerich Pact and Banner of Peace, because his very being radiated peace. He foresaw grave calamities before they descended upon humanity—two World Wars—and he warned, with great sorrow in his heart, against a third universal disaster. Yet he sent messages of peace to all parts of the world, to purify the space, to help the growth of human consciousness. He was a builder, creating many majestic structures, visible and invisible. He scattered many benevolent milestones in the countries through which he passed. These blessed magnets remained and kindled many a noble striving in human hearts. His creativeness, his art, his thought, all were imbued with a holy fire. His was a cosmic consciousness.

My Master is ever-living. He taught me that there is no death, no ending—that there is Infinity. A rare privilege has been given me in this life: to meet a Great Soul, a Master, and to be allowed to become his disciple.

With inexpressible gratitude in my heart, I hope to follow in his steps. I know I will meet him again in ever-flowing life.

Select Bibliography

Sina Fosdick, Letters, New York, 7 July 1948.

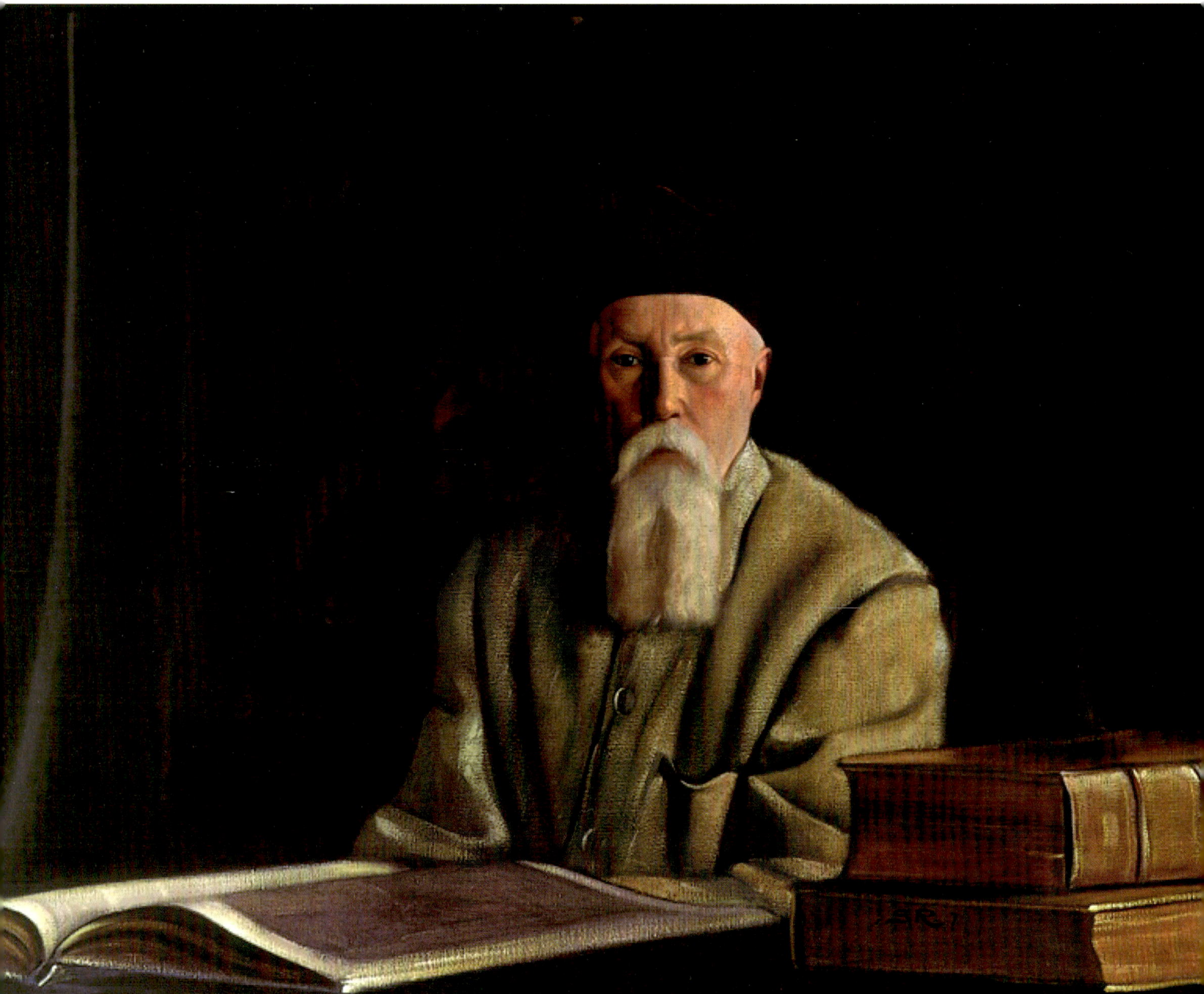

Nicholas Roerich, by Svetoslav Roerich, 1937

The Roerich Family and Altai

A.V. Ivanov and I.V. Fotieva

The name of Nikolai Konstantinovich Roerich, and that of his prominent family, is inseparably tied to the Altai. The master's sketches and paintings conveyed the beauty of this mountainous country, his words about Altai are found in articles and books, and one of these books bears the symbolic title, *Altai–Himalayas*. What was it about this place that so impressed and attracted this artist, who was born in St. Petersburg; worked in Europe, the United States and India; and won international fame?

One reason was a search for evidence of cultural and historical commonalities amongst the peoples of Eurasia: Russians and Indians, Turks and Mongols. And the Roerich family succeeded in finding

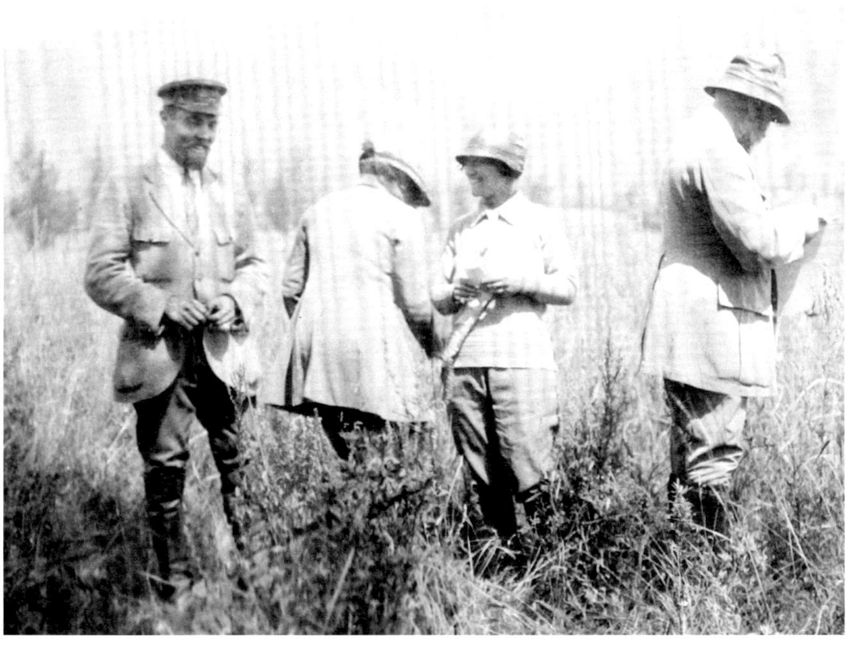

Left to right: George Roerich, Helena Roerich, Sina Lichtmann, Nicholas Roerich August, 1926. Altai (Nicholas Roerich Museum Archive, NY)

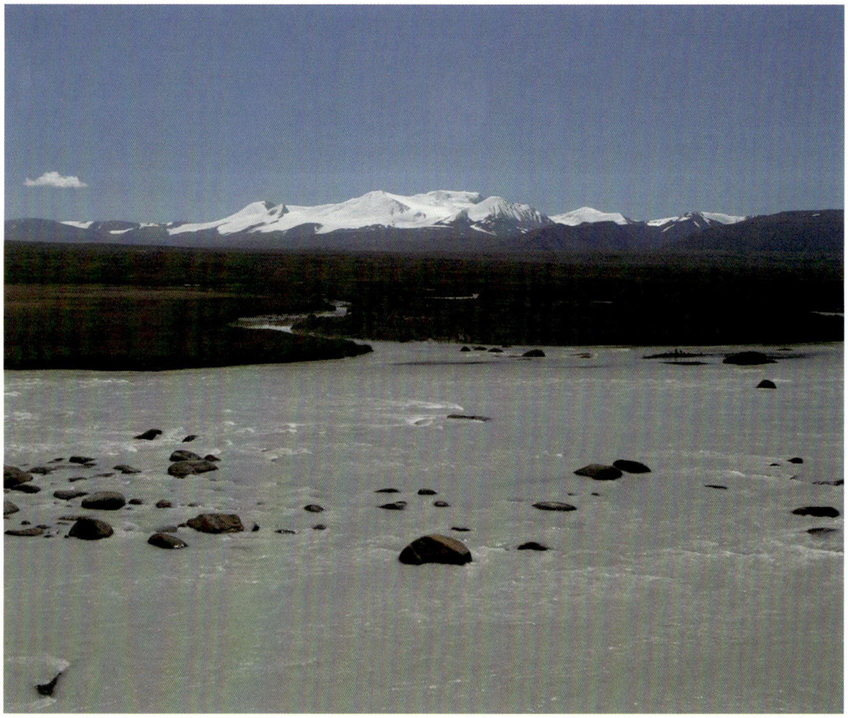

Ukok Plateau in the Altai region of southwestern Siberia with Akalaha River (Belovodye – the area of White Waters) (photograph by A. Ivanov)

irrefutable facts about these ancient cultural connections, revealing, among other things, the animistic statues common to the Himalayas, Altai and the European part of Russia. The Roerichs took great interest in the ancient migratory paths of the nomadic peoples, who carried knowledge and cultural values both from East to West and from West to East. Along these routes, Altai was particularly a key point, as both a birthplace of, and as a place of cultural exchange between Eurasian cultures. In fact, just as N.K. Roerich conjectured, it is to Altai that modern Koreans, Hungarians, Turks and even Japanese trace their origins. He wrote:

> 'In the migration of peoples, Altai is one of the most important points. Interments built with large boulders, or the so-called Chudian graves (or burial mounds), the inscriptions on the rock, all of this brings us to that time when from the far Southeast, full of glaciers and sand, people gathered to the avalanche, in order to fill and recreate Europe. Prehistorically as well as historically, Altai represents an untripped treasurebox. The Great Lady of Altai, Mount Belukha, who feeds all rivers and fields, is ready to give of her treasures.'[1]

And, of course the great artist was certain that the cultural essence of Russia, the middle Eurasian power, could not be understood without detailed study of her Eastern roots. So, he wrote of the interwoven European and Eastern cultural elements in the story of Russia's formation:

> 'You know that after prehistoric times, the great plain of Russia and Siberia became the thoroughfare for a procession of migrating peoples….If today you can count over 300 dialects in Russia, then how many languages, living or dead, must have once existed in her immense steppe? In the periods following the universal hieroglyphs of the Stone Age, we have made the most unexpected discoveries in the layers of Russian subsoil; these archaeological surprises help us conjure an image of real Russian life…
>
> '…Even now in the Tversky and Moscovian provinces we see ornaments with ancient reindeer. Imagery of such animals instantly calls to mind the Stone Age. At the same time, in the very same places, you will find decorations with clear expressions of Mongolian embroidery, or obviously Gothic forms.
>
> 'In the southern steppe, the remains of skiffs astonish us with artifacts of the classical Hellenic world.
>
> 'In the upper Volga Region and on the shores of the Dnieper, you will be struck by the combination of beautiful Romantic styles with the ruins of the Byzantine Empire. And in the Byzantine ruins you will sense the cradle of the East, Persia and Hindustan. You will feel that the clever Arabian merchants sailed every river of Russia just to spread the entire tale of the East, through to the coast of China.
>
> 'Since the 12th century, Kievan Russian was under the Mongol yoke. But even in times of unhappiness, Russia learned new tales, new songs of the triumphant, nomadic East. In the glint of Tartar swords, Russia decorated and carved these wonderful new symbols.

> '...In Russian icons we see reincarnations of Italian primitivism and Asiatic miniatures. But these elements are full of national images as well, and create a new whole. They give way to the Russian icon, before which the world rightly bows.'[2]

But the Roerichs were interested not only in the Asiatic—including the very strong Indian—roots of Russian culture, but in the East as a whole, as a living, inexhaustible spring of knowledge, beauty and wisdom. Through paintings, scientific works, practical research, and the unique philosophical-ethical study of the Agni Yoga, the members of the Roerich family conveyed the power of the artistic forms and the depth of Eastern thought, and their importance in our times.

One of the Roerichs' most significant achievements was the Trans-Himalaya Organisation, or the Central Asian Expedition, from 1924 to 1928. The travellers were challenged not only by the elements. Local authorities, distrustful of the Russian researchers, also presented countless obstacles. Such circumstances called for not only extraordinary courage, but also inexhaustible patience, restraint, and constant composure. Roerich wrote of this subject:

> 'Just like anywhere, on the one hand, you can find wonderful relics, fine ways of thinking and expression based on ancient wisdom, and friendly human relations. You can enjoy beauty and be easily understood. But in those same places, do not be surprised if you are horrified at the perverse forms of religion, at the ignorance and the degeneracy.
>
> 'We must accept things as they are. Abandoning traditional sentimentalities, we must welcome the good and fairly denounce the harmful and the bad. We should carefully distinguish narrow-mindedness and superstition from hidden symbols of ancient knowledge. We will welcome all endeavours towards creation and constructiveness, and deplore any barbaric or destructive nature and spirit.'[3]

Later, a scientific research institute 'Urusvati' or 'Light of the Morning star', symbolically named by Helena Roerich—both wife and closest collaborator of Nikolai Konstantinovich, would be established in the Kullu valley in India to study the results of the expedition The Institute maintained close contact with several scientific centres in

India, the United States and Europe. To this day, only a small portion of the important materials, travel notes, theoretical and philosophical works housed in its archives have been studied.

Many questions arise. India, Tibet, the Himalayas, China, Mongolia—such was the route of their grand expedition—but why did the Roerichs approach Altai specifically, subjecting themselves to dangers of pursuit and even arrest in Moscow? What could this distant, little-known, intractable part of Asiatic Russia add to the gigantic volume of materials that had already been collected on it? Many answers come to mind. First, it led to an understanding of the importance of Siberia as a whole—not only its history and culture, but the Siberian taiga, lakes and rivers, mountains and glaciers—literally our life source, and among the few remaining on the planet. They discovered that both the culture and the natural environs of Siberia are invaluable treasures. 'Russian power will grow beholden to Siberia'—each member of the Roerich family would agree with these words of scientist-writer Mikhail Lomonosov's which articulate that Siberia should not be exploited, but studied, valued, and protected, her worth proclaimed to the whole world.

The second answer is directly connected with the Roerichs' worldview, expressed in their philosophical legacy, the books of 'Living Ethics' which contained ideas far ahead of the times. However, today these ideas have received convincing scientific support, restoring to scientific thought the ancient idea of an animate Universe, of the cosmic role of humans, the substantiation of thought, and many others. Also included is the salient idea that existence on our planet

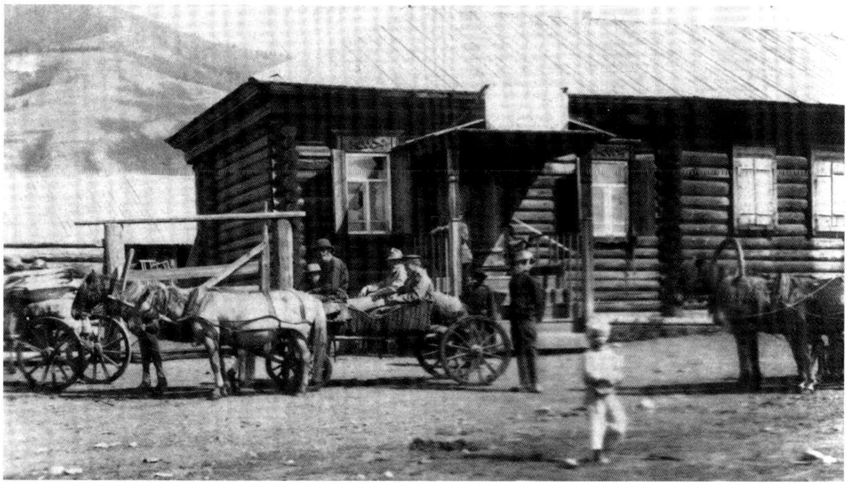

Right to left in the carriage: George Roerich, Nicholas Roerich August, 1926. Altai (Nicholas Roerich Museum Archive, NY)

is similar to a living organism, and there are special places on which our existence, and the life of the planet itself, depends. Accordingly, like vital organs, these require special study, protection and care. In these places, a human spirit that has not yet lost its natural keenness, is elevated, cleansed and can acutely feel its connection to the world. Although these ideas are new for us, our ancestors knew them long ago. In fact, it was specifically in these places that temples and sanctuaries were built, the dead buried and sacred rites performed.

The Roerichs were convinced that Altai was one such place. It was no mere coincidence that so many legends and beliefs were connected to this mountainous country—for example, the prophecy that the valley of the sacred Katun' River is the exact site where the final battle between good and evil will transpire. And it was not just its geographical location that led Roerich to call Altai the 'Heart of Asia'; in this expression was concealed a precisely intended meaning.

The expedition left from Moscow on 22 July 1926. Four days later the travellers arrived in Novosibirsk, where, Roerich's comrades who were just returning from the United States joined them: the journalist Maurice Lichtmann and his wife Zinaida (Sina) Fosdick, and a future collaborator on the Roerich Museum in New York. The path from Novosibirsk to the Altai plateau ran along the great Siberian River Ob'. On 28 July, the travellers arrived in the town of Barnaul, and began their trek along the Ob' reaching the town of Biisk after two days of trekking. From Biisk, they began the journey into the deep mountainous country, in the direction of the highest peak in Altai, Mount Belukha. The old Russian village, Upper Uymon at the foot of the Katunsky Ridge, had been chosen as the Expedition's base camp.

Along their route, the Roerichs stopped in many villages, recording data and conversing with people. Beyond the Mariinsky settlement, Altai opened forth in all of its majestic beauty. Most of all, the Roerichs were astonished by unbelievably tall grasses and flowers, 'clear, golden, blue, purple,' in which a horse and its rider could easily disappear from view. Not far from the village of Kyrlyk, as Roerich clarified in his journal, was the celebrated region 'where began the studies of the White Burkhan and his good friend Oyrot,' who brought the Altaians—the indigenous people of the area—news of the beginning of a beautiful new era, if only they would reject the bloody shamanistic sacrifices and respect all living things. Beyond the village Abay, they came across the camps of nomadic Altaians more frequently, 'conic yurts' covered in larch bark. From thereon began the deepest region of Altai, rich in 'beautiful forests, thundering rivers, and snow-capped ridges'. Roerich was worried that a Tibetan member of the expedition would not be able to survive the arduous journey through Altai. But, the Tibetan patiently bore the hardships, and calming his companions, said, 'This is only right—to have obstacles on the road to Shambhala.' For him, the trip to the foot of Katunsky Ridge was a voyage to the secret country of holy sages and righteous men, 'keepers of the future world' where the teachings of the great Buddha would reign.

Trekking on the left bank of the Katun' Valley, late at night the expedition arrived in Ust'-Koksa, the final point on the journey. Tales of this sacred river, as of the three-peaked Mount Belukha, were dispersed all over Central Asia. The Roerichs had heard the first story back in Urumchi. The Katun' fascinated H.K. Roerich: 'The Shambation river rolls over boulders and passes. Who can resist her call?' After fording the Katun', the Expedition finally arrived at Altai—Upper Uymon.

Uymon, one of the most ancient settlements in the kray, was founded by peasants who had fled to Siberia three hundred years ago during the church reforms of Patriarch Nikon. Here you could expect to find that which was almost lost in European Russia: old Slavonic legends, arts and crafts, applied artwork, the old styles of clothing, and of course, ancient icons and handwritten books. Besides all this, Roerich knew that the Old Believers of Altai had ties with the villages of Old Believers in Mongolian Altai. Another important reason to reach Upper Uymon was to get the perspective on the rest of the expedition route from the famous guide—well known even in scholarly circles in Novosibirsk—Vakhramey Atamanov, an unsurpassed trekker,whom specialists came all the way from Moscow to consult with.

The Roerichs often conversed with him about different issues. After hearing from him an old song about Prince Iosaf, Nikolai Konstantinovich asked, 'Do you know, Vakhramey, about whom you are singing? In fact, you are singing about Buddha. And the Bodhisattva was changed over in translation from Greek by Iosaf…' This did not surprise Atamanov, who in turn talked of the distant world of Whitewater. Reminiscing about it, Zinaida Fosdick comments that in Upper Uymon 'everyone spoke, as if all of the Old Believers from all of the ends of the Earth converged upon Altai, in search of Whitewater'. In fact, Atamanov's grandfather had undertaken just such an endeavour. It was becoming clearer that distant lands of wise men are known under different names: Whitewater amongst the Old Believers; the sacred peaceful mountain Meru amongst the Hindus; and the land of immortality and justice—Shambhala—amongst Central Asians and Tibetans. While in medieval Europe, the quest for the mysterious Christian Holy Grail was the symbol of heroic dedication and selfless service. The Roerichs were deeply convinced that this similarity of legends was not coincidental.

The abundance and variety of grandiose burial constructions in Altai astonished Nikolai Konstantinovich. In his journal, he wrote about the *kereksura* (arrangements of vertically erected stones), 'steles of anonymous peoples,' 'deer rocks,' and 'stone figures'—'kezera.' Roerich specially conducted excursions to Belukha, mostly to make sketches. 'Of course my main aspiration, as an artist, was to produce artistic works,' Roerich wrote. Belukha—'The Great Lady of Altai, the snow-capped mountain, who feeds all rivers and fields, ready to give of her treasures'—was known far beyond Siberia, perhaps since the time of the creation of the holy Vedas in India, in which researchers discovered with surprise distinct signs of 'northerly motives'.

Far to the south of Asia, they knew that in the north, in the mountainous country of Altai, on the right shore of the Katun', high in the sky there rose a many-peaked mountain, the source of the legendary river, the turquoise Katun'. This mountain was Kelukha, Uch-Sumer, 'about which the deserts whisper,' Roerich wrote in his journal. On 17 August, Roerich crossed the Katunsky Ridge from north to south through the pass on the frigid white and walked out into the southern side of Belukha. On that day, both the eastern and western crests of the mountain were clearly visible. It is likely that this sight inspired the idea for a future painting, *Unspilled Vessel.*

Much later, upon the completion of the expedition, Zinaida Fosdik wrote on 27 September 1929:

> '...in one of the halls of the Roerich Museum in New York, there was a meeting of Siberians and friends of Siberia. Nikolai Konstantinovich was present at this gathering, and in his greeting, said, 'The Country of the great future is Siberia, and the living embodiment of her beauty is Altai!''

End Notes

1. Roerich, N.K. *Chosen*. 1979. p. 124.
2. Roerich, N.K. *The Path of Blessings*. Minsk, 1991. pp. 47-48.
3. Roerich, N.K. *Chosen*. 1979. p. 99.

Diamond of Consciousness:
A Practice of Agni Yoga

V. Khvorostov

Nicholas and Helena Koerich, from 1920 onwards, became followers of a spiritual teaching called Agni Yoga , also known as Living Ethics, believed to be passed down to them by Master Morya. He was the acknowledged guru of the Russian born spiritual scholar Helena Petrovna Blavatsky (1831-1891 A.D), who along with American spiritualist Col. Henry Steel Olcott founded the Theosophical Society in 1875 in New York.

Under the direct guidance of these spiritual Masters, the Roerichs expounded upon the Agni Yoga teaching and practice in several books. This Sanskrit term is taken from the Hindu Vedic god of fire or 'Agni' and the Teaching is derived from the divine transformative power of 'agni' as a vehicle of self-realisation and self evolution. They point toward a unique possibility for self development and defined the method of broadening of one's consciousness and its ability to receive the ever expanding vibrations of the Universe. As a consequence the practitioner is able to perceive and interact with different energies in a more significant way. One of the main features of this Teaching is that it expresses knowledge of the Laws of the Universe which allow us (practitioners) to guide the development of humanity in unity and harmony with the development of the Universe itself.

Among the several methods of broadening of one's consciousness as outlined in the Teachings of Agni Yoga, one practice is specifically emphasized (in the books of *Supermundane*): the state of 'diamond of consciousness'. This state stresses the importance of focusing on the moment between falling asleep and waking, so as to allow us to be in touch with subtle energies which, in these moments, reveal their existence. Through this practice one can perceive the subtle world almost in the same measure as one had earlier perceived the gross world. During this intermission—between the state of waking and of sleep—the work of our energy centres transfer or switch over to the vibrations of the subtle world. Correspondingly, returning to the gross world leads to the loss of vision of this other world.

According to the Agni Yoga Teachings, this potential to perceive the energies of different worlds—gross and subtle—is inherent in each one of us. On the ordinary, mundane level of consciousness, perception of mainly one world prevails—either of the gross world while we are in the waking state, or (of) the subtle world when we are in a dream state, or in the state of meditation. However, there exists another interesting phenomenon of human consciousness. It manifests in the moment when the subtle body crosses from one field of energy to another. The previous moment of existence in the subtle world is superimposed upon the beginning of the waking state in the physical world (gross level). This superimposition of both worlds leads to their interpenetration. *Supermundane*, the last book of the Agni Yoga Teaching states:

'During such transitory state of consciousness, man equally belongs both to the gross and subtle world'.

The intention of this practice is to show the unique possibility of staying simultaneously in two worlds during the transition from dream state to waking. It is available to everyone. During this shift from one energy level to another, 'for an instant [a person] becomes aware of the quality of the subtle world'. It is verily a special moment when the otherwise invisible world is revealed.

Of course, we enter this invisible world every time we plunge into sleep or into deep meditation. But this state of consciousness, referred to as the state of 'diamond of consciousness', is strikingly different from both these states. Being in the state of 'diamond of consciousness' allows a person to see and even take limited action in both worlds simultaneously. A mindful attunement by the practitioner to any activity or process occurring in his/her physical life can produce a corresponding vision on this level of subtle energy as well. Once one acquires the ability to see, one also acquires an ability to influence what one sees.

On the gross level, one usually takes notice of an occurrence only when one directly encounters it. Whereas on the subtle level, thoughts and feelings are perceived as currents of energy, rays intertwined into diverse patterns, that unite people who have a karmic connection (from past/previous lives). By envisaging through physical consciousness an occurrence currently manifest on the gross level, a person, if in the state of 'diamond of consciousness', can simultaneously perceive on the subtle level the progression of all energy processes which surround the event that is transpiring. A practitioner, by directing a part of his consciousness to this, can instantly comprehend the event's essence and content. He/she can also understand the nature of how it occurred, and the interaction of other fields of energy related to it.

Such a two-tier vision (that is both gross and subtle) allows one to cross the threshold to new levels of human understanding, and to the realization that life is a process of infinite and diverse permutation of vast numbers of different energies. With this understanding a conviction arises of mankind's multiple connections with the myriad manifestations of all worlds. But this is not the only result of developing such a quality of consciousness.

The state of 'diamond of consciousness' enhances the demand to raise the ethical level of our thinking. The practitioner is clearly able to perceive each and every consequence of thoughts, consciously or subconsciously projected or released into space. Through this it is evident that malevolent words, even if pronounced unintentionally, or a constant negative attitude towards a task, activity or person, can release similar negative vibrations and become a powerful destroyer of one's field of energy. Conversely, thoughts of support, love and

The Command of Rigden Djapo, 1926 (International Centre of the Roerichs, Moscow)

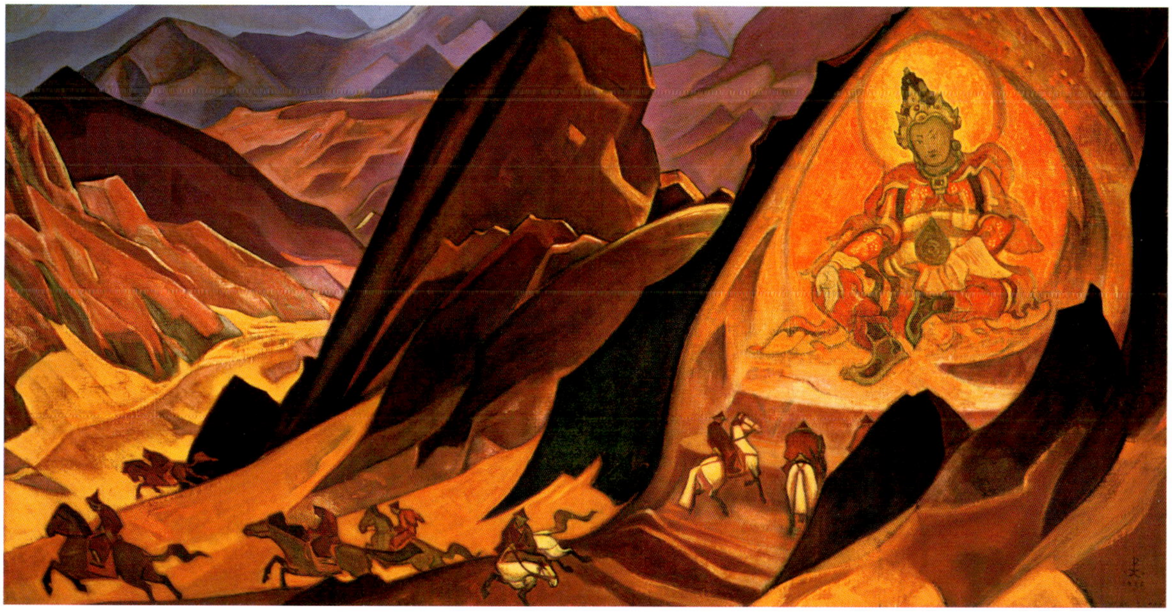

trust that carry a beneficial spiritual charge are also transmitted and revealed to the recipient.

Having experienced and being aware of the consequence of these states, a practitioner will, no doubt, try and avoid even the unmindful projection of adverse thoughts or feelings. But if unable to do so, more serious karmic consequences are called forth because this enhanced understanding or knowledge presupposes a new level of responsibility. Thus, instead of a narrow material understanding of physical phenomena, this practice enables one to breakthrough to the world of subtle energies to the causal world.

This state of consciousness can impart real knowledge of all that is happening in this world. One begins to perceive the origin of, and understand the essence of earthly occurrences, and the shrouding veil of physical appearance (or reality) falls off. A new horizon to the possibility of life opens up. It is not by chance that Helena and Nicholas Roerichs' teaching of Agni Yoga call these moments the 'diamond of consciousness', a crystal clear and pure vision of life that is devoid of the distortion of 'maya' or the illusions of our earthly life.

It is interesting to note that a phenomenon similar to the state of 'diamond of consciousness' can be noticed in nature as well. It relates to the premonition of the first rays of the sun, when for a short instant the whole natural world appears to be still; night shadows have fled, and first light is on the threshold of a new day that has not yet encompassed the whole world. In the Agni Yoga Teaching, this moment is expressed in the following words:

'One may also observe interruptions of the currents. As in aviation one may encounter air pockets, so, too, in the observation of currents, sudden cessations may be noted. In ancient times such manifestations were called the silences of nature.' (391. AUM, Agni Yoga Teaching)

Special importance is given to these concepts—the dividing line of the passage of movement between plus and minus, passivity and activity—in the Hindu treatise *Precepts of God Shiva to his Consort Devi*: 'When everything is breathed out and the breathing stops by itself...... during such a universal pause a small 'I' disappears.'

There is a fading of the preliminary state of consciousness while the following state has not yet fully manifested itself. At such a moment, one who listens to the voice of nature is receptive to subtler levels of thought, and can receive answers to questions one has pondered upon, and even have a premonition about future events.

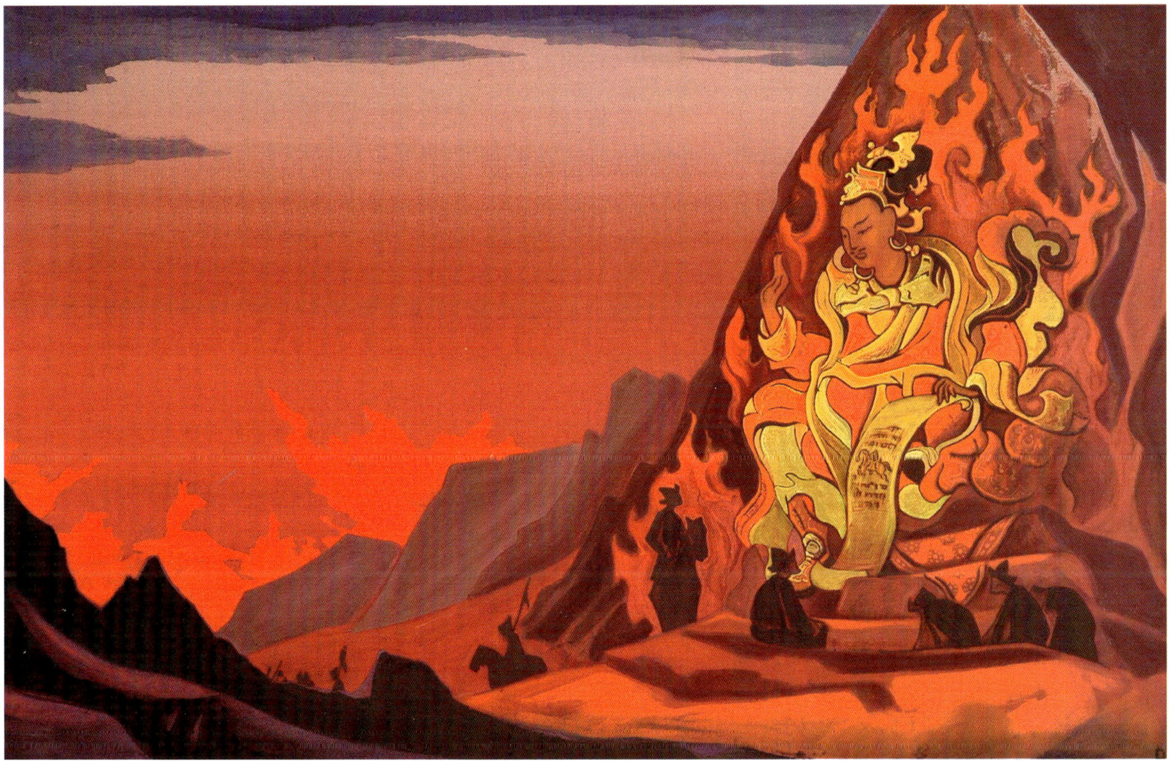

Command of Rigden Djapo, 1933 (Nicholas Roerich Museum Archive, NY)

Such points of silence in the consciousness of man as in nature, allow us to penetrate new fields of energy. In remembering that each recollection of the subtle world may be very helpful for human evolution, we should place this task of penetration to the subtle world even more urgently before us. One has only to recognize it.

How does one manifest in oneself this unique state of consciousness? Having discussed the features of the state of 'diamond of consciousness' one is already closer to an answer.

It is useful if we train ourselves to wake up slowly and consciously when awaking from slumber, dividing our attention between the two worlds—the dream state and the waking state. Exactly at this point when we are beginning to be conscious of the physical world while still lingering in the dream state, we have to pause for as long as possible. We have to get accustomed to this new quality, so that our consciousness is able to recognize its own new state. If practiced consistently, this new quality of consciousness will assume clarity, bringing us slowly towards a level of constant awareness of both worlds. Such an ability will bring forth a qualitatively new attitude towards one's physical or outer reality, helping to transcend in part, the world of 'maya'. It

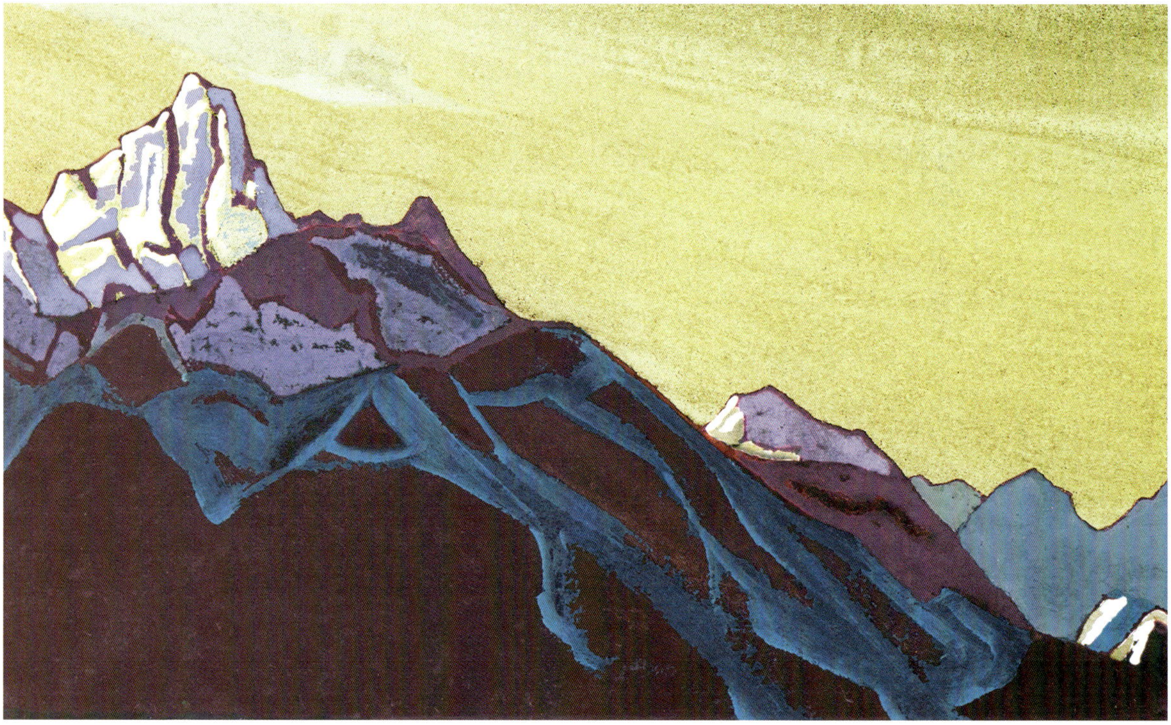

Study of Mountains series (International Roerich Memorial Trust, Naggar, Kullu)

is then that signs of the 'New Era' will unhesitatingly approach our world and 'Truth' will shine through.

Obviously, the above mentioned possibilities are not the only ones that will arise as a result of developing this state of consciousness. The path of one's inner development is clearly outlined in the book *Supermundane* of the Agni Yoga Teachings: 'When a man brings impressions from the Subtle World to the gross level, he can also receive a premonition about the Fiery Gates'. This allusion can be explained by defining the Fiery World to mean the 'pure' world, into which entry is achieved, not through the Vedic sacred self-purification fire-ritual, but through a symbolic meditation on its power, a simple visualization for peace, a technique that helps a believer to overcome all obstacles. This state can also carry us forward to the perception of the 'Fiery World' in unity with all other worlds. Here the fiery world would signify the 'pure' world. 'Conditions of the three worlds may be manifested in earthly life as well'. The whole process of the 'idea' crossing through all worlds—from its inception in the pure Highest Fiery spheres, through its saturation by thoughts on the mental level, and by feelings and forms on the astral level, till the materialization of the 'idea' on the physical level—all this will be revealed to the Man of the Future. Verily, infinite are the horizons of the knowledge of the spirit revealed through the aspiring consciousness!

The number of people who are consciously able to receive and assimilate the vibrations of subtle, invisible worlds is growing. Awareness of subtle energies in strengthening people's hearts too is progressively enhanced. Indeed this task of enlarging consciousness is the challenge placed before mankind.

Select Bibliography

'Aesthetic Aspect of Labour Activity in the Career-guidance of Schoolchildren'; Laboratories of schoolchildren career-guidance; Komi State Pedagogical Institute, Syktyvkar, Russia.
'Connection with the Highest '; Banner of Peace newspaper.
'Diamond of Consciousness '; Banner of Peace newspaper.
'From Delhi to Kulu Valley' Roerich bulletin 'Svyatogor'; The exhibition of Nicholas and Svyatoslav Roerichs' paintings Reproduction in Syktyvkar, Russia 'Let's protect names and heritage of the Roerichs', V.5.
'How to read Agni-Yoga books' Literary miscellany 'Ural Roerich Bulletin', Roerich Movement Bulletin 'Svyatogor'
'Master vs Teacher'; Banner of Peace newspaper.
'That's how we work'; Banner of Peace newspaper.
'The Role of Egregore in setting up and functioning of Roerich societies'; Banner of Peace newspaper.

'The great Azaras who know the Teachings of India, know the origin of Kalachakra. They know vast things which, when they will be revealed to help humanity, will completely regenerate life! Many of the Teachings of Kalachakra are unknowingly used both in East and West, and even in such unconscious utilization, much that is wonderful results. It is therefore comprehensible how incomparably great would be the possibilities made manifest by a conscious achievement, and how wisely could be used the great eternal energy, this fine imponderable matter which is scattered everywhere and which is within our use at any moment. This Teaching of Kalachakra, this utilization of primary energy, has been called the Teaching of Fire. The Hindu people know the great Agni—ancient teaching though it be, it shall be the new teaching for the New Era. '

Roerich, N., *Shambhala,* Nicholas Roerich Museum: New York, New York, 1985, pg. 28.

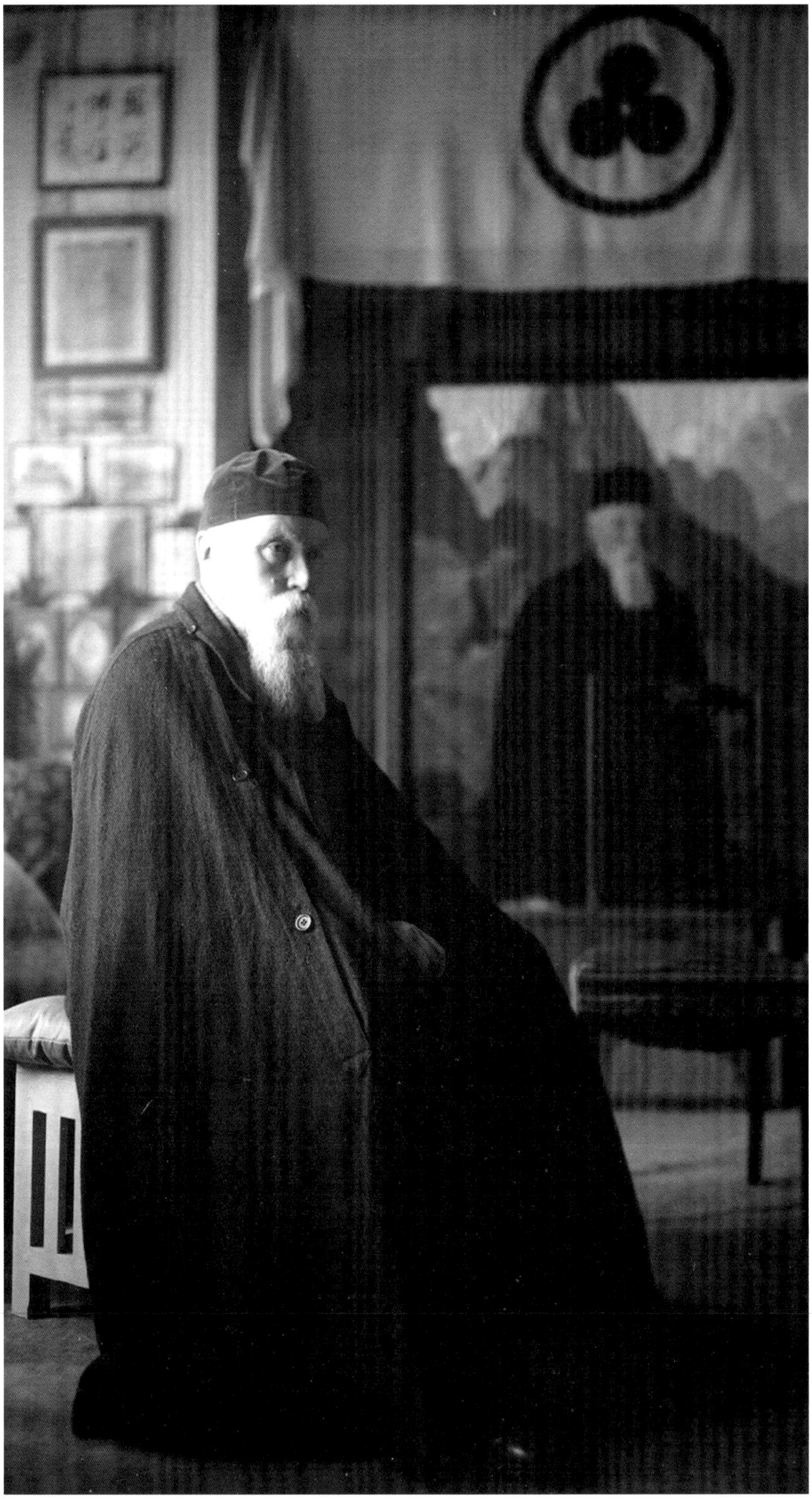

Nicholas Roerich, ca. 1937. Naggar, India. In background: his portrait by Svetoslav Roerich (Nicholas Roerich Museum Archive, NY)

The Roerich Pact and the Banner of Peace

Marga Koutsarova

The Roerich Pact—the Treaty on the Protection of Artistic and Scientific Institutions and Historic Monuments—was the first international treaty to provide a comprehensive solution to the problems of how cultural property should be protected. It has become the foundation of the contemporary international legal system for the protection of cultural treasures. A comparison between the Roerich Pact and the 1954 Hague Convention for the Protection of Cultural Property in the Event of Armed Conflict, and in particular, the nature of the protection provided for in these treaties, the protected objects, the criteria for their registration and the symbol for the protection thereof also establishes the larger vision of the Roerich Pact.[1] Considered alongside will be the 1977 Additional Protocol I to the Geneva Conventions, the 1999 Second Protocol to the 1954 Hague Convention and other international legal instruments.

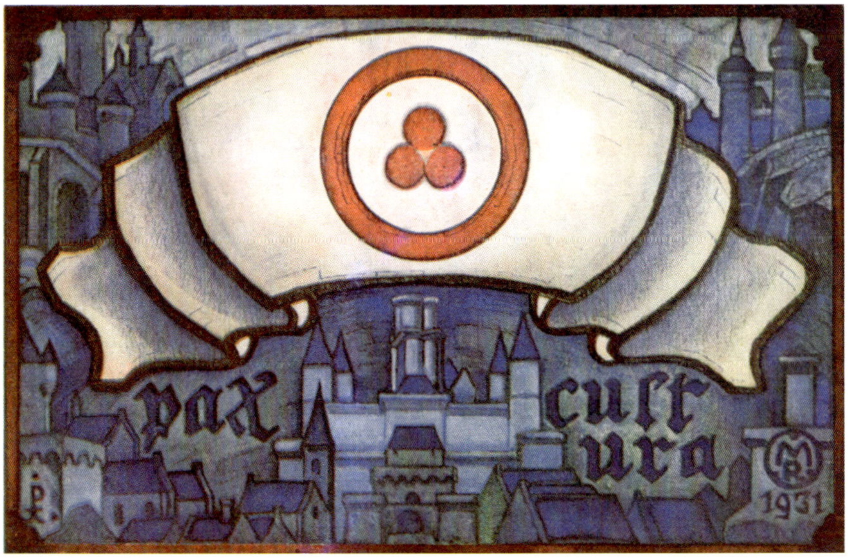

Banner of Peace, Pax Cultural 1931 (International Centre of the Roerichs, Moscow)

The 1954 Hague Convention provides in the first paragraph of its Article 4 that no act of hostility should be directed against cultural property and that such property should not be used for purposes which are likely to expose it to destruction or damage in the event of armed conflict. However, the second paragraph of the same Article states: 'The obligations mentioned in paragraph 1 of the present Article may be waived only in cases where military necessity imperatively requires such a waiver.' This reservation relates to cultural property enjoying *general protection* in accordance with the 1954 Hague Convention. The Convention also provided for *special protection* to movable and immovable cultural property of very great importance. But this is also conditional protection as it may be waived 'in exceptional cases of unavoidable military necessity'. The 1954 Hague Convention has borrowed this limitation from the 1907 Hague Regulations Respecting the Laws and Customs of War on Land, where the destruction and the seizure of the enemy's property is forbidden unless such destruction or seizure be imperatively demanded by the necessities of war.[2] However, these notions—'imperative military necessity' and 'exceptional cases of unavoidable military necessity'—were not clearly defined in the 1954 Hague Convention and their content has thus remained vague.[3] Adopted in 1977, the Protocol additional to the Geneva Conventions of 12 August 1949, and relating to the Protection of victims of International Armed Conflicts (hereinafter: 1977 Additional Protocol I) withdrew the approach of the 1954 Hague Convention.[4] According to this Protocol, only military objectives are to be made the object of military attack. Civilian objects and therefore cultural objects may be attacked *only* when they have become military objectives. No exception to this rule is permissible.

The Diplomatic Conference, which adopted the 1977 Additional Protocol I, succeeded in defining the notion 'military objective' and this is considered one of its major achievements. According to Article 52 (2) of this Protocol, the definition of military objective includes two criteria that need to be fulfilled cumulatively if an object is to be considered a military objective. The first criterion relates to the nature, location, purpose and use of an object—and whether any of these characteristics lead to it making an 'effective contribution to military action'. The second criterion relates to the military advantage to be gained by destroying, capturing or neutralising a given object and this military advantage has to be 'definite, in the circumstances ruling at the time'.

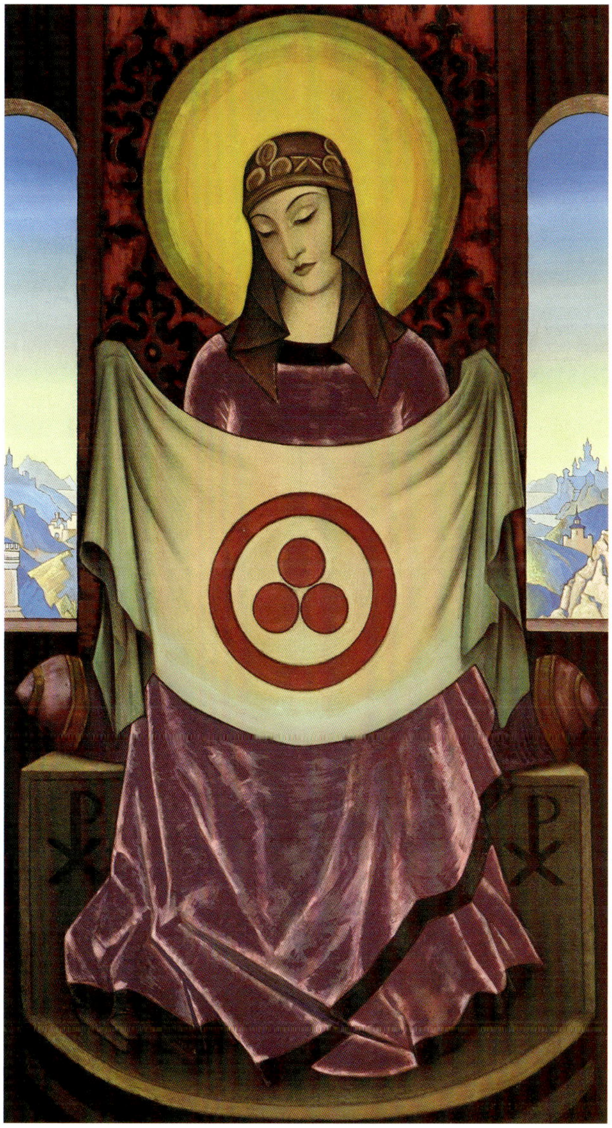

Madonna Oriflamma, 1932 (Nicholas Roerich Museum, NY)

In 1992, the Government of The Netherlands and UNESCO jointly commissioned Professor Patrick Boylan to undertake a 'wide-ranging review of the apparent failure of the 1954 Hague Convention and its Protocol (now the First Protocol) to achieve the clear and honourable objectives which this important International Legal Instrument was intended to achieve'.[5] Following the recommendations contained in Boylan's report and the enormous preparatory work done by the Government of The Netherlands and UNESCO, a Diplomatic Conference was convened, and within the framework of that the Second Protocol to the 1954 Hague Convention was signed on 17 May 1999. This Protocol entered into forcc in 2004.

The 1999 Second Protocol to the 1954 Hague Convention adopted from the 1977 Additional Protocol I to the Geneva Conventions the rule that there may be no hostile attack against cultural property except in cases, when such property becomes a military objective. Building further on this premise, the 1999 Second Protocol restricted the criteria for considering a cultural object a military objective. That was achieved as a result of considerable effort at the Diplomatic Conference in the Hague in 1999. Unlike other civilian objects, the nature and the purpose of a cultural object cannot make it a military objective, whereas its use can—there have been no arguments during the Conference on this point. However on the issue of the location of the cultural property, heated debates took place. The Greek and the Egyptian delegations, as well as the International Committee of the Red Cross firmly opposed the approach whereby the mere location of a cultural property defines it as a military objective, because such an approach would greatly diminish the protection of cultural property.[6] Although the criterion of the location of the cultural property did not carry much conviction, several delegations, mostly from NATO countries, vigorously insisted on it. A compromise was eventually reached by way of the following wording: an act of hostility may be directed against cultural property which, by its *function*, has *been made into* a military objective. One cannot but agree with Jean-Marie Henckaerts, the lawyer of the International Committee of the Red Cross who participated in the elaboration of the 1999 Second Protocol,[7] that only by a stretch of imagination it is possible to assert that the notion of 'function' covers not only the use, but also the location of the cultural property.

It may be stated here that the debate on the location related only to those cultural objects which, in accordance with the 1954 Hague Convention and the 1999 Second Protocol to it, enjoy *general protection*. As regards the cultural property which by virtue of the 1999 Second Protocol is entitled to *enhanced protection* there were no disputes whatsoever: the enhanced protection of such cultural property may be lost only if *by its use* it becomes a military objective.[8]

The Roerich Pact, signed on 15 April 1935 at the White House in Washington provides for the protection of cultural property *without reservations*. The Roerich Pact, clearly and categorically, introduced for the first time in international law, the principle of the priority of the protection of cultural property over military necessity. This principle enshrined in itself the fundamental idea that cultural property has an imperishable significance for the whole of humanity, whereas military necessity is of a transient and time-serving

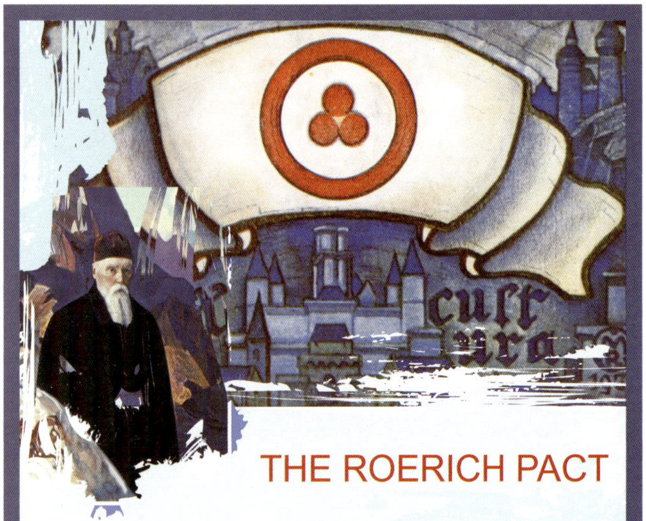

THE ROERICH PACT

In the last few decades, cultural heritage has faced destruction and plunder globally as a result of war and strife. On account of ethnic and religious cleansing, timeless archives, mosques, temples and churches have felt the severe tremors as well. In such a situation, preservation of cultural heritage from armed conflict has become a major concern.

Nicholas Roerich was one of the most remarkable peace activists. He believed that wars were dangerous in innumerable ways. Apart from killing countless innocent people, they destroy symbols of art and culture. In spite of initial hurdles like minimal international and government support, he continued developing his idea of preserving cultural treasures of the world. He moved around the world with his message of peace and preservation of art. Roerich incessantly worked towards sensitizing and uniting all nations, their governments and people engaged in war, through his idea of culture based on 'Living Ethics'.

During the Russian-Japanese War of 1905, Roerich realised the need for a special treaty for the protection of monuments of culture. Immediately after the First World began, Roerich applied to the government of Russia and other countries suggesting to them to reach an international agreement for the protection of cultural values. However, his suggestion never gained the desired support. Yet, he continued with his efforts.

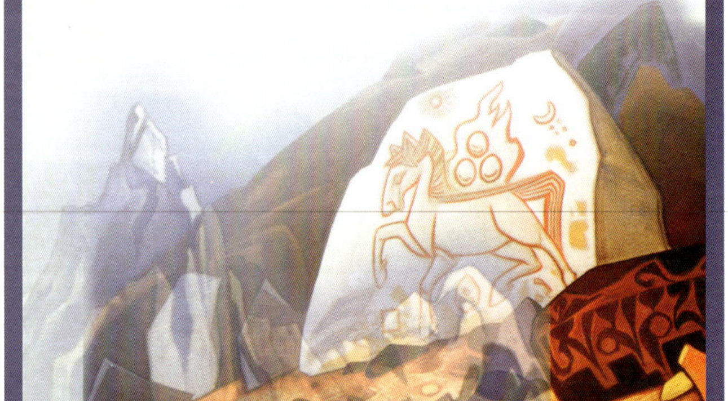

nature. This very approach to the problem of the protection of cultural property shows the tremendous difference between the Roerich Pact and the 1907 Hague Conventions respecting the Laws and Customs of War on Land and concerning Bombardment by Naval Forces in Time of War.

The Roerich Pact was conceived and elaborated as a universal international treaty. Its adoption in Washington in 1935 gave to all mankind the exceptional possibility of saving many invaluable treasures of world culture in the forthcoming World War. The intended universal character of the Roerich Pact has to be particularly stressed. The Pact introduced for the first time legal principles and rules which were then and are today also of worldwide significance. The resolution of the Third Conference on the Roerich Pact convened in November 1933 in Washington, recommended the adoption of the Pact by the governments of all nations as a demonstration of the noble attitude of their peoples towards protection of culture.[9] Furthermore, the Treaty offered that States, which do not become signatories to the Treaty on the date it was opened for signature, may sign or adhere to it at any time.[11] The Preamble of the Roerich Pact states the object of this international treaty: the universal adoption of a flag (the Banner of Peace), already designed and generally known. At the signing of the Treaty, President Roosevelt, endorsing its importance said: 'In opening this Pact to the adherence of the nations of the world, we are endeavouring to make of universal application one of the principles vital to the preservation of modern civilisation.'[11]

That many countries, and in particular the European countries, did not adhere to the Roerich Pact on the eve of the Second World War,[12] lead to the loss of invaluable and irreplaceable treasures of human genius. The 1907 Hague Conventions did not help protect the treasures of culture as was demonstrated by the First World War. In his address to the 1933 Third Conference on the Roerich Pact, Michel de Taube specifically mentioned that '...both 1907 Conventions have demonstrated clearly enough during the World War their incapability' to effectively protect cultural objects.[13] Unfortunately this was confirmed in the Second World War as well. After the Second World War, yet another opportunity to retain the highest standards in the international legal protection of cultural property achieved by the Roerich Pact was missed. The Pact was not offered for adherence to all the countries in the world and therefore it remained a regional treaty.

During the Diplomatic Conference, which adopted the 1954 Hague Convention, it was the US and the United Kingdom that insisted on the 'military necessity' reservation. [14] An interesting fact at the Conference is worth mentioning—the representative of Romania pointed out that no such reservation exists in the Roerich Pact and it is striking that the US in particular, which had signed and ratified the Roerich Pact earlier, insisted on the inclusion of this reservation.[15] 'The position of the United States at the Conference,' notes Professor P. Boylan in 1993, 'seems particularly illogical since it was (and remains) a Party to the 1935 Washington Pan-American Treaty ('Roerich Pact'), which requires unconditional 'respect and protection' with no hint of any 'military necessity' exemption.'[16] A substantial number of states represented at the 1954 Hague Diplomatic Conference were opposed to the 'military necessity' reservation, including France, Greece, Spain and the countries of the former 'socialist' block. The Anglo-Saxon countries, however, made it clear that this reservation is a *conditio sine qua non* for their acceptance of the Convention.[17] As a result the Conference adopted the reservation and it was included in the text of the 1954 Hague Convention which, in this respect, made a step backward in comparison to the Roerich Pact. And it took another half a century before the Second Protocol to the 1954 Hague Convention managed to achieve, in 2004, the level of unconditional protection that the Roerich Pact had envisaged as early as 1935!

Article 5 of the Roerich Pact provides that cultural property shall cease to enjoy the protection envisaged in the Pact in case *it is made use of* for military purposes. *It is to be noted, that neither the location of the cultural property, nor any other factor, apart from its use for military purposes, may serve as the reason for waiving the protection granted to cultural property by the Roerich Pact.* This approach, which is simple and the only correct one, has been accepted by the Second Protocol to the 1954 Hague Convention in relation to the cultural objects enjoying enhanced protection. One could say that as a whole, due to compromises in the wording, it has been adopted also in relation to cultural objects enjoying general protection. This was accomplished more than sixty years after the signing of the Roerich Pact.

The Second Protocol to the 1954 Hague Convention contains new rules, which are not in the Roerich Pact and the 1954 Hague Convention, and which provide for additional guarantees for the protection of cultural property. In accordance with this Protocol, a cultural property which has become a military objective may be attacked only if there is no alternative and only after an effective advance warning has been given whenever circumstances permit. Another significant achievement of the Second Protocol to the 1954 Hague Convention is the provision for attributing individual criminal responsibility on persons responsible for violation of the international rules on the protection of cultural property.

List of protected cultural property. *Criteria and procedure for inclusion in the list*:

> As per the 1954 Hague Convention, when cultural property is subject to *general protection*, it is not listed and its protection may be waived in cases of 'imperative military necessity'. *The special protection*, which has been established with a view of preserving such treasures of culture as the Versailles Palace, the Taj Mahal or the Hermitage, requires listing of the respective cultural property in the International Register of Cultural Property under Special Protection. This too may be waived 'in exceptional cases of unavoidable military necessity'. However, this system of special protection proved to be unviable.[18] In over fifty years after the adoption of the 1954 Hague Convention only five objects have been listed in this International Register—the Vatican and four refuges of cultural property (in the Netherlands and Germany).[19]

Several reasons account for the extremely limited success of the special protection system under the Hague Convention. First of all, in order to be included in its list, a cultural object has to be situated at an adequate distance from any large industrial centre or from any important military objective. Apart from the fact, that there is no agreement on what 'adequate distance' actually designates, the above condition is almost impossible to fulfill, since many treasures of culture are located in city centres, where they are surrounded by potential military objectives.[20] In the second place, any state which is Party to the Convention may lodge an objection to the entry of cultural property in the Register.[21] The practice of the past years has shown that often objections are raised to the entry of cultural objects in the International Register on grounds which may have no relation to culture whatsoever.[22]

While preserving the special protection under the 1954 Hague Convention, the 1999 Second Protocol established a new system of *enhanced protection* of cultural property which has to be entered into a separate list. States party to the Protocol have the right to object to an entry proposed by another State party only on grounds that relate to the significance of the cultural property, to its protection on national level and to the obligations of the proposing state not to use the respective cultural property for military purposes.

On comparing the criteria and procedure for entry in the list of protected cultural property as envisaged by the Roerich Pact and as by the 1954 Hague Convention, the Roerich Pact formulated a much more flexible system, which corresponds to the complexities of life. In accordance with Article 4 of the Roerich Pact, the signatory Governments and those which accede to the Pact are required to send to the Pan American Union[23] a list of the monuments and institutions for which they desire protection. Thus, unlike the 1954 Hague Convention and the Second Protocol to it, the Roerich Pact provides for the listing of *all* cultural property requiring protection. Each State that has signed or acceded to the Pact independently draws its list and there are no conditions or restrictions regarding inclusion of monuments or institutions in this list.

The Second Protocol, that aimed at eliminating the imperfect provisions of the Hague Convention, provided solutions which are closer in spirit to the Roerich Pact: it revoked the onerous and unrealistic requirement of adequate distance of a cultural object and has limited the number of those entitled to take decisions on inclusion in the enhanced protection list.

The Convention concerning the Protection of the World Cultural and Natural Heritage adopted in Paris in 1972, established the World Heritage List. The 1954 Hague Convention, regulates the protection of cultural property only during armed conflicts—its International Register of Cultural Property under Special Protection is valid in wartime.

Thus, in accordance with these two conventions, two lists of cultural property exist. The success of the World Heritage List served as an incentive to try and alleviate the criteria for entry to the list in time of armed conflict. Hence the creation of a list of cultural property under enhanced protection by the 1999 Second Protocol to the 1954 Hague Convention.

In the absence of a wartime list, UNESCO successfully availed itself of the World Heritage List. During the war in the former Yugoslavia, UNESCO referred to the World Heritage List in relation to Dubrovnik and as a result this city was more or less spared.[24] It needs to be stressed that a list which was not intended for wartime purposes served to protect during armed conflict. The worldwide renown and the authority of the World Heritage List helped to protect Dubrovnik. This attests Nicholas Roerich's idea of the greatest *educational importance* of the legal protection of cultural property in time of peace. The very fact of such protection cultivates in the consciousness of people, respect for cultural property and appreciation of its significance.

In 1993, the Executive Board of UNESCO adopted a decision inviting States party to both the Hague Convention and the 1972 Convention concerning the Protection of the World Cultural and Natural Heritage which had sites listed on the World Heritage List to consider the possibility of nominating them for the International Register of Cultural Property under Special Protection.[25] Although this decision of the Executive Board of UNESCO did not bring about concrete results, the initiative itself is welcome as it testifies to an orientation towards a single list for the treasures of culture of mankind.

The Roerich Pact provided for the protection of cultural property both

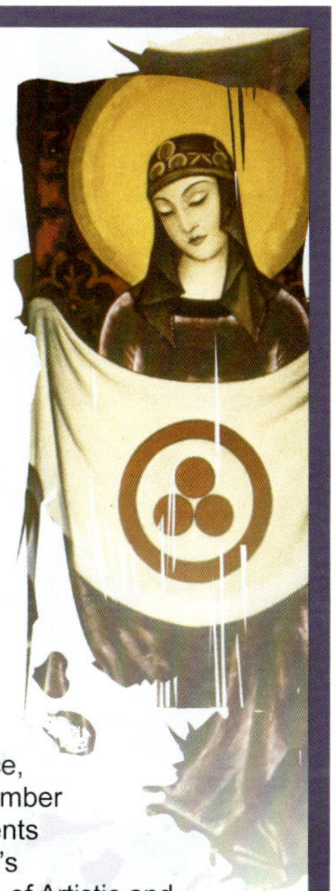

In 1929, in collaboration with a number of lawyers and artists, Roerich drafted a pact for the protection of artistic and scientific treasures of the world. While appealing for help and support, he did not only go to the governments but also to the people of various culturally rich countries. According to Roerich, the pact was to protect the values of human genius. In 1931, in the Belgian city of Bruges, the Roerich Pact International Union was founded. In September of the same year, the First International Conference took place in Bruges. Roerich's idea of the establishment of the 'League for Protection of Cultural Artifacts' was discussed and the 'Day of Culture' founded. This Pact gained worldwide fame. The Third International Conference, which took place in Washington in November in 1933, recommended to the governments of all countries to sign the Pact, Roerich's Pact—International Treaty on Protection of Artistic and Scientific Institutions and Historical Monuments—was signed on April 15, 1935, in Washington, in the White House, in the presence of the then American President Franklin D. Roosevelt.

The Pact consisted of eight clauses and called for the protection of cultural values not only during was but in times of peace as well. The USA and twenty countries from Central and South America signed the Pact. Active movements in support of Roerich's Pact renewed after the World War II ended. In 1950, the Roerich Pact Committee in New York handed to UNESCO all the documentation related to the pact. In 1954, on the basis of Roerich's Pact, the international 'Convention for the Protection of the Cultural Property at the Time of Armed Conflict' was passed in the Hague. The representatives of six countries, including the Soviet Union, signed the convention.

Painter, archaeologist, explorer, visionary, peace activist Nicholas Roerich devoted the last two decades of his life to research expeditions in Central Asia and his passion for painting in his Himalayan home in India. He painted the majestic mountain peaks of the Himalayas, the far-flung landscapes and their peoples, together with their history, legends and spiritual traditions. Most of his paintings were made available on the internet in late 1990's and enabled art-lovers the world over to appreciate his artistic creations.

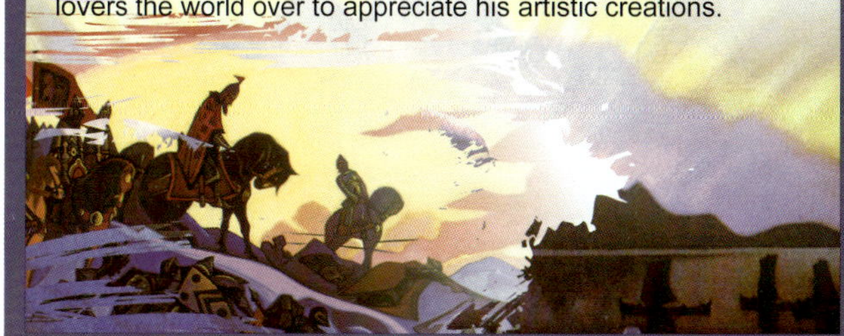

in times of peace and in wartime and it envisaged a single list for this purpose. The latter provision of the Pact demands our special attention. The events of the last fifty years confirm the viability and correctness of this approach. Cultural property should be protected, as it is written in the Pact, 'in any time of danger' and a single list should direct such a protection. Different lists imply that it is not the principle of protection of culture that is being followed but rather military considerations.

Objects of Protection

The Roerich Pact provided for the protection of the most comprehensive range of objects of culture: historic monuments, museums; artistic, cultural, scientific and educational institutions.[26]

It is worth noting that the Roerich Pact protects both movable and immovable cultural property. Some authors have expressed the opinion that the Roerich Pact envisages the protection of just immovable cultural property.[27] It is not possible to agree with this opinion. In the draft of the Roerich Pact published in 1929 it is said:

> 'The historic Monuments, educational, artistic and scientific Institutions, artistic and scientific Missions, the personnel, *the property and collections* of such Institutions and Missions above mentioned shall be deemed neutral and, as such, shall be protected and respected by belligerents.'[28]

The wording of the text clarifies that the draft of the Pact provided for the protection of movable cultural property. In the text of the Pact adopted in April 1935, the words 'the property and collections' are no longer present, but it is inconceivable that the international legal protection of movable cultural property was abandoned. The protection of the museums stipulated in Article 1 of the Roerich Pact presupposes the protection of the buildings of the museums and of their exhibits, that is, of all movable cultural valuables preserved therein, since a building on its own is not a museum but at best a monument of architecture or history. This argument applies as well to the movable cultural property preserved in the scientific, educational, cultural and artistic institutions protected by the Roerich Pact.

The Roerich Pact also provides for the protection of the *personnel* of the above mentioned institutions.

Finally, as is rightly pointed out by E. Alexandrov, the protection accorded by the Roerich Pact covers not only the material substances of the Institutions, but also their *non-material* characteristics—their legal status, the achieved recognition, the nature of their activity, their place in social and cultural life, the conditions for developing the institutions' specific activities, etc.[29] This broad interpretation of the protection envisaged by the Roerich Pact pertains also to the protection of the personnel of these institutions: not only their physical integrity, but also *their mental integrity* is entitled to protection. The latter implies securing the possibilities and conditions for the work of the personnel and for the manifestation of their creative potential.[30]

It follows from Article 1 of the 1954 Hague Convention, that the Convention protects—using the legal terminology of the Roerich Pact—historic monuments, museums and *some cultural institutions* (large libraries and depositaries of archives; refuges, intended to shelter, in the event of armed conflict, the movable cultural property enumerated in Article 1 of the Convention). The Convention uses the descriptive method of detailed enumeration of these objects. The 1999 Second Protocol to the Hague Convention did not introduce any changes as to the scope of the protected objects and personnel. It is evident from the above provisions of the Hague Convention, that unlike the Roerich Pact it does not protect:

> Scientific institutions (except for scientific collections); educational institutions; the personnel of the museums and of the cultural, artistic, scientific and educational institutions, that is, persons engaged in creative work.

The Roerich Pact, it may be concluded, provides for a much broader scope of protected objects than the 1954 Hague Convention:

To Carry the Banner of Culture

Today one can say with confidence: in spite of the regional character of the Roerich Pact, it is the fundamental international treaty in the field of cultural property protection. The Pact introduced for the first time and established in international law the following principles and rules:

- cultural property, irrespective of its ownership and state allegiance, belongs to all mankind as its cultural heritage;

- cultural property enjoys unconditional protection and respect in time of armed conflict;
- cultural property loses the protection it is entitled to only in cases when it is used for military purposes;
- cultural property must be protected in time of peace;
- cultural property has to be registered and included in list with a view of its protection both in time of peace and in wartime;
- generally known and obligatory sign for the protection of cultural property in time of peace and in time of armed conflict is to be established (the Banner of Peace);
- application of the national regime of protection to the foreign cultural property.

It should be added that the provisions in this treaty relating to the protection of cultural property 'in any time of danger' (the Preamble of the Roerich Pact), in wartime and in time of peace (Article 1, Paragraph 3) are extremely important. It is owing to them that the Roerich Pact is applicable both to international armed conflicts and to conflicts of non-international character. At the Third Washington Conference on the Roerich Pact official representatives of states as well as lawyers pointed out to this purpose of the Roerich Pact.[31]

Not only is the Roerich Pact a tremendous achievement of mankind, it is a matter of true pride for the signatory countries, particularly the country which was the leader in the cause for its advancement and adoption—the United States of America. Due to a number of circumstances, the US has discontinued its patronage of the ideas of the Roerich Pact and has not taken further upon itself the leading role in the field of the protection of cultural treasures.

The 1954 Hague Convention at present is the universal international treaty for the protection of cultural property in the event of armed conflict, ratified by many countries in the world.[32] The Convention has taken over many of the most important principles and rules of the Roerich Pact, however it differs from it in a fundamentally important point: it subordinates the protection of cultural property to military necessity. The 1977 Additional Protocol I to the Geneva Conventions has made a very important contribution to the protection of cultural property. The adopted in 1999 Second Protocol to the 1954 Hague Convention, which came into force in 2004, is a significant achievement of contemporary international law.

The 1972 Convention concerning the Protection of the World Cultural and Natural Heritage undoubtedly consolidated and developed the principle of the Roerich Pact of protection of cultural property in time of peace, even though it does not refer to the Roerich Pact.

Cultural property is threatened, as we all know, not just by armed conflicts, but also by shortsighted government policy in time of peace—for example by 'imperative financial necessity' to cut down on the required funding for the maintenance and development of cultural objects. Let us recall the words of Nicholas Roerich, that most important for us should be the spirit and creativity, then comes health and only in the third place—wealth.[33] The Roerich Pact bears in itself the potential for integrating these ideas of Nicholas Roerich in international relations. We should note that in the Pact there is no reservation of imperative financial necessity which could waive the obligation to protect cultural property and respectively allow the systemic cutting down on the funding of the culture institutions and their personnel.

Nicholas Roerich's idea for establishing a Banner of Peace Fund, to a certain extent, has been implemented —the 1972 Convention concerning the Protection of the World Cultural and Natural Heritage set up a Fund for providing financial support to states to supplement their efforts at the preservation of cultural treasures of world significance. The 1999 Second Protocol also provides for the setting up of a Fund, aiming to assist the protection of cultural property during armed conflict. Let us recall however that the Roerich Pact provides for an all-embracing protection of the objects of culture as well as of the personnel of the artistic, scientific and educational institutions. Let us also recall the words of Nicholas Roerich that the Banner of Peace Fund shall provide financial support to those who are carrying the message of Beauty, and of knowledge to the broad sections of the public. The above said makes it clear that an International Fund working under the aegis of the Banner of Peace and aiming at the development of the cultures of the peoples of the world and *an all-embracing education* has not yet been established and its establishment, when this happens, shall become the true possibility for the development of many countries–of all the human family on our Planet.

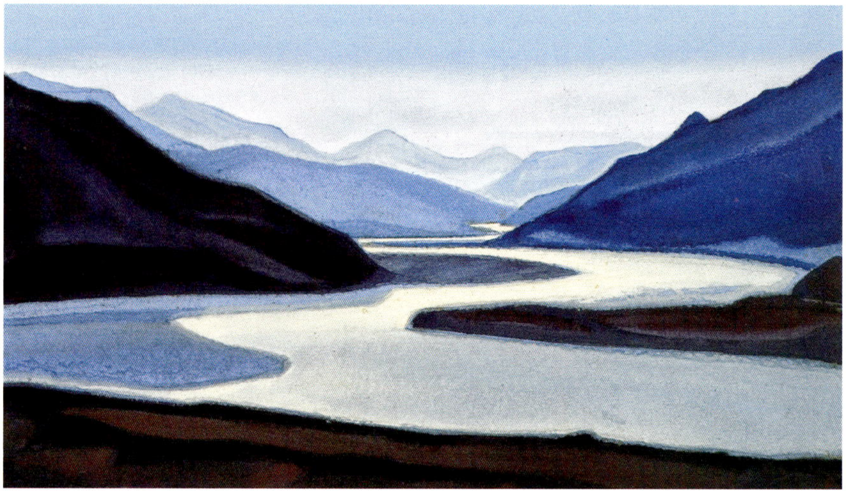

Brahmaputra, 1946 (International Centre of the Roerichs, Moscow)

'But a world-wide fund, in which everyone shall contribute one's voluntary mite,' writes Nicholas Roerich, 'shall be the sign that humanity has already become mature enough and is capable of carrying the Banner of Culture.'[34]

This, of course, is a task which is enormous in its scale and extremely difficult. Its fulfilment requires the united efforts of the international community, states and people. Even though it may be a long way to go before humanity becomes capable of carrying the Banner of Culture, there is no doubt that this is the only way forward.

End Notes

1. As this paper is published in abridged version, the section on the sign for protection has been omitted.
2. Regulations Respecting the Laws and Customs of War on Land, Article 23 (g). The Regulation is the Annex to the Hague Convention (IV) Respecting the Laws and Customs of War on Land (done at the Hague, 18 October 1907).
3. *Hladik Jan*. The 1954 Hague Convention for the Protection of Cultural Property in the Event of Armed Conflict and the notion of military necessity. International Review of the Red Cross, No. 835, p. 621-635.
4. *Henckaerts Jean-Marie*. New rules for the protection of cultural property in armed conflict. International Review of the Red Cross, No. 835, p. 593-620. The Electronic version of this article at: http://www.icrc.org (Info resources\International Review\1999-No. 835).
5. *Patrick Boylan*, 'The Significance of the 1954 Hague Convention and its 1999 Second Protocol in relation to the Protection of Cultural Property in the Event of Armed Conflict', *Cultural Policy, Criticism and Management*, 2005, Issue 1. City University, London, p. 2. *The First Protocol to the 1954 Hague Convention was also adopted in 1954.*
6. Jean-Marie Henckaerts at http://www.icrc.org. (Info resources\International Review\1999-No. 835).
7. Jean-Marie Henckaerts represented the International Committee of the Red Cross at the 1999 Diplomatic Conference, which has adopted the Second Protocol to the 1954 Hague Convention. The International Committee of the Red Cross had the status of observer at the Conference.
8. Jean-Marie Henckaerts at http://www.icrc.org.
9. Documents of the Third International Conference on the Roerich Pact and the Banner of Peace in Washington, 17-18 November, 1933, Archive of the International Centre of the Roerichs, p. 102.
10. Article 6 of the Roerich Pact.
11. Znamya Mira. Mezhdunarodnyi Tsentr Rerihov. Moskva. 1995, p. 145.

12. The Roerich Pact was signed by the United States and 20 American Republics, namely: Argentina, Bolivia, Brazil, Chile, Colombia, Costa Rica, Cuba, Dominican Republic, Ecuador, El Salvador, Guatemala, Haiti, Honduras, Mexico, Nicaragua, Panama, Paraguay, Peru, Uruguay, Venezuela.
13. Address by Michel de Taube, member of the International Law Institute and of the American International Law Institute, member of the International Law Academy in the Hague, to the 1933 Third Conference on the Roerich Pact. Znamya Mira. Mezhdunarodnyi Tsentr Rerihov. Moskva, 2005, p. 137. Michel de Taube refers to the 1907 Hague Convention respecting the Laws and Customs of War on Land and the 1907 Hague Convention concerning Bombardment by Naval Forces in Time of War.
14. *Boylan Patrick.* Review of the Convention for the Protection of Cultural Property in the Event of Armed Conflict (The Hague Convention of 1954). Paris, UNESCO, 1993, p. 56.

15. *Emil Alexandrov*, International Legal Protection of Cultural Property, 1979, Sofia: Sofia Press, p. 145.
16. *Boylan Patrick.* Review of the Convention for the Protection of Cultural Property in the Event of Armed Conflict (The Hague Convention of 1954), pp. 56-57.
17. The United States ratified the 1954 Hague Convention for the Protection of Cultural Property in the Event of Armed Conflict on 13.03.2009. The United Kingdom has not yet ratified it.
18. Jean-Marie Henckaerts at. http://www.icrc.org.
19. Since the adoption of the Hague Convention in 1954 there have been registered 9 objects in the International Register of Cultural Property under Special Protection. The registration of four of these objects (refuges for cultural property) has been subsequently cancelled on the request of the states which have jurisdiction over them. See UNESCO document CLT-2005/WS/6 'Report on the implementation of the 1954 Hague Convention for the Protection of Cultural Property in the Event of Armed Conflict and its two 1954 and 1999 Protocols. Report of the activities from 1995 to 2004. p. 2
20. Jean-Marie Henckaerts at. http://www.icrc.org.
21. If an objection has been lodged there has to be initiated a procedure of arbitration or of voting, in the latter case the Parties to the Convention may vote. If the voting procedure has started the objection will be confirmed only if the Parties so decide by a two-third majority of the Parties voting. See Article 14 of the Regulations for the Execution of the Convention for the Protection of Cultural Property in the event of Armed Conflict.
22. Jiri Toman. *The Protection of Cultural Property in the event of Armed Conflict*, 1996, Dartmouth, Unesco, Aldershot, Paris, pp. 108-109. Cited in: Jean-Marie Henckaerts, at http://www.icrc.org.
23. At present: General Secretariat of the Organization of American States.
24. *Jean-Marie Henckaerts*. New rules for the protection of cultural property in armed conflict. http://www.icrc.org
25. UNESCO document CLT-2005/WS/6 'Report on the implementation of the 1954 Hague Convention for the Protection of Cultural Property in the Event of Armed Conflict and its two 1954 and 1999 Protocols. Report of the activities from 1995 to 2004', p. 2.
26. Article 1, Paragraph 1, of the Roerich Pact.
27. *Boguslavskyi M.M.* Pakt Reriha. // Mir cherez Kul'turu. [Sb. St.], Moskva: Sov. Pisatel', 1990, p. 15.
28. Italics added.
29. Emil Alexandrov, 1979, p. 92.
30. *Ibid*
31. Materials of the Third International Conference on the Roerich Pact and the Banner of Peace in Washington D.C. 17-18 November, 1933. / Znamya Mira. Moskva. 2005, p. 115, 127.
32. The 1954 Hague Convention has been ratified at present by 123 states. See the UNESCO website: http://portal.unesco.org/culture/en and the International Humanitarian Law database of the International Committee of the Red Cross. http://www.icrc.org/ihl.nsf
33. *Rerih N.K.* Derzhava Sveta. Sviaschennyi dozor. Riga, 'Vieda'. 1992, p. 62.
34. Znamya Mira. Mehzunarodnyi Tsentr Rerihov. Moskva, 1995, p. 76.

The Roerich Pact Committee in India

Marga Koutsarova

India responded affirmatively to the idea of an international treaty for the protection of treasures of culture. In 1948, distinguished representatives of Indian culture and science became members of the Roerich Pact Committee in India which aimed at the advancement and the adoption of the Pact. Among its members there were: Honorable R.K. Shanmukham Chetty, Finance Minister; Shanti Gurjar, Barrister-at-law; Honorable S.P. Muckerjee, Supply Minister; Honorable Amrit Kaur, Health Minister; Honorable Vijaya Lakshmi Pandit, Ambassador to Soviet Russia; Lady Sigrid Hydari, Wife of the Governor of Assam; Svetoslav Roerich, Vice-President of All India Association of Art, and others.

In January 1948, at the opening ceremony of the exhibition of Nicholas Roerich's paintings in Delhi,

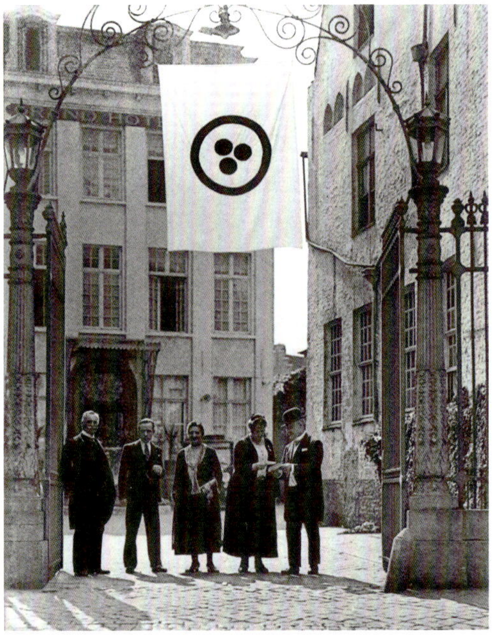

Delegates to the 2nd Conference of the International Union for the Roerich Pact in Bruges. August 1932 (International Centre of the Roerichs, Moscow)

Jawaharlal Nehru made a splendid speech on the significance of Roerich's art and he particularly stressed the idea of the Banner of Peace. And in August 1948, the Government of India headed by Nehru took a decision to adopt the Roerich Pact.

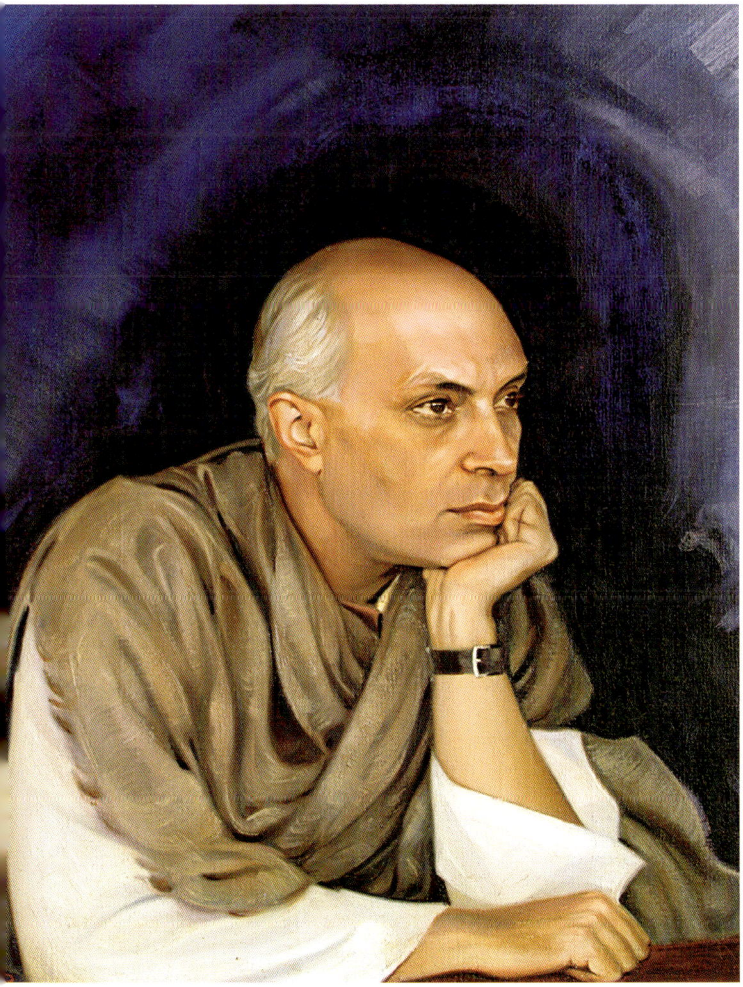

'When I think of Nicholas Roerich, I am astounded at the scope and abundance of his activities and creative genius. A great artist, a great scholar and writer, archaeologist and explorer, he touched and lighted up so many aspects of human endeavour. The very quantity is stupendous—thousands of paintings and each one of them a great work of art. When you look at these great mountains which have towered over the Indian plain and been our sentinels for ages past. They remind us of our spiritual heritage so much not merely of the India of the past but of something that is permanent and eternal about India, that we cannot help feeling a great sense of indebtedness to Nicholas Roerich who has enshrined that spirit in these magnificent canvases.'

Pandit Jawaharlal Nehru by Svetoslav Roerich, 1946 (International Centre of the Roerichs, Moscow)

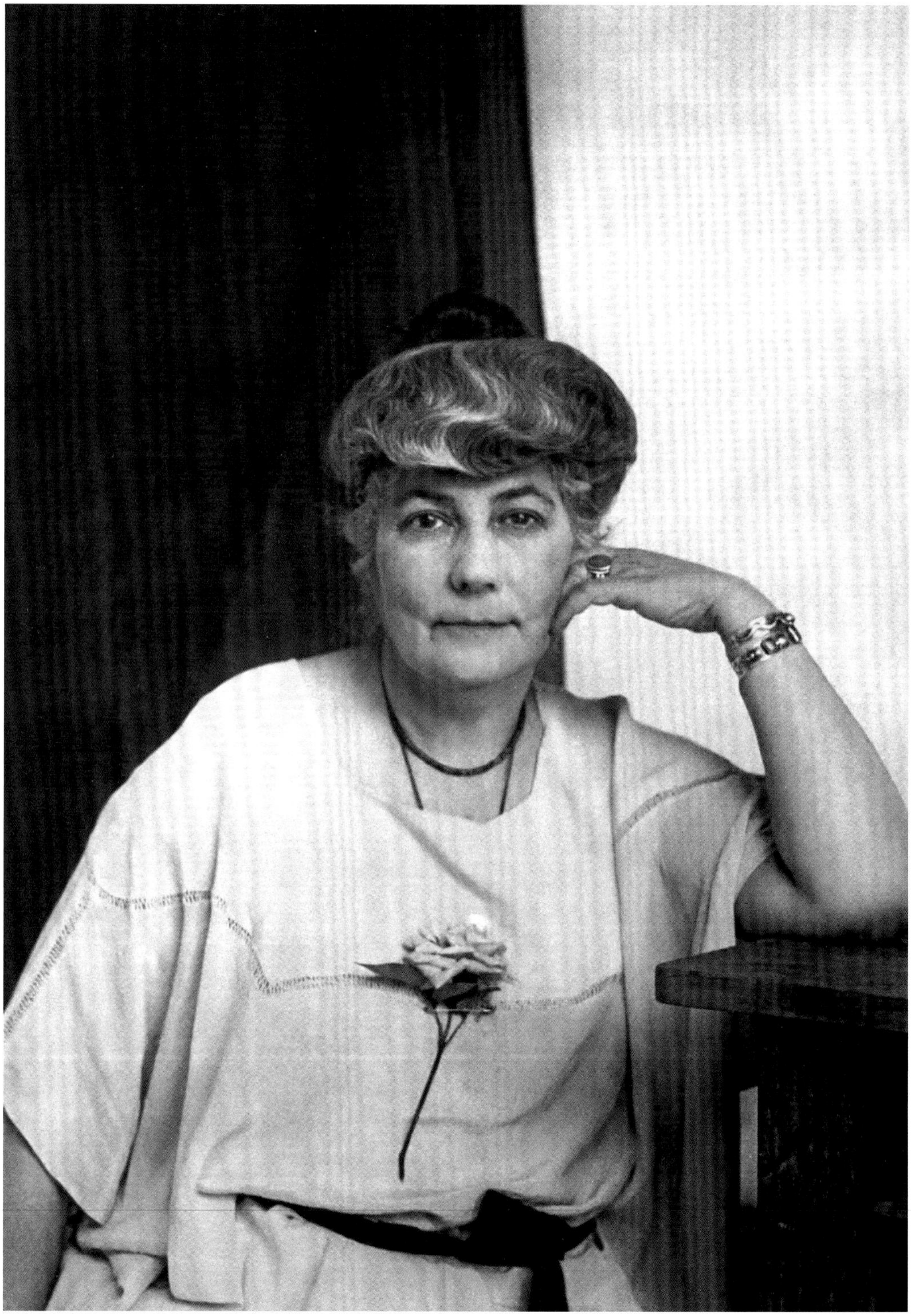

Helena Roerich ca. 1940, Naggar, India. (Nicholas Roerich Museum Archive, NY)

Living Ethics:
An Aspect of Agni Yoga

Marina Bernardi

The Russian artist Nicholas Roerich was a multifaceted personality who expressed himself in several fields, through arts, science, politics and religion. Behind each, shone through the unifying thread of his vision. It was a vision that was shared by all the members of his family, so much so that although they gave expression to their personalities through different fields, it is impossible to draw a distinction among them when it comes to their fundamental ideas and thought.

Iskander and the Hermit, 1938 (International Centre of the Roerichs, Moscow)

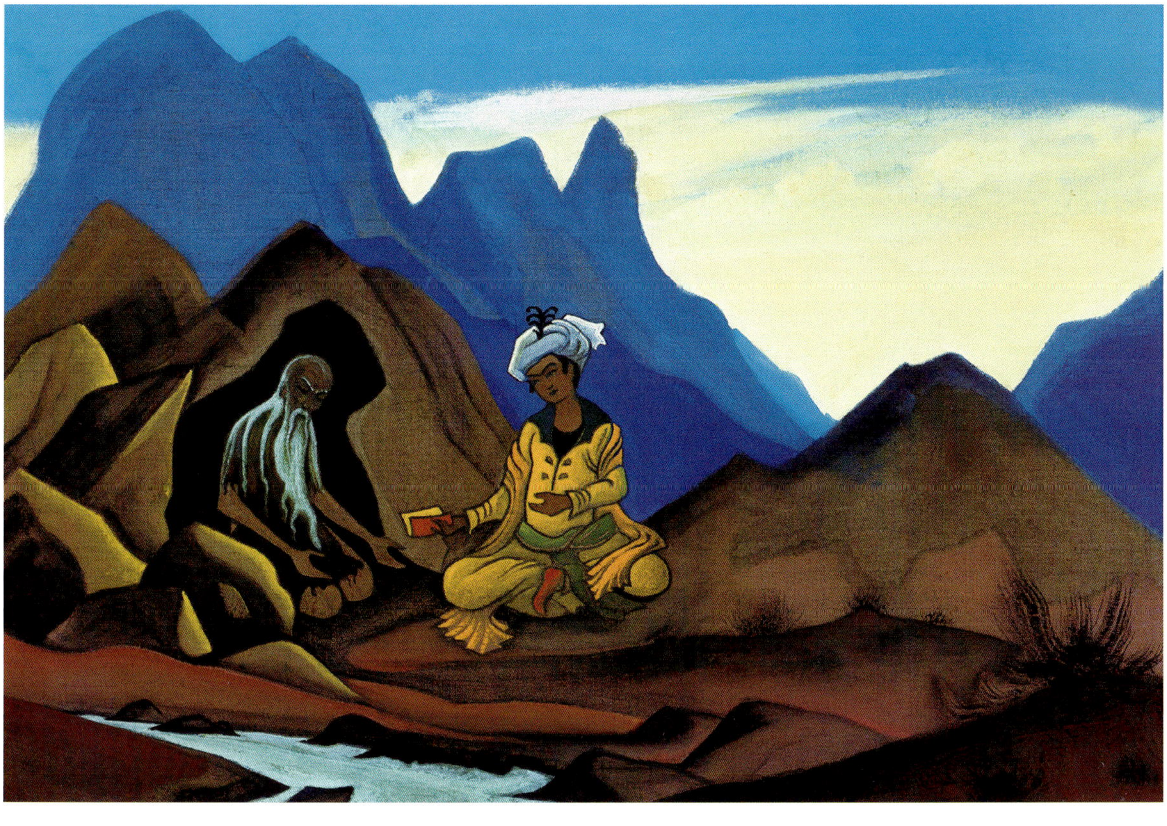

Nicholas Roerich's vision made him a precursor and visionary of a New Age. His philosophy set man inside a dense network of relationships: with himself, with his mentor or Guide, with other human beings, with other kingdoms, both subhuman and superhuman, that is to say, the kingdoms of heaven, manifested through the planets, the sun, the stars, and through the vast space verging on the Infinite.

What are the fundamental points of this philosophy?

First of all, we find the hypothesis of the existence of a guiding principle, which orients, coordinates and synthesises both macro-cosmic and micro-cosmic life. If the individual understanding can sense and access such a principle, it will strive to live by an ethical vision, in which all singularity is united with and ascribable to the Whole.

From this concept comes the term 'Living Ethics', a name attributed to the overall philosophy of the Roerichs. It indicates a free, spontaneous, voluntary adherence and application to the higher principles and values that guide cosmic evolution. The first step in living in correspondence with the light of Living Ethics is to persistently cultivate an internal attitude of attention to the subtle and invisible aspects and meanings of everything that happens on the physical level. This implies a bifocal view in each moment of one's life: commitment to acting and building on the concrete and manifested field, and concentration on perceiving and understanding the 'hidden aspect' of things, the subtle meaning and value of each event. The latter is an activity of the conscious mind.

These perceptions of elevated consciousness can be expressed through 'work'. Therefore, 'work' acquires a sacredness as it becomes an instrument between the subtle world of higher ideas and the concrete world of matter. This awareness can turn even the humblest job into a sacred and creative activity. Consequently one realises that the fulfilment of one's potential does not depend on the social or economic value of a craft or profession, but on an awareness that man and his work is a means between heaven and earth. In order to fulfil such a sacred function, work must be conscious, intense, dynamic, orderly, rhythmic and joyous. Work, in all its aspects, should represent human commitment towards the building of a new world. No matter how humble work may be, it is an invaluable contribution to the creation of the future, if it is performed in obedience to the Higher Laws.

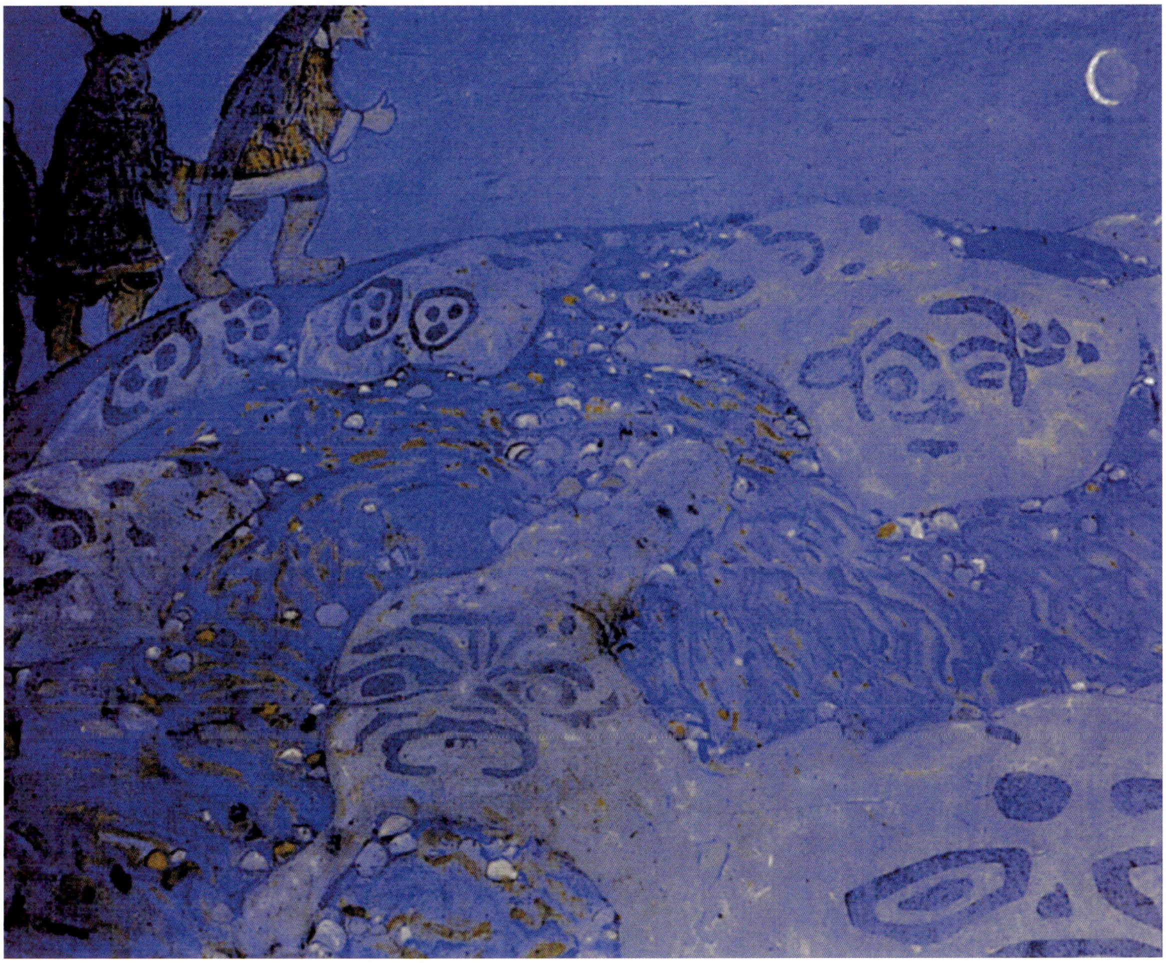

Conjuration of the Earth, 1907 (State Russian Museum, St. Petersburg)

The word obedience evokes an apparently opposite term: freedom, a core value in Roerich's philosophy. Man can set himself free from the chains of the material world only in so far as his consciousness is able to intuit the higher Laws, which have a universal and absolute value, and in so far as he decides to abide by them.

The Higher Laws ruling the universe aim at guiding the evolutionary process of man towards a unitary point of synthesis, in which the multiplicity and differentiation of existing forms of life are reabsorbed into a fundamental unity. Each being in each kingdom has an essential nucleus; all these nuclei are connected, and together they form One.

Man can consciously experience such essential unity by deliberately cultivating the value of brotherhood which finds its expression and manifestation in co-operation. Co-operation means working together towards a common goal, for Common Good, and acknowledging the interdependence of everybody's work. The individual is asked to find his own role in the joint work, and to perform it to the best of his capability, thus contributing to a final result which transcends the individual good and asserts a 'Higher Good'. Co-operation works as an antithesis to competition, so widespread and destructive in today's world.

Beauty is another fundamental value in Living Ethics. Beauty is evident everywhere: in nature, in art, in interpersonal relationships, in words, in daily events. It is considered a powerful instrument for the elevation of the spirit and transformation of one's consciousness.

Culture in particular—the composite sum of the most beautiful and profound things man has produced in the history of mankind—is the epitome of Beauty. Culture is also an instrument of transformation of human consciousness. Since by its very nature, it is the fruit of inspiration—that is to say the artist's contact with the most refined area of her/his consciousness. Culture has the power to arouse and evoke the latent potential in man's heart, thus enabling a new vision of life and new channels of self expression. The Roerichs also attribute to Culture the foremost capacity of healing and overcoming society's evils, of initiating peace and through it the salvation of humanity. Another function of Culture is to orient and train thought to vibrate towards wider and subtler spaces.

The correct use of thought is another foundation stone in the Roerichs' philosophy. Thought is the instrument that can elevate and refine human consciousness. First, it must be purified, and freed of the shadows of the past. It is then necessary to empower thought by constant attention and concentration. Finally, it must generate ideas of higher quality, which can be the initial seeds of beautiful and luminous works.

The concept of elevation and ascent often recurs in the philosophy of Nicholas Roerich. Human life is viewed as an ascending progression, with continuous conquest of new inner peaks, and of an expansion of consciousness. All on this ascending route, have their own place and can rely on those who have preceded them, at the same time assuming the task of stimulating, through their own example, those who follow. From this derives the concept of a mentor or Guide: 'Without a Guide, evolution is not possible,' states Nicholas Roerich. Devotion to the Guide and dedication of one's life to a greater and impersonal aim are a natural corollary of this concept.

Nicholas Roerich believed fire is the essence of life in all its manifestations, and is a unifying element for all beings in all kingdoms. According to him, the concept of 'fire' was not only a metaphor or an abstract idea or symbolic element, but also a concrete, tangible reality which man could consciously experience. Once man intuitively perceived this deep-seated core of his identity, he could express it in his actions, from actions taken in everyday life to the most complex activities. The conscious connection to his internal fire, or at least the intuition that such a contact exists, enabled man to acknowledge fire in all of that which surrounds him, and to relate to the beings around him so that a 'reciprocal fire exchange' could be activated.

The Roerichs' philosophy aims at promoting evolution, improving and transforming consciousness. Through his writings and paintings, Nicholas Roerich suggested the kind of behaviour and qualities that were needed to be cultivated in order to light the fire in one's own psyche. Therefore, 'lighting the fire in the psyche' had a concrete and pragmatic meaning, directed at making life more beautiful and valuable. It is a matter of finding 'fire sources' to draw fire from, which allow one to absorb fire in oneself, thus increasing one's psychic energy. The external manifestations of a man, who has ignited his psyche in this manner, actually gives out sparks of light, which act as activators or catalysts for his own spiritual growth and that of others.

All these tenets of Nicholas Roerich's philosophy are reflected and powerfully evoked in his paintings.

Select Bibliography

Eridano Bazzarelli, Maria Cristina Lopez, Joanna Spendel, Elemire Zolla. *Scritti Italiani Su Nicholas Roerich* (Messina, 1993)
Garabed Paelian, *Nicholas Roerich*, (Sedona, Arizona 1974)
Nicholas Roerich, International Centre of the Roerich, Moscow, (Moscow, 1997)
Heart 1932, Agni Yoga Society Inc. (USA 1944)
New Era Community 1926, Agni Yoga Society Inc (USA 1951)
Agni Yoga 1929, Agni Yoga Society Inc (USA 1952)
Leaves of Moyra's Garden 1925, Agni Yoga Society Inc (USA 1952)

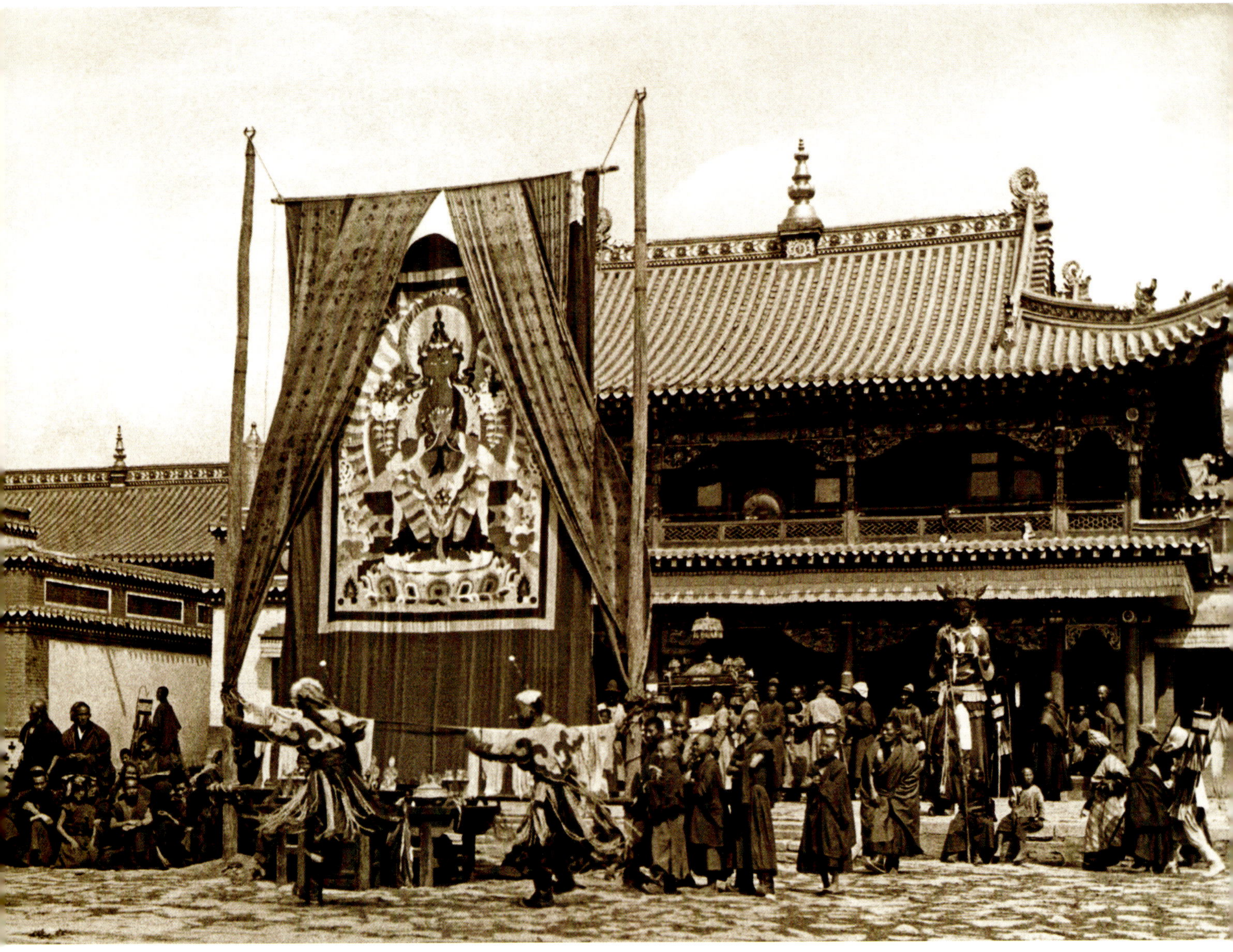

Ritual Dance of Lamas in Mongolia, 1935 (International Centre of the Roerichs, Moscow)

Across the Gobi Desert

Ruth Drayer

Locked in the heart of Central Asia, Tibet challenged Russian artist, Nicholas Roerich's imagination as no other country did. In 1904, Tibet and Great Britain had signed a treaty granting the British government control of entry, but it had maintained Tibet's policy toward strangers. It was almost possible to count on both hands the western foreigners who had entered the kingdom: Sir Charles Bell, a friend of the Dalai Lama; Lieutenant Colonel F.M. Bailey, the political officer in Sikkim;

Study of Mountains (series) (International Roerich Memorial Trust, Naggar, Kullu)

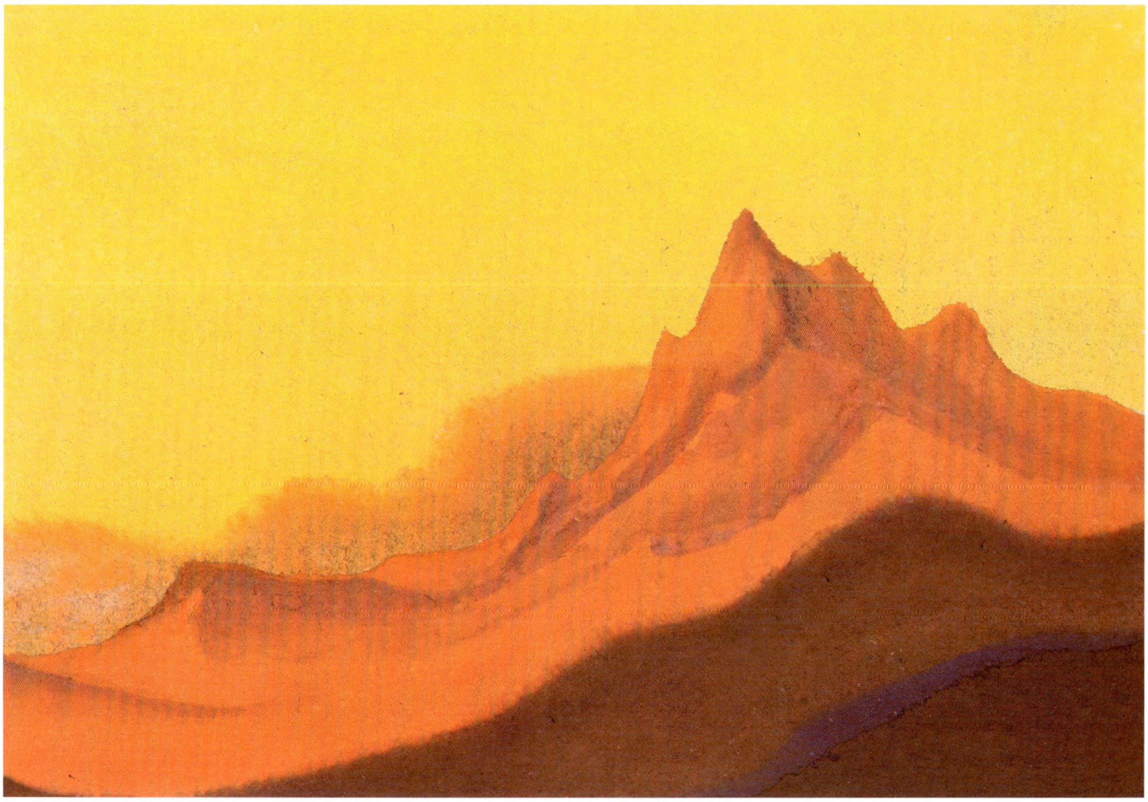

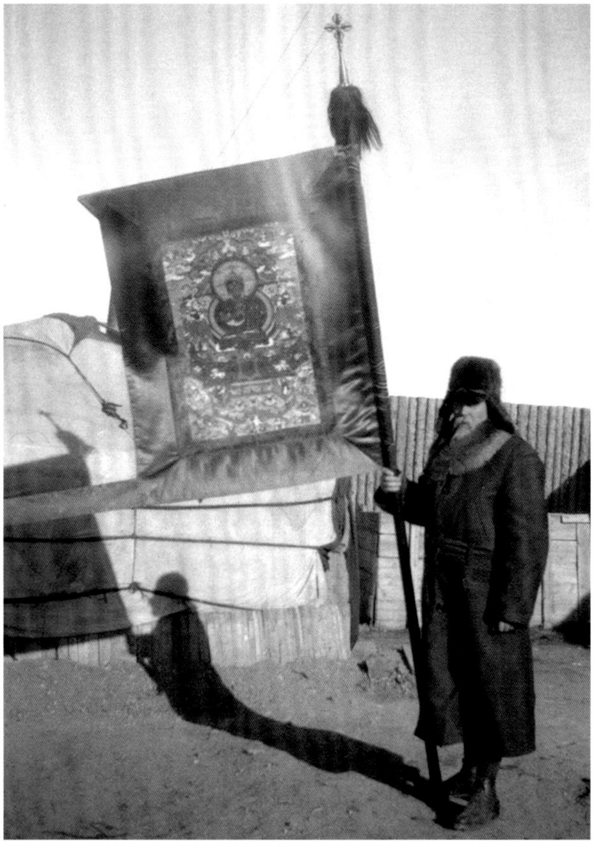

Nicholas Roerich March–April, 1927. Ulan Bator, Mongolia (Nicholas Roerich Museum Archive, NY)

some English officials; the adventurers who were climbing Mount Everest; and a few others. The two famous women—Helena Blavatsky, Russian spiritualist and Theosophist, and Alexandra David-Neel, the intrepid French explorer and scholar of Buddhism—who had managed to penetrate the country had only done so in disguise and under the greatest secrecy. Tibet was forbidden to most outsiders, and Lhasa, its capital, was even more closely protected. Not one of the great explorers who had set out to reach Lhasa had been admitted. The Russian explorer Colonel Przhevalsky and his men had gotten within 150 miles before they were halted by Tibetan officials and ordered to leave the country. Neither Sven Hedin, the Swedish explorer and geographer, nor Sir Aurel Stein, the Hungarian archaeologist, had gotten even that close.

If the Roerichs were able to visit Lhasa, it would be a brilliant achievement. While in Urga in the fall and winter of 1926, they met with a representative of the Dalai Lama who was willing to try to secure permission for them to enter Tibet and visit Lhasa. After waiting three months, they received an encouraging reply. Official passports would be issued, as well as a letter of introduction to the Dalai Lama. The family was thrilled, for mysterious Tibet was where Mme. Blavatsky had met her Masters and obtained the *Stanzas of Dzyan* that form the basis of her foundational book *The Secret Doctrine* (1888). Meanwhile, the Lichtmanns, then two of the trustees of the Nicholas Roerich Museum, New York, had gone back to America and then managed to return to Urga, bringing the mountain of supplies needed to continue the Expedition. Everything from tents to toilets, guns to paints, canvas to canned goods, was brought from America. The Roerichs were completely outfitted to resume 'encircling inner Asia' to search for future fields of artistic and scientific work—and Shambhala. Roerich was aware that the regions of Mongolia and the central Gobi were an explorer's and archaeologist's paradise—with whole cities hidden beneath the sands—but nothing could be planned beforehand. As the route to Tibet was unmapped, all they knew was that if they steered toward Central Tibet, their path must cross the formidable but uniquely interesting Gobi. Even the stretch of the journey after Tibet could not be known in advance. As George explained, 'The chaotic state of affairs in inner Asia and China made all sorts of unexpected events possible and the only thing left to us was to trust Providence and proceed on our journey, leaving details to be decided on the spot.' So with the good wishes of the Mongolian authorities, the Expedition set off on 23 April 1927, heading southwest toward a Mongolian frontier post and the Yum-Beise monastery. The gear and supplies were packed in three trucks, and light baggage was strapped to the running boards of the two Dodge touring cars that would carry the group. The Lichtmanns said their good-byes; they were returning to New York with plans for the new Roerich Museum building.

The banner of Maitreya, fastened to a Mongolian spear, had joined the flags leading the procession. The party had grown considerably, now consisting of the Roerichs, their caravanners, several lamas,

Mountain Glacier (International Roerich Memorial Trust, Naggar, Kullu)

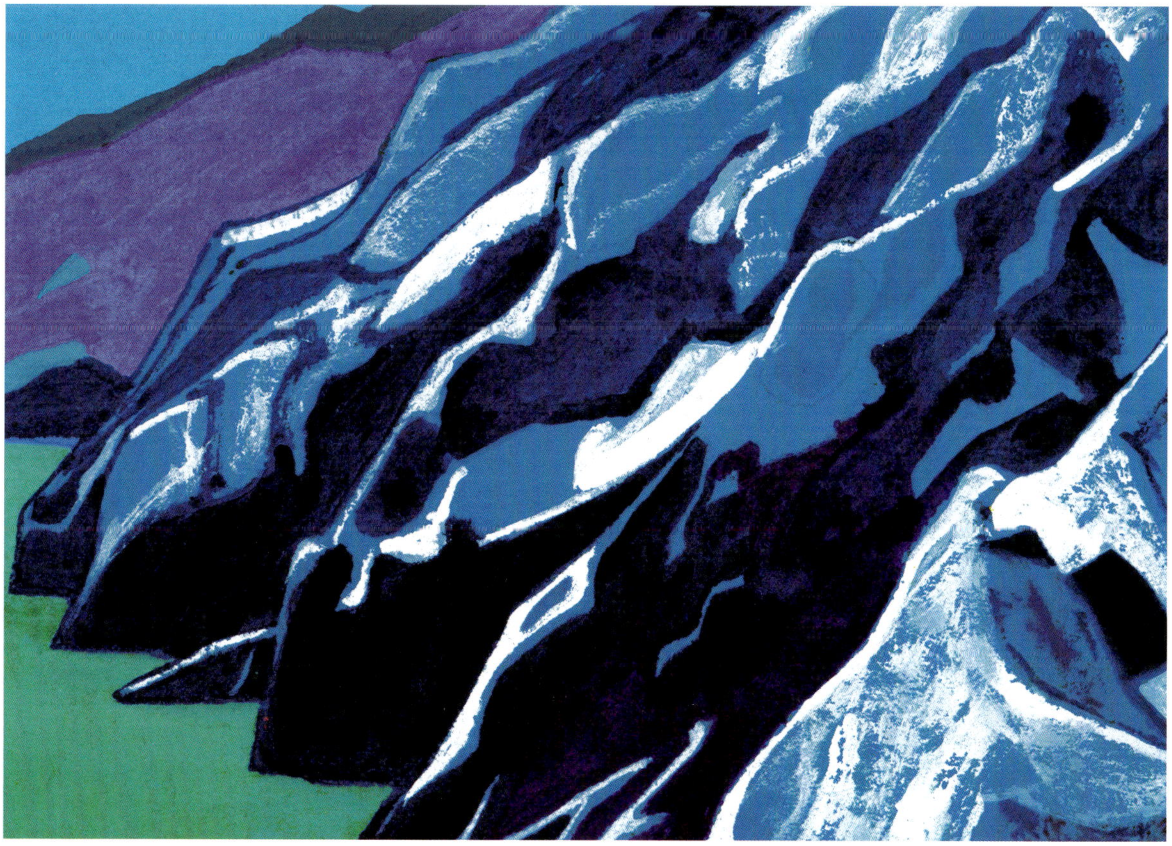

Dr. Ryabinin, the chief of transport, several army men, and two Cossack girls, Ludmila and Iraida Bogdanova, who were to help Helena Roerich. (The sisters became part of the Roerich household and continued with them for the next thirty years.)

George wrote:

> '...People had told us we could easily cross the Gobi by car, but it was impossible. With difficulty, we covered the nearly 600 miles to Yum-Beise in twelve days. There was no actual road, and with troublesome river crossings, stony ridges and car problems some days we did no more than ten or fifteen miles. Here and there we travelled on a camel path, but most of the trip we had to scout our way through virgin land. When our guide took us to an ancient, destroyed city fifty miles to the west, by mistake, we learned two important things: that all existing maps were inaccurate, and that we could not trust the local guides.'

Himalayas: The Disturbed Flame of Sunset, 1946 (International Centre of the Roerichs, Moscow)

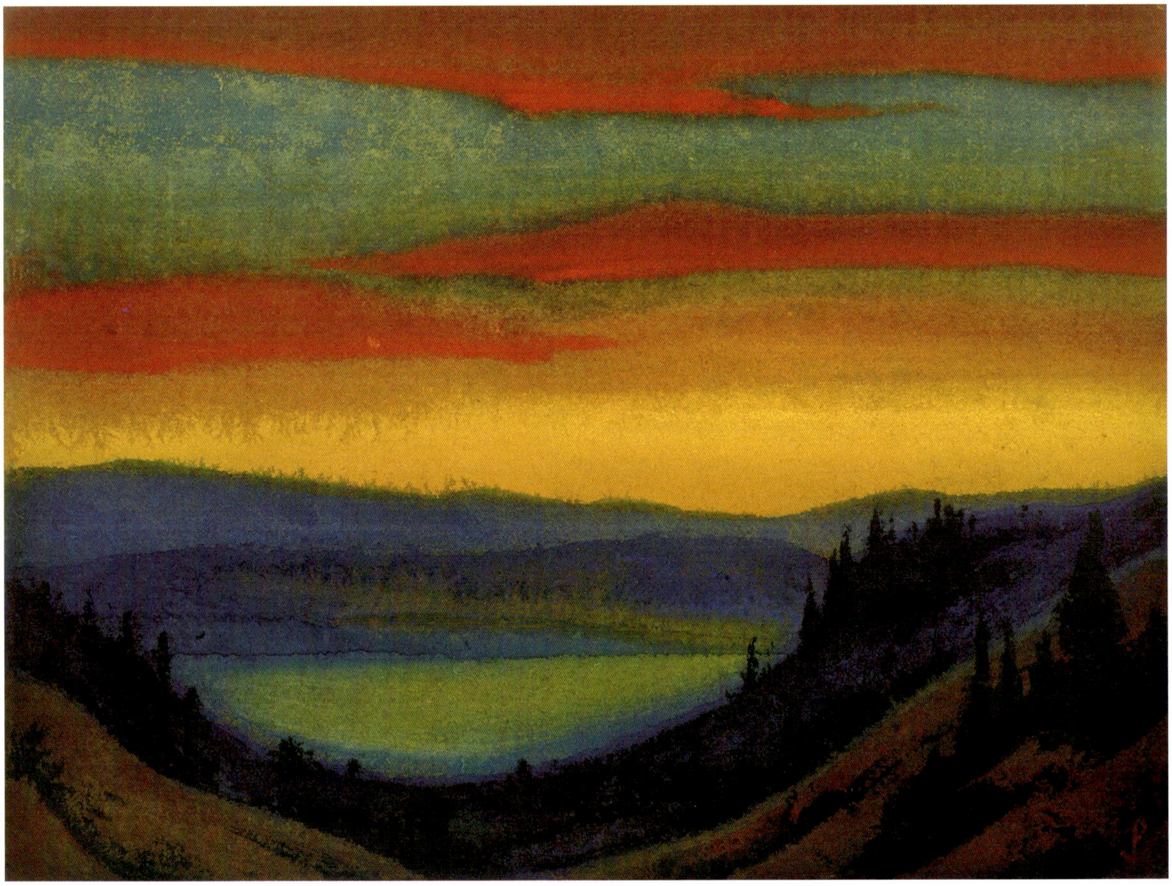

After endless negotiations, they managed to reach the Chinese border and continued by camel from there. Roerich wrote:

> 'Draw a line from the South Russian steppes and the northern Caucasus across the steppes of Semipalatinsk, Altai and Mongolia, then turn south, and you will have the main artery of our migration....The Central Gobi seems limitless. White-pink-blue sands, slate black. The fierce gales bury the flat slopes under a layer of stones, and we soon learned not to be caught by it. The danger of continuing on this route was that the wells might be dry or filled with dead animals; the only other way would be toward the east, but that area was infested with Chinese bandits.'

George described the region:

> 'The Gobi between Yum-Beise and An-hsi represents a succession of mountain ridges of crystalline rocks, intersected by desert. Most of the mountain ridges belong to the Altai system, which stretches northwest by southeast across the arid region situated between the southern branches of the Khangai Mountains and the eastern slopes of the T'ien Shans and the Barkol Mountains. I am confident that if explored properly, the numerous canyons that flank the desert ridges would offer ample opportunities to discover fossils.'

On 1 June 1927, the Expedition arrived at the edge of the central Gobi and set up camp on the silvery banks of the Shih-pao-ch'ang. Roerich noted:

> 'It is good, the Nan-Shan Mountains glow at sunrise, the mountain streams murmur, and the herds of goats and rams gleam white in the sun. Riders speed by us—is there any news? Rumours fill the air; they try to frighten us by giving us many reasons why we should wait here until September: the grass must thicken, the camels must fatten, their wool must grow, the treacherous swamps of Tsaidam must dry out, and the Blue River must subside.'

Waiting would also give them time to study future routes and complete preparations for their great march in August. As always, there was much to keep each of them busy. Just as Portniagin, their headman, was leaving to buy provisions and handle the cables to and from America, their Tibetan guide rode into camp on a fine black horse, driving a big herd of horses and mules to add to the caravan. They were advised that Lhasa had requested that all European travellers be prevented from coming any closer, but since the Expedition carried Tibetan passports and letters of introduction, and was escorted by a deputy of the Tibetan representative in Urga, the Roerichs were confident this would not apply to them.

Ten difficult days followed. They had problems obtaining more animals. Helena and several of the caravanners suffered health problems. Therefore, they decided to move their camp into the upper Sharagolji Valley, where all the conditions were better. They climbed 9,000 feet, crossed the 'Three Mountain Pass,' and entered the valley beside the snow-clad Humboldt Mountains (locally called the Doyugu), then continued until they set up camp in the foothills of Ulan Davan (16,000 feet).

In *Heart of Asia*, Roerich remembered it this way:

> 'A long march for the camels. The song of Shambhala rings again through the air. Even here on the stony mountain passes and frozen uplands, we are not left without signs of Shambhala. Bending over a stony slope, our lamas were collecting pieces

Nicholas Roerich February, 1926. Yarkand, Chinese Turkestan (Nicholas Roerich Museum Archive, NY)

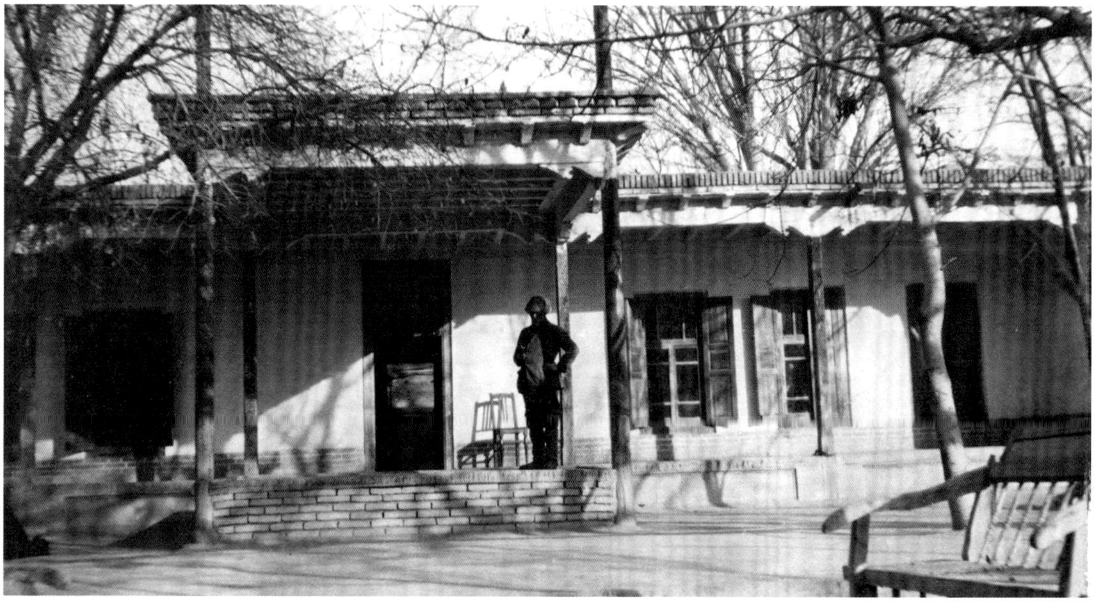

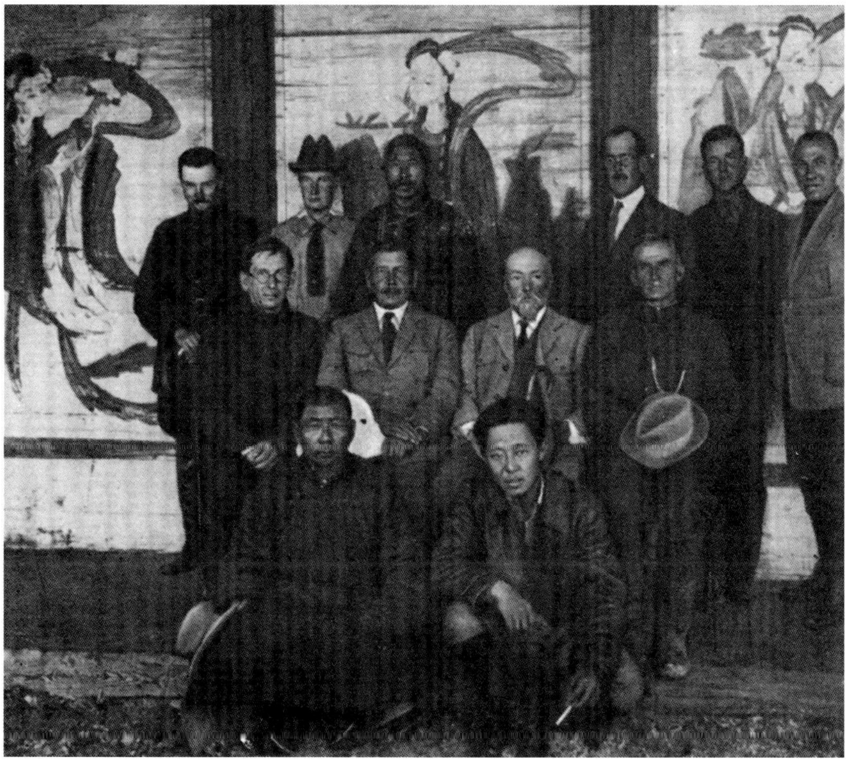

Second row, right to left: Pëtr Kozlov, Nicholas Roerich; third row, first from left: George Roerich September, 1926. Ulan Bator, Mongolia (Nicholas Roerich Museum Archive, NY)

> of white quartz and carefully designing them into something on the neighbouring rocks. It was the monogram of Kalachakra they had embedded into the sands. 'Henceforth, this white inscription that invokes the Great Teaching will be visible from afar to all travellers'.'

The six weeks in camp waiting for the camel caravan season to begin were a special time. The Mongols, whose solitary tents were scattered wherever water and grass was best for their herds, loved occasions to socialise. The Roerichs had a great tent erected and invited everyone to join in the Festival of Maitreya, observed annually on 5 July. The long service was conducted by the Expedition lamas. In return, the group was invited to join several days of festivities when the scattered people came together to enjoy themselves.

It was a peaceful time. Roerich painted the Bogdo-Ulas several times, then sketched and painted *Guardian of the Entrance, The Great Horseman* and others. The Humboldt peaks glowed white with snow, and the air was invigorating. The stillness reminded them of the Himalayan heights. At night, the group held wonderful discussions on the new prayer to Shambhala, the prophecies of the Panchen Lama, or the need for a pan-Asiatic language to reconcile, at least elementally, the three hundred dialects of Asia. Roerich yearned to convey to the West through his paintings and books—and through the establishment of the New Country—the importance that Maitreya, Shambhala and Gesar Khan have in Asia.

They were camped in the area where the Mahatma had rested on his way to Mongolia forty years before, so they decided to commemorate the spot with a suburgan of Shambhala. The suburgan was completed on 24 July. 'The Elder Lama of Tsaidam comes to consecrate it,' wrote Roerich.

In front of the tent of Shambhala, the lamas prayed for the coming of the Blessed Rigden Djapo and placed a polished mirror before the image. The altar was filled with gifts of turquoise, coral and beads, an image of the Buddha, a silver ring with a most significant inscription, prophecies for the future, and other precious objects that had been placed there by an old lama who had helped with the construction. That night news arrived that Colonel N.V. Kordashevski, a Lithuanian and long-time friend of the Roerichs who was to head the convoy, was crossing the Gobi after leaving Peking. Of vital importance, they also heard that the Panchen Lama and his Chinese escort were on the way to nearby Kumbun monastery and that his luggage was already there.

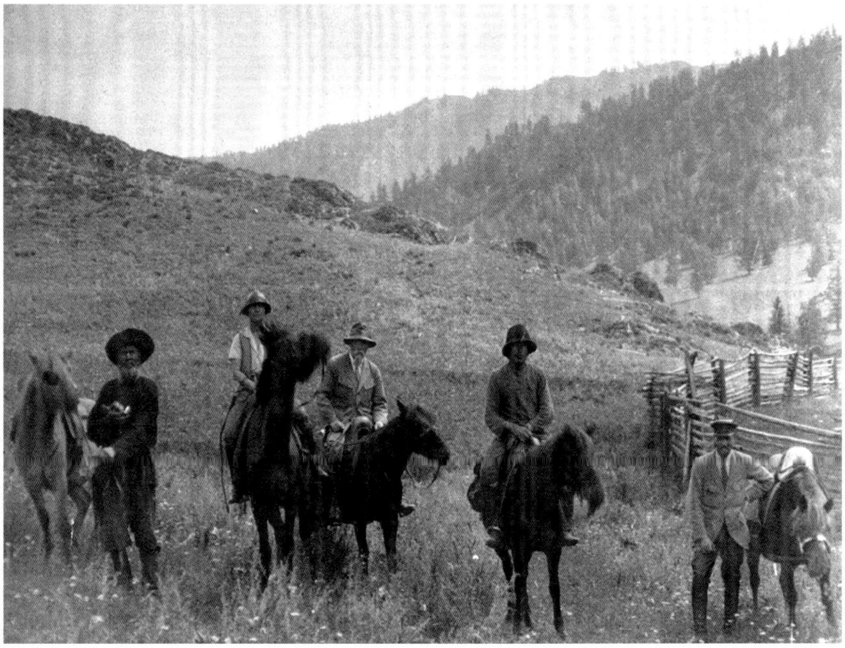

Right to left: George Roerich; third: Nicholas Roerich; fourth: Sina Lichtmann August, 1926. Altai (Nicholas Roerich Museum Archive, NY)

Other things happened during this extraordinary time. Many remarkable incidents which were considered significant signs were recorded by Roerich and George—flashfloods that destroyed property and animal life, and the sighting of a beautiful bird to which the lama said, 'Rigden Djapo is himself looking after us.' Other incidents were whispered by a few of the party or repeated by the co workers in New York. For instance, one warm day, when travelling in the desert, their caravan guide covered his nose and mouth with a scarf, explaining that precautions were needed. 'We are approaching the forbidden lands of Shambhala,' he said. 'We will soon encounter Sur—the poisonous gas that guards the frontier.' Lowering his voice, he continued, 'We are close to the place where all the people and animals of the Dalai Lama's caravan started to tremble while travelling with him from Tibet to Mongolia. The Dalai Lama reassured everyone and explained that they had approached the forbidden zone of Shambhala, and unfamiliar aerial vibrations were touching them.' Another time, the group was roaming through the desolate rocks of the desert when many of them became simultaneously aware of an exquisite breath of perfume in the air—like the best Indian incense. 'From where does it come?' they asked, 'for we are surrounded by barren rocks'. The high lama with them whispered, 'Can you smell the fragrance of Shambhala?' They also came to an area which the caravanners refused to enter, yet the Roerichs rode into it and remained there for a few days. Upon their return, the Asians prostrated themselves, exclaiming they must be gods, for no mere people could have penetrated that territory without divine credentials. Since Roerich's travel diary was kept for himself and the co workers in New York, it is doubtful that he thought it might ever be published or read around the world for decades to come. We must, therefore, assume, he did not intend to cause the frustration many feel while studying *Altai–Himalaya, A Travel Diary*, wishing he had confided the entire story behind the mysterious accounts of these few days. What they uncovered in the desert remains a mystery, for unlike other explorers who trumpeted their finds and filled the newspapers with stories of their adventures, the Roerich Expedition sought much that was only spoken of in secrecy.

Perhaps they found Shambhala, ancient cities or artifacts, or even a figurine of the Great Mother. Due to the diligent work of several Russians now translating the Roerichs' diaries and the writings of others involved with the Expedition, more may come to light. On

19 August 1927, they broke camp and started for the salt desert of Tsaidam, accompanied by several Mongols travelling in the same direction. They crossed a 17,000-foot high pass without difficulty, pausing to view the panorama of mountains and rocky crags ahead. This was the trail taken by the Dalai Lama in 1904, and it was comforting to come upon the many sacred sites marking his journey. Then, the dreaded salt desert of Tsaidam stretched before them. They decided to cross it at night:

> 'We could not stop but had to continue for a hundred and twenty miles without a halt. In the darkness of the night, the road was invisible and fortunately, we crossed the most dangerous spots without realising it. There were bottomless pits on either side of the narrow path, and if a horse had tripped, it would have been impossible to save him—one false step and we would have been finished. It was forbidding, but we made it and crossed Tsaidam in a new direction—the shortest way.'

In his diary, Roerich wrote:

> 'None of it was as the maps had indicated. After we were across, I chanced to look toward the west and saw endless pink sands glowing there. Although entirely unexplored, the maps show it as completely desert area; but this does not seem true to me. There may be much of the remarkable in the folds of those hills; maybe the ancient Buddhist monasteries expanded in that direction, with interesting hermitages and monumental caves. The Mongols seldom mention these regions, but they do tell stories of caravans lost in the sands and of buried cities.'

By the time they neared the Tibetan border, both Helena and the recently arrived Tibetan commercial agent were experiencing heart problems, no doubt exacerbated when robbers attacked the caravan. Colonel Kordashevski led a counterattack that drove them off, and when the Expedition expected another attack the next day, 'in blew a terrific snow-storm mingled with thunder, and the superstitious robbers dispersed.' Roerich described their approach to the border:

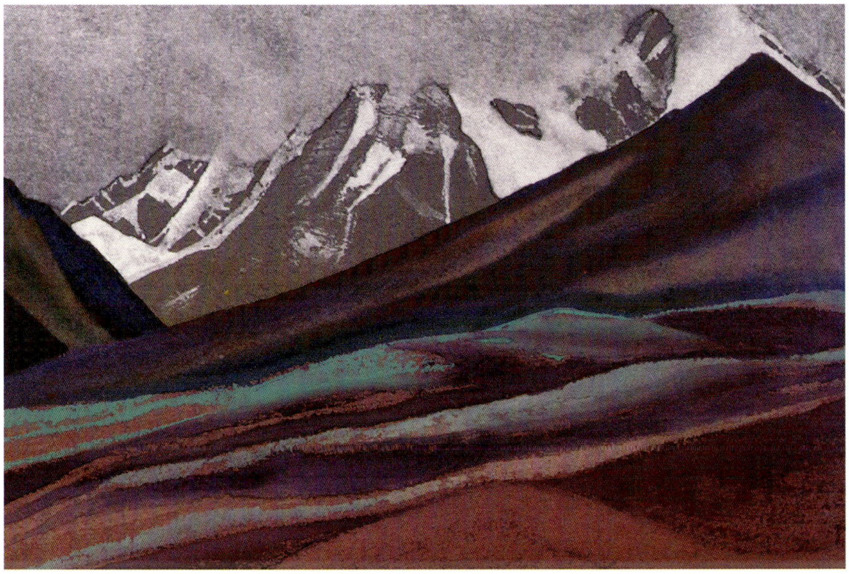

Mountain Pass (International Roerich Memorial Trust, Naggar, Kullu)

> 'We looked for Tibetan outposts, but instead, we saw something shining against the gray background of the hilly desert.'

Attempting to identify it, they wondered, 'Is it a huge tent?' But the white spot was too big for a tent. 'Perhaps it's snow?' But why would there be so much snow in only one place? As they approached, it seemed to increase in size, and whatever it was, 'was truly superb.' Getting closer, they realised they were looking at a huge pyramid, formed by the drippings of a gigantic geyser of Glauber salt. Roerich remarked, 'A snowy mass—glistening in the sun—verily, a sacred boundary.'

They had reached Tibet at last.

Select Bibliography

Bailey, F.M. *No Passport to Tibet*: Rupert Hart-Davis, 1957.

Cable, M. and F. French. *The Gobi Desert*. New York: Macmillion, 1944.

Hedin, Sven. *Across the Gobi*. New York: Greenwood Press, 1969.

_________Central Asia & Tibet. 1968.

Przhevalsky, N.A. *From Kulga Across the Tian Shan to Lob-Nor*, New York: Greenwood Press, 1969.

Roerich, George N. *Trails To Inmost Asia*, New Haven, CT: Yale Univ. Press, 1933.

Roerich, Nicholas. *Altai–Himalaya*, Brookfield, CT. Arun Press, 1983.

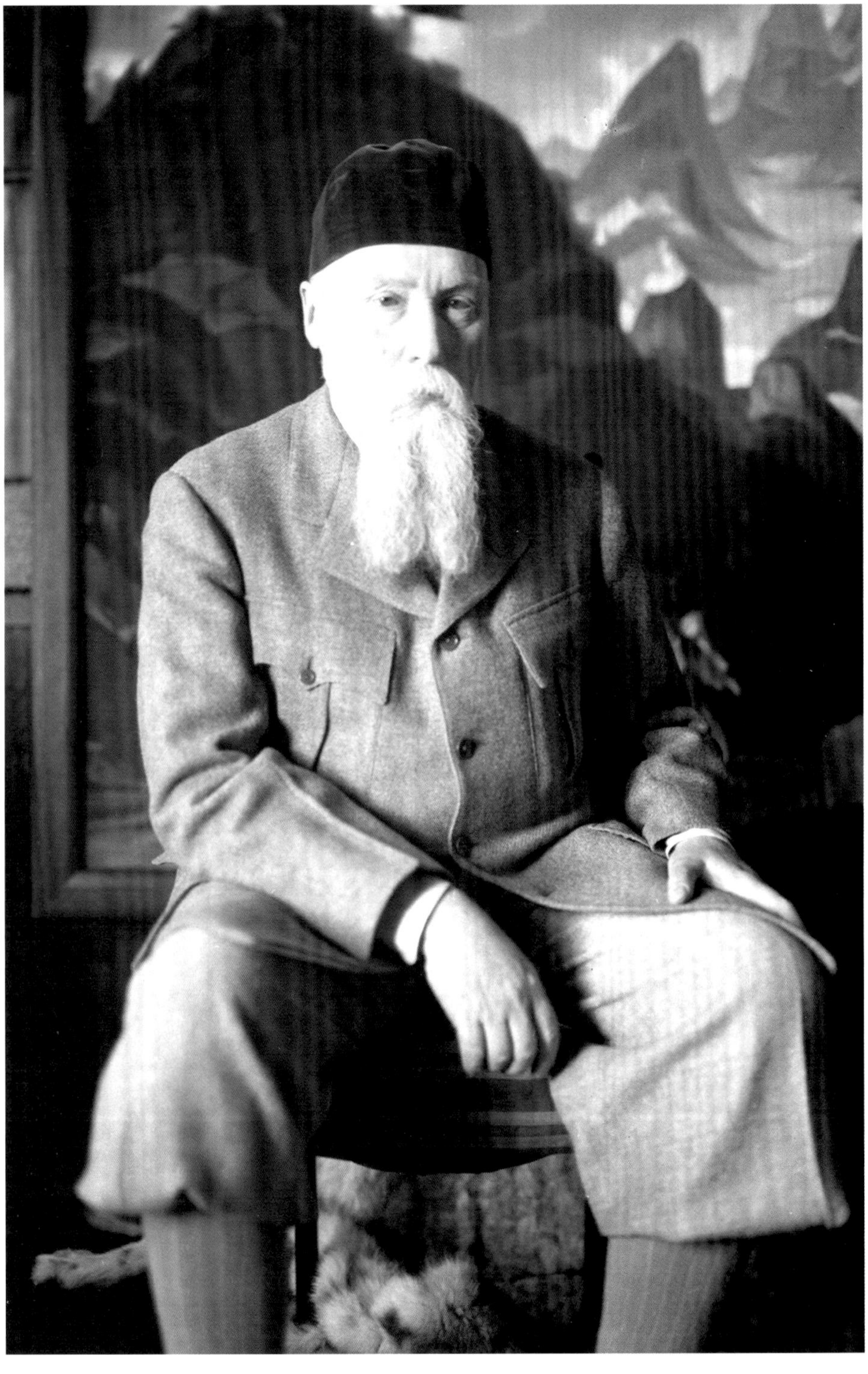

Nicholas Roerich, ca. 1937. Naggar, India. In background: a painting by Svetoslav Roerich (Nicholas Roerich Museum Archive, NY)

Mysticism and the Art of Roerich

Lokesh Chandra

The words of the French painter Cezanne, 'The landscape thinks itself in me, and I am its consciousness' could well have been said of Nicholas Roerich, the Russian artist who made India his home.

The Himalayan paintings of Roerich are a hymn to the vital strength of Life and Nature, a dynamic potential for the biosphere and psycho sphere. Like Lord Buddha, Roerich sees with his 'divine vision' (*divya-chakshus*) that every stone, every drop of water, every cell of the body is an endlessly flowing river of deep consciousness that enriches *Homo sapiens* in trans-utilitarian values.

His depiction of mountains show they are the lofty visual aspect of nature that is co-present in the ordering of the world and unites humanity with cosmic ambience. Everything on earth, including its skies and waters, is alive and our planet is a single life sphere as Gaia,

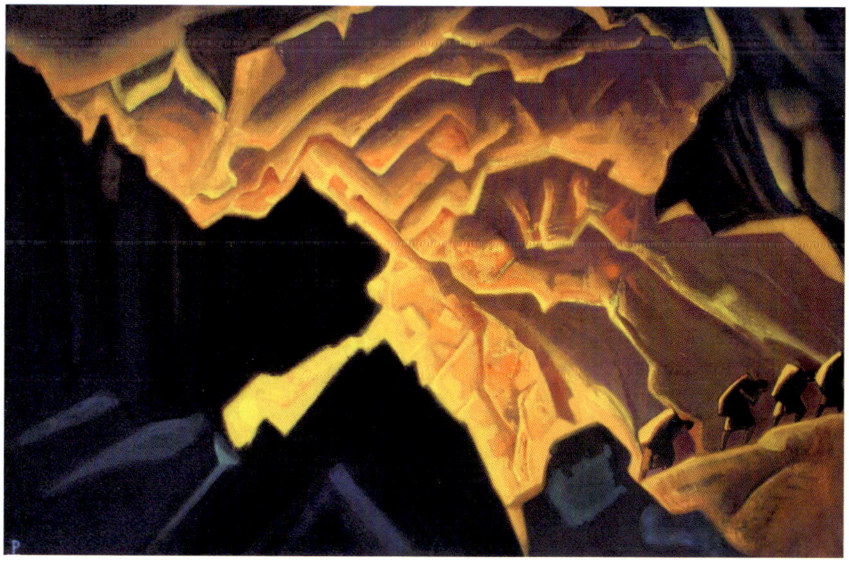

The Treasure, 1938 (International Centre of the Roerichs, Moscow)

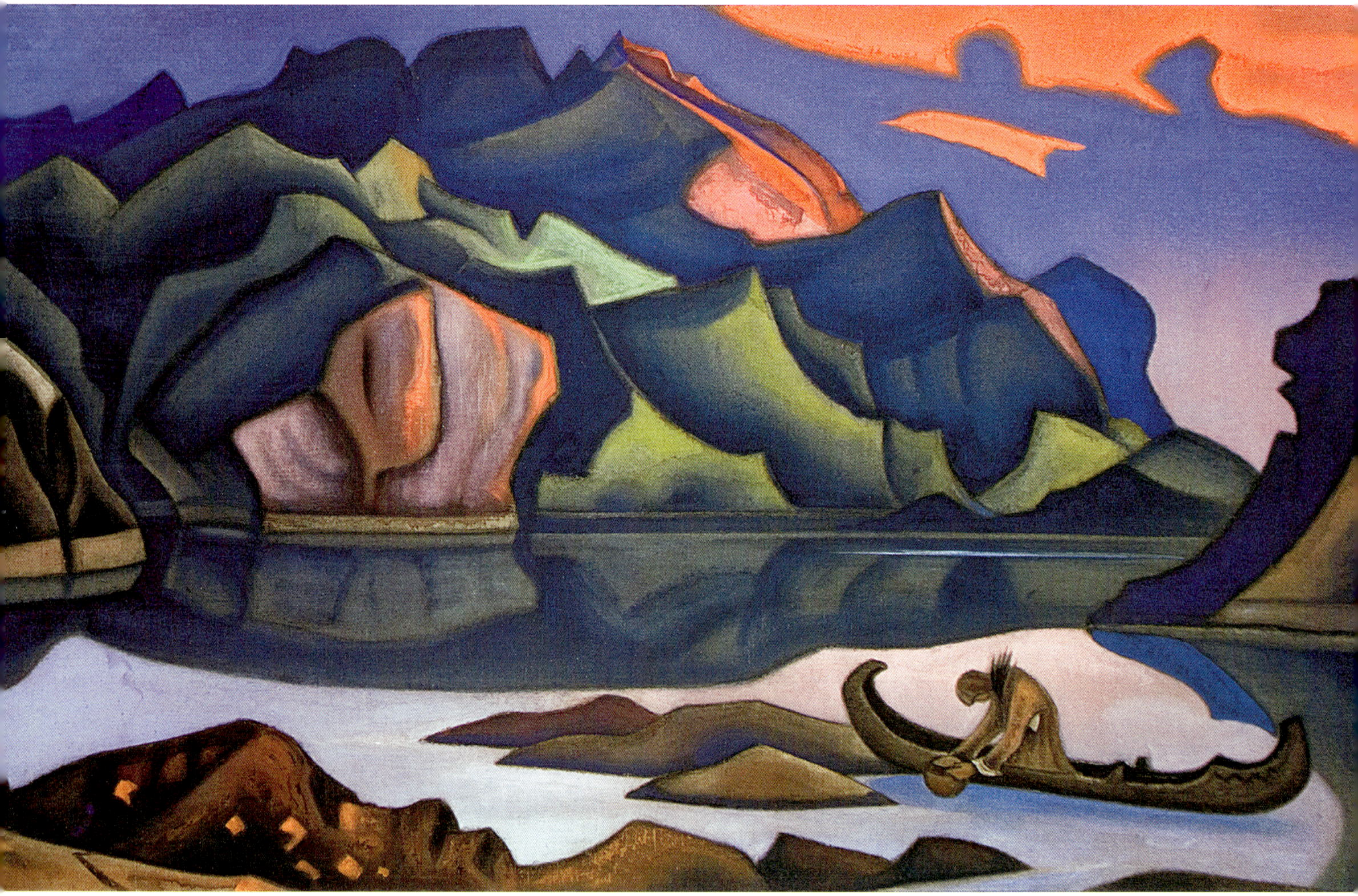

The Last Angel, 1942 (International Centre of the Roerichs, Moscow)

the ancient Greek goddess of the Earth. Gaia reflects concepts of the Rigveda: *gaya* is 'vital strength', 'Life', and *gayatra* is 'hymn'.

His mind opened to the entire universe, where coexistence of sentient beings, nature and consciousness are woven together like the diaphanous veil of Kuan-yin. The hushed peaks of the Himalayas in Roerich's colours of silence are like the flight of birds, or a nightingale singing among flowers. They are a new vehicle of spirituality for perceiving the ordering principle of a many-sided reality. Only an artist of the sensibility of Roerich could see the invisible threads of life, nature and universe and reproduce them in the vibrant colours of his paintings so that they become a vehicle to guide us to the essence of life itself. He interweaves the ecological and spiritual system into an interconnection of humanity, nature and the divine.

The *Samyuktagama* and *Ekottaragama* texts of the Chinese Buddhist Canon relate the encounter of Lord Buddha with a leaf of the *pippala* tree. These sutras were translated from Sanskrit originals which were destroyed in the political holocaust of the 10th century. To transcreate the sutras in English: In his meditation Siddhartha looked up at a *pippala* leaf imprinted against the blue sky, its tails blowing back and forth as if calling him. Looking deeply at the leaf, he saw clearly the presence of the sun and stars—without the sun, without light and warmth, the leaf could not exist....He also saw in the leaf the presence of clouds: without clouds, there could be no rain, and without rain the leaf could not be. He saw the earth, time, space and mind—all were present in the leaf. In fact, at that very moment, the entire universe existed in that leaf. The reality of the leaf was a wondrous miracle.

Likewise, Roerich focusses his formidable powers of concentration to look deeply into the endlessly flowing river of natural forms. Each and every peak of the Himalayas in his canvasses harbour the sublime universe within man. His great message is the convergence of utility and values, the merger of essence and appearance, the decolonisation of our being from dogmas, and constant self transcending activity without being haunted by theorisation.

Mysticism, with its very first characteristic of 'ineffability', is the liberation of spiritual experience from the dogma of scriptural doctrines. The writings and paintings of Roerich own the secular and the sacred as a biunity so that the forms and figures of *maya* establish our contacts with transcendent consciousness.

Roerich creates his mountains in mysterious outlines, in subtle luminous colours so that the viewer has to concentrate his mind on them to discover the infinite diffusion of his experience of beatitude (*ananda*), creativity (*isana*) and the wave (*urmi*) or the power of the autoconscious. His paintings try to capture the enhanced state of consciousness from an unparalleled variety of forms and deep speculation to intense experience of present Life. The paintings of Roerich are the *alaya-vijnana* of Buddhism, which is the collective psyche in which individual experiences reappear in a single flux, even over vast distances and across several centuries. In it, past and present live together and form a fruitful soil on which grows the plant of an individual.

The paintings of Roerich show his distant forefathers, the Vikings, the Russian saints and Buddhist themes: all are the interior light (*antar-jyoti*) of his Super-Consciousness. Mountains, incarnate beyond theological dogmas, in the soft light of Roerich's brush as a leap from the plane of *samsara* to that of *nirvana*. He conveys the message that our psychic Life reflects that of the universe: nothing vile or mean can tarnish the evolution of humanity towards the advent of Maitreya, or the manifestation of the Kulika Kings of the Kalachakra, or the Second Coming of Christ.

Nicholas Roerich led a US Department of Agriculture expedition to Mongolia and Manchuria in 1934 with the co-operation of the Secretary of the Department, Henry Wallace who wanted him to search for signs of the Second Coming of Christ. Roerich and Wallace shared a deep interest in the mystical and occult from 1931 to 1935. Roerich's attraction to Buddhism, Mongolia and Tibet arose because of the occult symbols providing clues to the Utopian Shambhala. Roerich encouraged the proclivities of Henry Wallace to mysticism which led to a change in the one-dollar bill. On its reverse side is the Great Seal replete with mystical symbolism. The eye is the all-seeing eye of God and the birth of the United States is the birth of a new era for mankind under the watchful observation of God: suggesting the Second Coming of Christ.[1] This change introduced in 1935 is in use till today.

Nicholas Roerich was in search of 'Sacred Signs' and was sure to find them: 'I know we shall see them.' To him Shambhala was a coming Paradise where Goodness would rule and Virtue would triumph.

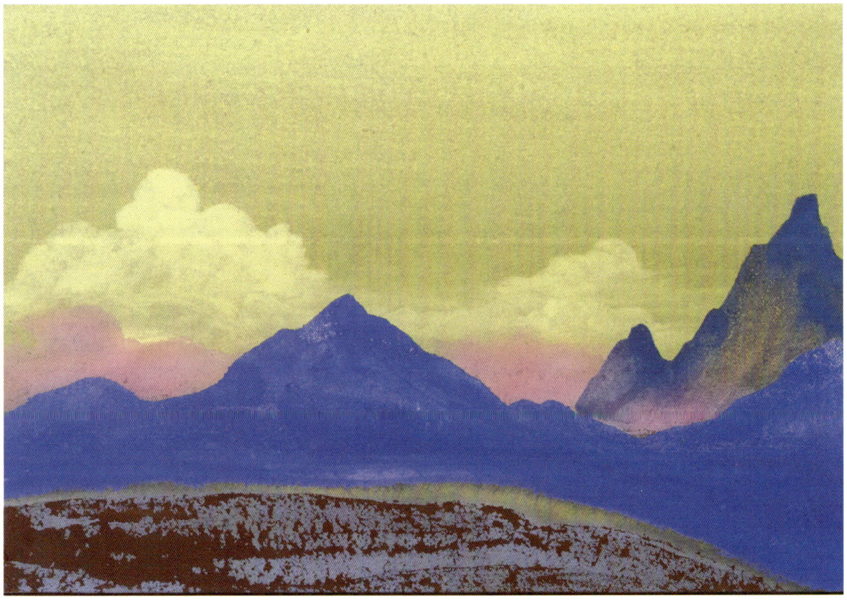

Study of Mountains (series) (International Roerich Memorial Trust, Naggar, Kullu)

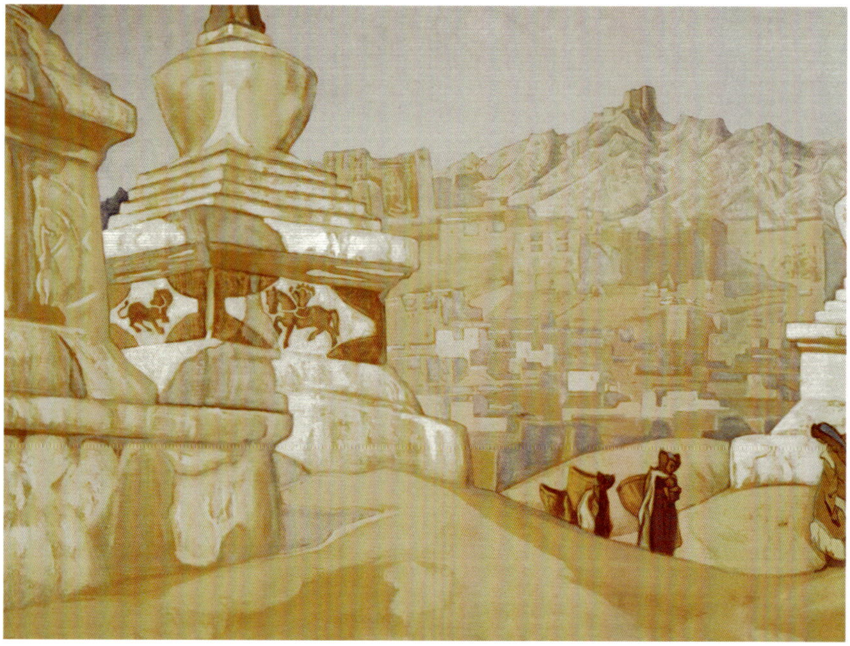

Steed of Good Fortune, 1925 (Nicholas Roerich Museum, NY)

It was the New Era, a symbol of the radiant future. Shambhala was the metropolis of the Kulika kings who promoted the doctrine of Kalachakra as a syncretic faith when Buddhism was destroyed by Islam in Central Asia. Shambhala was located on the Sita River or Syr Darya. It was a haven of peace and prosperity governed by wise and compassionate Kulika rulers, who are depicted by Roerich under their Tibetan name Rigden-Djapo. The kingdom of Shambhala vanished into a celestial realm, but the Kulika Kings continue to watch over human affairs and will return to save humanity from the forces of darkness, says the legend. In 1926, at Urga in Mongolia, he painted a prophetic image of a horseback rider, leading the country towards a new epoch in accordance with the legend of Shambhala. This painting was presented to the Mongolian government. 'The image is ready to rise....When the image will reach Urga, then will flash the first light of the New Era truth.' He painted the Rigden-Djapo or Kulika Kings of Shambhala, or Gesar Khan the hero of the Tibetan epic, of whom was said the neighing of his sacred horses were signs of approaching events. His paintings of Lhasa, Tibetan monasteries, his arduous expedition to the Himalayas, Gobi Desert, Mongolia and Tibet were to trace the elusive secrets of the theosophist, Helena Blavatsky's famous *The Veil of Isis*.

Roerich gave words and form to the human desire for an enlightened

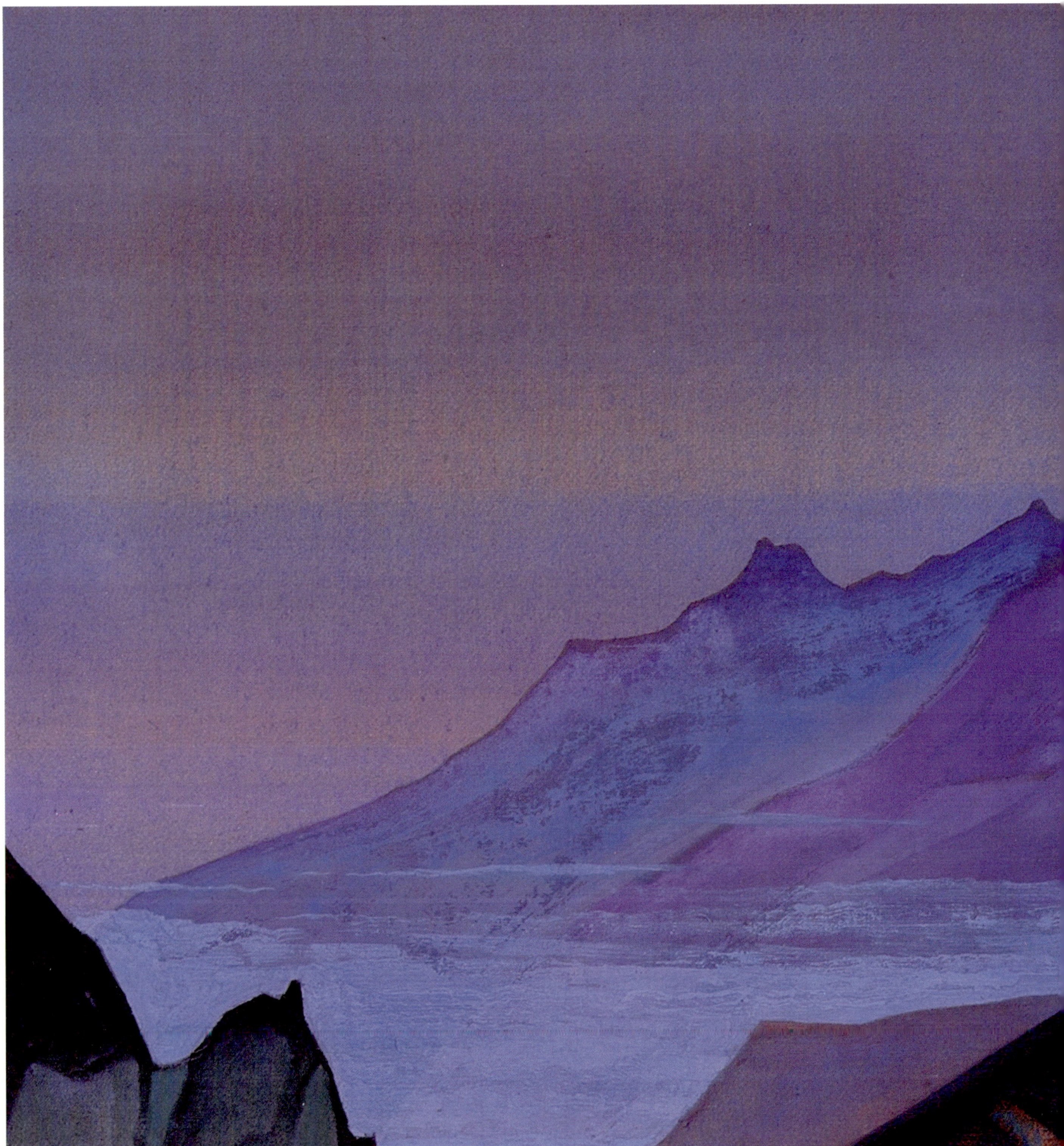

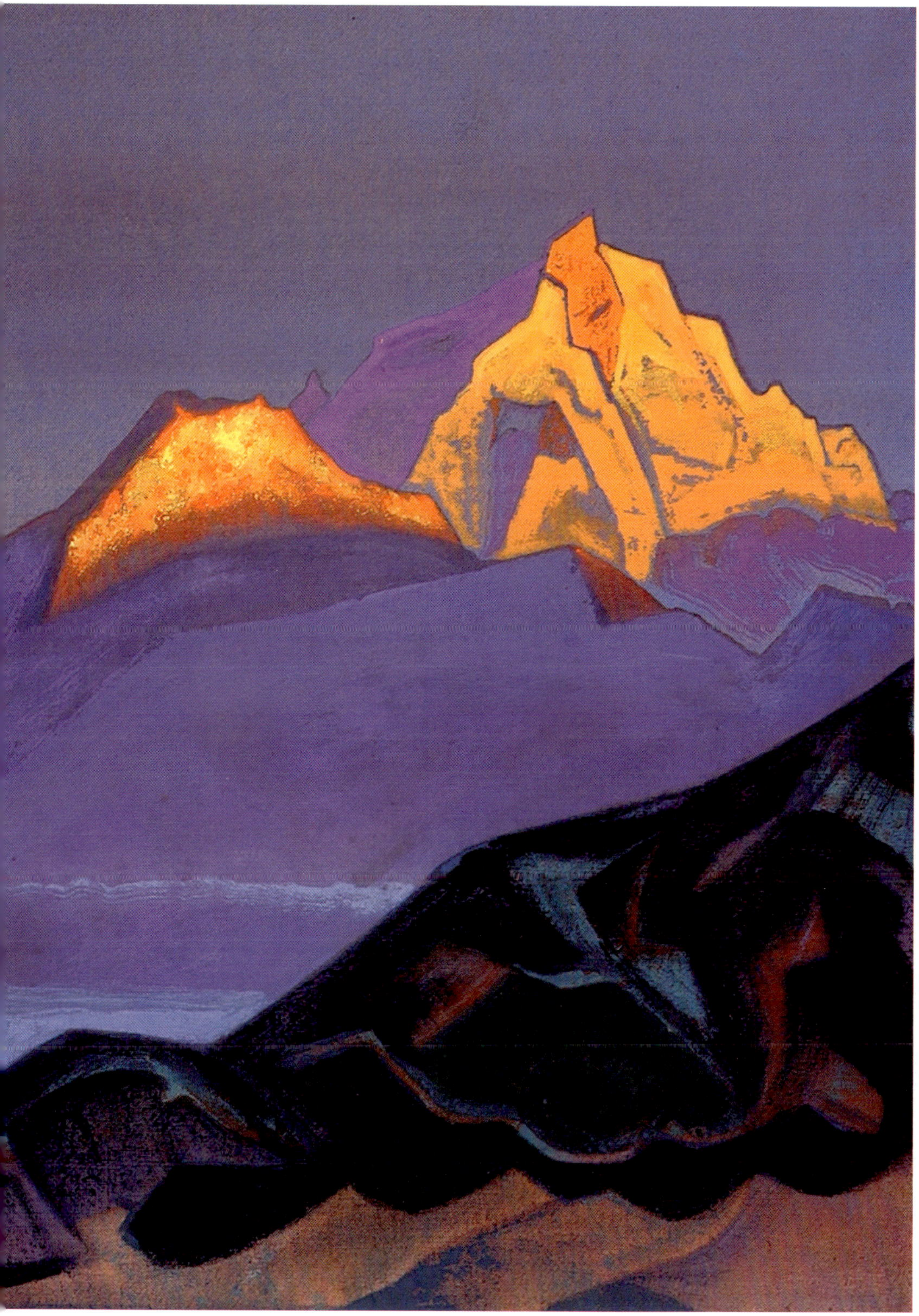

Path to Shambhala, 1933
(Nicholas Roerich Museum, NY)

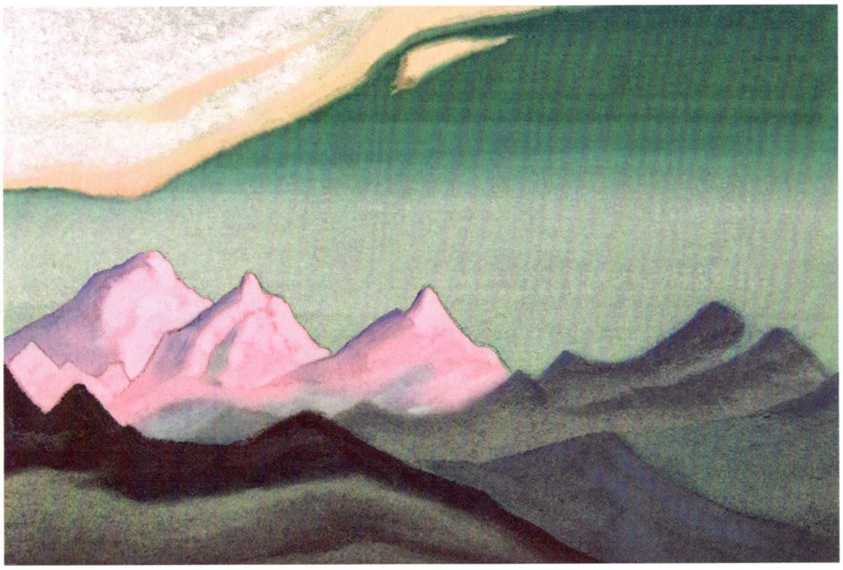

Study of Mountains (series) (International Roerich Memorial Trust, Naggar, Kullu)

era in Tibetan symbols of Shambhala, or Maitreya, or Gesar Khan. To him the sacred was the very essence of the profane, out of which always appears a new dynamism that melts into light and dissolves into human consciousness. Shambhala had a deep imprint on the Russian mind since the beginning of the 19th century as it came very close to their vision of *belovodye*. When the fame of Roerich was at its height, James Hilton wrote the novel *Lost Horizons* in 1933 and popularised the legend of Shambhala in the English-speaking world as the Shangrila.

The Great Soviet Revolution shook the world of culture and Roerich naturally held the hope that one day this homicidal ideology would be vanquished. The deep patriotic-nationalistic roots of Roerich led to his search for Russia's pagan beginnings and folklore and they were the subject of his earlier paintings. As the terror of communism reached its heights, Roerich painted his hopes and aspirations in gentle clouds, visionary landscapes, evocative colour sweeps, and in the vastness of overwhelming nature. The harmonious application of colour was integrated into an organic tonality.

The charming consistency of his figures, mountains, landscape and architecture was the powerful presence of an inevitable bliss that would be the golden ground of Life. His light, warm colours create other-worldly effects. Translucent blues contrasted with the subdued colours of surrounding hills, clouds, deer and other natural manifestations express a powerful presence of an Ideal soon to ripen our mental continuum to the finale during the reign of the 25th Kulika King Rudracakrin when:

Subduing the darkness of troubles through the blazing rays of his deeds Firm in the sky of the mind (cid-ambaram*)*
Dance of compassion of the oceans of Tathagatas will pervade space

The paintings of Roerich are mystical in the sense that they lead us from the seen to the unseen which was and still remains the tremendous civilising influence against dogmas, absolutism and consequent violence. In his paintings, we visualise the world as a cathedral. They are infused with spiritual greatness, beyond horizons of the noetic mind, towards the mysterious horizons of the unknown. Contemplating the paintings of Roerich, we encounter a spirtual depth which few artists have attained in history. Consummate shimmering outlines, the cosmic tranquility of his canvasses lead us to the imaginative conception of the Supreme in terms of Life and the Future of Culture.

His paintings are the vortex of Life in a state of continual becoming, in a space-silence continuum with a haunting sense of being and eternity. They are reminiscent of the first Tibetan monastery of Samye where in each storey the statues of gods symbolise a further metaphysical sphere, from the roughest on the ground floor to the ever subtler on the ascending storeys. It is a spiritual journey from the world of space and time to the timeless omnipresence of cosmic consciousness. Roerich's paintings with projective delineations of mountains, monasteries, epic heroes, the Maitreya Buddha, kings of Shambhala and the immense treasure of Pagan Rus and Orthodox Russia are patterns of forces that unfold creativity, compassion and wisdom.

End Note

1. Robert A Rupen, *The Canada-Mongolia Review*, 1979:5 (1). p. 1-36.

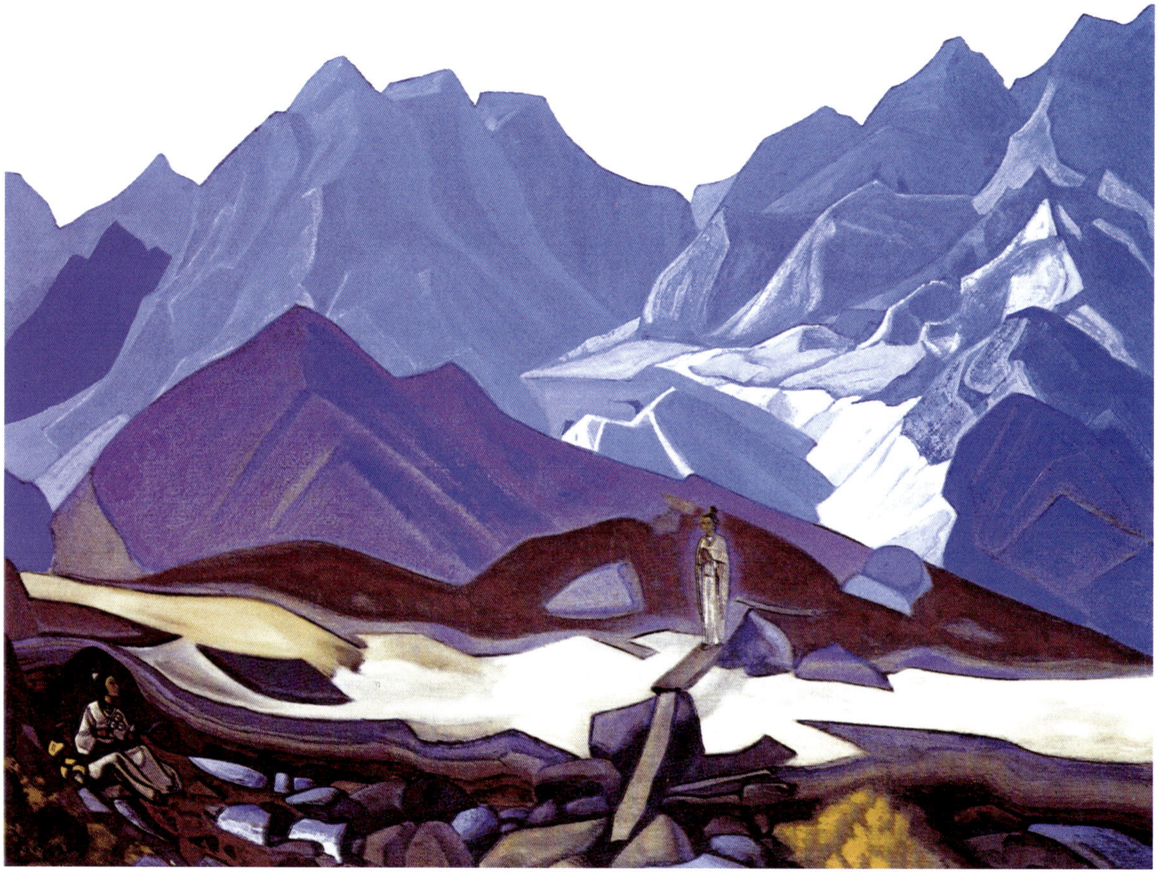

Tibet (Holy Stones). 1935-1936 (International Centre of the Roerichs, Moscow)

The Legend of Shambhala

Tashi Paljor

Researchers of the spiritual heritage of the Roerichs are well aware, through their writings, of the connection that existed between them and the Spiritual Centre of our planet, known in Tibetan texts as 'Shambhala'. Shambhala is a mythical kingdom located in Inner Asia according to both ancient Hindu and Buddhist spiritual and religious traditions. In previous centuries, Western travellers and spiritualists such as Hungarian Alexander Csoma de Koros, Portuguese Jesuit missionary Estêvão Cacella, German Albert Gruenwedel, the French Alexandra David-Neel, enchanted by accounts of the East, tried to discover its exact location. Shambhala is a Sanskrit term taken from the root Shambak, name of the Sakya tribe that ruled Shambhala then, and is generally understood to be a place of 'peace, tranquility, happiness'.

In the Tibetan Buddhist system of the Mahayana tradition, Shambhala is believed to be a 'pure land' with enlightened inhabitants that are said to be wise, clever and adept. They are also well built and energetic and can walk ten 'yojanas' a day. The Hindu Vedic age epics of the Mahabharata and Puranas, that pre-date Buddhism, refer to the 'Kalki' Kings of Shambhala. Ancient spiritual texts from the Tibetan Zhang Zung culture, that too pre-date Buddhism's entry into western Tibet, also mention its existence. Shambhala makes a central mention in the teachings and practice of the Kalachakra Tantra and its many commentaries.

The long line of Kalki Kings are known to uphold the integrity of the Kalachakra Tantra, a philosophical practice said to have been taught by Shakyamuni Buddha himself. The Buddhist scriptures refer to these line of kings as Rigden. This tantra or teaching was one of the last to be brought to Tibet from India at the request of King Suchandra, (Tib. Dawa Zangpo), the first King of Shambhala who played a pivotal role in its promotion. Renowned Tibetan scholar Thuken Rinpoche (1737–1802 A.D.) reiterates in his writings (*The Crystal Mirror*) that the Kalachakra Tantra, a complex tantric system, was introduced in Shambhala during the time of Lord Buddha, and continues to prevail there.

The Kalachakra Teaching prophesizes that when the world will decline due to man's gargantuan greed and the ravages of war, the 25th Kalki King (Tib. Rigden Djapo) will emerge from Shambhala around 2424 A.D., and with a huge army vanquish the evil forces to usher in a worldwide Golden Age. The concept of the Second Coming is prevalent in other spiritual traditions too: Christianity, Zoroastrianism, Islam, Hinduism and Buddhism where we have mention of the Messiah, Saoshyant, Muntazar (Mahdi), Rudra Chakrin and Maitreya Buddha.

The Kalachakra Tantra is a shorter form of an original text, the *Kalachakra Mulatantra* which is no longer in existence. The teachings extrapolate the concept of time and cycles. They explain the method and practice of harnessing the most subtle energies within one's body to channel them towards one's path to enlightenment. The concepts of the Kalachakra Tantra have multiple symbolism and meanings.

Shambhala too is said to have many meanings. In its physical connotation it is a geographical space, but in its meta-physical sense it is an extra dimensional spiritual reality. There are also alternative meanings. But in this diverse understanding the underlying principle remains that only those with a karmic connection (through past lives) or inherent merit can experience this Place. His Holiness, the present and 14th Dalai Lama gave an 'Initiation' to a large audience aspiring to understand the Kalachakra Tantra in 1985 at Bodh Gaya, Bihar, India. It is one of the many he has given. On the occasion he noted that only those who practice the Vajrayana school of Buddhism, a system of tantric Buddhism, with serious intent, can reach Shambhala without obstacles. Such an Initiation is accompanied by the making of a Mandala—a sacred art form drawn in a circle which depicts the deity of the same name—the Shri Kalachakra's sacred residence, along with other resident deities.

There are four divisions of teachings or tantras that make up the philosophical treatise of the Vajrayana system of Buddhism. These divisions are known as Kriyatantra, Charyatantra, Yogatantra and Annuttaryogatantra. The teachings of Shri Kalachakra form part of the last two, Anuttaryogatantra and Yogatantra. All four teachings and practices are essential for Buddhist practitioners.

In its physical attributes Shambhala is believed to be surrounded on all sides by snow clad mountains. It is shaped like an eight-petalled lotus with water bodies dividing each petal. The centre of the lotus appears like an elevated snow-clad peak. On each petal-like peak, there exist twelve billion cities, making it ninety-six billion cities in all. In the middle of these cities are four islands divided by snowy mountains. Crowning these mountains is the capital of Kalapa. South of Shambhala lies the garden Malaya; in the east and west the lakes of Lesser Manasa (Tib. Nyive Tso) and the White Lotus, respectively. In the north are situated the residence of all the great religious kings.

A Tibetan text by Acharya Panchen Lobsang Palden Yeshi (1738–1780 A.D.), of the line of Panchen lama lineage, describes Shambhala as a place of great enlightenment and states the reason behind the vast spread of Buddhism is the kings and enlightened beings of Shambhala.

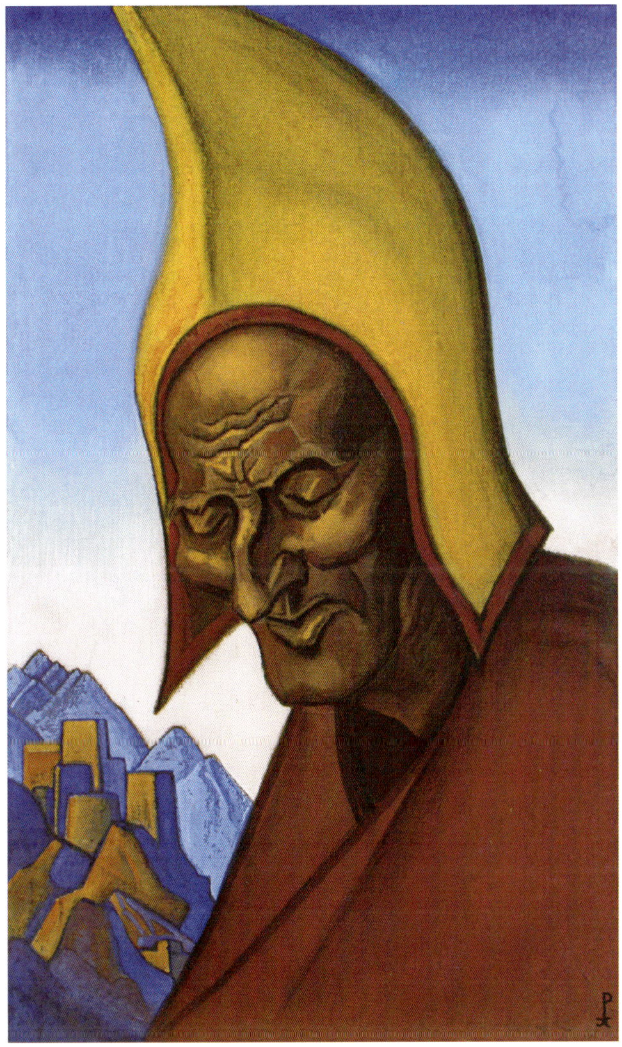

Lama, 1941 (International Centre of the Roerichs, Moscow)

However, to reach Shambhala, one must have acquired the powers of virtuous merit or one may meet with various hindrances on the way, for example, hostile non human spirits, yakshas, or angry murderous Nagas may kill those who take this path according to Buddhist texts.

According to Tibetan Buddhist texts, Lord Buddha gave his second Sermon, the Dharma Chakra Parvartan at a place called Rajgriha (Rajgir, Bihar, India). He made sixteen kinds of Mandalas of the Kalachakra on top of the mountain in Rajgriha. The Buddha seated himself in the middle of the Mandala. The chief disciple to receive this auspicious offering or Kalachakra Abhishek, was the king of Shambhala, Dawa Zangpo. Since then countless others received initiation. Following, the Multantra or principle tantric teaching of Shri Kalachakra was taken by King Dawa

Zangpo in the form of a book to Shambhala. He is said to have written the commentary on twelve thousand roots of the Kalachakra Tantra thereafter. When the Rigden King Pema Karpo (White Lotus) (176-76 B.C.) also known as the Kalki King Pundarika ascended the throne, he preached the Multantra. The Vimalaprabha, a commentary to the Kalachakra Tantra, was composed by him as well. This Vimalaprabha commentary, together with the Laghutantra or the Abridged Kalachakra Tantra form the basis of the Kalachakra practice as it is known today in Tibetan Buddhism, as part of the Vajrayana practices.

It is said that from here others spread the preaching of Shri Kalachakra to India. When the 19th Rigden king of Shambhala ascended the throne, different classical translators or Lotsawas, born in Tibet, preached and spread the Kalachakra Tantra in Tibet.

In his sacred teaching, Panchen Palden Yeshi says that not only Kalachakara Tantra, but all the teachings of sutras and tantras were widespread in Shambhala. Celestial beings, Dak and Dakhinis, miraculously took all the teachings of Je Tsongkhapa Lobsang Dakpa, the 14th century founder of Gelukpa school of Buddhism, to Shambhala. In Shambhala scholars study and teach various texts of, and commentaries on the sutras and tantras. Eighteen different forms of spiritual understanding are represented here.

The works of Madame H.P. Blavatsky, co-founder of The Theosophical Society, and author of *The Secret Doctrine* (1888), alluded to the Kingdom of Shambhala, which drew the interest of many westerners to Inner Asia where it was said to be located. Later 'Shambhala' reverberated in Helena Roerich's books on the spiritual philosophy of Agni Yoga (Living Ethics) and was extensively written about in Nicholas Roerich's Diaries on his Central Asian Expeditions : 'Shambhala', 'Heart of Asia' and 'Altai Himalayas'.

The Transcendent as Theatre in Roerich's Paintings

Joe Troncale

It would not be an exaggeration to say that much of Russian artistic culture in the first two decades of the 20th century was theatricalised.[1] The work that Russian painters did in the theatre was intimately integrated and synthesised with all of the other elements of a production. Many artists of the World of Art Movement were instrumental in revolutionising the theatrical arts in Russia at the invitation and under the direction of Sergei Diaghilev. Following the pioneering steps of Konstantin Korovin, many artists, including Nicholas Roerich, Alexander Benois, Leon Bakst, Mstislav Dobuzhinski and later the

Himalayas, 1933 (Nicholas Roerich Museum, NY)

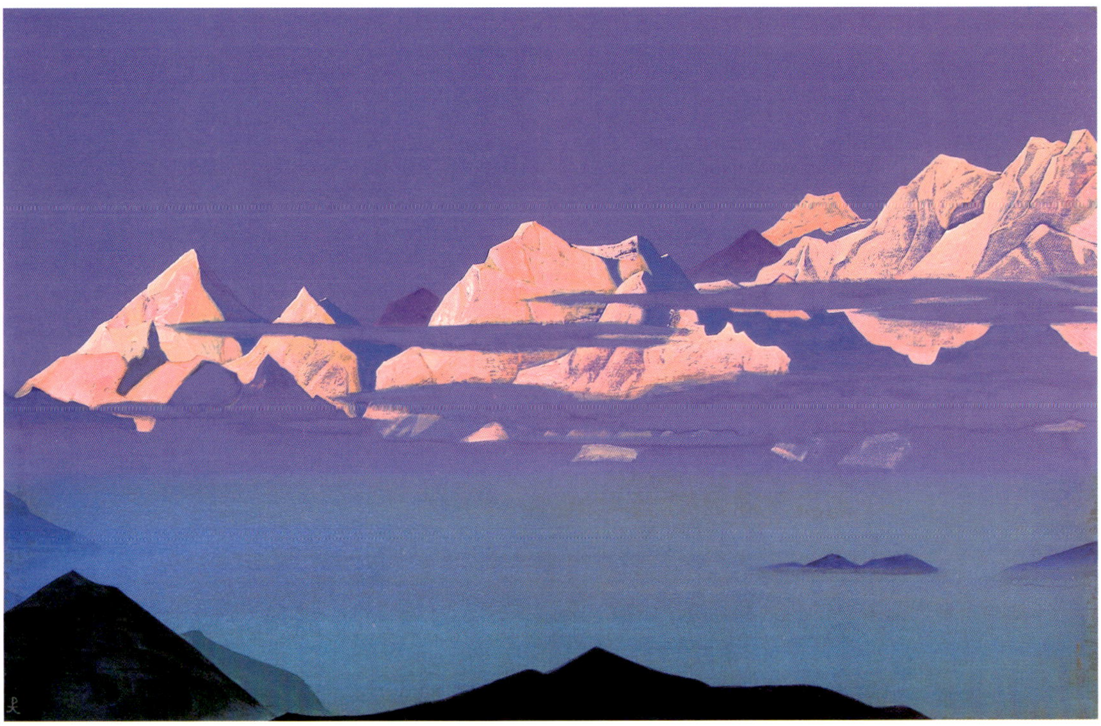

avant-garde painters Natalia Goncharova, Mikhail Larionov and Kazimir Malevich, among others, incarnated in their work a synthesis of the arts with music at its heart. They combined composition, visual design and colour with word, movement and music to express a fundamental unity between the arts that not only transformed opera and ballet as evidenced by the success of the Ballets Russes in Europe, but also transformed their painting.

Russian painters expended enormous creative energies to transform the theatre through the prominent introduction of painting as the significant unifying element in the synthesis of the performing arts. The argument might be made that when the artists returned to their art form outside of the theatre, they could not remain entirely within the same boundaries, personal or aesthetic, that were in place before they began their collaborations. The innovative spirit that characterised their collaborative work in the theatre was too permeating an influence to leave behind. Something of the dramatic, the musical, the movement of dance, the costuming and the notion of their synthesis remained with them. How this synthesis found expression in their painting outside of their theatrical work is an important question, particularly in the case of Roerich who continued to work on theatrical productions even in the later years of his life. To some degree, the theatrical remained within the aesthetic laboratory of those painters and significantly affected their artistic expression. For Roerich, it seems to have provided a means of discovery that transformed his work into a form of theatre beyond the stage, and that suited the expression of his worldview.

The age of the *miriskussniki*, as the World of Art painters were called, was being en-acted, mis-en-scened on the stages of Europe through the genius of their sense of the ornamental in the decorative and graphic arts and of the symbiotic relationship that existed when they were brought into synthesis. In the words of one of the chief ideologues of the World of Art, Dmitri Filosofov, after the group accepted Stanislavsky's invitation to collaborate at the Moscow Art Theatre, the 'World of Art' became the 'World of the Theatre'.[2] Nekhlyudova adds that 'the 'set designer' or, more accurately, the 'dekorativist' becomes synonymous with 'major artist'...; it always meant 'a grand style' and 'complex content'.'[3] The collective efforts of the *miriskussniki* modernised and legitimised theatrical design and decorative art (sets and costumes) to the point of raising them to the level of an art form itself. Through painting, the *miriskussniki* also brought ancient and primeval

Slavic myths to the fore, as well as connections between Russian art, past and present. This was particularly true of Roerich's work. As Syrkina notes:

> 'Roerich's artistic work in the theatre is invariably linked with his painting. The two are bound together by that general circle of interests, ideas and themes, as well as those particularities of the way he thinks in images, all of which come together as one in him as a historian, an archaeologist and an artist—a unique interpreter of ancient eras.'[4]

As Roerich began his work in the theatre one can see the boundaries between easel painting and set design begin to evaporate in his work, and his focus on set design becomes more and more central to his painting. After his successful collaboration with Stravinsky on the Rite of Spring in 1913, Roerich departed noticeably from a strictly Slavic and Russian historical narrative as his primary framework. His focus shifted to what can be called an esoteric narrative that was informed by his enduring interest in the East. His departure from Russia's historical narrative, appropriate as it was for his earlier work, signals the appearance of what appears to be a new non-Russian transcendental narrative. His earlier intuitive archaeological understanding of the roots of Russian culture facilitated this shift to a study of the origins of Eastern culture.

He did not find himself in the theatre, nor did he, as Syrkina writes:

> '...seek to discover himself in the theatre. He already knew his amplitude and it immediately defined his place. The historical epic beginnings of his painting as never before took effect on the heroic repertoire, the attraction to the monumental could not but arrive with him on the musical stage....'[5]

It might be said, however, that it was during the course of his work on more than fifteen theatrical productions that he may have discovered the final dimension that complemented his work and imbued it with the fullest possible expression of his vision.

Once Roerich had achieved success through his work with the 'Russian Seasons' in Europe, the idea of synthesis remained a creative principle and became a distinct quality of his paintings for the

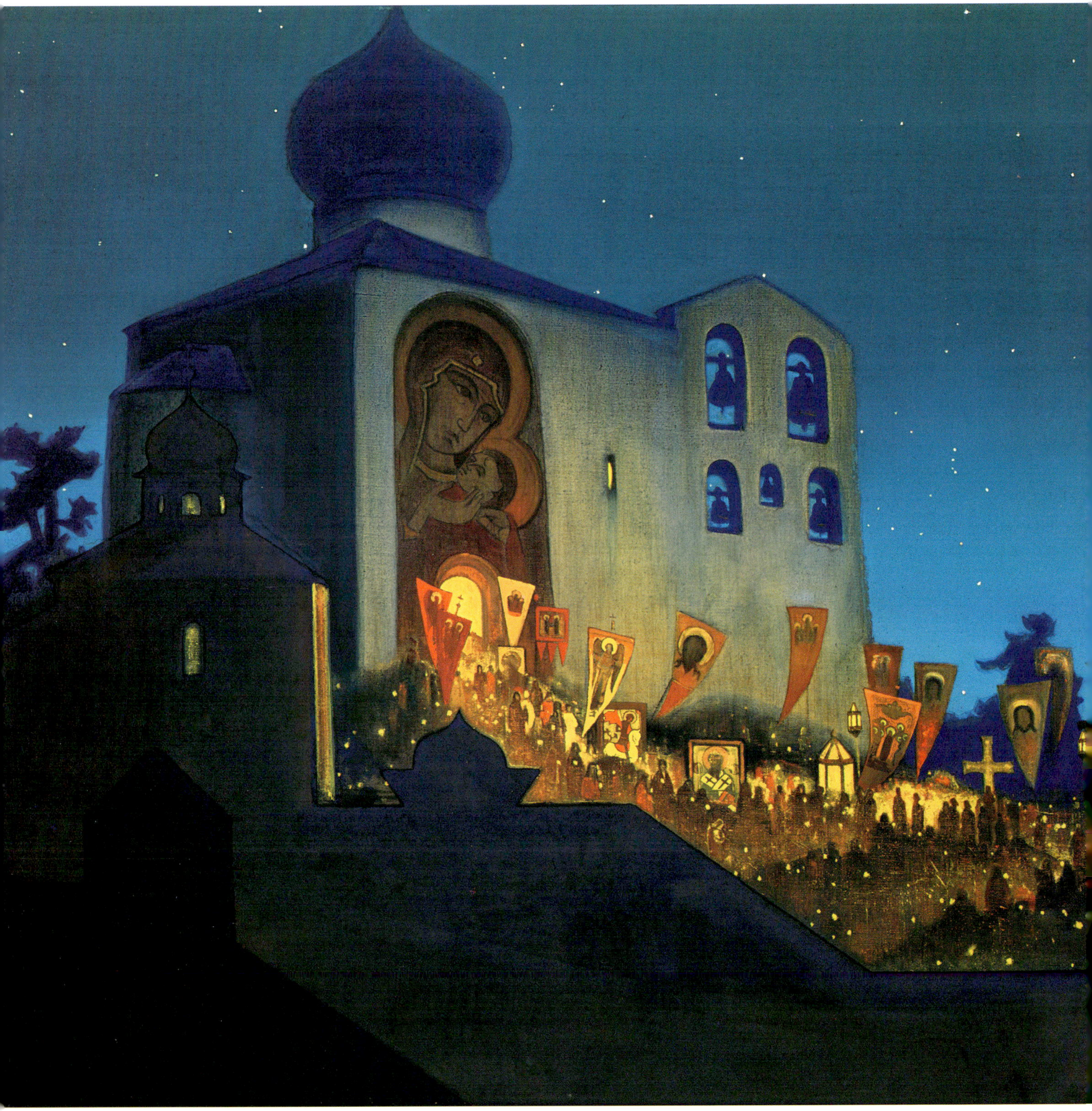

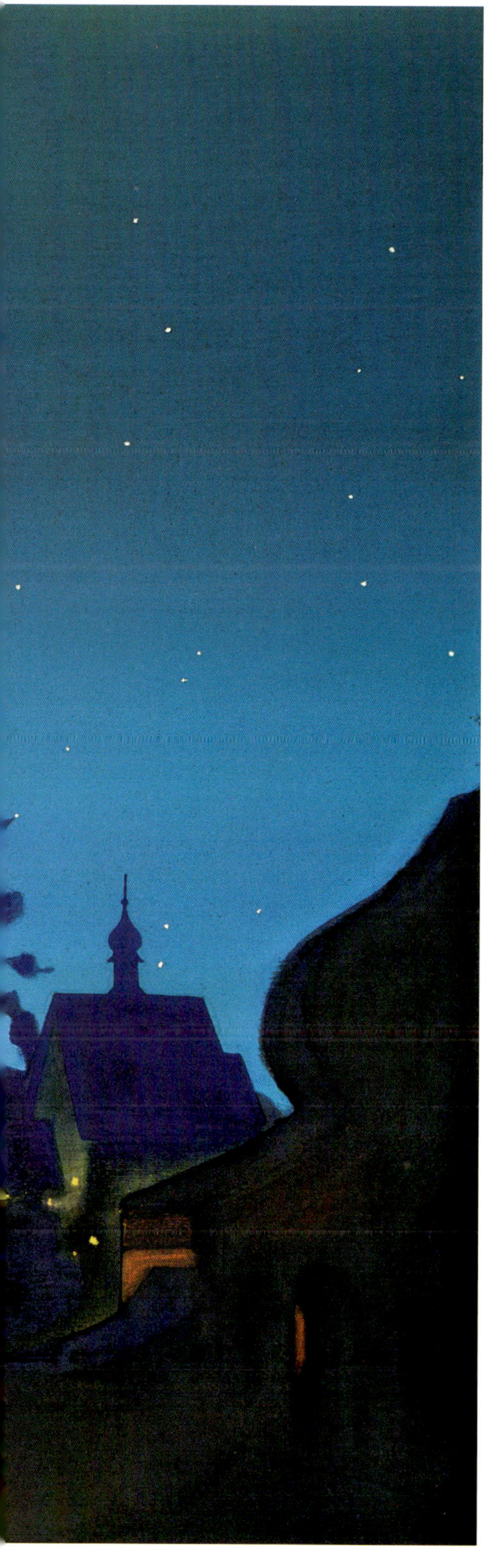

remainder of his life. Such a characterisation of his work provides a way of understanding it not only within the context of his artistic acculturation and contributions as a member of the World of Art but beyond it. Yakovlevna refers to this in her observation that 'Roerich comes out of an age that is being re-created on the stage.'[6] Integrating themselves and their work into the theatre, artists were acting on their intuitive aesthetic sense and not on the theories of theatrical design. There is nothing theoretical in the native aesthetic response of an artist's work because there is nothing theoretical about an artist's aesthetic sense and act of creativity. That is all external to the creative act itself, which is intuitive.

Roerich distinguished himself among his contemporaries by the accomplished quality of the paintings he completed for his theatre designs. Scholars note that when Roerich was working on designs for a theatrical piece, whether for opera or ballet, he typically produced easel paintings that were considered masterpieces in their own right. One scholar writes that Roerich's 'sketches' for set or costume designs can be seen as such only 'provisionally' or 'conditionally' since the boundary between easel painting and theatrical decorative art all but disappears in his work. This symbiotic fusion of easel painting and theatrical decorative art in his painting, as Yakovleva concludes, is one of the particular characteristics of Roerich's oeuvre.[7]

The notion of 'theatricalisation' provides a more grounded entry into the painter's mind to discover the prism through which his ideas were filtered and found final expression in paintings. Theatricalisation is the act of making theatre of something, of

Facing page: The Heavenly Forces are now Invisibly Serving with us (Easter Night), 1934 (International Centre of the Roerichs, Moscow)

dramatising or focussing the spotlights, as it were, on the crucible of human existence where various contours of life emerge as most significant. As the meaning of images emerges, it is acknowledged within the painting itself as something common to all human beings. In the course of 'theatricalisation', the epiphanies of the process of self-understanding are singled out with the purpose of rendering a particular service to humankind and the cosmos. In his work, Roerich is pre-occupied with capturing those, seemingly, random epiphanies that occur in moments of identification with Beauty Itself or ultimate Reality. As Diotima explained to Socrates in Plato's 'Symposium', from that moment on, true virtue can exist and the process of transforming the world can begin because images themselves have become superfluous. For Roerich, the very nature of this moment is dramatic: it is the ultimate goal of human existence. It is an ecstatic event when a human being 'stands outside' of him/herself, prior to the conditionality of forms.

Human evolution and the development of human culture as part of the evolution of the cosmos were central to Roerich's scholarly interests as an archaeologist. As a painter he seemed compelled to monumentalise moments in which evolution coalesces in time. Monumentalism was an important device of Roerich's early period, a time when his paintings captured historically mythical features of ancient Slavic culture and memorialised them. Gradually as he began to include elements of eastern esotericism, the nature of that monumentalism changed. His interest in the conscious evolution of the cosmos became more pronounced, and by the mid-1910s that interest became a fundamental theme of his paintings. Dramatic images of that process, reaching one's full potential through moments of transcendence and ecstasy, began to dominate his work. Combining spectacular mountain views and lavish, other worldly colours, Roerich evoked the context or philosophical landscape of those moments. He explores and emphasises the fundamentally ontological and archetypical nature of the human and aesthetic processes, and enables us to consider the relationship between the two.

Roerich regarded the extraordinary setting of the Himalyas as an integral part of the monumentalisation of the experience of becoming one with that which, from his point of view, is prior to all other events of human existence. Druzhinkina concludes that '[Roerich] successfully synthesised the legends that come from the depths of time with a vital sense of reality, of the landscape of the exotic natural beauty of the East and he fused them into the new artistic reality of his own creative work''.[8] Known as the 'Abode of the Gods', the Himalayas play a significant role in the depiction of the theurgic moment when the divine and human are combined and all human endeavours, including art itself, become a divinely-human instrument of cosmic evolution. From this point until the end of his life in 1947, the transcendental process of human realisation became the corner stone of his aesthetic.

As an artist whose life's work can be considered an important vein of Russian cosmism and as a practitioner of an esoteric school of yoga, Roerich redefined the role of humankind as coincident and coefficient with the cosmos rather than as dominant. He moved from a specific traditional scientific approach of archaeology to an approach that was 'scientific in another way' of transcendental philosophy. He verified this role with images from 'the other side'.[9] A contemporary writes that '[Roerich's] images of the world...serve only as the plastic means to tell people some secret: an ancient secret of the spirit that is in communion with or complicit with other worlds' which Dostoevsky's Alyosha Karamazov and Father Zossima experience. He concludes that:

> '...in the works of the latter period...the themes were as before —'Roerich themes', but one could feel that the main attention of the artist was focussed on the search for...[a] decorative exterior [which] combined with a petrified form and a mesmerised determination of a sense of direction, perhaps, gave his later works a particular edge of fantasy…Nevertheless, one misses the 'former' Roerich, less affected and theatrical and more submerged in his element.'[10]

Undertaking a study of Nicholas Roerich and his work must take into account some of the criticism that has shadowed his work from the beginning of the 20th century to the present day. The character of that critique has evolved from what has been called the 'Benois complex'.[11] Essentially, this 'complex' is, at best, a rather dismissive attitude toward Roerich's work that began with statements as early as the 1910s by Alexander Benois. This complex has coloured the dominant disposition of many western critical approaches to the artist's work. While it is no surprise that the generally universal apotheosis which the painter enjoys in Russia is met with scepticism in the West, the 'Benois Complex', as the name implies, is more often than not an automaticity in response to the specific nature of Roerich's work.

What some critics consider problematic in Roerich's work is that his prolific repetition of what might be called transcendental moments in generalised images tends to profane those images and robs them of an intrinsic aesthetic fullness and meaning that they might otherwise possess. Within the context of world painting that question might have some true relevance. However, within the context of Russian art, it begs the question of what art's purpose or mission is.

As one of the leading artists in the World of Art movement and a pioneer in Russian art history as well as a self-appointed arbiter of Russian art, Benois held very strong views about what was admissible as art and what was not. A harsh critic of individualism as heretical in art, Benois withholds from Roerich the designation as a St. Petersburg artist, but, instead, puts him and his 'Muscovite' sense of art in a class with V. Vasnetov. However, he acknowledged that Roerich sometimes succeeds at climbing to significant heights and his current works are filled with a vigorous epic spirit.[12]

Echoing Benois' critique of Roerich's 'endless visions' and 'painterly meditations', a Russian art historian recently wrote that 'after 1920, Roerich's work no longer belongs to Russian culture. It is worth noting that it barely still relates to art.'[13] Even John Bowlt, a preeminent scholar of early 20th century Russian painting, suffered a momentary lapse when he succumbed to the 'Benois Complex' as recently as the early 1990s.

His role in the development of Russian culture is considered formidable. Torn from the roots of a worldview ineradicably bound to the transcendent by more than seven hundred years of Russian Orthodox traditions and the art of iconography, Russian painting would be unrecognisable. Roerich's work possesses the deepest, most primal elements of that Russian artistic character and reflects those traditions. He devoted his life to the principle of creating a perfect world in concert with all other worlds. He was convinced of the power of art and a consciousness of beauty to effect such a transfiguration. Criticised for the overt and overly philosophical qualities of his work from the beginning, he did not relinquish his vision.

Given the limited discussion of Roerich's work in western scholarship, one might conclude that many western critics, particularly

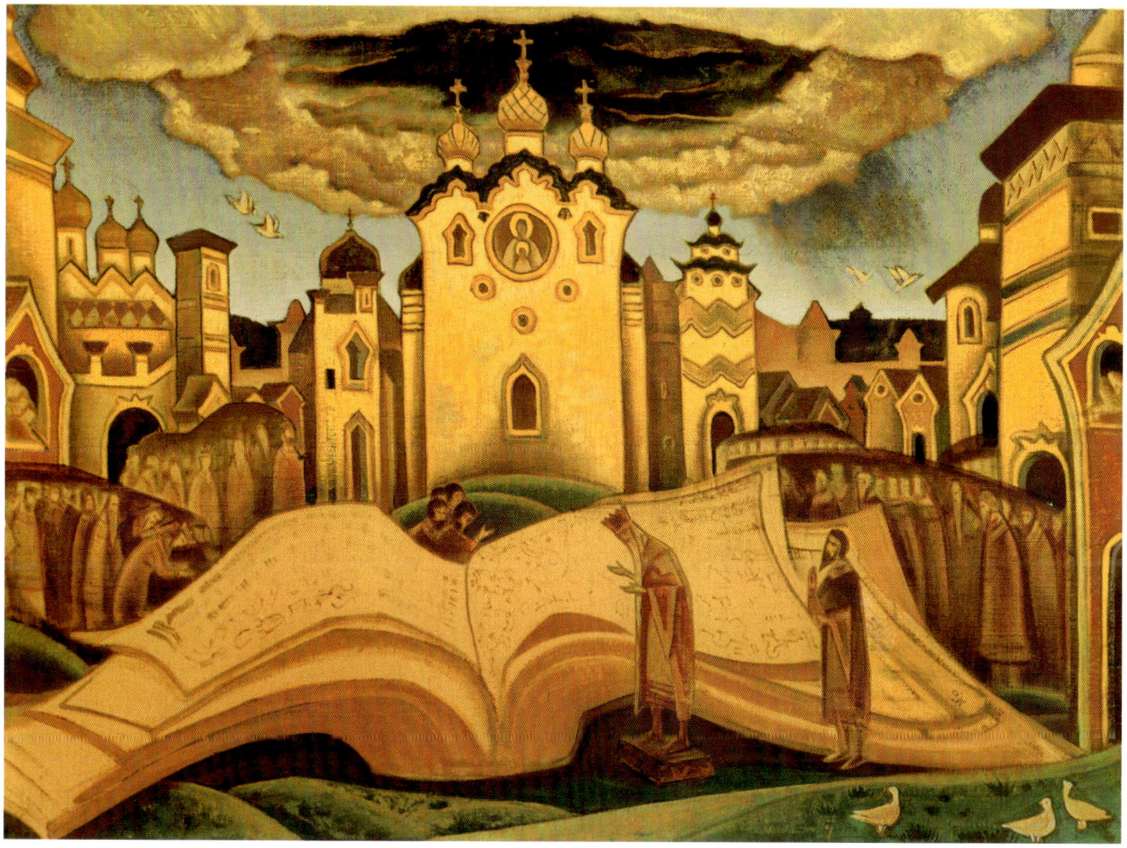

The Book of Doves 1922 (International Centre of the Roerichs, Moscow)

specialists in Russian culture and art, concur with Benois and for this reason choose largely to ignore the artist's work. Whatever validity it may have, Benois' point of view ignores the fact that Roerich's paintings from approximately 1915 until the end of his life were essentially a part of his own yogic practice of Agni Yoga rather than some nod to the 'fashion' of esotericism, as Bowlt suggests. Dedicated to the 'cosmic' notion of art as something sacred and thus purposed towards the expansion of human consciousness and humankind's evolution toward perfection, Roerich produced an oeuvre intended to serve humankind on this path. His was a sacred art as practiced in the Great Eastern tradition and must be considered in that context. Addressing the complexities of research on the occult or the esoteric in Russia, one must acknowledge stumbling blocks inherent in western criticism that we as western observers have assimilated in the course of our own western acculturation in the 'rational'.[14] One can conclude that the Russian proclivity for the esoteric and toward an eastern and theosophical worldview is not something that can be ignored in a culturological study of Russian culture, no matter what cultural or intellectual artifacts are the object of that study. So rather than struggle with or dismiss what is inherently a part of the 'non-rational' Russian heart as it spontaneously arises in the images of Roerich's work, we might consider his theatricalisation of the transcendent as a natural

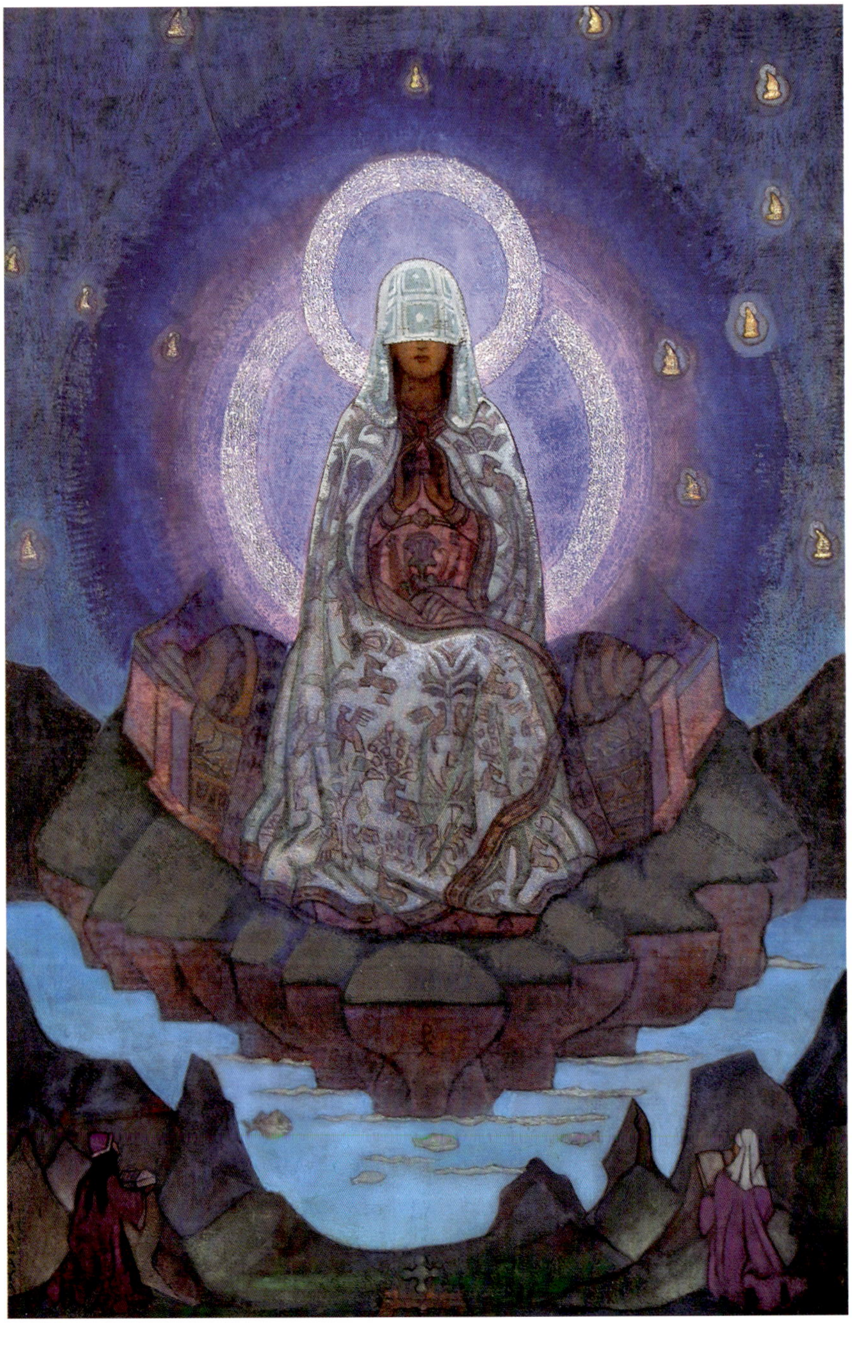

Mother of the World. 1930s (Nicholas Roerich Museum, NY)

way of perceiving and accomodating that as crucial to understanding the aesthetic of his work.

Inspired by Utopian hopes, many of the important political and social figures in early 20th century Russia were, as Stites calls them, 'revolutionary dreamers'.[15] Among those dreamers were the artists of the period who, avant-garde or not, carried on the long Russian tradition of creating art that directly affected fundamental changes in their society and, ultimately, its re-creation. In his own unique way, Nicholas Roerich was also a 'revolutionary dreamer'. His utopian vision was from an esoteric rather than exoteric point of view. Rather than engaging in social daydreaming, Roerich entertained what might be called transcendental visions.

When seen within the context of the sweeping tide of the Russian avant-garde in all of the arts, particularly in painting, of the second and third decades of the 20th century, with its deconstructive mode of fragmentation and rejection of conventional modes of form and colour, Roerich's canvases seem to be an anomaly. However, if, as Mikhail Epshtein defines it, the avant-garde 'represents an anti-art'[16] that displaces art from its rightful sphere with some other force or power which then takes its place, we might also argue that Roerich's work is merely a representation of an extreme at the other end of the spectrum from Malevich and other Russian avant-garde artists.

Considering the spiritual foundation of Roerich's work beginning in 1915, one might argue further that since 'the avant-garde is the artistic assimilation of precisely those zones of existence which are invisible, intangible and ineffable, Roerich's paintings could be seen simply as the articulation of the invisible, the intangible and the ineffable, which is, after all, the specific character of art, particularly the art of the avant-garde.'[17] Both extremes of the avant-garde were 'spiritual', that is, both were attempting to realign humankind with some higher truth, whatever it might be called, whether it was the divine, a cosmic consciousness, etc. Roerich, however, seems to have been sitting on the edge of imagination, not picturing either the divine or the truth as sought by humankind or even the conditional reality in which it lives. His focus seems always to be on the space between the two, and his intention was to bridge the gap between them. His artistic eye is preoccupied with the etheric heights imaged in the Himalyas where one *might* experience the transcendence to pure energy and consciousness, or where those who have experienced it, visually or psycho-physically, are poised on the edge of the precipice of their psycho-physical existence savouring their vision and the experience of it. However impenetrable those images might seem, their 'logic' derives apparently from the painter's decision to place his aesthetic expression at the service of such experience.

The most powerful principle that drove the development of both idea and form in Russian painting of the last half of the 19th century was the artist's 'consciousness' as part of the intelligentsia of the civic and moral responsibility to ameliorate the condition of the Russian people through the creative and regenerative process of art. Even though the *miriskussniki* attempted in vain to establish the primacy of art for art's sake at the beginning of the 20th century, the idea of art as purposed to transform humankind was maintained as a part of the aesthetic in the work of the majority of artists outside that small circle. From 1905 to 1917 it was reaffirmed with a vengence. It can be said that Kazimir Malevich and Pavel Filonov, two of the most dynamic proponents of modernism in Russian painting, pursued this principle in their highly experimental work. They were both intent on changing the world, and most particularly their own Russian world, through their work. Malevich chose the path of the geometrisation of all form, Filonov—the anatomical autopsy of all form. The work of Roerich stands in sharp contrast to that of Malevich and Filonov. Although Roerich did not pursue experimentation in form to the degree that the Russian avant-garde did, from approximately 1915 until his death his work was another kind of experimentation that is no less significant in philosophical and formal terms in the history of Russian painting. As one of the artists whose work defined and inspired the exploration of the landscape of Russian cosmism for more than one generation of painters, Roerich was concerned not only with the renewal and regeneration of Russia's life poential through his work as were the artists of the 19th century, but also, and more broadly, with the evolution of the entire cosmos and man's role in it. Roerich's main concern was not art itself, but what art as Beauty does to 'consciousness', how it alters, clarifies, and expresses 'consciousness' of the Beautiful. His work is a measure not of the effects that art may have directly on the cosmos in order to change or somehow 'reorder' it, but, rather, it is a measure of how art alters and clarifies 'consciousness' in humankind. Human 'consciousness' would then have to go about the arduous task of reordering itself within the cosmos.

In a much broader sense of 'theatricalisation', one could say that Roerich's life was a theatre. He was on stage with high-level Bolsheviks and high-level American political figures, and roamed the Mongolian deserts in search of a New Russia. He played a role necessary to gain the needed support for his visions to become reality. There is the necessity for an inherent non-conventionality to remain focussed on the visions of an unconditional nature while dealing forcefully with the details of conventional life. So argue scholars who repeatedly appeal to our sense of this when tracing what might be considered by some to be the more questionable contours of Roerich's life after the October Revolution.

Roerich was, indeed, every bit as much a visionary as was any self-professed and self-obsessed avant-garde Russian artist of the pre- and post-Revolutionary period. However, there was a difference. That difference is what makes Roerich unique. Whether one finds Roerich's work convincing intellectually may not be as important as finding it perceptually enthralling as one merely engages its etherially attractive qualities. After all, it was Malevich who defined 'perceptual feeling' as supreme in art.[18]

End Notes

1. V. Petrov-Stromsky, Tysyacha let russkogo iskusstva: istoria, estetika, kul'turologia (Moskva, 1999), 304.
2. Elena Panteleevna Yakovlevna, *Teatral'no-dekoratsionnnoe iskusstvo N.K. Roericha* (Sankt-Peterburg, 1996), 62.
3. M.K. Neklyudova, Traditsii i novatorstvo v russkom iskusstve kontsa xix—nachala xx veka (Moskva, 1991), 25.
4. F. Syrkina, 'Roerich i teatr' in M.T. Kuz'mina, ed., *N.K. Roerich: zhizn' i tvorchestvo* (Moskva, 1978), 79.
5. *ibid*, 80.
6. Elena Panteleevna Yakovlevna, *Teatral'no-dekoratsionnnoe iskusstvo N.K. Roericha* (Sankt-Peterburg, 1996), 10-11.
7. *ibid*, 10-11.
8. N.G. Druzhinkina, 'Mif v iskusstve N.K. Roericha' in *Smysly mifa: mifologiya v istorii i kul'ture: Sbornik v chest' 90-letiya professora M.I. Shakhnovicha, Seriya* 'Mysliteli" vypusk #8 (Sankt-Peterburg, 2001), 300.
9. M.C. Kagan, ed., Filosofiia kul'tury kak teoreticheskaia distsiplina (Sankt-Peterburg, 1998), 369.
10. Sergei Makovsky, *Siluety russkikh khudozhnikov* (Moskva,1999), 92.
11. N.V. Tyutyugina, 'Комплекс Бенуа', или к проблеме оценки творчества Н.К.Рериха 1920–1940-х гг.', 2. Electronic Library of the International Roerich Center at http://lib.roerich-museum.ru/node/848.
12. A.N. Benua, *Russkaya Shkola Zhivopisi* (Moskva, 1997), 110-111.
13. V. Petrov-Stromsky, Tysycha let russkogo iskusstva, 304.
14. There are two rather good studies by western critics of the occult in Russia that warrant mentioning here. The first of its kind was *The Occult in Russian and Soviet Culture*, ed. Bernice Glatzer Rosenthal (Ithaca, 1997) and the second was 'The Occult Revival in Russia Today and Its Impact on Literature' by Birgit Menzel in The Harriman Review, Vol. 16, No. 1 (Spring 2007), 1-14. Each breaks new ground in the scholarship on this topic.
15. Richard Stites, Revolutionary Dreams: Utopian Vision and Experimental Life in the Russian Revolution (New York, 1989).
16. Mikhail Epshtein, 'Avant-Garde Art and Religious Consciousness,' *Five Fingers Review: Vanishing Points* #10, (San Francisco, 1991), 166-169.
17. *ibid*, 166-169.
18. Kazimir Malevich, *The Non-Objective World: The Manifesto of Suprematism* (New York: Dover Publications, 2003).

Nicholas Roerich: Artist and Humanist

Shri Prakash

A holistic analysis of the life and the times, the philosophy, work and activities of Nicholas Roerich provides at one and the same time his vision of building a global society and culture with its roots going deep into existing national and ethical sources. Roerich was born into a prosperous Russian family settled in St. Petersburg. His great attachment to rationalism, humanism, art, archaeology, philosophy, poetry and international public activity to preserve peace and conserve culture in its finest meaning as a basis and expression of a multi-cultural human civilisation were not inherited virtues. Members of Roerich's family mainly served as prominent military and administrative employees in Russia since the reign of Russian monarch, Peter I, also known as Peter the Great, who was famous

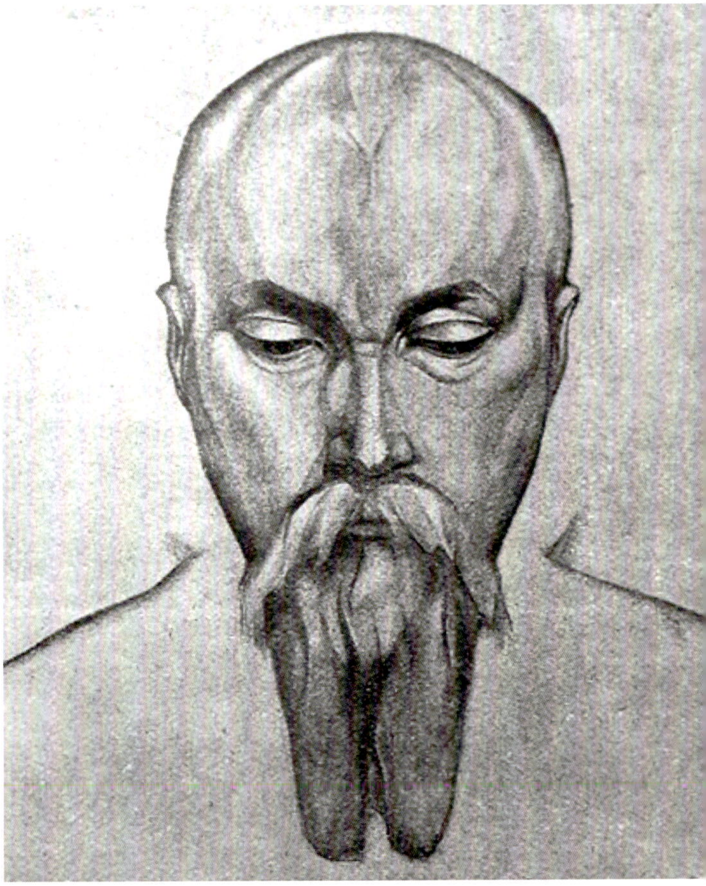

Portrait of Nicholas Roerich, ca. 1930 (International Centre of the Roerichs, Moscow)

for building a strong and prosperous Russia, employing many Western engineers and architects. His father Konstantin Fedovorich was a well-known notary and his mother Maria Vasilevna Kalashnikova was descended from a long line of merchants and traders.

Nicholas Roerich's multifarious interests and abilities developed from childhood inspirations and dedicated hard work. For example, when he was just nine years old, a noted archaeologist came to explore the St. Petersburg region. Knowing the Roerich family and seeing Nicholas' enthusiasm, he asked him to accompany him on his excavations of the local tumuli, which helped him to develop a lifelong interest in archaeology, starting with Russian archaeology as revealing a visual inheritance of human culture all over the world. He studied law as his family wanted him to, but his heart was set on training as a painter. In 1897, Nicholas Roerich graduated from the Emperor's Academy of Arts, St. Petersburg and for a few years he further studied painting in the studio of the famous Russian landscape painter Arkship Kuindzhi.

There is an underlying and unifying theme of Roerich's universe. One of the clearest statements of his philosophical quest and conclusion was made by Nicholas Roerich in his address to the Dalton School in 1930. It is worthwhile quoting parts of his speech for the striking rationality that underlies his philosophy. Nicholas Roerich said that he was once asked, 'What was the difference between the East and West?' He answered, 'The best roses of the East and the West have the same fragrance, so while we are speaking about opposition and differences, essentially we have the great 'One', because really all law is one and, under this law, everything is one.' In essence, Roerich is referring in his own way to the similarity of all human beings and their right to equality and freedom. For a person from his social background, his views represent a radical revision of values which he might have been taught in his childhood. His rational philosophy and humanism demonstrated the achievements of Russian civilisations epitomised by the likes of Leo Tolstoy. The same universality is expressed by Roerich in his view on how to build a happy life. He emphasised that after visiting more than twenty-five countries, he had come to the conclusion that happiness could be had only through the pursuit of the beautiful. The concept of the Beautiful was not for Roerich any addiction to a pursuit of beauty per se but the idea of what a happy and beautiful society used interchangeably should be and the freedom to construct it as individuals and groups.

It was this inspirational philosophy which provided a common ground for Roerich and Rabindranath Tagore, one of India's leading poets (1861-1941) and winner of the Nobel Prize in Literature in 1913. Roerich met Tagore and modelled some of his paintings on famous texts like *Gitanjali* and Tagore's notion of freedom and fearlessness as the basis for human creativity and happiness.

Select Bibliography

Shaposhnikova L.V. 'Scientist, Thinker, Painter,' Moscow, International Centre of the Roerichs, 2006.
Roerich, Nicholas. *Realm of Light*, International Roerich Memorial Trust, Naggar, Himachal Pradesh, 2009.

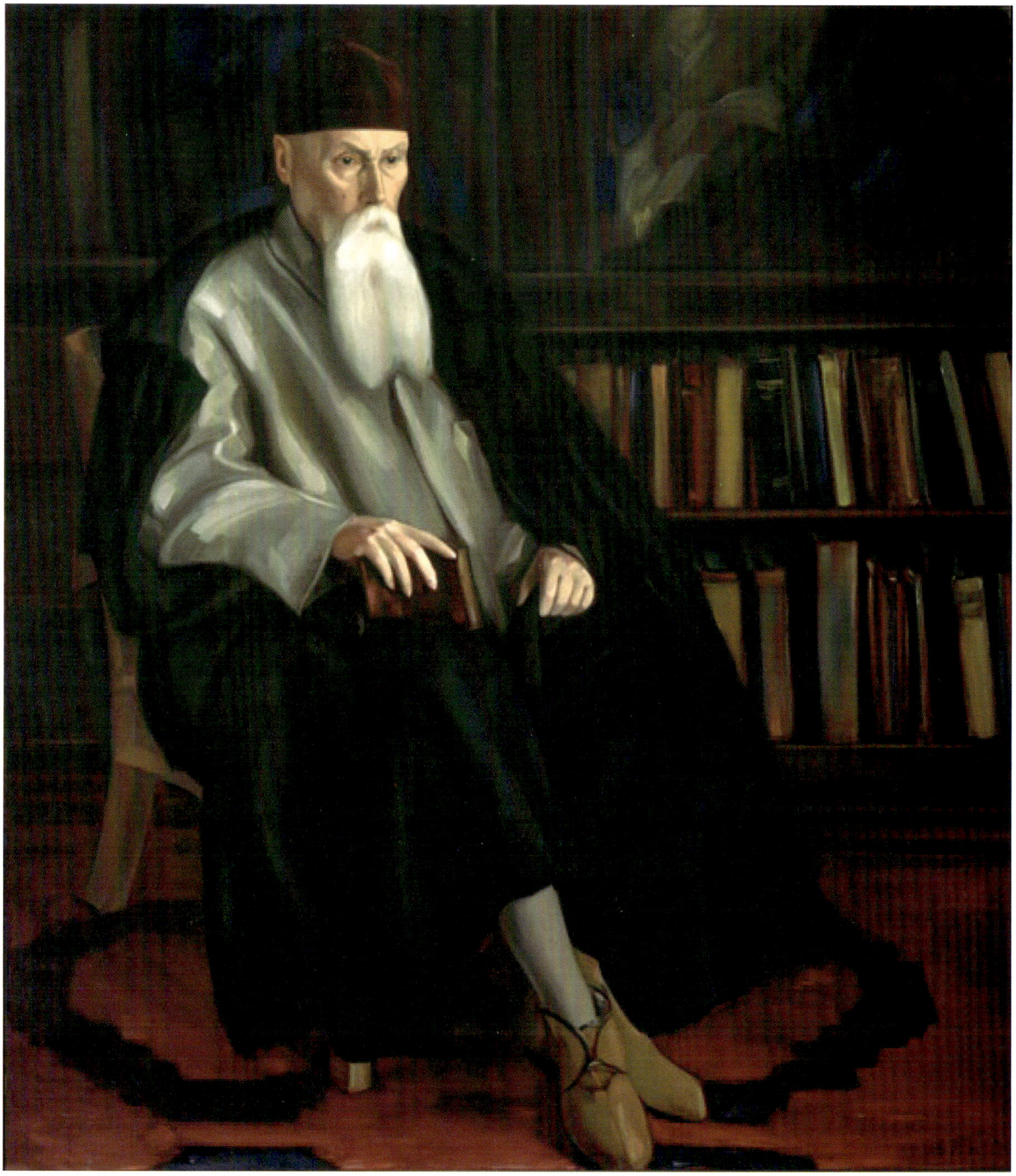

Nicholas Roerich, by Svetoslav Roerich, 1937

Nicholas Roerich: Influences and Experiences

Ven. Lama Doboom Tulku

Russian artist Nicholas Roerich witnessed the outbreak of World War I and a revolution that upturned the Romanov monarchy in his native land. New political ideologies threatened to shatter the fragile peace. Perhaps it was as a result of these events, that he began to advocate a return to the ancient roots of human wisdom, which assert the importance of spiritual life and of peaceful co-existence. He found those messages in the different religious and artistic traditions of the world. Through his paintings and writings, he sought to interpret for his contemporaries all that was edifying and uplifting in their own prehistoric culture and in the unfamiliar cultures of the peoples of Central Asia, Tibet and India.

Roerich's philosophical evolution began at a time when many European thinkers including Russian Indologists were discovering

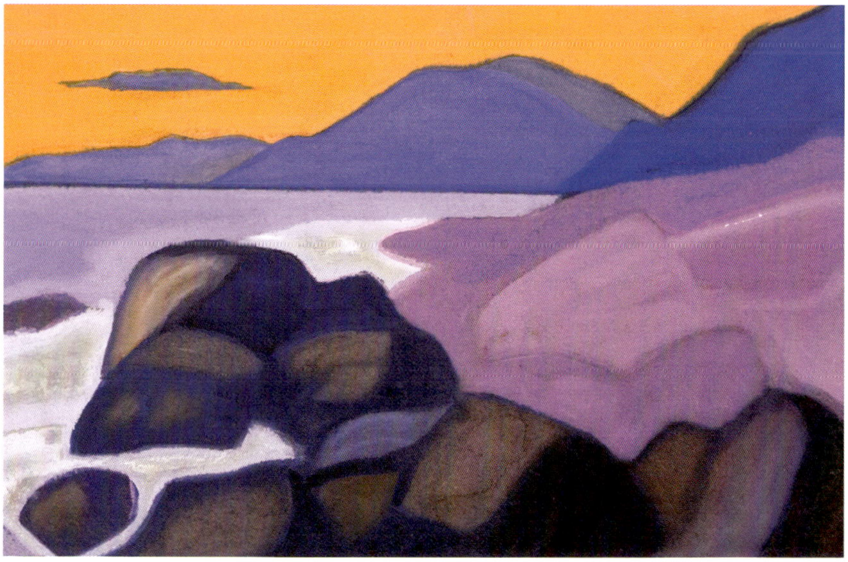

On the Shore of Pongola Lake (International Roerich Memorial Trust, Naggar, Kullu)

the civilisations of the East. He and Helena Roerich were also much influenced by the work of theosophist, Madame Blavatsky and together they read the sacred scriptures of India and Tibet. Their study of ancient ideas and modes of life drew them East, towards the vast steppes of Mongolia and the Himalayan regions.

Why did Roerich choose to explore those strange lands to the East and South of the Great Russian Federation? His 'orientation', so to speak, began early: in the Roerichs' country house with its Sanskrit name, *Isvara,* where hung a picture of the Himalayan peak of Kanchenjunga, which he was to paint many times over in later life. He was a member of the Committee that supervised the building of a Buddhist temple in St. Petersburg. Speaking of that time in relation to his later quest, he said: 'it was during the construction of a Buddhist temple in the Russian capital that I first heard of Shambhala...from a very learned Buriat Lama...It will be known some day why this name pronounced under such circumstances had a great significance.'[1] Other 'coincidences' exist. In Darjeeling, he chose to live in the 'Talai Pho Brang', said to have once been the residence of the thirteenth Dalai Lama, which had become a pilgrimage site for visiting Lamas

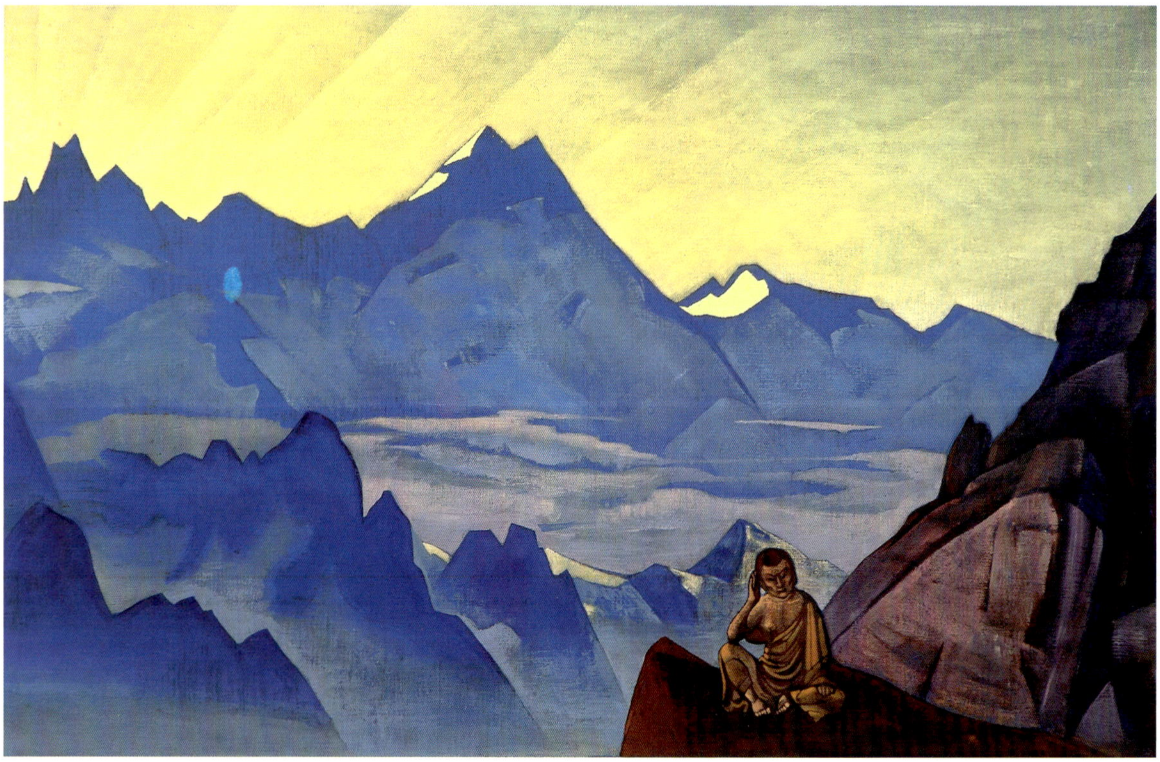

Milarepa, the One Who Harkened, from 'Banners of the East' series, 1925 (Nicholas Roerich Museum, NY)

and ordinary Tibetans. There he met the Geshe Rinpoche of Chumbi Valley with whom he established a long friendship. This Lama imparted to him some of the secret teachings of Shambhala.[2]

These impressions emerge from the narrative he penned during his journey. In an age of materialism, Roerich always upheld the primacy of spiritual things. He believed in the universality of the spiritual quest, which he saw as the ultimate goal of great and enduring civilisations. He linked the prophetic messages of Judeo-Christian and Islamic faiths with those of the older religious traditions of Asia and of the indigenous peoples of the Americas. In his essay, 'Maitreya' he spoke of 'the merging trends of thought of the most seemingly distant individuals.' To his early formula 'Maitreya, Massiah, Muntazar' as the names of the coming teacher of 'the New Era', he added a long list of other names from different lands. His paintings and travelogues are a narrative of that journey.

Roerich felt that denial and disparagement of the forms and goals of alien religious expression only led to an impoverishment of one's own understanding. They were 'the most hideous aspects which obscure the light of the heart'.[3] He saw connections between the wisdom traditions of others with the writings of Russian theologians and discoveries of material scientists of his day. He wrote, 'This is not a casual eclecticism. On the contrary, it is just the opposite: from all directions—to the one. Because in every human heart, in the entire human kingdom, exists one and the same striving to Bliss...'[4]

He also believed that the path to the future regeneration of human civilisation would be totally inclusive. All the people of the world and all classes of people should and would have access to the treasures of the Path—to beauty, learning and light. He believed that art alone could unify humankind. As Director of the Art School run by the Society for the Encouragement of the Arts in 1906, he insisted on opening the doors of this institution to all children regardless of their social class.[5] In America, he introduced for the first time lessons in music and sculpture for the blind. The credo of the school must have been inspiring for donors, faculty and students alike.[6]

A third impression that emerges is that Roerich always points to the future, to the New Era to come, full of unimaginable energies. He was among the first Europeans to take this legend seriously. Scholar-explorers of the previous centuries, Alexander Csoma de Koros,

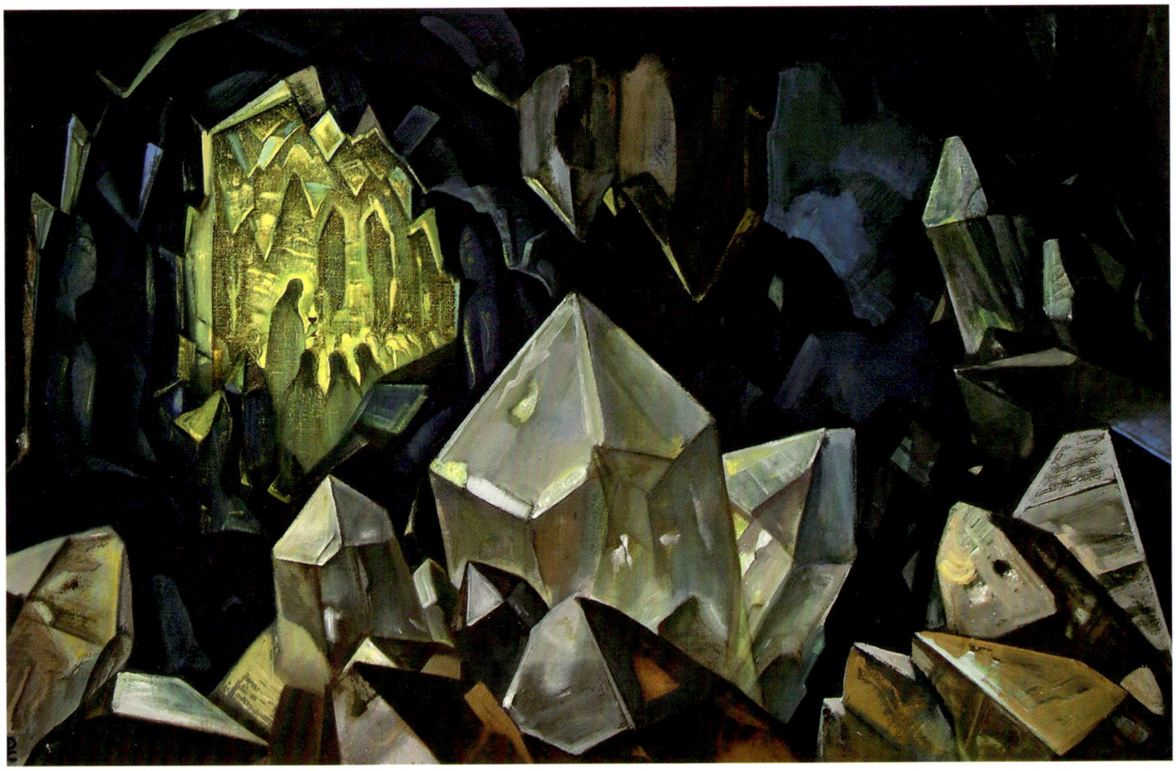

Most Sacred (Treasure of the Mountain), 1933 (Nicholas Roerich Museum, NY)

the Hungarian pioneer and scholar, had mentioned it and Albert Gruenwedel, the German explorer of Central Asia had published a translation of the Panchen Lama's *Path to Shambhala*. Roerich never doubted its existence on some plane, whether material or mental. But he could link the prophecies of Shambhala, its warrior king Rigden Jyapo and the coming of the future Buddha Maitreya to every other known messianic teaching, to the Hindu Kalki avatar of the Vishnu Purana, the Belovodye of Siberia, the Christian book of Revelation, the Islamic and Christian legends of the Black Stone and the Grail. His enthralling Himalayan paintings show the Messengers of the coming age, or the Keepers of the Secret, the 'Mahatmas', who will stay in the mountains till the Age of Kali, of Hindu mythology, ends.

Roerich may have learnt about the Kalachakra teachings, which are closely connected to Shambhala from Dromo Geshe Rinpoche who left Tibet after the flight of the Panchen Lama in 1923, an event foretold in the Shambhala prophecies. He summarised them thus: 'The Teaching of Shambhala is a Teaching of Life. As in the Hindu Yogas, the Teaching shows how to use the finest energies filling the macrocosmos, which energies can as mightily be manifested in our microcosmos.'[7] He saw the signs of the immanent manifestation of this state everywhere. They 'exultingly impel us towards the future'. It is possibly this messianic promise of a different, more perfect world that makes his collection of paintings in different art galleries and his own home in Naggar, Kullu, Himachal Pradesh, a province North India, a place of pilgrimage for young seekers of today.

Many of Roerich's convictions find an echo in the teachings of Tibetan Buddhist masters. Writing somewhere in the highlands of Central Asia, he says: 'The essential nature of people is fundamentally good... Everything evil and hideously harmful is primarily sediment resulting from ignorance.'[8] As often as he could, he tried to stop his Mongolian sharp shooters from killing wild yaks and kyang. He wrote later about the need to protect all living beings from slaughter. Living in the chaos of Indian cities, he wrote: 'Two lives are evident in Asia and for that don't be discouraged by the sights of everyday life. Easily you can be rewarded with the Great Truth that will enwrap you forever.'

An enduring legacy is the work of Roerich's son George (Yuri), who accompanied him on the Central Asian Expedition of 1923–28 and translated, with Gendun Choepel, one of the most important intellectuals of Tibet in the 20th century and considered a lama incarnate, *The Blue Annals*. Had he lived longer, he would have been among the foremost interpreters of Asian cultures to the Western mind.

End Notes

1. Nicholas. Roerich. *Himalayas – Abode of Light*, London: David Marlowe. 1947.
2. *ibid*, p. 110.
3. Nicholas. Roerich. Maitreya, New York: 1932, reprinted 2006 by IRMT, Naggar, Kullu.
4. *ibid*. pp. 4-5.
5. Jaquelene, Decter. *Nicholas Roerich: The Life and Art of a Russian Master*. Inner Traditions International and Nicholas Roerich Museum. 1989. p. 67.
6. *ibid*.
7. Nicholas. Roerich. (n.d.) *Altai–Himalaya: A Travel Diary*. London: Jarrolds Publishers. p. 121.
8. Nicholas. Roerich. *The Invincible*, New York: Nicholas Roerich Museum. 1974.

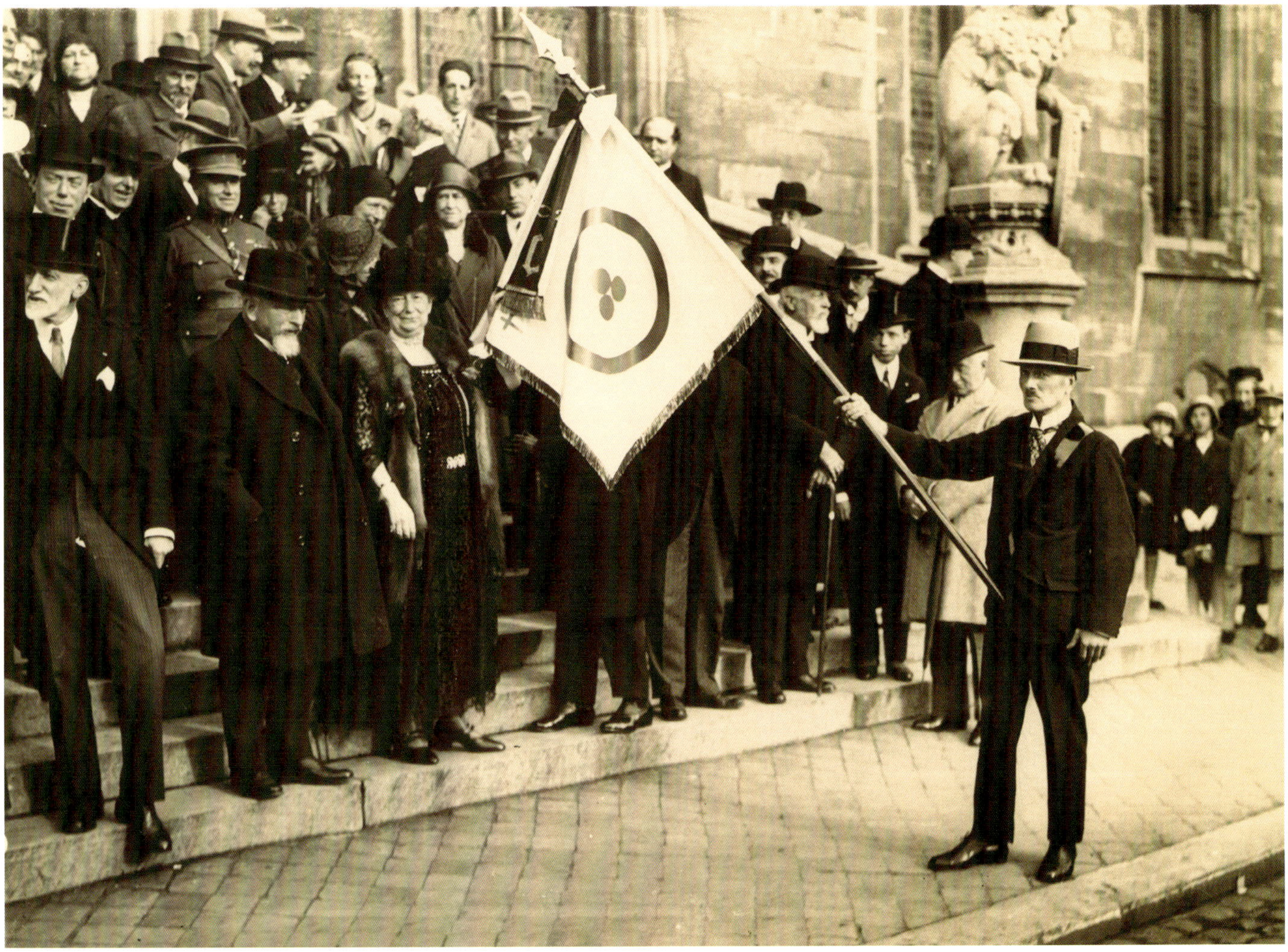

Participants of the 1st Conference for the Roerich Pact at the reception, given by the Bruges municipality in the City Hall (Gothic Hall). September 13, 1931 (International Centre of the Roerichs, Moscow)

The Roerich Pact: Original Collaborators

Kenneth Archer

It is not surprising that the Russian painter, Nicholas Roerich (1874–1947), the son of a lawyer and a graduate of the Faculty of Law at the University of St. Petersburg as well as a graduate of the Academy of Art, would create a legally binding international agreement to protect works of art. He did not study law by choice but, once committed, did his best to make it serve his artistic and historical interests. His law school thesis on cannon law and aesthetics resourcefully combined law and art. It was just the first step towards the eventual peace pact that would bear the name Roerich.

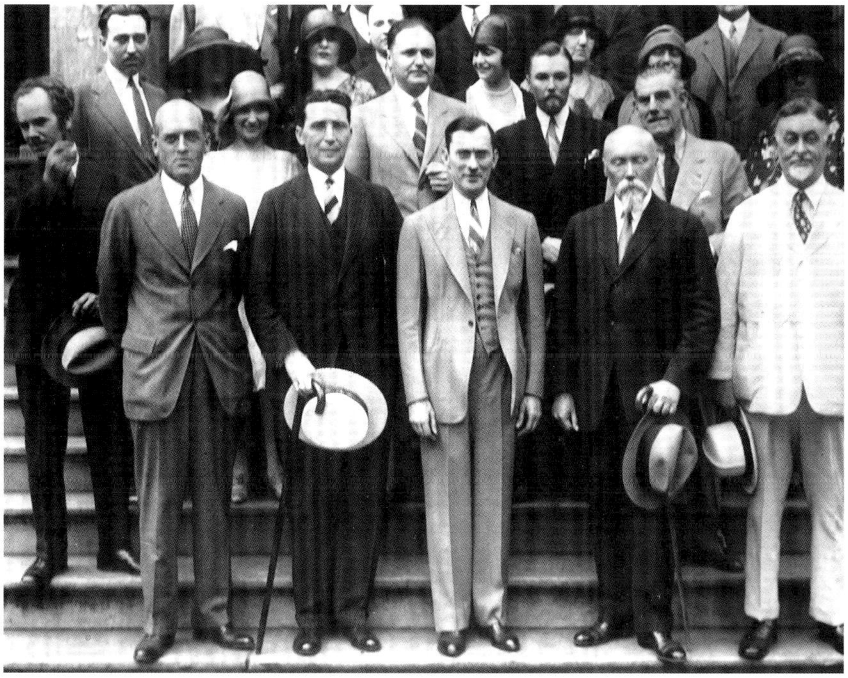

Left to right, first row, starting with second: Louis Horch, James Walker, Nicholas Roerich, Charles Crane; second row: Georgiy Grebenshchikov, Sina Lichtmann, Maurice Lichtmann, George Roerich; behind him: Sofie Shafran; to the right of her: Nettie Horch June 20, 1929. City Hall, New York: Reception given by New York City Mayor, James Walker, at City Hall in honour of Nicholas Roerich (Nicholas Roerich Museum Archive, NY)

In 1903 and 1904, the artist, accompanied by his wife Helena, toured the ancient cities of Russia—Yaroslavl, Rostov, Vladimir, Pskov, Novgorod and others. During these trips he executed in oil a series of around 90 architectural paintings, some of which still survive at the Oriental Museum in Moscow. While Roerich was painting, his wife—the daughter of Ivan Ivanovich Shaposhnikov, a Russian architect—took photographs of the buildings.

Tsar Nicholas II was so pleased with Roerich's architectural paintings that he arranged for them to be shown as a special exhibition in Moscow in 1904. Concerned about the condition of these buildings, Roerich used this opportunity to campaign for their preservation. His initiative, which included a formal proposal to the Society of Architects, contained the seed of the Roerich Pact, which he was to campaign for worldwide twenty-five years later. The artist's concern for the safety of ancient buildings, and indeed all works of art, came to the fore again in 1914, at the start of the First World War. He made a proposal at that time to the Russian Government for a treaty of protection among nations. The proposal was met with interest, but warfare prevented the necessary multilateral negotiations. Sina Fosdick, the Executive

Nicholas Roerich and Svetoslav Roerich amidst the New York Museum co-workers, 1920 (Nicholas Roerich Museum Archive, NY)

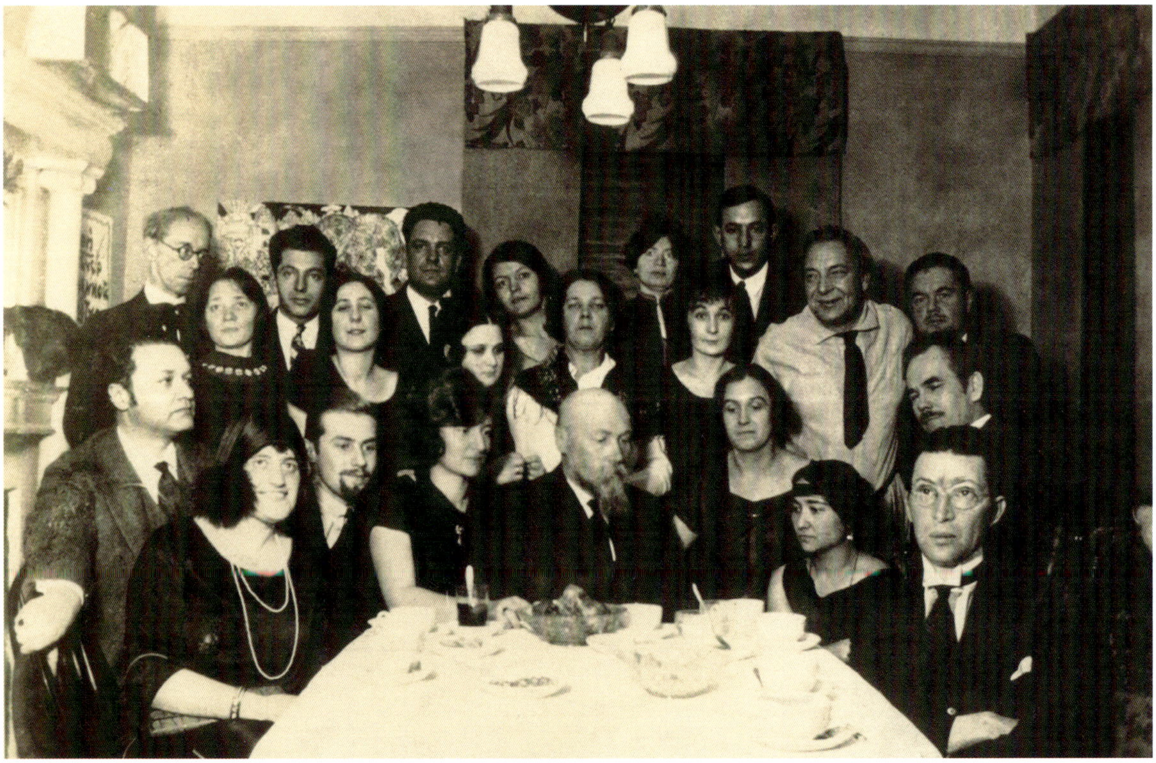

Vice-President of the Nicholas Roerich Museum in New York, and a member of the organising committee for the Roerich Pact in the 1930s, confirmed the dates of Roerich's early initiatives from which the idea of the Pact originated:

> 'In 1904 – it was a plan for the international protection of cultural sites and institutions in war and peace. He proposed it to the Imperial Society of Architects at that time and, later, in 1914, to the state authorities.'[2]

A number of Roerich's paintings at that time reflected his response to world events: notable examples are, *The Cry of the Serpent, The Doomed City, The Crowns, The Lurid Glare* and *Human Deeds*, all executed in tempera in 1914. Fosdick regarded these canvases as premonitory:

> 'From 1912 one can detect a prophetic trend in Prof. Roerich's work. In that year he painted *The Last Angel*, in which the world is in conflagration. In 1914 he painted *Human Deeds*, which showed a group of terrified wise men looking at a destroyed city. In these and other canvases of a similar character, he portrayed the threatening catastrophe he had foreseen.'[3]

Roerich and his family left Russia around the time of the Revolution in 1917, and lived for a while in Finland and Scandinavia. He left much of value behind in St. Petersburg: his collections of artworks and artefacts; the well-remunerated administrative and pedagogic positions at the institution where he worked; clients and sponsors; as well as his standing and reputation in Russian society. It was to take a decade and more for Roerich to build a base strong enough on which to propose and campaign for his Pact. He needed to secure income, reputation and stature in the West to match what he had in Tsarist Russia.

The artist's former secretary, Vladimir Shibayev, detailed the chronology and conditions of Roerich's life in the years that led up to the Pact. He explained that in 1919, the artist had come to England to do theatrical work with Sir Thomas Beecham at Covent Garden and with Sergei Diaghilev for the Ballets Russes. Interviewed in 1972, at Cardiff University, Wales, where he lectured in Russian studies,

Shibayev said that he had first met Roerich in London and had assisted him in various ways until becoming his full-time secretary in 1928. Sometimes referring to memoirs drafted in Russian, Shibayev related how the Roerich family had planned to go to India in 1920:

> 'I accepted with joy his suggestion to join him and his family in going to India, where on the invitation of the Indian poet, Rabindranath Tagore, he soon intended to go. With my knowledge of English, I was to join him as his private secretary.'[4]

Shibayev explained how there had been a change of plan and the artist and his family had postponed their trip to India and gone to the US instead:

> 'Prof. Roerich received an invitation from Dr. Robert Harshe, Director of the Chicago Art Institute, to visit America on a tour of 30 cities in the USA. This was a chapter of Prof. Roerich's biography in which I did not participate, because he did not require the services of a secretary in America, and I temporarily remained in Europe.'[5]

Sina Fosdick, in the course of the interviews at the Nicholas Roerich Museum's premises, gave details of institutions the artist had set up during his three-year stay in the United States. As she did so she leafed through and quoted from publications she had authored:

> 'In 1921 Prof. Roerich founded *Cors Ardens*, the International Society of Artists. Later that same year he founded the Master School of United Arts, which embodied his belief that all the arts should be united under one roof. A number of artists, musicians and teachers joined him in these cultural enterprises. In 1923, the year he left to embark on his Central Asian Expedition, the Roerich Museum opened.'[6]

The Roerich Museum in New York was the centre of Roerich's international work as a cultural activist. It was the hub of several institutions. There was the Museum itself, which was open daily and free to the public. There were the International Art Centre, which set up exhibitions; the Master Institute, with classes in music, painting,

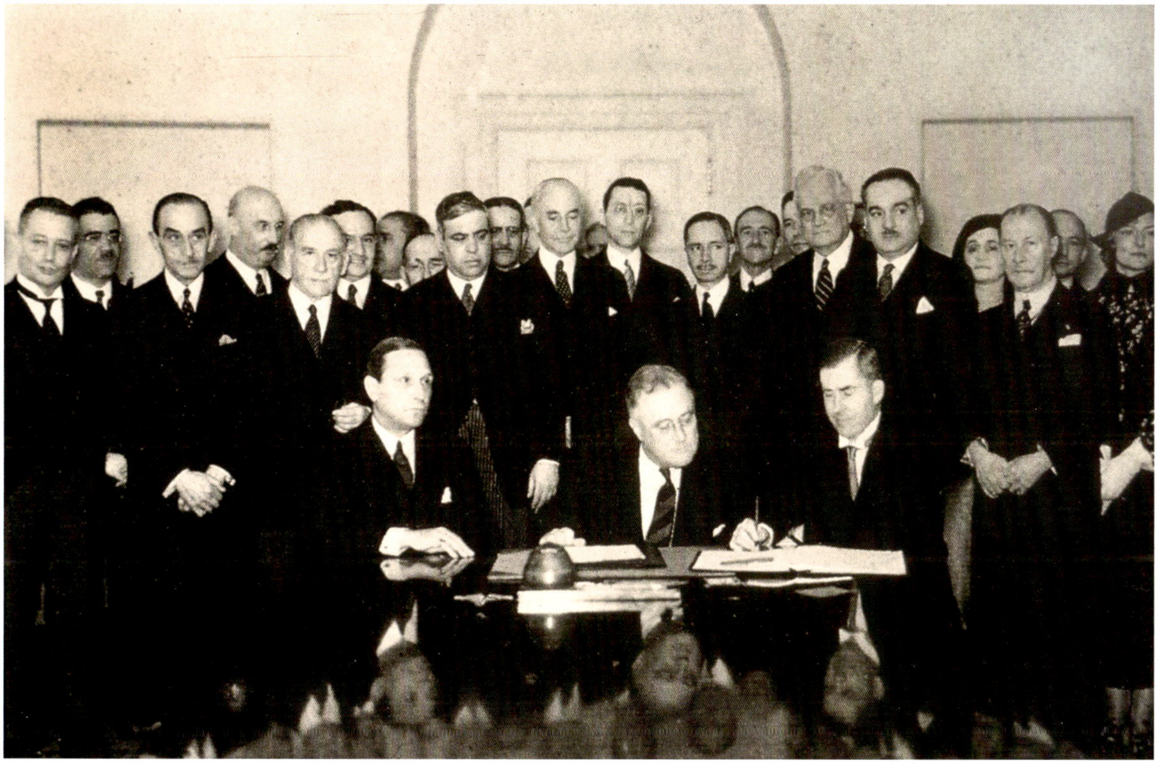

Signing of the Roerich Pact in the Oval Room of White House in presence of the President of the USA Franklin D. Roosevelt. Washington, the USA. April 15, 1935 (International Centre of the Roerichs, Moscow)

sculpture, architecture, opera, ballet and drama; the Roerich Museum Press, which published books on culture; and the Roerich Society with its affiliated branches in other countries, which spread the vision of international brotherhood through beauty. The Museum also housed the American headquarters of the Himalayan Research Institute, which Roerich and his wife set up at Kullu in 1929, to explore that region.

Responding to questions at his office in Bangalore, Nicholas Roerich's younger son, Dr. Svetoslav Roerich, outlined the roles and responsibilities of the administrators at the Roerich Museum and its related institutions. It is important to note their names now, in view of the destructive schism that was to occur in the mid-1930s, which severely impeded the progress of all Roerich's activities, including the Roerich Pact. Beginning with his own functions in these organisations, the artist's son said:

> 'First, I was director of the International Art Centre. Later on, I was vice-president of the Museum. The president was Mr. Horch. Father was the honourary president. Everyone had

> a field of responsibility. We all had our departments, our own particular responsibilities. Mrs. Fosdick and her first husband, Mr. Lichtmann, were at the Master Institute of United Arts. Miss Grant was at the Roerich Museum Press. Mr. Horch was active in an executive capacity. His wife was in charge of the Roerich Societies and the Society of Friends of the Roerich Museum. That was her field, really. It was a very good working unit. Mr. Horch was a good executive, and he worked very well in that capacity. Mrs. Horch worked there—she also worked well...Everyone fitted into the various groups.'[7]

It was in 1929, when Roerich had settled in India and the activities of the Roerich Museum were flourishing, both in New York and through its affiliates in other countries, that he proposed his idea for the Roerich Banner of Peace. The banner was for the protection of all the cultural treasures of the world. The Roerich Peace Pact Committee, which promulgated the idea of the Banner and the legally binding Pact, was based at the Roerich Museum in New York. The campaign for the Pact constituted yet another department of work at the Museum and was an integral part of the overall activity that took place there. In his 1983 interviews at Bangalore, Dr. Roerich made clear his own allegiance to the Pact as well as that of the other department heads:

> 'As members of the Roerich Museum and the other institutions, all of us in one form or another naturally played some part in the organisation or formulation of the Roerich Pact. Every one of us understood the importance, the significance, of the project, and, of course, was happy to contribute something to its consummation.'[8]

The text of the Pact had been drawn up by Georges Chklaver, doctor of International Law and Political Science at the University of Paris, who was instrumental in the promotion of the Pact in Europe. In 1930, committees similar to the one in New York were set up in Paris and at Bruges in Belgium. Vladimir Shibayev, the artist's secretary from 1928 to 1939, gave details of the Pact during his interviews at Cardiff in 1972. As he spoke he referred to documentation kept in files since his days in India. Asked how he would define the Pact, Shibayev said:

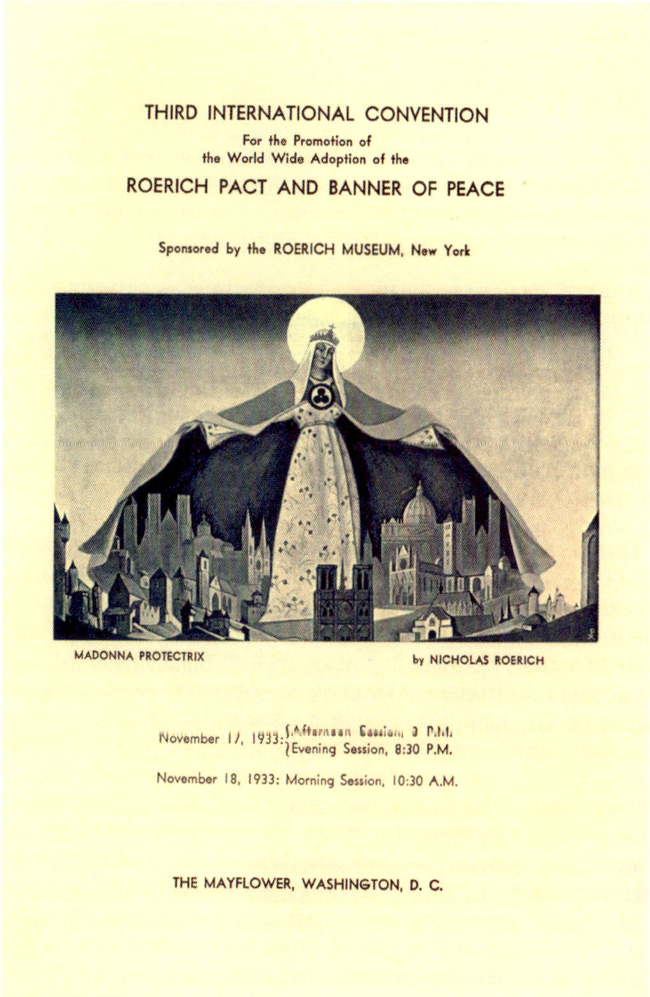

THIRD INTERNATIONAL CONVENTION

For the Promotion of
the World Wide Adoption of the

ROERICH PACT AND BANNER OF PEACE

Sponsored by the ROERICH MUSEUM, New York

MADONNA PROTECTRIX by NICHOLAS ROERICH

November 17, 1933: Afternoon Session, 3 P.M.
Evening Session, 8:30 P.M.

November 18, 1933: Morning Session, 10:30 A.M.

THE MAYFLOWER, WASHINGTON, D. C.

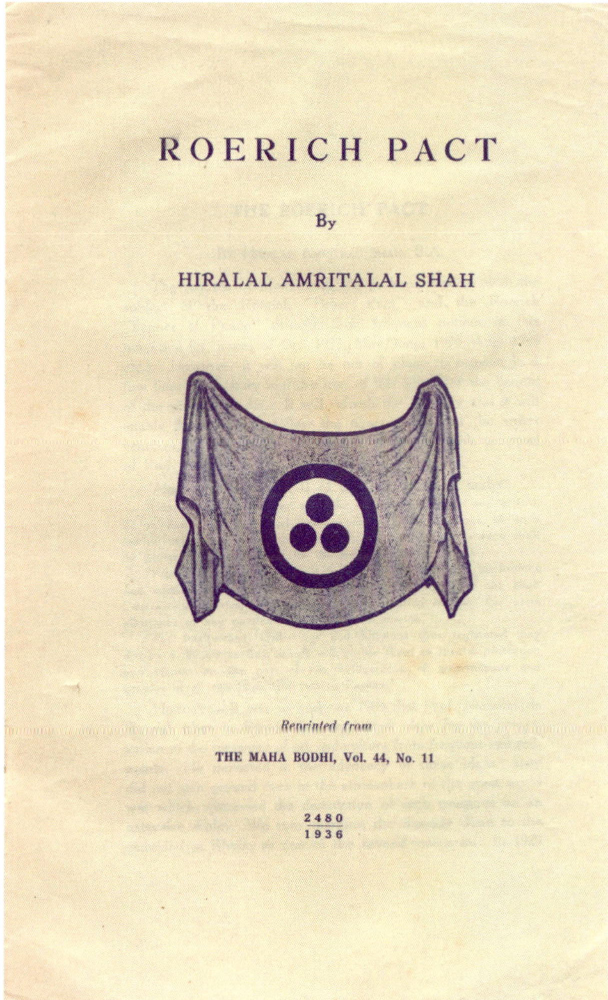

ROERICH PACT

By

HIRALAL AMRITALAL SHAH

Reprinted from

THE MAHA BODHI, Vol. 44, No. 11

2480
1936

The invitation card for the III Conference of the International Union for the Roerich Pact. November 17-18, 1933 (International Centre of the Roerichs, Moscow)

'It was an international treaty to protect ancient buildings, works of art and cultural institutions in times of peace and war. Known as the Roerich Pact and Banner of Peace, it was a kind of Red Cross of culture. Under the provisions of the Pact, the Banner was meant to fly over monuments, museums and other cultural establishments in the same way as a red cross is used to protect hospitals and ambulances. The Banner was designed by Prof. Roerich. It was a white flag on which were three magenta spheres enclosed in a magenta circle. The symbol could be interpreted in various ways. It could be taken to represent religion, science and art as expressions of culture. Or it might be seen to show the past, present and future creations of man protected within the circle of eternity.'[9]

Roerich painted a number of times on the theme of the Banner of Peace. In the collection of the Nicholas Roerich Museum in New York are two particularly relevant canvases. Both were executed in tempera in the Himalayas in 1932. *Madonna Oriflamma*—a monumental work reminiscent of the Italian medieval painter, Duccio, in its humanising of the Byzantine icon style—comprises a Madonna with a fiery golden halo holding the Banner of Peace to her breast. *St. Sophia – the Almighty's Wisdom* is a Symbolist painting and arguably in homage to the Swiss painter, Arnold Böcklin, whose works Roerich admired. The artist depicts a warrior on a white horse riding across a flaming sky holding the Banner of Peace. The walled city beneath him is thrown into contrast by the blazing light. When answering questions about this canvas, Fosdick gave her own view:

> 'A messenger is bringing the message of peace: 'There should be no war, only the preservation of culture in each country.' Prof. Roerich's idea was to bring Russia and America together and to teach everyone the meaning of culture. The buildings of various countries are depicted in this painting, including two from Russia.'[10]

Although the main activities in promoting the Pact took place in America and Europe, Roerich spent much of his time in India at the Himalayan Research Institute—an active outpost of the Roerich Museum. In a time when global contact was nothing compared to what it is now, there was a high degree of international communication.

The campaign for the Pact and Banner progressed in Europe through the convening of two international conferences held in the medieval city of Bruges. The first took place in 1931 and the second in 1932. These events were followed up by circulating their proceedings, which contained messages of support from cultural institutions and celebrities in many parts of the world.

The third international convention on the Roerich Pact was held in Washington in 1933. Representatives of 35 countries participated—artists, scientists, teachers, priests, politicians—and gave their endorsement. The proceedings were published in the United States and Europe. Soon afterwards, at a conference of the Pan-American Union, a resolution was passed urging its member states—the 21 countries of the Americas—to sign the Pact. Fosdick, checking through her papers during the 1981 interviews and passing on documentation to support the information she gave, outlined how the involvement had begun of Henry Wallace, the United States Secretary of Agriculture:

> 'He had admired Prof. Roerich's art and ideas for quite sometime and started to come to the Museum regularly in 1933. He became a great friend of Frances Grant and took an interest in her work and writing. It was through Miss Grant that he persuaded Prof. Roerich to lead the Department of Agriculture Expedition to Asia [1934/35].'[12]

Fosdick explained how Wallace had been instrumental in getting the Pact adopted:

> 'Secretary Wallace became enthusiastic about the Pact and helped Frances Grant with it. She had corresponded with all the Latin American countries and had contact with all their ambassadors in Washington. Wallace felt they should be the first countries to enter into the Pact, and it was arranged that they should do so in Washington on Pan-American Day in 1935. It was the culmination of an enormous amount of work in many countries.'[13]

On 14 April 1935, in the President's office at the White House in Washington, representatives of the US and 20 Latin American countries signed the Roerich Pact. Five of the Museum's seven trustees were present: Louis and Nettie Horch, Sina Fosdick, Maurice Lichtmann and Frances Grant. Neither Roerich nor his wife was there: he was leading the US Department of Agriculture Expedition in Mongolia; she was writing on Agni Yoga in India.

Francis Grant was the foremost campaigner for the Pact in the United States. A professional writer and publicist, she joined Roerich in his cultural enterprises soon after his arrival in New York and became a trustee and Vice-President of the Roerich Museum as well as Director of the Roerich Museum Press. Since the late 1930s Grant had lived in the New York apartment that had once been the Roerich family home. Interviewed there in 1982 she spoke of her work on the Pact and her frequent visits to the capital:

> 'I was *persona grata* in Washington. I am not talking about areas. I'm talking about the Pan-American Union and all the ambassadors of Latin America. I was much in Washington, I went often...working on the Roerich Pact.'[14]

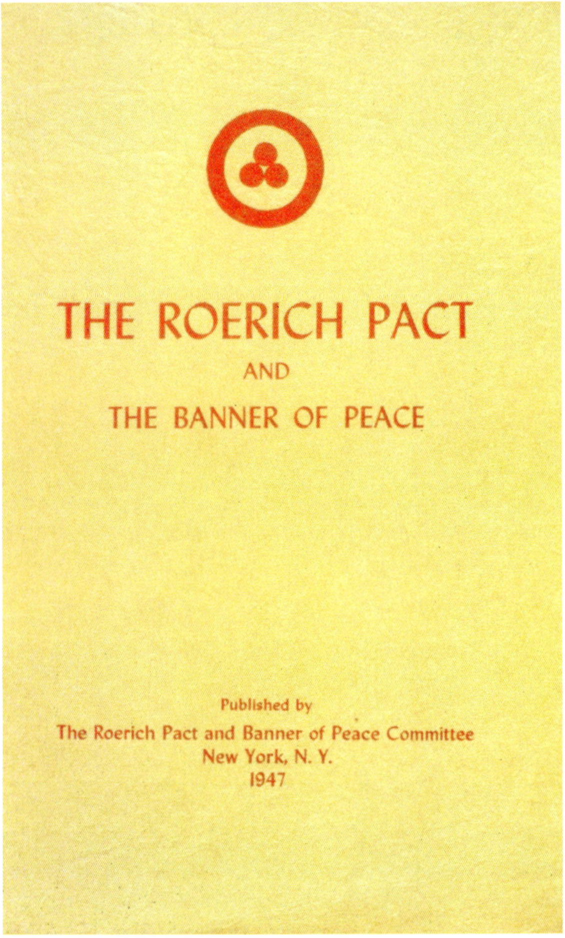

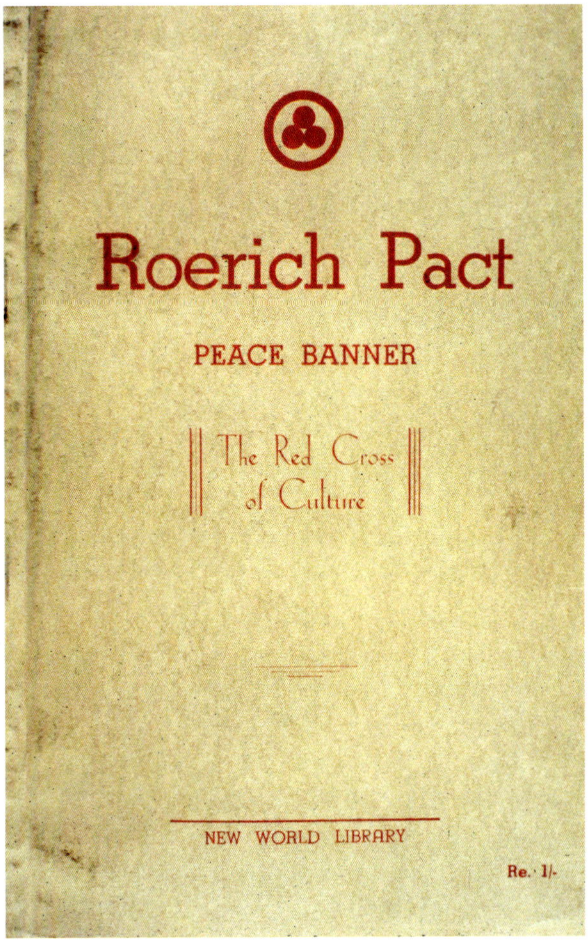

The Roerich Pact publication, 1947 (International Centre of the Roerichs, Moscow)

Bringing out a large file from her archive, Grant revealed evidence of her achievement:

> 'You see, the Pact was ratified...if you look through the file, you won't find the work...but it was thorough, I assure you. I have however, in the same file, the letters of the governments, who wrote to me saying, 'We will ratify it.' Practically all of the governments communicated with me—most of them, the democratic governments. They were friends, and we got the ratification.'[15]

After describing her work on the campaign, Grant gave a frank account of the events that followed the signing of the Pact. She related that Louis Horch, their close collaborator for more than a decade, had ousted Roerich from his Museum. It was a valuable piece of real estate, which she said, Horch, a Wall Street broker by profession, then rented out for profit as an apartment building. The story, as Grant told it, rang with elements of Greek tragedy:

> 'This is a great wrong, which has been done to a very great person. It was done in such an ugly way...I know the story, because I was a witness to it all. I was there through the whole thing, and there wasn't anything I wasn't privy to.'[16]

Grant, who became a dynamic campaigner for human rights after the demise of the Museum, related the story from its beginning:

> 'You know, there appeared suddenly in the New York papers an item that Roerich was a spy and that the expedition was stopped. I went to Washington and demanded that Wallace make a denial, which he did. But the intrigue was already beginning here [in New York] too, with the Horchs. Something had been happening with Wallace and the Horchs.'[17]

In July 1935, Horch called a meeting of the Museum's trustees—the ones who were in New York. He told them he had decided to break away from Roerich and run the Museum and its institutions without him. In her interviews, Grant continued the story:

> 'While Prof. Roerich was in Inner Mongolia, Horch decided to possess the Roerich Museum building. I, who was one of the trustees, do not hesitate to say that this was one of the most fraudulent actions that I have ever known...'[18]

It is inconceivable that these events were taking place within weeks of President Roosevelt's international broadcast in which he had said that the treaty of the Roerich Pact possessed a spiritual significance far deeper than the text of the instrument itself. A short time later, the Inland Revenue Service audited the Roerich Museum. It reported that Roerich had failed to file returns of his income for three consecutive years and had underpaid his taxes. In her interviews, Grant described the occurrence as blatant injustice:

> 'This is going into what is, in my opinion, the greatest diversion of justice...Horch was Prof. Roerich's agent and responsible for all his transactions and taxes while Prof. Roerich was in Mongolia

> and could hardly pay taxes from there. Horch had his power of attorney. He never filed, and then accused Prof. Roerich of not paying.'[19]

The Roerichs and the trustees who remained loyal to them—Fosdick, Lichtmann and Grant—were unsuccessful in all the litigation that ensued. Speaking of the matter in retrospect, Dr. Roerich said that it was a long story, which one must know in all its details and ramifications. He commented poignantly: 'It was a time in America when justice went only to those who had the most money.'[20]

During their interviews, Shibayev and Fosdick had referred to the Horchs' actions as 'the Great Betrayal'. Grant did likewise and described how the Museum, the other institutions and their cultural activities had been deliberately sabotaged in an attempt to discredit Roerich:

> 'Everything we did they tried to eliminate—things we had accomplished...You know, afterwards, Wallace tried to have removed the name of Roerich from the Pact. My friends in Latin America told me. Of course, he wasn't able to do that, but he tried very hard. They did the most insidious things, and Wallace helped Horch in the whole deception...'[21]

None of the Roerichs ever returned to America. Discussing the difficulties his father met in promoting the Peace Pact, Dr. Roerich mentioned the crises faced by Jean Henri Dunant, the man who first conceived the idea of the Red Cross, and who was expelled from that organisation and was forced to leave Geneva:

> 'We must remember that Jean Henri, when he was introducing the Red Cross, had so many difficulties, poor fellow. He was put in jail for it and had to stay in jail for that idea, which has now been accepted and agreed by everybody.'[22]

The Roerich Museum in New York, a 29-storey skyscraper on Riverside Drive, was lost. It was a unique complex of cultural institutions. However, despite the loss of its international base, the Roerich work continued. The campaign for the Pact also prevailed, though weakened by the blows to Roerich's reputation and the decimation of his resources.

In 1937, the Congress of Roerich Baltic Societies in Riga, Latvia, voted to set up Banner of Peace Committees in all the Baltic States. In 1946, the Sixth All-India Cultural Unity Conference in Calcutta resolved to adopt the Pact. And in 1948, the Indian Government declared it would adopt and adhere to the Pact and its Banner. Furthermore, in 1954, at an inter-governmental conference at The Hague, the Pact and the Banner formed the basis of an agreement signed by its 39 member states. The agreement later ratified in Paris by all these states, concerned the defence of cultural property in the event of armed conflict.

Nonetheless, Roerich's original intentions were never realised. He wanted the provisions of the Pact to be observed by all nations. And he intended the Banner of Peace to be used throughout the world in the same way as the flag of the Red Cross. Nowhere is this the case. During the 1983 interviews in Bangalore, Dr. Svetoslav Roerich analysed the current position regarding the Pact. He acknowledged what had been achieved, and he indicated what he considered the next step ahead:

> 'Everything was done. It became a pact. That is already a great achievement in itself. Now we have to extend it like the Red Cross...The Red Cross we remember worldwide, because we see the Red Cross before our eyes all the time. We are reminded of it because we see the Red Cross used every day. The symbol of the Banner of Peace is not used now, although it could have been used quite effectively.'[23]

In the 21st century it is no longer unusual for artists to commit themselves as cultural activists on a global scale. In this regard Nicholas Roerich was well ahead of his time, and although his Banner may not fly above the monuments he sought to save, he has preserved it for posterity through his writings and paintings.

End Notes

1. Sina Fosdick, unpublished interviews by the author, November, 1981, New York, USA.
2. *ibid.*
3. *ibid.*
4. Vladimir Shibayev, unpublished interviews by the author, February to December, 1972, Cardiff, Wales.
5. *ibid.*
6. Sina Fosdick, interviews, *op. cit.*
7. Dr. Svetoslav Roerich, interviews, *op. cit.*
8. *ibid.*
9. Vladimir Shibayev, interviews, *op. cit.*
10. Sina Fosdick, interviews, *op. cit.*
11. Vladimir Shibayev, interviews, *op. cit.*
12. Sina Fosdick, interviews, *op. cit.*
13. *ibid.*
14. Frances Grant, unpublished interviews by the author, November and December, 1982, New York, USA.
15. *ibid.*
16. *ibid.*
17. *ibid.*
18. *ibid.*
19. *ibid.*
20. Svetoslav Roerich, interviews, *op. cit.*
21. Frances Grant, interviews, *op. cit.*
22. Svetoslav Roerich, interviews, *op. cit.*
23. *ibid.*

Select Bibliography

Heart, 1944 (1932), Agni Yoga Series, Agni Yoga Society, New York.
Helena Roerich, *Letters of Helena Roerich*, Vol. 1 (1929-38), Vol. 2 (1935-39), 1954 and 1967, Agni Yoga Society, New York.
Helena Roerich, *At the Threshold of the New World: Dreams,Visions and Letters of Helena Roerich*, 1998, White Mountain Education Association, PO Box 11975, Prescott, Arizona 86304, USA.
Hierarchy, 1933 (1931), Agni Yoga Series, Agni Yoga Society, New York.
Kenneth Archer, 'Nicholas Roerich: An Idol With Feet of Clay?' 1989, Review of *Nicholas Roerich: the Life and Art of a Russian Master* by Jacqueline Dector, with the Nicholas Roerich Museum, New York, Thames and Hudson, London. Included in *Art History*, Vol. 13, Number 3, September 1990, pp. 419-422.
Kenneth Archer, 'Pictures by Nikolai Roerich Found in an American University' (in Russian), *Pinakotheke*, 8-9/1-2, 1999, Moscow, pp. 73-79.
Kenneth Archer, Nicholas Roerich—Roerich, East and West: Paintings from the Nicholas Roerich Museum, New York, 1999, Parkstone Press, Bournemouth, England.
Nicholas Roerich, *Fiery Stronghold*, 1933, Stratford, Boston, Massachusetts.
Nicholas Roerich, *Himavat*, 1946, Kitabistan, Allahabad.
Nicholas Roerich, *The Invincible*, in Russian, 1936, Urguns, Riga, Latvia. English translation, 1974,Nicholas Roerich Museum, NewYork.
Nicholas Roerich, *Realm of Light*, 1931, New Era Library, Roerich Museum Press, New York.
Paul Belikov and Valentina P. Knyazeva, *Roerich*, in Russian, 1972, Molodaya Gvardiya, Moscow.
Roerich Museum Press, *Roerich Banner of Peace*, 1931, New York.
Roerich Museum Press, *Roerich Museum Bulletin*, Vol. I, 1931, New York.
Roerich Museum Press, *Roerich Museum Bulletin*, Vols. II & III, 1932-1933, New York.
Roerich Museum Press, *Roerich Pact and Banner of Peace*, 1931, New York.
Sina Fosdick, *Nicholas Roerich*, A Brief Biography in Commemoration of the 90th Anniversary of his Birth, 1964, Nicholas Roerich Museum, New York.
The Roerich Pact and Banner of Peace Committee, *The Roerich Pact and Banner of Peace*, 1947, New York, USA.
The Roerich Pact: Banner of Peace, No. 1, 1931, Paris.
The Roerich Pact: Banner of Peace, Vol. II, Proceedings, Third International Convention for the Roerich Pact and Banner of Peace, 17 and 18 November 1933, Washington DC, New York, 1934.

Urusvati: Himalayan Research Institute

Mikhail Chiryatyev

Nicholas Roerich and his family's acquaintance with India and their study of its culture were connected with the activities and fieldwork of their Central Asian Expedition (1924–1928). The materials and data collected during the Expedition needed to be systematically collated, and further researched in a proper manner. In 1928, the Roerichs established the Institute of Himalayan Research, 'Urusvati', which in Sanskrit means 'The Light of the Morning Star'—*Uru* and *Svati* are names from the ancient Indian text 'Agni Purana'. The Institute was located in Naggar, in the picturesque Kullu Valley in the Himachal region of India where the Roerichs had settled after the Expedition. 'Urusvati' was planned as a different kind of Institute. An interdisciplinary research Institute, it aimed at an integrated

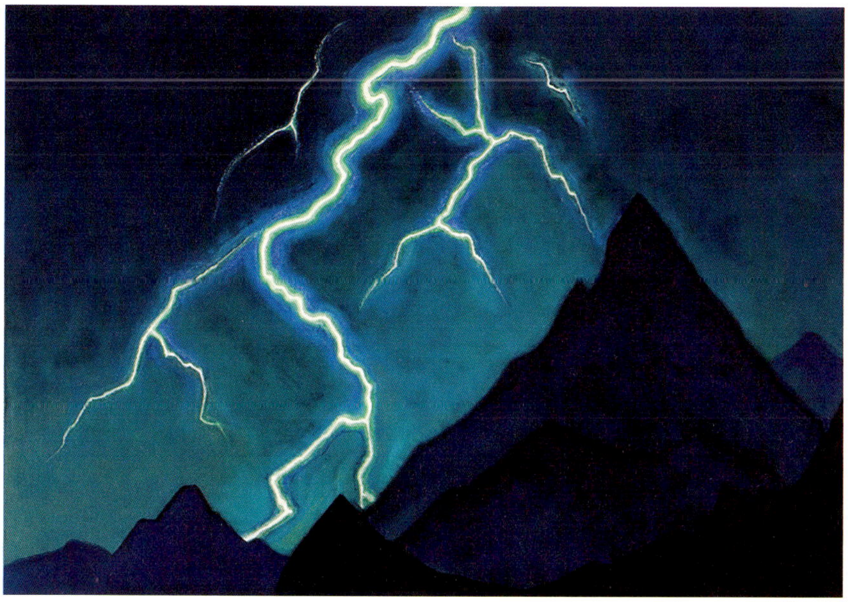

Heaven's Command, 1935-1936 (International Centre of the Roerichs, Moscow)

scientific study of the Asian region particularly its less studied and documented areas. The concept of the synthesis of natural sciences and humanitarian disciplines as well as that of traditional and modern knowledge was fundamental to the Institute and new in its idea. It also had the distinction of being the first high altitude scientifc centre.

Nicholas Roerich's eldest son, Yuri (George) was appointed the Director of 'Urusvati' and the main Editor of its Journal while Nicholas was President-Founder and Chairman of the Board. Much of his time was spent in painting and he was more of a mentor and inspiration to the Institute. His field was archaeology and comparative cultural studies. His search was for the similar sources of the arts of diverse civilisations. His wife, Helena Ivanovna, who was the Honorary President and founder of the Institute, collected and processed various sources of philosophical ideas of the East, and kept detailed notes. The youngest son, Svetoslav

Left to right: George Roerich, Nicholas Roerich, Svetoslav Roerich, ca. 1942. Naggar, India (Nicholas Roerich Museum Archive, NY)

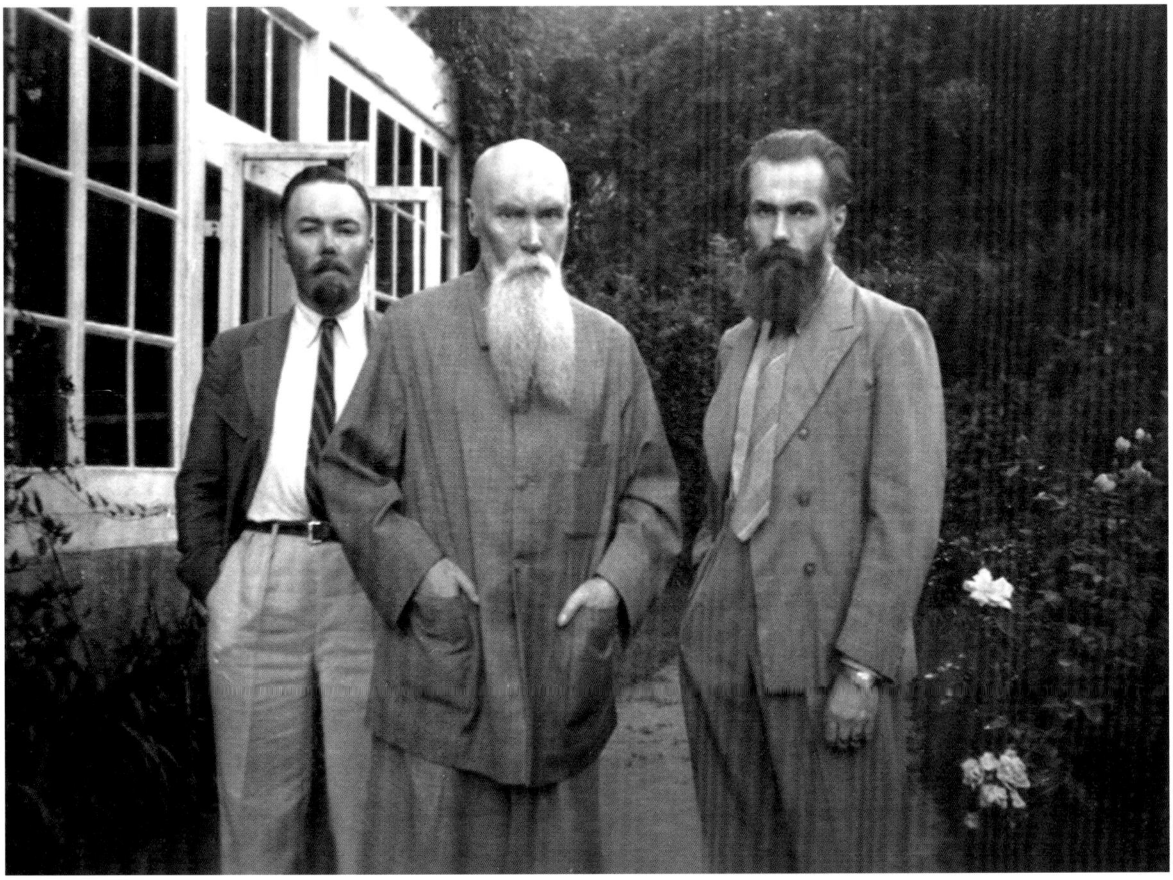

Nikolaevich, a painter and an expert in ancient art and local pharmacology, was a gifted botanist and ornithologist as well. He was in charge of the natural sciences. The Roerichs believed this Institute would be a new and future prototype of a 'Temple of Knowledge'.

Helena Ivanovna outlined the activities of the new research centre:

> 'The centre should be developed into a city of knowledge. In this city we wish to create a synthesis of scientific achievements. Therefore, all branches of science should eventually be established there. And, since the source of knowledge lies in the Cosmos, the co-workers of the scientific center should belong to the whole world—that is, should include all nationalities. And, as the Cosmos is indivisible in all its functions, the scientists of the world should be indivisible in their achievements. In other words, they should be united in closest co-operation.'[1]

The location was chosen due to the innumerable possibilities for research that the region opened up, for example in new cosmic rays, magnetic currents, meteoric precipitations, rare medicinal plants, and the unique opportunity for observation and the study of geological, archaeological and astronomical data. Other important research disciplines were botany, zoology, ornithology and ethnological-linguistic studies, etc. The Institute strengthened its relations with numerous scientific institutions, many of which actively cooperated with the Institute in its various fields of research.

After 1932, a science laboratory was built for the first time at the height of 4,650 feet above sea level. Experiments in physical, general and organic chemistry, pharmacology were conducted in the excellently equipped premises. The influences of cosmic factors and electro-magnetic fields of the earth on the properties of medicinal plants were investigated. The Roerich family, with their joint work and indefatigable energy, facilitated the recognition of the Institute in India as well as abroad.

Explaining the vision of the Institute, the intention of Nicholas Roerich is quite clear in his words:

> 'When we founded the Institute, the first priority was the permanent mobility of work. From the time of its foundation,

> expeditions and excursions are conducted each year. There is no need to stop the formed tradition. If all the workers and correspondents are attached to one place, so many unexpected and good opportunities will be frozen...What is needed is what Indians warmly call *ashrams*. It is a hub.'[2]

The Research Institute consisted of the departments of Archaeology, Natural and Medical Sciences and a Biochemistry Laboratory. The Department of Archaeology, related sciences and arts, planned to conduct scientific excavations on sites in agreement with the Indian Archaeological Survey, conducted archaeological surveys, linguistic and ethnographical studies in the Himalayan region, and the adjacent region of Western Tibet, and extensive excavations in different regions of the Middle East.

The Department of Natural and Medical Sciences and Applied Research aimed at extensive biological and botanical explorations of the Himalayan region and of the various regions of the Middle East and India, provided conditions were conducive for such expeditions. A Botanical Research Laboratory, extensive plantations and experimental botanical gardens were to be established.

The Bio-chemical Laboratory aimed at studying ancient Indian and Tibetan medicine and physiology in the light of modern research; maintaining a Herbarium and plantations of medicinal plants, for which purpose the Kullu Valley provided special possibilities; a Cancer Research Laboratory to experiment in new and local cures. In addition there was to be a Research Library with collections of books, pamphlets and manuscripts in various fields of arts and sciences, monthly issues listing Indian and western scientific publications. A book exchange programme with leading scientific institutions and publishers; a collection of Oriental books and manuscripts; as well as photocopies of rare manuscripts and editions were also part of the Library's activities.

This would be supported by a Museum which would house collections gathered by the different departments of the Institute during their exploration and research, and a photographic service to maintain photographic material of the various expeditions of the Institute. Considering the wide range of research conducted at the Institute, it required participation of scientists from different fields. Among the honorable advisers, corresponding members as well as permanent members of 'Urusvati' were world-famous scientists and Nobel laureates: Albert Einstein, R. Millikem, Lui de Broyle, R. Maggofin, the President of American Archaeology Institute, Sven Gedin, the eminent traveller, S.I. Metalnikov, professor of Pasteur Institute in Paris, Professor K.K. Lozinsky, E.D. Merill, the Director of Botanical Gardens in New York, and many others.

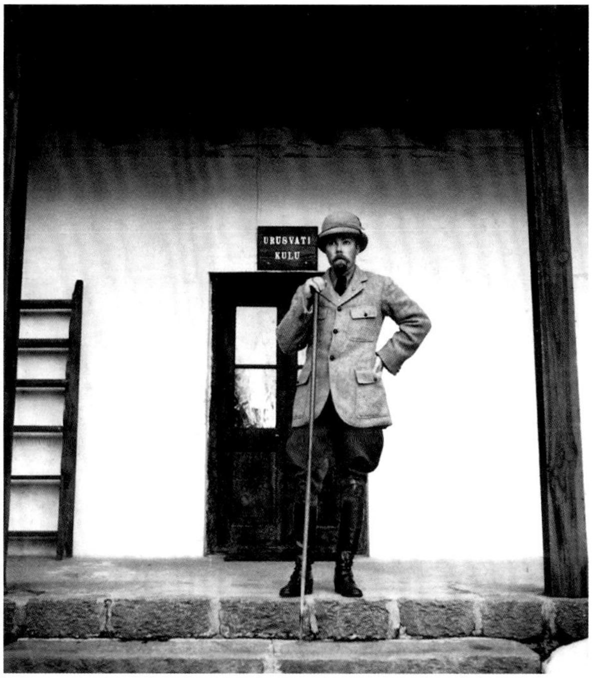

George Roerich at the Urusvati Institute, ca. 1935 (International Roerich Memorial Trust, Kullu)

Many renowned thinkers, scientists, religious figures and art personalities of India were connected with the Institute. Some of them were Chandrasekhar Venkataraman, Jagdish Chandra Bose, Rabindranath Tagore, Abanindranath Tagore, Pandit Rahul Sankrityayana, Ashit Kumar Haldar, Suniti Kumar Chatterjee of the Calcutta Univesity, Ramananda Chatterjee, Sarvepalli Radhakrishnan, Swami Satyananda Saraswati, Teija Singh, Kedarnath Dasgupta, K.P.P. Tampi, R.M. Raval, Tibetan scholars Lama Lobzang M. Dorje and Lama Gendun Choepel of Darjeeling and others.

The Institute maintained active co-operation and worldwide connections with two hundred and eighty-five institutes, universities, museums and libraries. In India 'Urusvati' collaborated with the Jagdish Bose Institute, the Asiatic Society of Bengal, the Mahabodhi Society in Calcutta, the Vishva Bharati University and others.

The vision of the Institute was to lay down the foundations of a synthesis of knowledge. Nicholas Roerich had foreseen 'the great future of powerful energy' as well as realised that any narrow pragmatic utilisation of it, could lead to the destruction of nature, and pose a threat to mankind. He appealed to scientists for a broad interdisciplinary co-operation, which would realise cultural foundation of all nations without prejudice and bias. In 'the most ancient teachings of Asia', he and his associates found 'the facts of exact sciences concealed in symbol'. These were identified as 'magnetic currents', 'psychic energy', 'the omnipresent element of cosmic Agni', the interaction of 'mental nervous energy with cosmic phenomena of great scale'. Through its work, the Institute attempted to synthesise knowledge of eastern philosophy with the contemporary discoveries of science.

Explaining the emergence of the new trends of thought, L.V. Shaposhnikova, a well known Roerich scholar, writes:

> 'That was a time when traditional science entered a period of crisis, when its great discoveries and findings could not be adequately explained either by the cognitive theory or by European philosophical thought. Some outstanding scientists, including Nobel Prize winners, began to express the idea that the end of science was coming, that all it could do had already been done, and that essentially it was turning into a technical tool for satisfying various human needs and did not need more fundamental research. Another group of equally famous scientists was seeking a way out of the existing situation and paid more and more attention to metascience, a field in which they guessed or intuitively sensed the prospects for further scientific advancement. The spiritual methods of metascientific cognition gave hope for the fruitful development of scientific research.'[3]

To elucidate this approach of Roerich and other scientists of the time, it is important to look at the prevalent streams of thought in Russia at the end of the 19th and beginning of the 20th century. A heterogeneous group of philosophers, scientists, artists, poets and even musicians through their art and scientific research strove towards an understanding of the purpose and source of life. Some

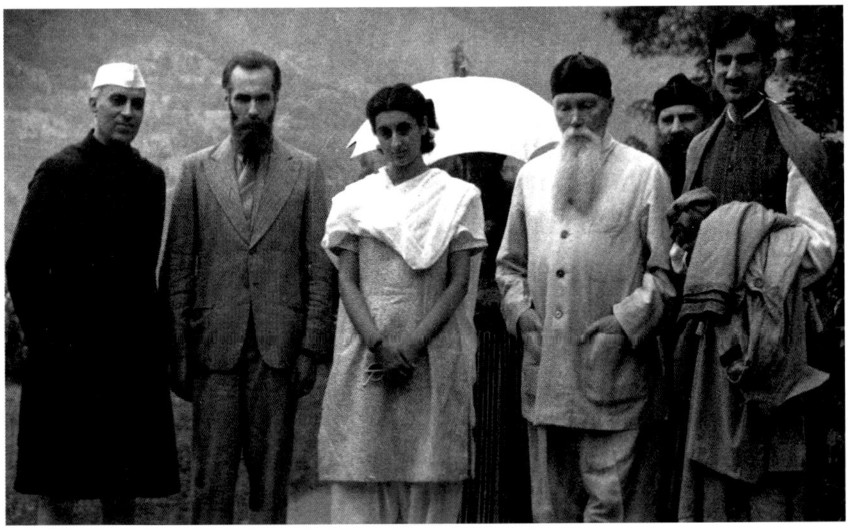

Left to right: Jawaharlal Nehru, Svetoslav Roerich, Indira Gandhi, Nicholas Roerich and Mohammad Yunus; with umbrella: Helena Roerich, 1942. Naggar, India (Nicholas Roerich Museum Archive. NY)

of the famous Russian cosmists were academician V.I. Vernadsky, the author of *The Concept of Biosphere and Noosphere*, who was the founder of disciplines such as geochemistry, bio-geochemistry, radio-geology; K.E. Tsiolkovsky, the constructor of space missiles, who proved the inevitable ascent of man into cosmic space and put forward the problems of the ethics of science; A.L. Chizhevsky, world renowned scholar, artist, poet; P.A. Florensky, clergyman, religious philosopher, eminent scholar, physicist, mathematician and philologist; V.S. Soloviev, religious thinker, poet, literary critic, who advocated ideas of unity of life, developed the theory of Christian Sofiology—a cult of the eternal femininity.

To this foundation of knowledge was added Helena and Nicholas Roerich's Teaching of Living Ethics, which reveals the scientific foundations of ancient concepts on the cosmic evolution of man and his destiny, the role of universal energy, and of thought in the evolutionary process. The Roerichs indicated the path of future progress of scientific and humanitarian thinking, and emphasised the pivotal role of culture in the evolutionary transformation of the world.

The whirlwind of the ordeals of the 20th century devastated Russia with unprecedented force. Russia was destined to become the focus of many contradictions, the arena of the most substantive world events; having ripened over centuries, they became a turning point in the spiritual transformation of life.[4]

The views of cosmists regarding the unity of Being and spiritual mission of man are comparable to the theories of certain ancient Indian philosophical schools with which the Roerichs were familiar particularly Buddhism and Vedanta, and which had been advocated in recent times by Swami Vivekananda, Sri Aurobindo Ghosh, Rabindranath Tagore, S. Radhakrishnan, Jagdish Chandra Bose and other outstanding sons of modern India.

In the 20th century, science increasingly began approximating religious-philosophical ideas of the East. It is particularly clear in the case of recent discoveries of quantum physics and astronomy. The intricate connections of subject (the observer) and object (the observed) by way of energy-information interactions, various fields and radiations, including biological ones, and finally of consciousness itself were becoming clearer by the day.

In the view of some scientists, the boundary between matter and energy was becoming blurred, while substance, wave, field and particle were becoming more and more mutually conditioned. Quantum physics has 'forced us to look at the world not as at a collection of physical objects but as a complex network of interrelations of various parts of a united entity'.[5]

The development of new science, synergetics, led to the necessity of revising the entire scheme of research methodology. The greatest scientists of the world engaged with Eastern thought. In his remarks on the ancient Indian text, Rigveda, V.I. Vernadsky expresses the qualitative leap in the rapprochement of the modern physical picture of world with the views of Eastern philosophies. In 1902, he wrote to his wife from Klampenburg: 'I am sending to you the amazing Rigveda hymn...in the metrical translation by Deussen. It seemingly corresponds quite exactly to the content. It is the creation of an unknown poet (and a great thinker) who lived at least 1,000 years before Christ, many years before the Buddha, Socrates and all of the Greek philosophy and science. And how modern it is, how it makes our thoughts pulsate even today! I see in the author the first leap into infinity...and the root of life is transferred into the existing beyond the world (Nichtsein)—into the originating and disappearing, elusive and inexplicable attraction of the heart, into the emotion of love.'[6]

Similarly, the Nobel Laureate, Brian Josephson, Professor of Physics at Cambridge University, wrote: 'All matter seems to possess a secret unity, which scientists cannot explain, but which is often talked about in different Eastern religions.'[7]

The 20th century was marked by rapid development of science and enormous scientific accomplishments. Its characteristic feature is the substantial broadening of the boundaries of knowledge, and importantly, the substantiation of the opinion that all knowing is not restricted to scientific explication. And, that any data and knowledge which is perceived through different methods and modes, is equally valid. It is obvious that what Roerich had envisioned, synthesis of ancient and modern science, of knowledge, religion and philosophy, was becoming more and more plausible.

Thus, scientific thought, having travelled the tortuous path of analysis of the manifested external forms of nature, gradually returned to the path of synthesis in search for that common, eternal base which determines the existence of all changeable and ephemeral forms.

At the First World Parliament of Religions (Chicago, 1893), Swami Vivekananda had expressed this in his brilliant speech:

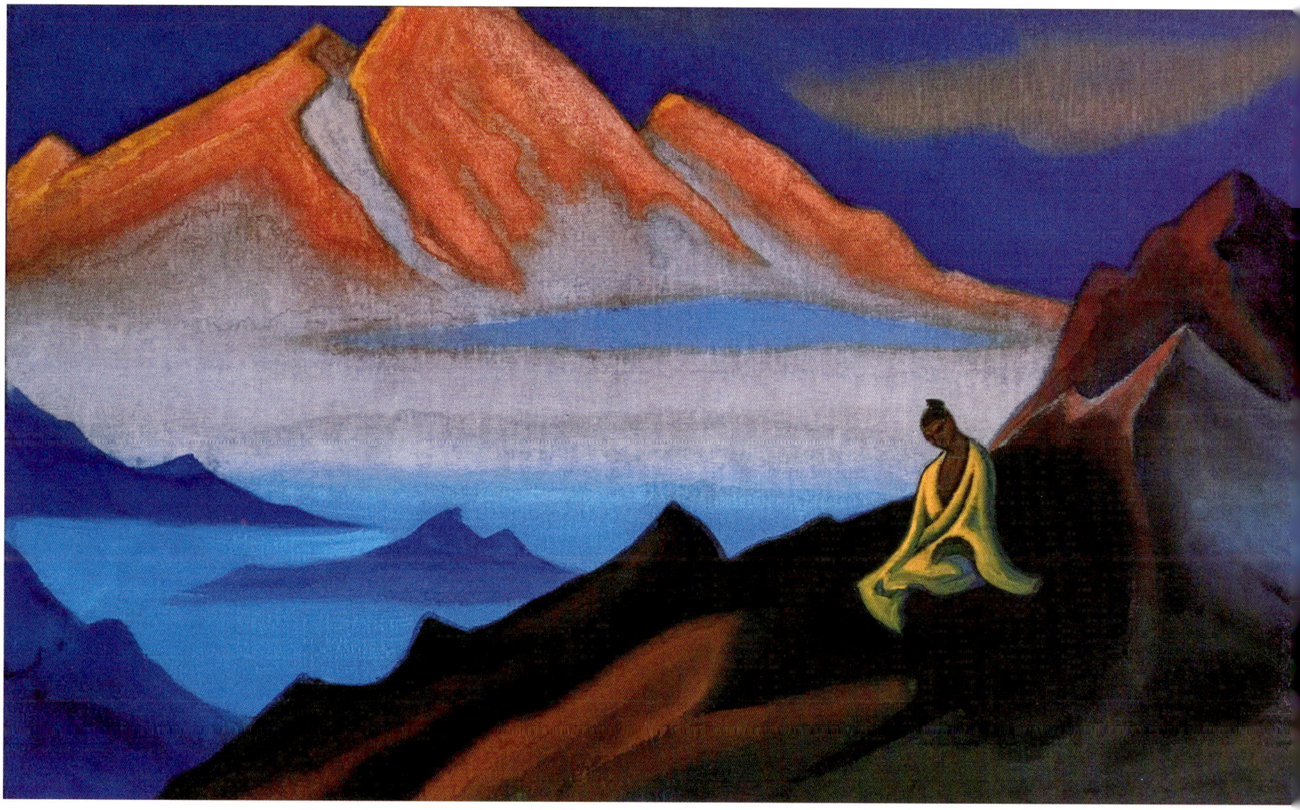

The Teacher, 1946 (International Centre of the Roerichs, Moscow)

'Science is nothing but the finding of unity. As soon as science would reach perfect unity, it would stop from further progress because it would reach the goal. Thus chemistry could not progress farther when it would discover one element out of which all others could be made. Physics would stop when it would be able to fulfill its services in discovering one energy of which all the others are but manifestations, and the science of religion become perfect when it would discover Him who is the one life in the universe of death, him who is the constant basis of an ever changing world, One who is the only Soul of which all souls are but delusive manifestations. Thus is it, through multiplicity and duality, that the ultimate unity is reached. Religion can go no further. This is the goal of all science.

'All science is bound to come to this conclusion in the long run.'[8]

The 'Urusvati' Institute had been active for about ten years when it had to wrap up its activities due to the onset of the World War II.

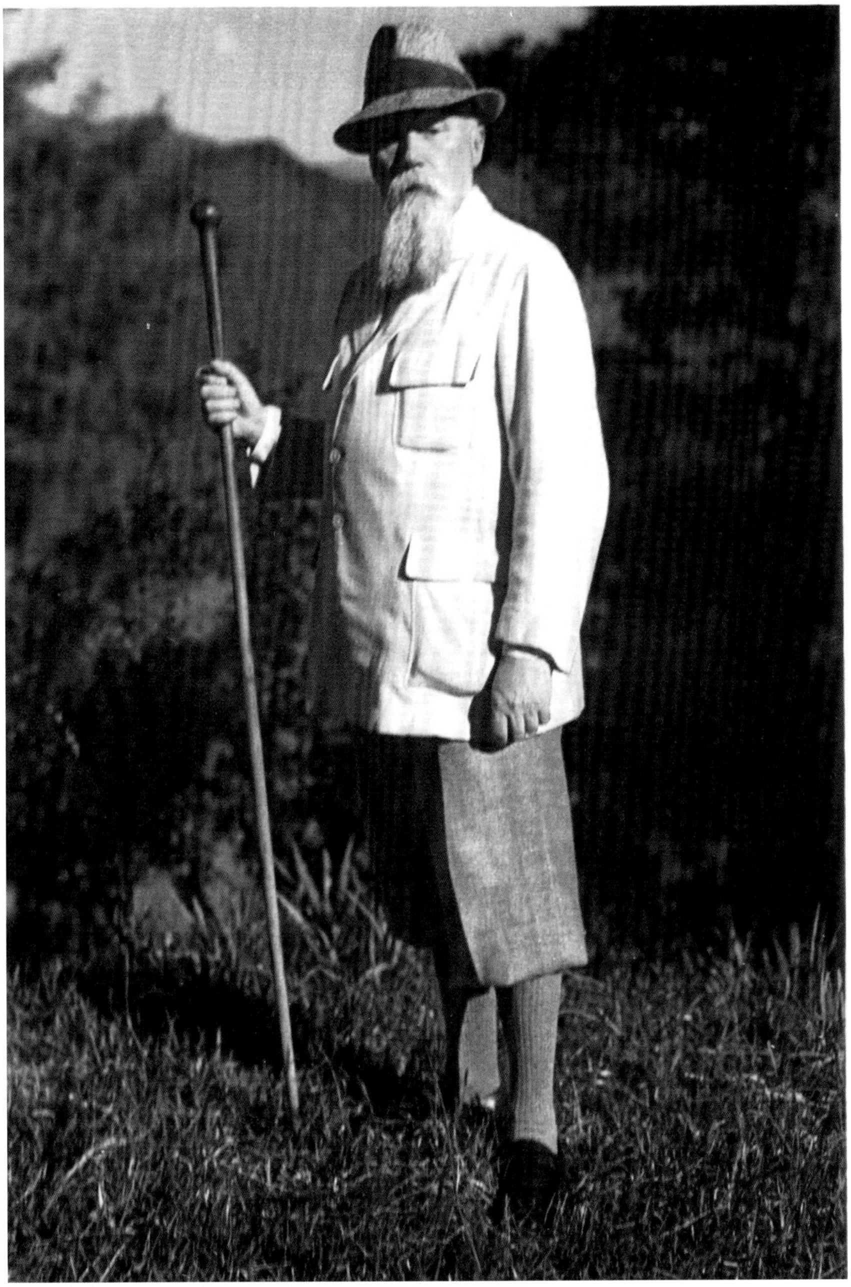

Nicholas Roerich in Kullu, ca. 1943 (International Roerich Memorial Trust, Kullu)

International events interrupted the achievement of its full potential. However, a number of local expeditions in the valleys adjacent to Kullu were undertaken during that time. A number of publications saw light. In 1934-35 an expedition to Manchuria was undertaken which, among other things, collected data on drought-resistant crops. Svetoslav Roerich and his colleagues planted rare medicinal herbs and prepared

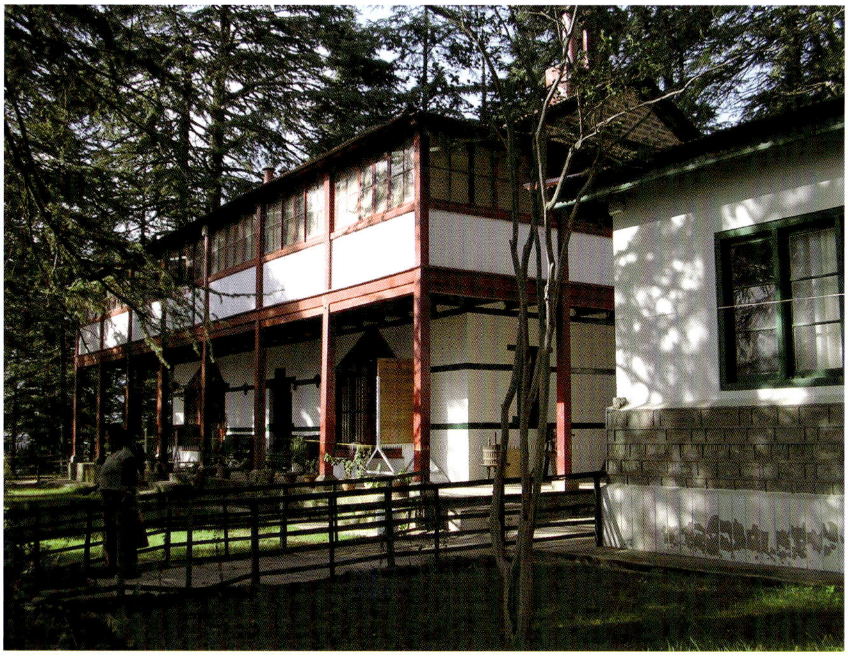

Two buildings of the Institute of Himalayan Research Urusvati (International Roerich Memorial Trust, Kullu)

curative balms and essences, and engaged in chemical research with reliance on the knowledge of the alchemists of the past as well as philosophers from East and West. For many years the International Roerich Memorial Trust (IRMT) has been working for the preservation of the Roerichs' former estate in the Kullu Valley which comprises the Nicholas Roerich house-museum and the 'Urusvati' Institute, an idea that was well ahead of its time.

End Notes

1. Letters of Helena Roerich (1929-1938), Vol. 1, 1954. Lett. N 13 on 13.10.1930. *Agni Yoga Society Inc.*, New York.
2. From the Conversation between N.K. Roerich with L. Lubimov in Paris in 1929 on the eve of the former's departure to America.
3. Shaposhnikova L.V. *The Light of the Morning Star*, The Unified Scientific Centre for Problems of Cosmic Mentality. The International Centre of the Roerich's. Moscow: ICR; Master-Bank, 2005.
4. See Chapter 2. Authored by M.Chiryatyev in: G.N. Fursey, E.I. Ryumtsev, M.N. Chiryatyev, Science and education in a general cultural context as the determinative factor of stable development of Russia. It is written with the assistance and participation of academician D.S. Likhachev. Published by St. Petersburg State University, Russian Academy of Natural Sciences, Non-Government Foundation by name of V.I. Vernadsky. St. Petersburg University Press 1999. (in Russian).
5. Kapra F. Dao fiziki…SPb., 1994. s. 116 (in Russian).
6. Vernadsky, V.I. Posviatit' svoi sily rabote nad istoriei razvitiya nauki: (from the letters to wife). Priroda. 1988. No. 2, s. 48.
7. Interview with Josephson, B. in *Detroit Free Press*. 1983. 25 October.
8. Swami Vivekananda. Addresses at the Parliament of Religions—3 Paper on Hinduism/ http://www.belurmath.org/swamivivekananda_works.htm.

Contributors

Manju Kak is an author, and an art and cultural historian.

Madhavan K. Palat was at the School of Social Sciences, Jawaharlal Nehru University, from 1974 to 2004. He was engaged in teaching and research in 19th and 20th century Russian history. His main areas of interest are workers from imperial and revolutionary Russia, the relation between bureaucracy, intelligentsia and workers, concepts of working class, forms of integration and domination, and the processes of mobilisation; the multi-national union in the Russian Empire and the Soviet Union, the principles and techniques of integration in Muscovite Russia, the late Russian Empire, the early revolutionary state, Stalinism, and the late Soviet system; conservatism as in Slavophilism, civilisation theory, and Solzhenitsyn; current affairs and international relations. He has contributed papers in various edited volumes on Russian history.

Suchandana Chatterjee is a Fellow, Maulana Abul Kalam Azad Institute of Asian Studies, Kolkata. A student of history, she was awarded a Ph.D from Calcutta University in 2002. Her research interests include regional histories of Eurasia and reflections on transition in Eurasia. She is currently engaged in the debates about Inner Asia as a nationalist and spiritual space and has written books on the subject and conducted several research studies. She has presented papers and participated in national and international conferences and has collaborated with research groups abroad.

L.V. Shaposhnikova is Director General of the Nicholas Roerich Museum in Moscow, First Vice-President of the International Centre of the Roerichs, Honored Artist of the Russian Federation, Member of the Russian Academy of Natural Sciences and Russian Academy of Cosmonautics named after K.E. Tsiolkovsky, Editor-in-Chief of *Culture and Time*. Awarded the Jawaharlal Nehru Award for International Understanding, she is an indologist, philosopher, researcher and populariser of the Roerichs' philosophic and artistic heritage.

Andrea Loseries studied in Paris, Santiniketan and Vienna. She received her Ph.D for research on Tibetan Bone Lore from Vienna University. She has curated exhibitions on Tibet, produced ethnological film documentaries and authored books on Tibet and Buddhism and published research papers. Since 2006 she is Head of the Department of Indo-Tibetan Studies and Director of the Centre for Buddhist Studies, Visva-Bharati, Santiniketan. Presently she is researching on the Sahaja traditions in Ancient East India and translates Rabindranath Tagore's dance dramas into Tibetan.

Alexander Vitalievich Stecenko was Chief Executive Officer of Helena Roerich Charitable Fund and Assistant Director General of Nicholas Roerich Museum of International Centre of the Roerichs. He is the first Deputy Director General of Nicholas Roerich Museum, Moscow. His research area is Nicholas Roerich's life and creativity, especially his Central Asian Expedition. He graduated from the M.V. Frunze Military Academy, Moscow. He studied Public Policy and Public Administration in the Academy of National Economy under the Government of the Russian Federation.

Ringee Eden Wangdi is Member of the board of Darjeeling Goodwill Centre and Trustee of the Himalayan Institute of Goodwill and Living Ethics (HIGLE). A Ph.D in Nepali Literature, she writes on local history, religion and culture, and has written and dramatised many musicals and plays based on Buddhist philosophy. She is the recipient of the Baba Bhim Rao Ambedkar Fellowship Award for working for women and minorities (Scheduled Castes and Scheduled Tribes) in the region.

Ian Heron trained in architecture, taking a special interest in processes of analysis and problem-solving. He has since worked continuously in applied art and design. In the 1970s he studied the legends of the *graal*, and subsequently encountered the work of Nicholas Roerich, who associated the *graal* with the Stone. This led the author to research the possible identity of the Stone and other factual material about it which related to its role in Roerich's life and work.

John McCannon teaches history at Southern New Hampshire University, and is former Editor-in-Chief of the *Canadian Journal of History*. His publications include *Red Arctic* (Oxford University Press, 1998) and numerous articles on the history of Russian aviation and exploration. His many Roerich-related publications highlight various aspects of Roerich's paintings, his geopolitical aims, his spiritual search, etc.

Sina Fosdick, one of the Roerichs' closest and most trusted co-workers, was Director of the Nicholas Roerich Museum, New York, from 1949 till her death in 1983. She was also member of the Organising Committee of the Roerich Pact. Sina participated in the Altai and Mongolia parts of the Roerich expedition of 1924–1928; she was with them in Moscow (1926), Mongolia (1927), India (1928, in Darjeeling), and left many diaries and notebooks about the most important events and experiences of her life, especially about her times with the Roerichs, her meetings and discussions with them, their teachings, their personalities and their noble work.

A.V. Ivanov has many publications to his credit. He is the Vice-President of Altai Public Fund 'Altai—21st century'. The ideas of Nicholas Roerich form the basis of the Fund's spiritual outlook. He is also the coordinator of International Summer Student Schools of Big Altai, which organises scientific and public dialogue between students of different countries and nations concerning common Alta in problems and perspectives of development.

I.V Fotieva is a Professor at the Altai State University, Russia. Her publications include *Hour Pre-Dawn*, Bannal 2003 and *The Foundation of Spiritual-Ecological Civilization*, Bannal, 2002. She is Executive Director of the Altai Public Fund 'Altai 21st Century'. She also occupies the post of Expert at International Summer Students School of Big Altai.

Vladimir Khvorostov is a Professor at Komi State Pedagogical Institute, Syktyvkar, Russia, since 1980. He graduated from Schnittke Music College (Moscow) and Moscow State Pedagogical University. He founded and lead 'People's Collective' a button accordion orchestra. He heads the Komi Republic Roerich Society which he founded in 1991. In 2000 he was selected co-chairman of Roerich Societies Union of North-West Russia. He is a member of the Roerich bulletin *Svyatogor* editorial board.

Marga Koutsarova is the Chairperson of the National Roerich Society in Bulgaria, which is a member of the International Centre—Museum of the Roerichs. She holds a Master of Law degree from the Sofia University, Bulgaria (1994), LLM degree in development from the University of Warwick, United Kingdom (1996), and a Masters in eastern philosophy and culture from the Sofia University (2009). The National Roerich Society in Bulgaria has initiated and carried out in 2004 and 2008 a wide range of programmes devoted to the cultural heritage of the Roerichs, together with a number of Bulgarian cultural institutions, the International Centre of the Roerichs in Moscow and the Ukrainian and Estonian Roerich Societies.

Marina Bernardi graduated in Psychology and specialised in Psychosynthesis. She works as group trainer in areas connected with the growth of human consciousness. She is a member of the board of the Italian Community of Living Ethics, whose main aim is to develop and realise the ideas included in the Teachings of the Roerich family. Since 2005 she is in charge of the Centre in Kalimpong (India), Crookety House, the last residence of Helena Roerich.

Ruth Drayer, an art major, studied in Washington, DC, El Paso, Texas and Los Angeles, California. Her artwork has been shown in galleries and is in private collections in Spain, southwest USA and Canada. She is the author of *Nicholas & Helena Roerich, The Spiritual Journey of Two Great Artists and Peacemakers* (Quest Books, the Theosophical Society Press, USA). She also directed and produced a DVD based on the book.

Lokesh Chandra, a scholar of Tibetan, Mongolian and Sino-Japanese Buddhism, is Director, International Academy of Indian Culture. He has written critical editions of classical texts in Sanskrit, Tibetan, Mongolian, Chinese and old Javamer language. He was a member of the Rajya Sabha, the Upper House of Indian Parliament in 1974-80, and in 1980-86. He was Vice-President of the Indian Council for Cultural Relations and Chairman of the Indian Council for Historical Research.

Tashi Paljor was Principal, Institute of Buddhist Studies, Leh (J&K), India. He is now retired and lives in Manali, Kullu (H.P.), where he continues the pursuit of Buddhist philosophical studies.

Joe Troncale is an associate professor and co-director of Russian Studies at the University of Richmond, USA. A Ph.D in Russian Literature from Cornell University in 1979, he writes on 19th and 20th century Russian authors, Russian cinema and painting. He currently teaches Russian language and literature, Russian painting and cinema, and the history of Russian cultural and intellectual development. In collaboration with the Museum of Nonconformist Art in St. Petersburg, he has curated two exhibitions of Russian painting at the University of Richmond Museums. He has received numerous grants and fellowships for his research and has received honours in teaching from the University of Richmond and from the states of Arizona and Virginia.

Shri Prakash completed his M.A. and M.Phil from Jawaharlal Nehru University, New Delhi and did his Ph.D in economic history of modern India from the University of Cambridge, UK. Shri Prakash was awarded the INLAKS Junior Research Fellowship, Churchill College, Cambridge University, UK; Senior Fellowship, Centre for Policy Research, New Delhi; and Senior Fellowship, Japan Foundation, Tokyo. His research papers have been published in international journals like *China Report, India Quarterly,*

Cambridge Journal of South Asian Studies. He is Professor at the Academy of International Studies, University of Jamia Millia Islamia, since 1990.

Ven. Lama Duboom Tulku was Director, Tibet House, New Delhi. He joined the Institute of Higher Tibetan Studies, Sarnath. Later he studied Buddhist philosophy and received a Geshe Archarya degree from Sanskrit University, Varanasi. In 1977, he joined the Private Office of His Holiness the Dalai Lama as Secretary. In 1996, he was appointed by His Holiness as Director of the Foundation for Universal Responsibility. In 1999, he was awarded an honourary doctorate in Buddhist Studies by the Mahachulalongkorn Buddhist University of Bangkok. He is the author of *Buddhist Translations: Problems and Perspectives, Buddhist Path to Enlightenment* and *Gyalwai Chostsul*.

Kenneth Archer is a scenic consultant and art historian with a Ph.D. from the University of Essex, Colchester, UK. Along with his wife, Millicent Hodson, Archer runs a dance and design team based in London. They reconstruct modern masterpieces and create their own works through the partnership, *Ballets Old and New*. They have staged productions for companies such as the Royal Ballet Covent Garden; Birmingham Royal Ballet; the Mariinsky Ballet, St. Petersburg; Paris Opera Ballet; Les Ballets de Monte-Carlo; Hamburg Ballet; Royal Swedish Ballet; Finnish National Ballet; Zurich Ballet; Portuguese National Ballet; La Scala Ballet; Rome Opera Ballet; Les Grands Ballets Canadiens and the Joffrey Ballet, USA.

Mikhail Chiryatyev is Trustee of the Board of the International Roerich Memorial Trust, India, a member of the Scientific Council of the United Science Centre for Cosmic Thinking Problems under ICR and Co-Chairman of its Kullu-Urusvati Sector. He graduated from Faculty of Chemistry, Leningrad State University (now St. Petersburg State University, Russia).

Acknowledgements

Roerich's art respects universality and compassion. Certainly, that spirit helped me secure the support and encouragement of many people, only some of whom are acknowledged here.

My thanks are due to the University of Jamia Millia Islamia where the project was conceived at the Centre for Jawaharlal Nehru Studies under the Vice Chancellorship of Professor Mushirul Hasan. Subsequently Mr. Najib Jung, the next Vice Chancellor gave it full support and extended all courtesy. For this I am indeed grateful.

My appreciation to Smt. Sheila Dikshit, Chief Minister, Delhi, to Dr. Karan Singh, Chairman, Indian Council of Cultural Affairs (ICCR) for their constant generosity and help. Shri Jawhar Sircar, former Secretary, Culture, went out of his way to encourage, guide and troubleshoot—I owe him a debt of gratitude. I also acknowledge Mr. Ashok Vajpayee, former Chairman, Lalit Kala Akademi; Mr. Pavan Varma and Mr Virendra Gupta (in their previous capacities as Director Generals of I.C.C.R) for their co-operation.

I am immensely thankful to the International Centre for Roerichs, Moscow, the International Roerich Memorial Trust, Kullu, (H.P.) and the Nicholas Roerich Museum, New York, for, amongst other suggestions and kindnesses, the many visuals that illustrate the essays. The Russian Embassy at New Delhi, where Ambassador Kadakin is an avowed Roerich admirer, extended gracious help and co-operation, along with Sergey Karmalito.

Dr. Alena Adamkova, the former Director of the International Roerich Memorial Trust, Kullu, (H.P.) gave invaluable inputs that helped shape my understanding. Each contributor has taken admirable pains to write upon some unique aspect of the artist's life so as to give a holistic understanding of the man and his times. Consultation and detailed conversations with Ambassador Krishan Raghunath and Professor Madhavan Palat provided much needed insights. I appreciate too, the supportive presence of Rimpoche Dubloong Tulku, Virendra Jain, and Professor B.N. Goswamy.

Poornima Mehta's detailed eye, and perspicacity gave shape to many difficult papers translated from Russian. She went beyond the call of duty in her brief. Thanks are also due to Aradhana Pradhan and Asmita Chaudhari for their patience and editing skills. The talented Zeeshan Ali and his team designed some of the illustrations.

Early administrative support was given by Mr Faheem of the Centre for J.L. Nehru Studies, and later the staff of the Academy of Third World Studies, Jamia Millia Islamia—under former Acting Director, Professor Shri Prakash who extended me all co-operation. I would also like to thank Javed, Ram Niwas, Talat whose help was taken over innumerable cups of tea. In its final editing and feed back the inputs of scholars Dr. Rahat Hasan and Dr. Saiffuddin, have been useful. Finally, but most importantly it is the belief of Mr Bikash Niyogi and his super efficient and conscientious Editor, Nandita Jaishankar to whom I owe the production and final shape of the book.

Manju Kak

Index